# BEYOND INDIVIDUAL AND GROUP DIFFERENCES

# BEYOND
# INDIVIDUAL
# AND
# GROUP
# DIFFERENCES

## Human Individuality, Scientific Psychology, and William Stern's Critical Personalism

# James T. Lamiell
### Georgetown University

SAGE Publications
*International Educational and Professional Publisher*
Thousand Oaks ▪ London ▪ New Delhi

*For information:*

Sage Publications, Inc.
2455 Teller Road
Thousand Oaks, California 91320
E-mail: order@sagepub.com

Sage Publications Ltd.
6 Bonhill Street
London EC2A 4PU
United Kingdom

Sage Publications India Pvt. Ltd.
B-42, Panchsheel Enclave
Post Box 4109
New Delhi 110 017  India

Printed in the United States of America

*Library of Congress Cataloging-in-Publication Data*

Lamiell, James T.
Beyond individual and group differences : human individuality, scientific psychology, and William Stern's critical personalism / James T. Lamiell.
    p. cm.
Includes bibliographical references and indexes.
ISBN 0-7619-2172-9 (cloth)
  1. Psychology—History—20th century. 2. Psychology—History—19th century. 3. Stern, William, 1871-1938. I. Title.
BF105.L36 2003
155.2—dc211

                          2003008606

03   04   05   06   10  9  8  7  6  5  4  3  2  1

| | |
|---|---|
| *Acquiring Editor:* | Jim Brace-Thompson |
| *Editorial Assistant:* | Karen Ehrmann |
| *Production Editor:* | Sanford Robinson |
| *Typesetter:* | C&M Digitals (P) Ltd. |
| *Copy Editor:* | Carla Freeman |
| *Indexer:* | Molly Hall |
| *Cover Designer:* | Michelle Lee |

# Contents

Preface      xiii

1.   Introduction: A Lost Star      1

**Part I. Historical Beginnings**      27

2.   The Problem of Individuality
and the Birth of a "Differential" Psychology      29

3.   The Narrowing of Perspective in the Proliferation
of Standardized Testing and Correlational Research      55

4.   The Entrenchment of a "Common Trait"
Perspective on Human Individuality      82

**Part II. Statistical Thinking in the Post-Wundtian
Restructuring of Scientific Psychology**      111

5.   The Emergence of a "Neo-Galtonian" Framework
for Psychological Research: A Historical Sketch      113

6.   Contemporary "Nomotheticism" Within the
Neo-Galtonian Framework: A Methodological Primer      140

7.   Contemporary "Nomotheticism" in Critical Perspective      176

**Part III: Rethinking the Problem**      213

8.   An Introduction to Critical Personalism      215

9.   Some Models of Personalistic Inquiry
in Contemporary Psychology      243

10.   Our Differences Aside: Persons, Things,
Individuality, and Community      279

References 303

Author Index 319

Subject Index 323

About the Author 331

# Detailed Contents

1. Introduction: A Lost Star                                                    1
    Berlin Beginnings                                                           2
    During the Breslau Years, 1897–1916                                         4
        Marriage to Clara Joseephy and Early
            Contributions to Child Psychology                                   5
        Initiatives in Applied Psychology and Participation
            in the 1909 Clark University Conference                             8
        Engagement in the School Reform Movement
            and the Controversy Over Psychoanalytic
            Psychotherapy With Children and Adolescents                        10
        World War I and the Move to Hamburg                                    15
    During the Hamburg Years, 1916-1933                                        16
        The Personalistically Minded German Jew in
            the Face of the Imminent Catastrophe                               18
    Denoument                                                                  20

Part I. Historical Beginnings                                                  27

2. The Problem of Individuality and the Historical
    Emergence of a "Differential" Psychology                                   29
    Die allgemeine Psychologie in Late
        19th-Century Germany                                                   31
    The Birth of die differentielle Psychologie                                34
        Stern's Vision of the Scope and Mission
            of Differential Psychology                                         34
        Stern's Antimechanistic Convictions                                    38
        Transitional Summary                                                   43
    The Personalistic Perspective Within Stern's
        Broadened Conception of
        Differential Psychology                                                43

"Individual" and "Attribute" as Basic Concepts    46
The Concept of Dispositions    49
Summary    51

3. The Narrowing of Perspective in the Proliferation
of Standardized Testing and Correlational Research    55
Stern's Understanding of the Role of Standardized
Testing in Differential Psychology    56
Stern's Views on the Limits of Standardized
Psychological Testing    58
Investigating Individualities    62
The Ascendance of Standardized Methods in
Psychognostics and Psychotechnics    64
Edward L. Thorndike's Reformulation of the
Problem of Individuality    65
Hugo Münsterberg's Identification of
Applied Psychology With Psychotechnics    69
The Growing Disenchantment of a Critical Personalist    71
Summary    78

4. The Entrenchment of a "Common Trait" Perspective
on Human Individuality    82
Gordon W. Allport's Efforts Toward a "Psychology
of Personality"    84
Circumscribing the Discipline    85
Common Traits and Individual Traits as
Structural Elements of Personality    87
The Call to Supplement Nomothetic With
Idiographic Inquiry in Personality Studies    89
Major Contours of the Nomothetic-Idiographic Debate    92
Summary    105

Part II. Statistical Thinking in the
Post-Wundtian Restructuring of Scientific Psychology    111

5. The Emergence of a "Neo-Galtonian" Framework
for Psychological Research: A Historical Sketch    113
The Restructuring of Scientific Psychology's
"Two Disciplines"    114
In the Beginning . . .    114
Briefly on the Nature and Provenance
of the Pearson $r$    116

Redressing the Deficiencies of
  the Galtonian Model                                         119
  Solving the Metaphysical Problem: From
    Natural Categories to "Treatment Groups"    120
  Solving the Epistemic Problem: Statistical
    Patterns in Aggregate Data as Grounds
    for Generalizations About Individual
    Level Phenomena                                           122
An Overview of Some Major Developments in the
  History of Statistical Thinking                             124
  From Political Arithmetic to Social Physics                 124
  From Social Physics to Laws Governing
    Individual Psychological Functioning                      129
  Disagreements in Late-19th-Century
    Thought Over the Proper Understanding
    of Statistical Knowledge                                  132
Summary                                                       136

6.  Contemporary "Nomotheticism" Within the Framework
    of Neo-Galtonian Inquiry: A Methodological Primer         140
    The Rudiments of Neo-Galtonian Inquiry                    142
      The Statistical Comparison of Treatment Groups
        in Neo-Galtonian Experimentation                      142
      Extending the Research Design to Incorporate
        a Group Difference Variable                           149
      Extending the Research Design Further to
        Include an Individual Differences Variable            154
    The Establishment of Contemporary
      "Nomotheticism's" Periodic Table of Elements            158
      The "Lexical Hypothesis" and Its Systematic
        Investigation Through Factor Analysis                 160
      Convergent and Discriminant Validity
        of the Five-Factor Model                              163
    In Search of the Sources of Personality
      Differences and the Laws Governing Their
      Behavioral Manifestations                               168
      Isolating the Relative Effects of Nature Versus
        Nurture as Causes of Personality Differences          168
      Discovering the Lawful Regularities Governing the
        Behavioral Manifestations of Personality Traits       170
    Summary                                                   171

7.  Contemporary "Nomotheticism" in Critical Perspective          176
        *Geschichte und Naturwissenschaft*:
        A Brief Look at Windelband's (1894)
        *History and Natural Science*                              177
            Minting the Expressions: Nomothetic
                and Idiographic                                    179
            Probing Windelband's Meanings                          180
        Method as Metaphysics in the Explanatory
        Pretensions of Neo-Galtonian Inquiry                       184
        The Epistemic Limits of Neo-Galtonian
        Inquiry and "Nomothetic" Laws of
        Personality Functioning                                    191
            On Prediction                                          191
            On the Empirical Discovery of "Basic
                Human Tendencies"                                  197
            On Probabilistic Thinking as the Basis
                for Nomothetic Knowledge Claims                    201
            On the Alleged Commonality and Heritability
                of Common Traits                                   203
        Summary                                                    205

**Part III. Rethinking the Problem**                              213

8.  An Introduction to Critical Personalism                       215
        Toward a Critically Personal Individual Psychology         216
            The Person in Personalistic Perspective                216
                The Unitas Multiplex                               217
            Phenomena, Acts, Dispositions, and the 'I'            220
            The Psychophysically Neutral Person, the
                Telic Nature of Personality Development,
                and Person-World Convergence                       225
        An Early Example of Personalistic Inquiry: *Recollection,
        Testimony, and Lying in Early Childhood*                   228
            Some Methodological Considerations in the
                Conduct of Personalistic Research                  229
            Some Theoretical and Philosophical
                Issues Highlighted by a Personalistic
                Conception of Lying                                234
        Summary                                                    236

9.  Some Models of Personalistic Inquiry
    in Contemporary Psychology                                     243

Some Illustrative Quantitative Research: Modeling
the Psychology of Subjective Personality Judgments
on Alternative Rationales for the Measurement
of Personality Dispositions                                      245
Preliminary Considerations                                       247
Measuring Personality Dispositions                               249
   I.  From Behavioral Observations To
     "Raw Score" Assessments Measuring
     Personality Dispositions                             249
   II. From "Raw Score" Assessments
     To Traditional Normative Measures                    251
   III. From "Raw Score" Assessments to
     Interactive Measures                                 253
Revisiting the Question of "Idiographic"
   Intuitions: Studies on the Psychology of
   Subjective Personality Judgment                             256
Some General Observations on Hypothesis
   Testing in Personalistic Inquiry                            261
Some Illustrative Qualitative Research: Personalistic
Studies of the Experience of Alzheimer's Disease                 264
   The AD Sufferer as an Evaluating
   and Intentional Person                                      266
   Introception and the Establishment of Syntelic
   Goals in the Case of Dr. B                                  271
   Comment                                                     273
Summary                                                          274

10.  Our Differences Aside: Persons, Things,
Individuality, and Community                                     279
On Critical Personalism as a Foundation
   for Personality Theory                                      281
   Reviving the Project Within
     the Contemporary Context                             281
   Person Characterization Without
     Between-Person Comparisons                           282
   Individuality Versus Uniqueness                             285
   Positioning, Position Taking,
     and Personal Identity                                286
   Teleology Reconsidered                                      288
On Critical Personalism as a
   Framework for Social Thought                                291

*Menschenkenntnis* and
    *Menschenbehandlung* Revisited     291
Personalism Without Individualism     296
Individuality, Diversity, and Community     299

References     303

Author Index     319

Subject Index     323

About the Author     331

# Preface

In May of 1984, I participated in a symposium that was part of the program of the Second European Conference on Personality, held at the University of Bielefeld, in what was then West Germany. My invitation to the conference was extended by the symposium organizer, the late Professor Jean-Pierre DeWaele of the Free University of Brussels, and was prompted by an article I had published in the *American Psychologist* in March of 1981 under the title "Toward an Idiothetic Psychology of Personality." The paper I presented at the Bielefeld conference was essentially an elaboration and extension of the ideas I had set forth in the 1981 article.

After my presentation, during discussions with German colleagues Lothar Laux and Hannelore Weber, I was asked if I was at all familiar with the works of William Stern. "Oh sure," I quickly replied, "he was the IQ guy." Showing patience for which I shall be forever grateful, Laux and Weber explained to me that Stern's contributions to psychology actually extended quite a bit beyond the invention of the intelligence quotient and that, given my own developing perspective on the field, it might be well worth my while to familiarize myself more extensively with Stern's ideas.

Back home in the United States some weeks after the conference, I received a mailing from DeWaele that included photocopies of some pages from a work by Stern that had been published in 1906. In an accompanying note, DeWaele directed my attention to some mathematical expressions that appeared in Stern's work, noting the striking formal similarity between those expressions and equations which I had used to convey some of my own nascent ideas in the domain of personality measurement. I think it was exactly then when I decided that, for me at least, familiarity with Stern's writings was not merely an option but a necessity.

Unfortunately, I had long since passed up the opportunities presented to me during my student years to learn German, and the obstacle left before me by that youthful decision had not yet been overcome as I was writing *The Psychology of Personality: An Epistemological Inquiry*, which appeared in 1987 (Columbia University Press). Hence, that work contains no references at all to Stern or to that comprehensive system of thought he articulated over the course of his illustrious career, under the name of *critical personalism*. However, by the time I arrived in Heidelberg in January of 1990 to begin a semester's sabbatical there, I had advanced with my study of German sufficiently to begin reading Stern's works. The project I launched then has been a continuing one ever since, and I was able to progress significantly with it during a second sabbatical semester, spent at the University of Leipzig in 1998.

With this book, I hope to awaken a wider appreciation for Stern's perspective on human individuality and for the proper place of personalistic thinking within scientific psychology. I regard this contribution not as the completion of my project, but only as its culmination as I have been able to advance with it thus far.

In my 1987 book, I argued that as the basis for a scientific psychology of personality, the long-dominant and still hegemonic individual differences research paradigm is logically flawed in ways that are both fundamental and irremediable from within that paradigm. The present work underscores and further elaborates that same thesis. Going well beyond the earlier book, however, I have a great deal more to say here, both about the historical emergence of the paradigm that has dominated the thinking of mainstream personality psychologists for most of the 20th century and about the considerations that in my view should guide a reconceptualization of the basic issues in the 21st century. The largely ignored or forgotten contributions to psychology that William Stern made between 1900 and 1935 figure prominently in both lines of discussion.

Chapter One offers a biographical sketch of Stern's professional life. The remaining nine chapters are evenly distributed over three parts.

In Part I, I concentrate on the historical roots of modern correlational studies of individual and group differences in the subdiscipline of "differential" psychology that was formally proposed by Stern in 1900. Chapter Two treats of the emergence of Stern's proposal and its early development against the background of the turn-of-the-century general/experimental psychology typified by the research programs of prominent figures such as Wilhelm Wundt and one of Stern's own mentors, Hermann Ebbinghaus.

Chapter Three focuses on developments within differential psychology that considerably narrowed its scope relative to Stern's initial vision. There, the discussion highlights the influential ideas of E.L. Thorndike and Hugo Münsterberg, and considerable attention is devoted to Stern's ever-growing concern over the untoward influence that the ideas defended by those thinkers were having on differential psychology.

Following Stern's death in 1938, the most prominent spokesperson for views similar (though not identical) to his own was Gordon W. Allport. Accordingly, Chapter Four is concentrated on Allport's efforts to maintain among scientific psychologists an appreciation for many of the concerns that Stern had voiced previously. Because Allport's efforts in this regard were articulated mainly in terms of the distinction between *nomothetic* and *idiographic* personality studies, I concentrate in Chapter Four on the major contours of the debate fueled by Allport's writings on the topic.

Once Allport finally had been persuaded by his many intellectual adversaries to "cry uncle and retire to his corner" (as he himself put it), the way was effectively cleared for the vast majority within the mainstream of personality psychology to prosecute, virtually unopposed, a strictly "nomothetic" discipline tethered securely to the correlational research methods that had been pioneered by Francis Galton and Karl Pearson in their studies of individual differences in intelligence. By this time, the rest of the considerably broader vision of differential psychology that Stern had set forth in 1911, together with critical personalism, had vanished all but entirely from the disciplinary landscape.

Coeval with and indeed indispensable to these historical developments was the wholesale investment by scientific psychologists in general—including, but not limited to, those investigators proclaiming specific interest in the psychology of personality—in a research paradigm guided by the principles of statistical thinking. Part II of this book is organized around this enormously consequential fact.

Chapter Five treats of the historical emergence during the 19th century of statistical thinking itself and of the infusion of that style of thinking into scientific psychology. The discussion points to the ascendance among 19th-century scholars of two competing views of the nature of the knowledge generated when aggregates of individuals sampled from populations are examined statistically—a form of inquiry known originally as "political arithmetic"—and explains why one of those two competing views, but not the other, was serviceable to mainstream psychologists as they effectively reinvented their discipline during the first third of the 20th century.

Chapter Six is a rudimentary methodology. Through the introduction of simple, hypothetical research examples, it offers an exposition of the basic design and data analysis principles defining the procedural canon that continues to guide inquiry at the interface of what Lee J. Cronbach identified in 1957 as scientific psychology's "two disciplines." Major emphasis is placed here on the statistical methods that structure such inquiry, in an attempt to make clear how contemporary mainstream trait psychologists see those methods as serving their professed objectives of predicting, explaining, and understanding individual behavior.

In Chapter Seven, the canon described in Chapter Six is subjected to close critical scrutiny. My intent is to establish beyond all further doubt that the study of variables marking individual and group differences fails to advance scientific understanding of the behavior and psychological life of individual persons, and why this is so. Through an attempt at the beginning of Chapter Seven to set the record straight on what the German philosopher Wilhelm Windelband actually said in 1894 when he drew the distinction between nomothetic and idiographic knowledge objectives, I try to make clear why modern "nomothetic" personality psychology could not possibly be a truly nomothetic science of *persons* in the sense of nomothetic that Windelband originally intended. Pointing back to the "findings" of the hypothetical investigations introduced for illustrative purposes in Chapter Six, I then try to show why statistical knowledge of the sort issuing from studies of individual and group differences fails logically, and hence necessarily, at every turn as the basis for claims concerning the scientific prediction, explanation, and understanding of individual behavior.

Part III addresses the challenge of rethinking the problem of human individuality within scientific psychology, and in this section of the book, the historic contributions of Stern return to center stage.

Chapter Eight offers an introduction to critical personalism. In the first half of the chapter, the major concepts of that system of thought are introduced, following the lead provided by a monograph written by Stern himself for just such purposes and published in 1917 under the title *Psychology and Personalism*. In the second half of Chapter Eight, I have sought to illustrate several features of personalistic thought through a discussion of parts of a work completed in 1909 by William Stern in collaboration with his wife, Clara, titled *Recollection, Testimony, and Lying in Early Childhood*.

In Chapter Nine, two models of personalistic inquiry taken from the contemporary literature are introduced. The first of these is provided by experimental research on the psychology of subjective personality judgments that I have carried out in recent years in collaboration with various students. The findings of that research mount a direct empirical challenge to the long-standing belief that it is meaningless to characterize individuals without comparing them to one another. The same research also illustrates how quantitative methods can be implemented in research that is nevertheless fundamentally personalistic in nature. The model offered here is one I call "neo-Wundtian," and it is just such a model that I believe should guide the needed reconceptualization of the problem of individuality within scientific psychology.

The second example of personalistic inquiry discussed in Chapter Nine, illustrating nonexperimental work of a decidedly qualitative nature, is provided by Steven R. Sabat's recent investigations into the experience of Alzheimer's Disease (AD). Based on extensive interviews with AD sufferers, this work beautifully illustrates what can be accomplished when research "subjects" are regarded as *persons* rather than as mere instances of diagnostic categories such as "mildly" or "severely" cognitively impaired.

Chapter Ten concludes this work with a general discussion of the potential of personalistic thinking both as a foundation for personality theory and as a framework for social thought. Of surpassing importance in the former regard is an appreciation for the fact that meaningful characterizations of individuals not only *can* be achieved wholly apart from between-person comparisons but indeed *must* be achieved for there to *be* any such comparisons. To see this is to grasp the logical possibility of dispensing with between-person comparisons altogether in the scientific study of personality. This is the conceptual passageway leading out of the long-dominant but fatally flawed paradigm and into a framework decidedly more hospitable to the philosophical and theoretical tenets of Stern's critical personalism.

The distinction between person characterization, on one hand, and between-person differentiation, on the other, is also significant for the consideration of critical personalism as a framework for social thought. Within this framework, individuality is understood not in terms of behavioral "traits" seen to set one individual apart from others, but rather in terms of personal values that distinguish what an individual's character *is* from what it *is not but would otherwise be* were the individual's personal values other than they are. In this view, one's individuality cannot somehow be compromised by being *like* others in certain respects, because one's individuality does not hinge on being *different* from those others to begin with.

By embracing a conception of person characterization that sets aside considerations of between-person differences, it is possible to embrace individual-*ity* without endorsing individual-*ism*. In this light, critical personalism emerges as a framework nurturant of community in ways that, arguably, the contemporary emphasis on what separates individuals and groups from each other is not. This suggests that personalistic thinking may have something very important to offer as we seek, in this postmodern age, to come to terms with the various social issues raised by considerations of diversity and multiculturalism.

As the foregoing suggests, this book engages issues and incorporates material cutting across several subspecialties within contemporary psychology. In the main, the concerns of this work are philosophical and theoretical, but in the service of those concerns, the perspective adopted is in some parts historical, in other parts methodological, and in still other parts empirical. I recognize that in presenting for consideration such a work as this I have run the risk of disappointing, frustrating, and perhaps even losing altogether those readers who do not think of their interests as transcending the boundaries of these various perspectives.

Nevertheless, it has seemed to me that for the task at hand, this sort of multifaceted treatment is what is called for, and I can only hope that readers who come to this book with concerns that do not seem to articulate with all of the aforementioned facets of the material will invest the effort to engage the entire work nonetheless. For if nature herself cannot be partitioned as our universities are (I believe it was C. West Churchman who once said or wrote words to this effect), nor can every conceptual problem in 21st-century scientific psychology be relegated neatly to just one or another of the field's currently recognized subspecialties.

This much said, the multifaceted character of the book's contents has mandated some concessions by the author as well. For example, although I have written for an audience primarily comprising advanced students and established academic psychologists, the very specialization to which I have just alluded means that even among readers who are highly knowledgeable in the philosophical, theoretical, and historical areas of the field, there will be many whose familiarity with statistical concepts is quite limited. In an effort to accommodate these readers, I have written of technical matters in a way that might in places seem pedestrian to readers who are already relatively sophisticated in this subject. I must therefore beg the indulgence of those readers and invite them to skip over parts of the discussion that seem too elementary.

With regard to the historical aspects of this work, I recognize that the present treatment cannot be regarded as complete. For reasons indicated above, my focus has been on William Stern's identification of the "problem of individuality" within scientific psychology, on critical personalism as the system of thought in terms of which he proposed to engage the relevant issues, and on certain intellectual developments within psychology before, during, and soon after Stern's time that were of direct relevance to the fate of his ideas vis-à-vis mainstream 20th century thinking about individuality. Unquestionably, there is much more that could be said to augment the history I have traced here, and I hope that my work will heighten interest in furthering this line of historical inquiry beyond the limits of the present account.

In July of 2002, I participated in a symposium that was part of the program of the Eleventh European Conference on Personality, held at the University of Jena, in eastern Germany. The conference program was replete with papers discussing empirical findings issuing from studies of individual and group differences, carried out in full accordance with the procedural principles and interpretive traditions that have dominated thinking within mainstream personality psychology for nearly 100 years. Ubiquitous throughout the conference facility and its proximate environs were posters trumpeting the 5-day event and featuring a lengthy passage taken from William Stern's 1911 text, *Methodological Foundations of Differential Psychology* (quoted in the original German even though the official language of the conference was English).

Through its contents, the Jena conference program enabled participants to reinforce, both in themselves and in one another, long-standing and widely shared convictions concerning the aptness of modern differential psychology as a vehicle for advancing the scientific understanding of human individuality. What was more, the conference participants could do this while still invoking symbolically, through a quoted textbook passage displayed prominently throughout the conference venue (though opaque to a great many of the participants), the intellectual patronage of differential psychology's acknowledged Founding Father.

As I observed all of this, it struck me that the Jena conference could serve as the raison d'etre, in microcosm, for this book. First of all, the prevailing consensus among the Jena conference participants (as in the field at large) that statistical knowledge of the kind generated through studies of individual and group differences advances the scientific understanding of individuals' personalities is ill founded, and needs to be challenged anew. Second, had William Stern been present in the flesh at Jena, he would have rejected the suggestion, implicit in the conference posters, that he concurred with the prevailing consensus. Stern *never* embraced that view. Indeed, could he have attended the Jena conference himself, the Founding Father of differential psychology would have voiced dissatisfaction with virtually the entire conference program and would have urged instead a careful consideration of his other—and to his own thinking vastly more important—intellectual "child," critical personalism.

My mission in writing this book has been to explain thoroughly both that and why all of what I have said in the immediately preceding paragraph is so.

# Acknowledgments

In completing this project, I have received help from many quarters. Through the Georgetown University Graduate School, I have been supported by two summer research grants and a Senior Faculty Research Fellowship. I have also benefited greatly from a sabbatical granted to me during the Spring 1998 semester. A Fulbright Senior Scholar Award enabled me to spend that sabbatical semester in Leipzig, Germany, where I could make extensive use of the superb library facilities there. Most of the historical research that has gone into this book was completed in Leipzig.

I would like to thank Alison Kuhl for her help in compiling the bibliography, and for her technical assistance with the tables as well as Melisa Breiner-Sanders's.

I am grateful to Franz Samelson and Kurt Danziger for their critical comments on my initial ideas about this work. My Georgetown colleagues Norman J. Finkel and Steven R. Sabat provided very helpful feedback on some chapters. Beyond this, Norm and Steve have lent friendly support and encouragement over the entire duration of this lengthy project.

Through the earliest stages of the journey that has led to this book, my former departmental colleague Daniel N. Robinson was a valuable source of support, encouragement, and intellectual inspiration.

Several colleagues in Germany have assisted me in many ways, large and small, direct and indirect. Werner Deutsch, Siegfried Hoppe-Graff, and Frank Radtke deserve special mention in this regard.

As the project neared completion, my wife, Leslie, spent many hours scanning figures and helping me organize the electronic files that had to be created for transmission of the material to Sage. Leslie lent her assistance cheerfully, over and above the countless hours of patience and moral support that could come only from a true partner.

I am enormously grateful to the talented and consummately professional Ms. Carla Freeman for her thorough and sensitive copyediting.

Had I to thank the Senior Editor at Sage, Jim Brace-Thompson, only for his confidence in and backing of this project, my task would be quite large enough. But when our collaboration began, neither of us could have known that with several chapters of this work still to be written, much of my time and attention would be diverted to the care of my dying mother. Jim Brace-Thompson's message to me was clear and unambiguous: "Take all the time you need, and treasure all of it that you have. The book will wait, and Sage will wait for it." I cannot find the words to convey the full measure of my gratitude to Jim Brace-Thompson for his patience and understanding through that challenging time.

To my son Kevin, to my daughter Erika,
and to the memory of my mother,
Rita Jacobs Lamiell (1916-2002)

# Chapter One

## Introduction

### *A Lost Star*

Approaching the end of her distinguished career in the discipline long known as *differential psychology,* Leona Tyler (1906-1993) undertook a retrospective essay titled "Neglected Insights in Personology" (Tyler, 1984). She began as follows:

Last summer I had occasion to refer to *A History of Psychology in Autobiography,* a series I had not looked into for years. I was struck by the fact that many of these eminent psychologists of the past had used this opportunity to present the ideas they considered to be the culminating achievement of their long and productive careers. I was also saddened and intrigued by the realization that many of these ideas had afterward virtually disappeared from mainstream thinking in psychology. . . .

The first person whose ideas I should like to highlight is William Stern. . . . Because my teaching specialty has been individual differences I have known at least his name for a long time, paid due respect to him in historical introductions to textbooks, but never carried my acquaintance any further. As I read his autobiography, I realized that I had been giving him credit for just those things he did not wish to be remembered for.

Everybody knows, for example, that he invented the IQ. In his later years, he indicated in no uncertain terms that he did not regard this as a contribution. He is often called the father of differential psychology. But in his autobiography he talks about his realization, after his first book on differential psychology, that [here quoting Stern][1] "real individuality, the understanding of which I had made my goal, cannot be reached through the channels of differential psychology. The reason is that differential psychology *dissects* and *generalizes* and thus never really studies individuals." I myself came to that conclusion 20 years ago, and thought it was original! [But] most of Stern's books seem not to have been translated, and my graduate school German is not adequate for their comprehension. (Tyler, 1984, p. 2; emphasis in original)[2]

How could the historical developments Tyler identified in this passage have come to pass? Why is it that William Stern's acknowledged place in the history of psychology as the inventor of the intelligence quotient (IQ) is a place that he finally wished he did not occupy? What warrant could there have been for Stern's (and, years later, Tyler's) conclusion that the objective of understanding individualities could not, after all, be achieved through empirical investigations of individual and group differences? Just what was Stern's perspective on human individuality? What reasons might Tyler have had, so many years after Stern's death in 1938, for being not only intrigued but also saddened by the disappearance of that perspective from the landscape of scientific psychology? Why was the system of thought called *critical personalism*, gradually and painstakingly articulated by Stern over the course of his own highly productive career, so thoroughly obscured by subsequent developments within the discipline of differential psychology that he himself had founded? Why might his personalistic orientation merit our more careful consideration now as one from which to critically appraise—and possibly reorient—contemporary thinking about human individuality within mainstream scientific psychology?

In this book, I have sought to provide answers to these and related questions. But before delving further into these matters, we do well to ask this question: Who was this once prominent but now long-lost star of early 20th-century scientific psychology? Who was William Stern?[3]

## Berlin Beginnings

On April 29, 1871, Rosa Stern (1839-1896) gave birth to the son whom she and her husband, Sigismund Stern (1837-1890), would name Louis William. Bühring (1996a) has speculated that it was Sigismund Stern's affinity for France and things French that inclined him toward the names that were chosen for the boy, instead of their German counterparts, Ludwig Wilhelm. Whatever the validity of this view, the younger Stern would eventually dispense with his given first name altogether and have himself known simply as William.[4]

Sigismund Stern ran a small studio in Berlin specializing in design sketches for wallpaper. The studio employed several people, but the business was never especially successful, and there were times when the elder Stern had difficulty meeting the payroll. When he died in 1890, he left little money behind in the family savings, and so it became necessary for William, an only child who was by then engaged in university studies, to work as a tutor to help finance the care of his ailing mother until her death in 1896.

If William Stern found little to emulate in the life of his father, matters were altogether different regarding William's maternal grandfather, also named Sigismund Stern (1812-1867), even though he had died 4 years before his grandson was born.[5] After completing doctoral studies in philology and philosophy at the Friedrich-Wilhelm University, in Berlin (today the Humboldt University), the elder Sigismund Stern opted for a career in pedagogy. While directing a school for boys in Berlin, he became very active in the Jewish reform movement there and later continued his efforts on behalf of the Jewish community in Frankfurt am Main, where he moved in 1855 to assume the directorship of a high school. According to Bühring (1996a), William Stern's grandfather led the movement in Frankfurt to abolish corporal punishment in the schools and to base pedagogy on a better understanding of how children function psychologically.

Of this important figure in the Stern family, Bühring (1996a) wrote further,

> He was successful to a degree seldom matched by other Jews of his time. Beyond the borders of the Jewish community, he was accorded an honored place in German society. For example, he was a respected member of the "General Convention of German Teachers," and was first-named in the list of speakers at the Frankfurt Memorial Celebration held in 1859 in honor of the 100th anniversary of the birth of [the German poet and writer] Friedrich Schiller. (Bühring, 1996a, p. 12)

This passage sheds helpful light on the basis for William Stern's own characterization of his maternal grandfather as "a model and pillar for the entire family, a symbol to which one looked up with respect, the moreso because no one in the following generation (that of the writer's parents) would achieve such prominence" (Stern, 1925a, p. 7; parentheses in original).[6]

Given William Stern's great admiration for his Grandfather Sigismund and the latter's strong and abiding commitment to the Jewish community, one might think that William, too, would have become and remained an active member of that community. As will be discussed further, this turns out not to have been the case. However, Grandfather Sigismund's life as a scholar and intellectual certainly did serve as a model for young William's aspirations. In his boyhood diary, he noted with admiration his grandfather's scholarliness, achievements, and interests (Bühring, 1996a), and at age 14 wrote, "Oh, he must have been a great man! To imitate him is my greatest goal. I, too, will study philology" (Stern, 1925a, p. 58).

In 1888, William Stern did in fact enroll at the aforementioned Friedrich-Wilhelm University of Berlin to pursue studies in philology and philosophy, just as his respected grandfather had done many years previously. William soon found philology tedious, however (Stern, 1927), and after abandoning it, he was free for a time to devote his study efforts entirely to philosophy. Of this subject, he was deeply enamored, and indeed in his 1927 "self-portrait" (or intellectual autobiography), he referred to this period of his studies as "the happiest time of my life" (Stern, 1927, p. 132).

Stern's philosophical studies were guided primarily by Friedrich Paulsen (1846-1908), whose views were grounded in the tradition of Kantian rationalism, and Stern's personalistic outlook on psychological phenomena would likewise bear the marks of that intellectual tradition. Yet as Bühring (1997) has noted, Paulsen was also appreciative of the more empirically oriented approach to psychological questions that had emerged in the work of Gustav Fechner (1801-1887) and was being furthered under the intellectual leadership of Wilhelm Wundt (1832-1920). Stern (1927) wrote that Paulsen's utterly unmetaphysical outlook saved the student from being completely swept away by Hegelianism, and indeed, the less abstract, more empirical "strand" of Paulsen's thinking would also find expression in Stern's developing perspective (Schmidt, 1991a; Stern, 1927). By the third semester of his studies, Stern was not only continuing his coursework in philosophy but also attending lectures in psychology. He completed his doctoral dissertation on the topic of "Analogy in Popular Thought" *(Die Analogie im Volkstümlichen Denken)* under the mentorship of Moritz Lazarus (1824-1903), but none other than the prominent experimentalist Hermann Ebbinghaus (1850-1909) would have the greatest immediate impact on Stern's unfolding career.

## During the Breslau Years, 1897-1916

In 1894, Ebbinghaus left Berlin to direct the Psychological Institute at the University of Breslau.[7] Soon thereafter, he encouraged Stern to apply for a position as an instructor in the Breslau institute, and with no prospects in sight for securing an academic position in Berlin, Stern followed Ebbinghaus's suggestion. As part of his interview in Breslau, Stern spoke on the topic "Tasks and Methods of a Psychology of Individual Differences." He wrote in a letter to his friend, the philosopher Jonas Cohn (1869-1947), of the University of Freiburg, that after addressing his audience for "about an hour," there were only a few "easy questions" to answer, some of which had been skillfully put by Ebbinghaus (letter from Stern to Cohn, July 1, 1897;

Lück & Löwisch, 1994, p. 22). To the surprise of no one involved, Stern's candidacy for the position in Ebbinghaus's institute was successful, and Stern began his postdoctoral academic career as a *Privatdozent* there in 1897.[8]

Apart from his teaching and writing, Stern devoted some of his time and energy to the founding of the Breslau Psychological Association in November of 1897. Stern served as the first chairperson of the association, the stated mission of which was "to support, through lectures, reports, and discussions, the interest in psychological questions that has been awakened in the professional circles of widely varying intellectual disciplines, as well as to further psychological research through discourse and collaborative works" (Lück & Löwisch, 1994, p. 26; see also Bühring, 1996a, p. 39).[9]

## Marriage to Clara Joseephy and Early Contributions to Child Psychology

When not occupied by his intellectual pursuits and other professional engagements, Stern enjoyed making bicycle excursions into the countryside around Breslau, and this activity seems to have served him well both from the standpoint of physical health and as a welcome diversion from the monotony of bachelorhood in Breslau (Bühring, 1996a). Cycling also played a pivotal role in the next major development in Stern's life, for it was during an excursion on his two-wheeler through the Grunewald section of Berlin that he, then 26 years of age, chanced to make the acquaintance of a certain Clara Joseephy (1878-1945). Clara was the daughter of well-to-do Berlin parents who were not pleased about the developing relationship with "the poor wretch" (*der arme Schlucker;* Michaelis-Stern, 1991, p. 133). But Clara wanted William as her partner, and her strong will prevailed over her parents' wishes. She and William were married early in 1899 and immediately took up residence in Breslau. Soon, their family was under way.

On April 7, 1900, the Sterns' first child, daughter Hilde, was born, and William Stern recorded the following observations in writing:

> Born on 7 April, 1900, 2:00 a.m.
>     Observations before birth:
>     First movements were sensed around mid (13th?) Oct.
>     The movements were always more lively [when mother was] in the bath.
>     First day, 7 April.
>     Birth followed 24-hour labor. When only the head had appeared and the child's eyes were wiped with cold water, she grimaced as if to cry. First cry as the baby had completely emerged with the exception of one foot.
>     When laid on the table, she immediately sucked her thumb.

An *"aayhaay"* was clear in the cry of the first day, the *"aay"* sound inclining somewhat to *"ay,"* especially the second. The *h* unmistakably clear. Almost all cries had this form.

Immediately following birth the child reacted neither to sounds (hands clapping) nor to light (gas flame). On the other hand, at 5 hours of age she seemed to react to mother's short, sharp *"shhhh,"* by twice immediately suppressing her crying.

In the evening she was placed at the left breast and after a few seconds began to make the sucking movements correctly. (Stern diaries, April 7, 1900)[10]

With these lines, a project was begun that the Stern couple would maintain for 18 years. It would finally extend to more than 5,000 handwritten pages, preserving for posterity extensive diary observations on various aspects of the psychological development not only of Hilde but also of son Günther, who was born in 1902, and second daughter Eva, born in 1904 (see Figure 1.1). The Sterns originally planned a series of six "Monographs on the Psychological Development of the Child" based on the material that was gradually accumulating in the diaries. The topics on which they intended to write included (a) children's speech, (b) recollection testimony and lying in early childhood, (c) observing and portraying in childhood, (d) children's play, (e) the will and the emotions in childhood, and (f) thinking and the development of a worldview (Stern & Stern, 1999, p. xxxvii). In fact, only two of these six planned monographs were ever published: *Die Kindersprache* (*Children's Speech*) appeared in 1907 (Stern & Stern, 1907); and *Erinnerung, Aussage, und Lüge in der ersten Kindheit* (*Recollection, Testimony, and Lying in Early Childhood*) appeared 2 years later (Stern & Stern, 1909).[11]

In his intellectual autobiography, Stern (1927) commented specifically on the significance of the diary work for the larger mission that would center his intellectual life over the entirety of his career:

[In] the studies of my own children . . . I observed psychological life concretely, and in this way I was protected from those ivory-tower schemes and abstractions that we all too often encounter in the name of psychology . . . I came to see how a great diversity of psychological contents can exist within a single individual, either simultaneously or sequentially, and yet all converge on that developing person's unitary life line, thus endowing the highly variegated psychological contents of a life with meaning. The diary material impressed upon me the fundamental form of personal causality, which is the convergence of the propensities present in a child with the totality of outer influences. In short, the diary material provided me with a perspectival foundation for the philosophical theory I was gradually developing. (Stern, 1927, p. 17)

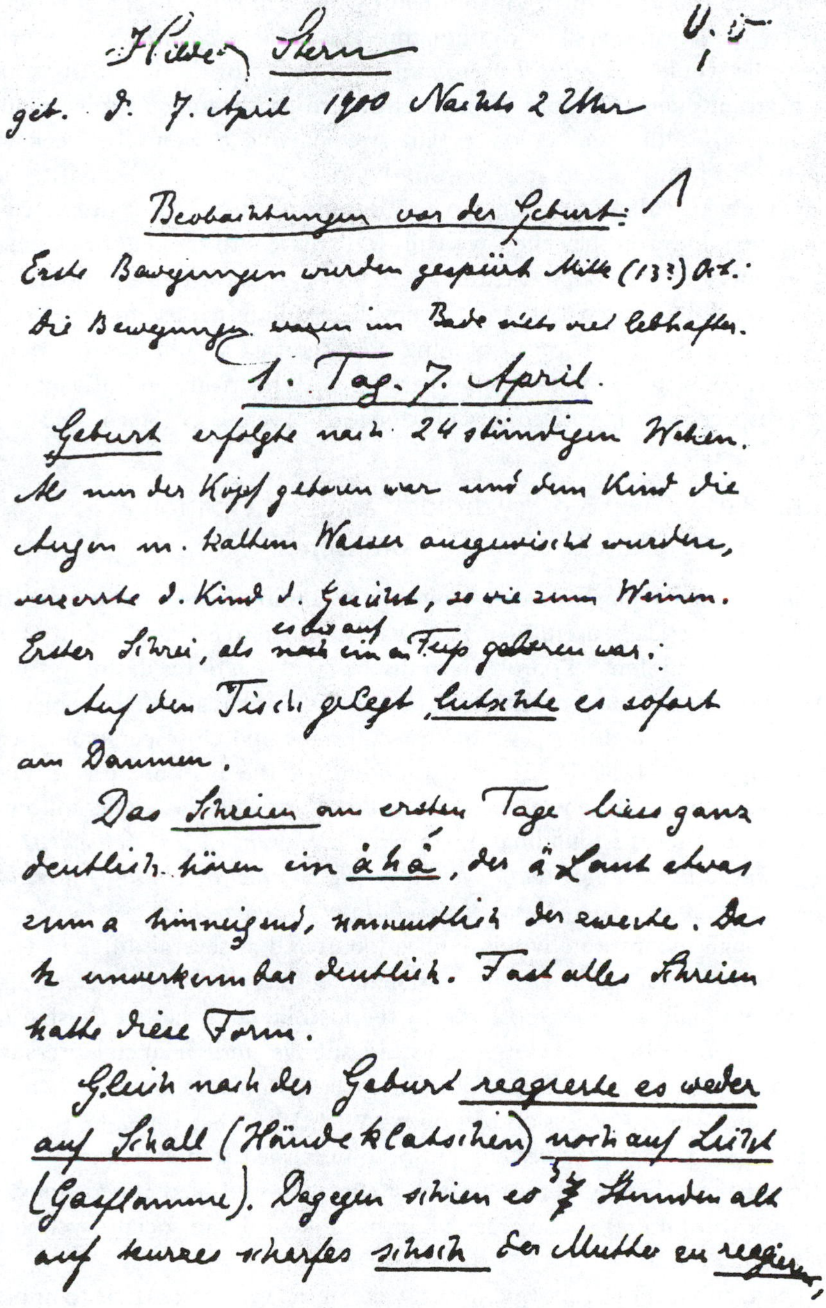

Hilde Stern

geb. d. 7. April 1900 Nachts 2 Uhr

Beobachtungen vor der Geburt:

Erste Bewegungen wurden gespürt Mitte (13?) Ct.:
Die Bewegungen waren im Bade viel ... lebhafter.

1. Tag. 7. April.

Geburt erfolgte nach 24 stündigen Wehen.
Als nun der Kopf geboren war und dem Kind die
Augen m. kaltem Wasser ausgewischt wurden,
verzerrte d. Kind d. Gesicht, so wie zum Weinen.
Erster Schrei, als ... noch ein ... Teil geboren war.

Auf den Tisch gelegt, lutschte es sofort
am Daumen.

Das Schreien am ersten Tage liess ganz
deutlich hören ein ä hä, der ä Laut etwas
zum a hinneigend, namentlich der zweite. Das
h unverkennbar deutlich. Fast alles Schreien
hatte diese Form.

Gleich nach der Geburt reagierte es weder
auf Schall (Hände klatschen) noch auf Licht
(Gasflamme). Dagegen schien es ... Stunden alt
auf kurzes scharfes ... der Mutter zu reagieren,

Figure 1.1    Facsimile of the First Page of the Stern Diaries, Written on April 7, 1900

The philosophical theory mentioned by Stern in this passage is actually the comprehensive system of thought—the *Weltanschauung,* or world-view—he would call *critical personalism,* a system of thought that would both ground and ever guide Stern's efforts to grasp human individuality. Ultimately, in the sources of certain irremediable tensions between the tenets of critical personalism, on one hand, and other intellectual trends that emerged within and soon came to dominate early 20th-century scientific psychology, on the other, we will find answers to the questions posed at the outset of this chapter. Circa 1900, however, these tensions could not have been fully anticipated, and the ambitious, industrious, and ever optimistic Stern was intent on fashioning a bridge that would join his philosophical convictions about human persons with his rising enthusiasm over the prospects for the new empirical science of psychology (Stern, 1927).

## Initiatives in Applied Psychology and Participation in the 1909 Clark University Conference

One of Stern's major objectives within psychology was to help make the discipline practically useful. During a vacation trip to Switzerland in 1902, accompanied by Jonas Cohn,[12] Stern discussed at length his desire to found an institute for applied psychology, and in 1906, he realized this objective in collaboration with his psychologist colleague and close personal friend Otto Lipmann (1880-1933). The founding of the Institute for Applied Psychology, with its central location in Berlin (not Breslau), was followed 2 years later by the founding, again with Lipmann, of the *Zeitschrift für angewandte Psychologie und psychologische Sammelforschung (Journal of Applied Psychology and General Psychological Research).*[13]

Although the institute would be headquartered at several different locations in Berlin during the ensuing years, and despite the fact that Stern himself would maintain only loose ties to the institute after he left Breslau for Hamburg in 1916 (see below), it would survive until financial pressures forced Lipmann to close it in 1930. The journal would continue for 3 more years, until Hitler's accession to power in 1933. By that time, 45 volumes and 68 special issues *(Beiheften)* had been published, containing articles on differential psychology, forensic psychology, and experimental pedagogy, as well as contributions in the areas of anthropological and social psychology (Bühring, 1996a).

These publications followed in the wake of the very first article to appear in the journal, a work authored by Stern himself, under the title *"Tatsachen und Ursachen der seelischen Entwicklung"* ("Facts and Causes of Psychological Development"; Stern, 1908). Stern's burgeoning interest in child/developmental psychology was undoubtedly part of the reason that he received an invitation to the international conference planned for the late summer of 1909 by G. Stanley Hall (1846-1924), the foremost American child psychologist of the day. But there is more to the story of Stern's involvement in that historic event.

The occasion for the conference organized by Hall was the celebration of the 20th anniversary of the founding of Clark University, in Worcester, Massachusetts. The invitation ultimately extended to Stern was actually made first to Ebbinghaus, who in 1905 had left Breslau to assume a professorship at the University of Halle. Hall's invitation had tentatively been accepted by Ebbinghaus, who then died suddenly in early 1909, and only then was the invitation redirected to his former student and junior colleague.

Stern wrote in a letter to Cohn on May 17, 1909, that he was enthusiastic about this opportunity but also expressed his sadness over the event that had brought the invitation about:

> I attended [Ebbinghaus's] burial in Halle, and as his eldest student and also the representative of [the institute at] Breslau I said some words of remembrance at the graveside. In spite of everything that has long since distanced me inwardly from him, his death has touched me deeply. He led me to psychology, and for 15 years my professional destiny was bound to his. (Stern letter to Cohn, May 17, 1909; Lück & Löwisch, 1994, p. 76)

In Chapter Two, we will further discuss the source of this "inward distance" from Ebbinghaus that Stern came to feel.

When in the late summer of 1909 the ocean liner named *George Washington* set sail from Germany, William Stern was not the only passenger bound for the Clark University conference. Three other invitees to the event, Sandor Ferenczi (1873-1933), from Hungary; Carl Jung (1875-1961), from Switzerland; and Sigmund Freud (1856-1939), from Austria, were on board as well. On the day after the ship reached New York, the August 30 edition of the *New York Times* published a list of prominent passengers arriving from abroad. Only one of the four psychologists headed for Massachusetts was named in this list—and this was neither Ferenczi, nor Jung, nor Freud. Presumably, Stern's early initiatives in applied psychology had won him at least modest notoriety (Bühring, 1996a; Deutsch, 1997). Unfortunately, he was incorrectly identified in the *New York Times* as William *Stein,* and Deutsch (1997) has pointed out that though this error was corrected in the records provided by the Clark conference archivist William A. Koelsch, one mistake was merely replaced by another, for in this latter instance Stern's first name was given incorrectly as *Wilhelm.*

Stern's lectures at the conference, which were delivered in German, were centered around two themes. One was the psychology of testimony, and the other was the study of individuality. In the published abstracts of Stern's lectures, which were prepared by Stern himself in German and then translated into English by E. C. Sanford (cf. Stern, 1910), one finds Stern beginning his remarks on the latter topic as follows:

> In addition to the main problem of Psychology (the investigation of the general uniformities of the mental life) two others now begin to engage attention, which until recently have been left almost entirely to other disciplines.
>
> *The Question of Differences (differentielle Fragestellung)* deals with the variations in the particular mental functions. Each may be studied with reference to the degree of its general variability; its qualitative differentiation into "Types," its quantitative differentiation into grades, its genetic differentiation into developmental stages, its relative variations in comparison with other functions, i.e., its correlation.
>
> The Question of Individuality *(individuelle Fragestellung)* has to do with the knowledge of a single individual personality in and for itself, whether in relation to its total psychical makeup or in relation to a particular aspect, as character, intelligence, etc. (Stern, 1910, p. 276; parentheses and emphasis as shown in originally published translation)

As we will see in Chapters Two and Three, this was neither the first nor the last time that Stern would point to the need for a distinction between the study of *individuals,* that is, *persons,* and the study of individual *differences,* that is, *person variables.* This crucial distinction would ultimately be blurred to virtual obliteration by major conceptual developments within the field of differential psychology during the first three decades of the 20th century. In Parts I and II of this work, these historical developments and their methodological consequences will be discussed at length, and I will argue that this turn of events finally doomed Stern's personalistic outlook to the obscurity that Tyler (1984) would later mourn.

## Engagement in the School Reform Movement and the Controversy Over Psychoanalytic Psychotherapy With Children and Adolescents

Still several weeks before sailing to America, Stern wrote in a letter to Cohn:

> In view of your plans to found a pedagogical society, I'd like to share with you the following. For a year already, efforts have been underway to found a large

'society for school reform,' *(Bund für Schulreform),* which would involve all of Germany and would have local chapters in various cities. The overall objective here is to organize collaborative efforts among all interested parties—school administrators, doctors, parents, and psychologists—to address problems on a scientific basis. The idea has originated in Hamburg . . . and the executive committee that is to be organized will include among its members Meumann and myself.[14] (Stern letter to Cohn, July 28, 1909; Lück & Löwisch, 1994, pp. 77-78)

At the turn of the 20th century, "old school" pedagogy, relying heavily on repetitive drilling to achieve learning objectives and on corporal punishment to control behavior, still prevailed in many places in Germany. As was true of his grandfather Sigismund before him (see above), William Stern's views of children and of pedagogical practices inclined him to oppose these traditions. Not surprisingly, therefore, he had scarcely settled in again at home following his journey to America before he was involving himself in the efforts of the society which he had mentioned in his earlier letter to Cohn. The pedagogical objectives of the society, Bühring (1996a) notes, were modeled as follows:

[A]fter educational ideals represented by Johann Fichte's philosophical idealism, Wilhelm von Humboldt's neo-humanism, and Johann Pestalozzi's popular notions about child-rearing. The overarching concern of these three great humanists was . . . *the humanization of human society.* "This meant self-initiative, self-determination, self-independence, and the coordinated development of all of the human being's mental resources: the intellectual, the moral, and the aesthetic." (Bühring, 1996a, pp. 61-62, quoting in part Probst, 1989, p. 14; emphasis added)

From the 4th to the 6th of October, 1913, the Society for School Reform convened in Stern's home city of Breslau. In coordination with this event, 2 days prior to the opening of the society's official sessions, Stern took it upon himself to organize a meeting of what was called the Commission for Youth Studies *(Kommission für Jugendkunde).* Stern's intention was to make this group into a subsection of the larger Society for School Reform, with a focal mission given in the public statement published the following year in the *Journal of Applied Psychology and General Psychological Research:*

The [Commission's] task is to gather together into one organization those persons and institutions dedicated to scientific research on children and adolescents, and in particular on their psychological lives. The Commission will fulfill this task through the sponsorship of scientific study groups, and by supporting, through the scientific expertise of its members, the official activities of the

Society for School Reform. (*Zeitschrift für angewandte Psychologie und psychologische Sammelforschung*, 1914, p. 380; original German quoted in Bühring, 1996a, p. 60)

Pointedly, psychoanalytically oriented child psychologists were excluded from membership in the Commission for Youth Studies. Indeed, that membership issued on October, 5, 1913—hence squarely in the middle of the Breslau meetings of the Society for School Reform—a warning about the practice of psychoanalytic psychotherapy on children and adolescents. The document that circulated would finally recruit 31 signatories, including William and Clara Stern's, and proclaimed the following:

> The members of the Section for Youth Studies within the Society for School Reform regard it as their duty to notify friends of youth and pedagogy of the dangers that exist as a result of attempts to apply psychoanalytic methods to children and adolescents.
>
> Without taking any position on the scientific significance of psychoanalytic theory and the therapeutic application of its methods with adults, the undersigned declare:
>
> 1. The claim that psychoanalytic methods prove that previously conducted research on children has been misdirected, and that only through psychoanalysis has a scientific child psychology become possible, is unjustified.
> 2. The extension of psychoanalytic methods to application in the course of normal child-rearing practices is to be rejected. The reason for this is that psychoanalysis can lead to a lasting psychological infection of the treated with premature sexual fantasies and sexual feelings, and thus deprive children of their innocence in a way that presents a great danger for our youth. The various successes in child-rearing that have been claimed by practitioners of psycho-analysis are greatly outweighed by the damages that will be done to the immature mind. (Reprinted in German in Graf-Nold, 1991, p. 69)

This was not Stern's first expression of opposition to Freud's views. Already in 1901, Stern had published a review of Freud's *Interpretation of Dreams,* which appeared the previous year (Freud, 1900), and though Stern's commentary was by no means entirely negative, he did level some rather harsh criticisms.

On the positive side, Stern wrote:

> [T]his novel perspective on dream life, with the analogies Freud makes in many places to pathological conditions, opens up to us many interesting considerations,

even if, for reasons to be discussed presently, the underlying theory itself must be rejected. What seems most valuable of all to me is the effort to extend the explanation of dream life beyond the sphere of imagination, the play of associations, the activity of fantasy, and the somatic relationships, and to point further to those little known strands leading down into the core of the world of affects. . . . In addition to this, the book contains many valuable and interesting details, fine-grained observations and points of theoretical perspective. But above all one finds here an extraordinary wealth of material on carefully recounted dreams, which any researcher in this area will greatly welcome. (Stern, 1901, p. 131)

But criticism followed:

There is so much wrong with [Freud's] procedure that it is difficult to know where to start. For one thing, "self observation" is not so simple, particularly when one is being influenced by, in the case of Freud himself, his own theory, or, in the case of his patients, probing questions and instructions [while the dreamer is relating the dream]. Nor is there the slightest reason to see in waking fantasies the repetition of dream work, so that what the former stumbles upon as an end- or tie-off point is to be regarded as the latter's unconscious starting point. Here, a bald claim is being offered in the place of needed evidence. [As the saying goes,] "if you can't prove something, just impose your interpretation on it"[15]. . . . The inadmissibility of this approach to dream interpretation as scientific method must be emphasized, because the danger is great that uncritical souls could get comfortable with this engaging mind game and that we, as a consequence, would slip into an entirely mystical and arbitrary exercise, whereby one could then prove everything with anything. (Stern, 1901, pp. 132-133)

Perhaps it was, at least in part, an enduring pique on Freud's part over this criticism that lay behind an unpleasant exchange that occurred in 1909, coincident with the aforementioned passage to the United States aboard the *George Washington*. Bühring (1996a) writes that at one point during the journey, Freud happened upon Jung and Stern while the latter two were engaged in a private discussion, whereupon Freud called out impatiently to his "crown prince" Jung, saying "Oh Doctor, when will you finally be finished with this conversation?"

But however uneasy the relationship between Stern and Freud may have been prior to 1913, matters were surely brought to a head in that year as a result of the publication by Hermine von Hug-Hellmuth (1871-1924) of a work titled *Aus dem Seelenleben des Kindes. Eine psychoanalytische Studie* (*From the Psychological Life of the Child: A Psychoanalytic Study*; von Hug-Hellmuth, 1913). This work appeared as the 15th publication in a series that was being edited by Freud, under the title *Writings in Applied*

*Psychological Studies.* In the work, von Hug-Hellmuth (and, by extension, Freud as series editor) sexualized the psychological life of the child to the point where Stern, outraged, determined to stand up in public opposition. On June, 9, 1913, he wrote to Cohn that he was just then in the process of formulating an essay protesting the practice of psychoanalytic psychotherapy with children: "What they have done now exceeds all comprehension. Psychoanalysis has become a pedagogical danger, and it is high time for the Commission for Youth Studies to stand up in opposition to this" (Stern letter to Cohn, June, 9, 1913; Lück & Löwisch, 1994, p. 91).

The "Breslau Proclamation" (see above) would give some voice to this opposition, but Stern himself would go further, publishing 1 year later an article in which he would argue that owing to its thin—indeed practically nonexistent—evidentiary base, the practice of Freudian psychotherapy with children "is not only a scientific aberration *(Verirrung)* but a pedagogical sin *(Versündigung)*" (Stern, 1914b, p. 91).

In her work, von Hug-Hellmuth (1913) charged that in deference to prevailing social conventions, the academic child psychologists of the day were closing their collective eyes to expressions of childhood sexuality. Bühring (1996a) notes that von Hug-Hellmuth "even dared to intrude into the Stern family by suggesting sexual motives behind Hilde's, Günther's, and Eva's innocent utterances—a [personal] affront to Clara and William" (Bühring, 1996a, p. 73).

Stern (1914b) responded directly to this criticism, stating,

> The fact that we have not written about sexual matters [in our works on child psychology] is not because we have concealed anything, but rather because through all of our intensive observations, we have not discovered the slightest trace of sexual undertones in our children's recollections. (Stern, 1914b, p. 86)

It must be remembered that by 1914, the Stern couple had recorded well over 4,000 handwritten pages of observations concerning the psychological development of their three children (cf. Behrens & Deutsch, 1991, p. 35). In light of this fact, it is not difficult to understand why Stern would have regarded himself as rather better positioned to speak, with at least a modicum of scientific authority, on matters of child psychology than were doctrinaire adherents of a theoretical perspective whose author could not have filled even one small notebook with his own direct observations of children.

Freud did not engage himself directly in the contentiousness under discussion here. There was a rejoinder of sorts to the Breslau Proclamation, authored by a Zürich minister named Oskar Pfister (1873-1956) and identifying 23 additional signatories. But Freud was not among those signatories, nor, apparently, was he consulted at any point during the drafting of the text (Graf-Nold, 1991).

Notwithstanding Stern's disagreements with Freud on certain fundamental issues—primarily infantile sexuality and the methods of psychoanalytic inquiry—Stern was also able to find aspects of psychoanalytic thought that were quite compatible with his views. Though in many respects, critical personalism more closely resembles the individual psychology of Alfred Adler (1870-1937) than it does doctrinaire Freudian theory, Stern's thinking readily embraced the notions of *depth* in mental life, including unconscious mental processes, and of *repression* (Bühring, 1996a). Perhaps these points of theoretical agreement helped to make possible the cordial meeting between Stern and Freud that took place some years later. On an undated postcard sent to Cohn from Vienna, probably written in May or June of 1928, Stern related that on the previous day, he had paid a visit to Freud and that the two had had "a two-hour conversation [that] despite all of our differences was most pleasant" (Lück & Löwisch, 1994, p. 161).

## World War I and the Move to Hamburg

The outbreak of World War I was certainly, to say the least, far from pleasant for Stern and for millions of other Europeans in the latter part of 1914. Fortunately for the 35-year-old Stern, he was declared physically unfit for military duty. However, he was assigned to supervise a dispatching station that served as a base for reconnaissance missions, and out of a sense of patriotic duty to the *Vaterland,* Stern forsook the salary that was due him in compensation for his services in this assignment. He also undertook to gather patriotic essays, poems, and drawings by school children in Breslau (Bühring, 1996a).

As a member of the teaching faculty at the university, Stern was affected most deeply by the war through the absence of so many students who had been drafted into the armed forces. Of course, a great many of those students would never return, and the magnitude of their sacrifice was by no means lost on Stern. In his letter to Cohn of July 19, 1915, Stern wrote,

> The reason it has been so long since I've written to you—or you to me—is surely an instinctive reticence to attend to private interests and relationships at this time, when world happenings push all such matters to the background, and make them seem unimportant. Neither of us can participate directly (I was found unfit for military service), and our indirect contribution seems to be, even in our own eyes, utterly insignificant in comparison to what others are doing out there. (Stern letter to Cohn, July 19, 1915; Lück & Löwisch, 1994, p. 92)

Yet even as war raged, the search was on at the Colonial Institute of Hamburg for a scholar with academic credentials and professional interests in pedagogy to replace Ernst Meumann, who passed away on April, 26, 1915. In November of that year, Stern was informed that he was the preferred candidate for the position, and the family made ready to leave Breslau for the bustling port city in northern Germany.

## During the Hamburg Years, 1916-1933

There was no university in Hamburg when Stern arrived in 1916. Instead, the city's academic life was centered by an entity known as the "Colonial Institute," and it included both a philosophical seminar and a psychological laboratory. Stern officially assumed directorship of both on March 1, 1916, and at that time also succeeded Meumann as editor of the *Zeitschrift für Pädagogische Psychologie und experimentelle Pädagogik* (*Journal of Pedagogical Psychology and Experimental Pedagogy*; Bühring, 1996a). In addition, Stern assumed leadership of the Institute for Youth Studies, which Meumann had established during the time between his own move to Hamburg in 1911 and his death in 1915. Combined with lecturing responsibilities, the demands of these many administrative and editorial duties left Stern, in the short run, with precious little time for research and writing. However, by moving to Hamburg, Stern did seem to have positioned himself better, in the long run, to significantly advance his scientific agenda.

Without doubt, a major component of that agenda was to further develop psychology as an *applied* discipline, that is, one addressed in practically relevant ways to the important issues of the day. In 1916, *the* issue in Germany was of course the war, and Stern's enduring sense of patriotic duty inclined him to support his native country's war effort as best he could. Research on the differential suitability of individuals of varying abilities and interests for specific jobs both within the military (e.g., as pilots of military aircraft) and in civilian life (e.g., as streetcar operators) defined an important part of Stern's contributions in this regard. In the years immediately following the war, Stern maintained his scientific interest in the topic of occupational suitability *(Berufseignung)* in a way that he hoped would contribute further to his country's reconstruction efforts. The goal of this line of research was to ascertain viable occupational possibilities for persons who were returning home with disabilities resulting from war injuries (Bühring, 1996a). The postwar years would also present Stern with the opportunity to renew his interest in the pedagogically important problem of identifying highly talented youth and providing for their proper education.

By Stern's own account, this concern over quality education for youth—and in particular for the young soldiers returning to Hamburg in defeat after many months of grueling military service and horrifying experiences—played a major role in his decision to join the effort to transform the Colonial Institute into a full-fledged university (Stern, 1927). That effort was finally successful, and in January of 1919, Stern was lecturing on "The General History of Philosophy" under the auspices of the new University of Hamburg (Bühring, 1996a).

That Stern would have chosen to lecture on philosophy rather than psychology would not have surprised Stern's colleagues, coworkers, or assistants. On the contrary, Bühring (1996a) notes that already during the negotiations that took place prior to Stern's acceptance of the offer in Hamburg, he made it clear to those concerned that he would not accept a teaching assignment that included only courses in psychology and none in philosophy.

To be sure, Stern was highly committed to the various empirical pursuits mentioned above (and others as well; Hardesty, 1976). They were, after all, projects designed to investigate individual and group differences in accordance with methodological principles that he himself had espoused in his second differential psychology textbook, completed well before the move to Hamburg (Stern, 1911). However, at no point in his academic life did Stern allow such pursuits to blind him to the crucial importance of philosophical considerations. On the contrary, throughout his years in Hamburg, he remained as committed as ever to realizing the larger vision he had begun to formulate many years earlier, during his student days in Berlin. That vision called for the development of a comprehensive system of thought by which it would be possible to reconcile the psychological realities (uncovered by careful empirical investigation) with the philosophical tenets (metaphysical, epistemic, and ethical) of a *Weltanschauung,* or worldview, predicated on an irreducible distinction between *persons* and *things.* Thus did he write in a letter to Cohn, dated October 5, 1916: "Volume two of *Person and Thing,* [titled] '*The Human Personality,*' is essentially finished. Together with a short work titled '*Psychology and Personalism,*' this volume should form the bridge between my philosophical and psychological ideas" (Stern letter to Cohn, October 5, 1916; Lück & Löwisch, 1994, p. 102; italics added).

The series Stern titled *Person und Sache* (*Person and Thing;* 1906) would consist finally of three volumes. Due to the paper shortage in Germany during World War I, the work mentioned by Stern in the above passage, *The Human Personality (Die menschliche Persönlichkeit)* did not actually appear in print until 1918 (Stern, 1918a). This was fully 12 years after the appearance of the first volume, *Ableitung und Grundlehre* (*Rationale and Basic Tenets;* Stern, 1906) and 6 years prior to the appearance of the third and last volume, *Wertphilosophie* (*Philosophy of Value;* Stern, 1924b).

In subsequent chapters, much will be said about Stern's efforts to further the personalistic perspective, both while in Breslau and later, in Hamburg. Indeed, that is an important part of the larger mission of the present work. For the immediate purposes of this biographical sketch, however, the point to be stressed is simply that even as Stern the research psychologist was devoting so much of himself to the various empirical efforts being carried out under the auspices of the psychological laboratory in Hamburg, Stern the philosopher was also somehow finding the time and energy necessary to develop that other facet of his scholarly vision. As will be seen, Stern would also have to devote much of himself during this period to defending the personalistic perspective in the face of other trends in scientific psychology that were antagonistic to it. As already indicated by Tyler's (1984) remarks cited at the outset of this chapter, this struggle was one in which Stern's views would not prevail.

## The Personalistically Minded German Jew
## in the Face of the Imminent Catastrophe

In "Recollections of My Parents," the youngest of Clara and William Stern's three children, daughter Eva (1904-1992), noted in a brief passage relevant to her father's Jewish heritage that he had felt "some sense of duty to the Jewish community" (Michaelis-Stern, 1991, p. 134). She hinted that it was perhaps this sense that led William Stern during his years at the University of Breslau to reject out of hand the suggestion that he renounce Judaism and permit himself to be baptized so that, in turn, he could become a tenured member of the faculty. Nevertheless, stressed Eva, her father was not a person who practiced the Jewish religion in any sustained way.

This view conforms to that of the Sterns' second-born child, Günther (1902-1994). For example, in an essay published in the *Süddeutsche Zeitung* on April 8, 1978, in commemoration of the 40th anniversary of William Stern's death, Günther wrote,

> No, the period of my childhood and adolescence was not really very Jewish at all... It was actually quite un-Jewish. The festive atmosphere of Friday evenings remained unknown to me. Never did I hear my parents speak of *Yom Kippur* or *Versöhnungstag* (Day of Reconciliation). And never was I brought to a synagogue by my father—as if I should say "brought" when he himself never set foot in a synagogue, at least not in my lifetime. (Anders, 1971, p. 115)[16]

Günther went on to point out that his father's religious beliefs actually took the form of an "utterly un-Jewish pantheism" (Anders, 1971, p. 115).

Perhaps this was in part a reflection of Stern's high regard for the views of the Leipzig physicist cum psychophysicist Gustav Fechner (1801-1887; Schmidt, 1991a). In any case, it is clear that although William Stern was born a Jew, the life he led was not "Jew-ish."[17]

On the other hand, mention has already been made of Stern's sense of duty to his native Germany. Another reflection of this is provided in the letter to Cohn of October 5, 1916, cited above. Immediately after conveying to Cohn that his (Stern's) most recently completed works would bridge the philosophical and psychological aspects of his thinking, Stern added,

> But when will humanity once again become interested in such problems? It is becoming more and more difficult to think beyond the next days, and to busy oneself with things that have nothing directly to do with the question of Germany's survival. (Stern letter to Cohn, October 5, 1916; Luck & Löwisch, 1994, p. 102)

Yet only a few lines later in the same letter, Stern expressed anew his sense of the relevance of his own efforts as an academician to the larger cause and, in the process, found reason to praise the German spirit:

> In the face of all that is happening, it is truly amazing how the German people engage with full intensity the practical intellectual tasks of the culture. In recent weeks I have been in Berlin and Leipzig. In Berlin I participated in a course for the care of small children that offered much that was informative. I spoke there to more than 800 persons about the psychology of early childhood. In Leipzig I spoke to the Association of Teachers about the issue of talent [among youth] and its significance in school and in work. (Stern letter to Cohn, October 5, 1916; Lück & Löwisch, 1994, p. 103)

The optimism that managed to seep through here, even in the midst of the horrible "war to end all wars," fairly gushed with the cease-fire, 2 years later. On November, 15, 1918, 4 days after the official cessation of hostilities, Stern wrote to Cohn,

> Thank you for your letter. Here we have experienced a few days of considerable unrest, but so far we have survived them well and without any personal difficulties. During the first days. . . one felt like a mere thing; an object of some sort being tossed about in a storm. But that ended soon, and now we are gathering our resources, especially our intellectual resources, in the awareness that the German people have never needed us more than they need us now, and that out of this new condition something great and enduring can emerge, if everyone is able and willing to contribute. (Stern letter to Cohn, November 15, 1918; Lück & Löwisch, 1994, p. 116)

Clearly, Stern's faith in the German people was strong at this time, as was his belief that he could, should, and would contribute positively to the postwar effort to revitalize German life and culture. It is important to appreciate, however, that Stern's hopes for accomplishing "something great and enduring" were grounded no more in his ethnicity than they were in his religious heritage. They were grounded in his personalistic worldview, that is, in his conception of the essential nature of human persons *as such*. To be sure, that conception *accommodated*—but also finally *transcended*—all considerations of individual and group differences issuing from contingent factors such as ethnicity, religion, culture, race, and natural endowment. Consistent with this view, Stern the critical personalist saw himself first and foremost *as a person rather than as a thing*. Relative to this fact, the additional fact that he was a German person was a matter of secondary importance at most, and the further fact that he happened to be a Jewish person was of scarcely any significance at all.

# Denouement

Very soon, the Nazis would make it clear that they saw things quite differently. Central to Stern's conception of the essential nature of human persons, however, was a firm belief not only in their inherent value but also in their basic goodness (Anders, 1950; Michaelis-Stern, 1991), and if this faith was fundamental to his nearly irrepressible optimism, it was undoubtedly also the source of his naïveté in the face of political developments unfolding in Germany in the early 1930s (Anders, 1950; Schmidt, 1991b). On January 6, 1933, Stern wrote to Cohn to congratulate him on the publication of his book *Wertwissenschaft* (*Science of Value;* Cohn, 1932):

> I hope that beyond the pleasure of seeing the finished book lying there in front of you, you will have the additional pleasure of sensing its impact on others near and far. . . For even if the immediate present is not exactly favorable for works of such a fundamental nature, which without being radical or laden with delusions of grandeur nevertheless address themselves to the most decisive issues of humanity, still we must hope that such times will return, because otherwise all of our objectives and accomplishments of the past 50 years will have been for nothing! History simply *cannot* be so senseless! (Stern letter to Cohn, January 6, 1933; Lück & Löwisch, 1994, p. 166)

Thus, mere weeks before Hitler's accession to power, on January 30, 1933, Stern was still inclined to focus attention on scholarly concerns and to express the hope that the intellectual atmosphere of the "immediate present" would soon enough give way to one more hospitable to those concerns. He continued the letter in this spirit:

> I, too, am trying to the best of my ability to emancipate myself as much as possible from the anti-scientific atmosphere of the times, and to work, admittedly only during extended pauses, on a "General Psychology," a work intended to give evidence of the fruitfulness of the personalistic perspective. Since no German-language general psychology text has appeared for quite some time, there is a need for this book. But I still cannot foresee how and when I will be finished with it. (Stern letter to Cohn, January 6, 1933; Lück & Löwisch, 1994, p. 167)

Stern would finally finish the work, but he would do so neither very soon nor in Germany. On April 7, 1933,[18] the Nazis officially declared that government employees, including university faculty and staff, not of Aryan descent were to be retired immediately. Of this *Blitzkrieg*-like invasion into William Stern's life, his son would later write,

> With one cruel stroke, the foundation for, and the sense of, all of his work seemed to be buried by this catastrophe. The friends with whom he was consulting, the students whom he was teaching, the colleagues whom he had helped to advance professionally, were warned about associating with him, an *undesirable (Schädling)*. The journals he was administering were ripped from his hands, his books were removed from the library, and from one moment to the next he was strictly forbidden to set foot in the Institute at the University of Hamburg which he himself had built up. (Anders, 1950, p. xxiv)

Within months of Stern's peremptory dismissal, he was grieving the deaths of two of his closest colleagues, Martha Muchow (1892-1933) and Otto Lipmann (1880-1933). Though neither of these individuals was Jewish, both were defamed as a result of their professional association with the Jew Stern, and both committed suicide in autumn of 1933 (Bühring, 1996a).[19] Soon thereafter, the Sterns traveled to the Netherlands, where William would at long last complete his general psychology text and arrange for its publication, which was in German, but by the Dutch publishing house Nijhoff (Stern, 1935). Efforts by Dutch colleagues to secure a permanent position for Stern at one of the universities in the Netherlands were not successful (Bühring, 1996a), and he finally accepted the offer by William McDougall (1871-1938) of a visiting professorship at Duke University, in Durham, North Carolina. In the winter semester of the 1934 to 1935 academic year, he taught his first course at Duke under the title "The Psychology of Memory."

In June of 1935, the Sterns returned to Europe and arranged to meet daughter Eva in Switzerland. Even then, as Eva would later recall, her father still had to be convinced that he was in danger of being arrested by the Nazis and that under no circumstances should he dare to return to Germany (Michaelis-Stern, 1991, p. 137). After a few weeks in Switzerland, it was decided that Clara would go to Hamburg to clear out the apartment, while William would go to the Netherlands and wait for his wife to meet him there. The couple did eventually reunite in Holland, and in the fall of 1935, they set sail again for the United States.

Bühring (1996a) has written that once they had returned to Durham, Clara and William Stern finally had to come to terms with the harsh fact that what they had originally envisioned as a temporary life in exile,

> [H]ad now become a permanent arrangement. No one believed any more that Nazi dominance in Germany was going to end any time soon. So there was nothing for the two emigrants to do except adjust . . . to their new circumstances. William held lectures at the university; Clara attended lectures at the university. He buried himself in small projects, she gave German lessons. Both tried to maintain correspondence, as best they could, with friends and relatives who had also endured the diaspora. (Bühring, 1996a, pp. 208-209)

There would be, however, yet one more trip back to Europe. In July of 1937, Clara and William Stern sailed to Holland and were met in Rotterdam by daughters Eva and Hilde. The latter had spent 2 years in prison in Germany as punishment for having sheltered communists who were fugitives from the Gestapo.[20] In a letter sent from Holland, Stern shared with Cohn the happy news that Hilde would be returning with her parents to the United States. He also informed Cohn that "during my current travels, the 'General Psychology' is being printed by the publishing company Macmillan, and it is supposed to appear in the fall" (Stern letter to Cohn, July 16, 1937; Lück & Löwisch, 1994, p. 180). This latter bit of professional news followed another announcement: "It will interest you to learn that next year [at Duke] I will also be a member of the Philosophy Department. This is especially pleasing to me because it is customary there for [the psychology and philosophy] departments to be sharply separated" (Stern letter to Cohn, July 16, 1937; Lück & Löwisch, 1994, p. 180).

But before the fall of 1938 arrived, Stern was dead, taken suddenly by a heart attack on March 27. To the very end, notwithstanding his status as an emigrant with limited skills in English, he had managed to keep one academic foot in philosophy even as the other was rooted in psychology.

For obvious reasons, there would be no appreciation of Stern published in Nazi Germany. In the United States, however, one of Stern's closest academic associates, Gordon Allport (1897-1967), wrote,

> William Stern was both a pioneer and a systematizer in psychology. . . . He will be remembered . . . for his sure-footed explorations in differential psychology, forensic psychology, psychotechnics, child psychology, and intelligence testing. But he will be remembered likewise and, I think, with increasing renown for his theoretical system of personalistic psychology wherein he ordered his manifold research, and which, in turn, he incorporated within his comprehensive philosophic doctrine of Critical Personalism. . . . It troubled him relatively little that his formulations ran counter to the trend of the times, particularly in American thought. . . . [H]e believed so intensely in the liberating powers of personalistic thought that he had faith in its ultimate acceptability to others. Thinking [personalistically], Stern became a monumental defender of an unpopular cause. [But] the personalistic way of thought will yet have its day, and its day will be long and bright. (Allport, 1938, pp. 770 and 773)

Contrary to Allport's confident forecasts, Stern is nowadays remembered, if at all, for an exceedingly small fraction of his substantively broad and conceptually deep contributions to psychology during the first third of the 20th century. Least of all can it be said that Stern's personalistic way of thought has ever yet had "its day." The chapters that follow comprise a systematic attempt to understand and to critically appraise this state of affairs.

# Notes

1. In mentioning *A History of Psychology in Autobiography* at the beginning of this quotation, Tyler (1984) was referring to a volume edited by Murchison (1930), which includes an English translation by Susanne Langer of Stern's *Selbstdarstellung* ("Self-Portrait"). This latter work was published in 1927 (Stern, 1927) as a contribution to a German language volume edited by Schmidt (1927). In this passage, Tyler was quoting Langer's English translation (Stern, 1930a).

2. Stern's last book, *Allgemeine Psychologie auf personalistischer Grundlage* (Stern, 1935) is among the few of his works that to date have been translated into English (*General Psychology from the Personalistsic Standpoint;* Stern, 1938). Another is *psychologie der Frühen Kindheit bis zum sechsten Lebensjahr* (Stern, 1914a), published in English translation as *The Psychology of Early Childhood up to the Sixth Year of Age* (Stern, 1924a); and a third is *Erinnerung, Aussage, und Lüge in der Ersten Kindheit* (Stern & Stern, 1909), published in English translation as *Recollection, Testimony, and Lying in Early Childhood* (Stern & Stern, 1999). But

as informative as these works are, a full appreciation for the scope and depth of Stern's thinking requires, as Tyler suggested, familiarity with works that are available only in German.

3. *Stern* is not only the name of the person on whom this discussion is focused but is also the German word for *star*. To date, no full-length biography of Stern has been published in English. However, in addition to the aforementioned intellectual autobiography (Stern, 1927, 1930a), a German language biography authored by Gerald Bühring did appear several years ago (Bühring, 1996a), and these works have served as the primary guides to the necessarily brief biographical sketch offered in this chapter.

4. In some of Stern's early publications, the author is identified as "L. William Stern," but from 1906 on, the "L." disappears altogether, and authorship is attributed to "William Stern." Under no circumstances is this individual properly referred to as "William L. Stern" (cf. Kreppner, 1992).

5. William's mother's maiden name was thus also Stern. In fact, William Stern's parents were cousins (Bühring, 1996a).

6. The work from which this passage has been quoted is one published by Stern under the title *Anfänge der Reifezeit: Ein Knabentagebuch in Psychologischer Bearbeitung* (*Beginnings of Maturity: A Young Boy's Diary in Psychological Perspective*; Stern, 1925a). In this work, the author of the diary mentioned in the title is identified by Stern as a youngster with whom he (Stern) was "well acquainted." And indeed he was, for it would be revealed years later by Stern's youngest daughter, Eva, that the boy who had written the diary was in fact William Stern himself.

7. The city known as Breslau during the time period under discussion here is located in the former German state of Silesia. Upon the conclusion of World War II, Silesia became a part of Poland, and Breslau was renamed Wroclaw.

8. As a *Privatdozent*, Stern's salary was entirely contingent on the fees paid by students who opted to attend his lectures. Stern developed a reputation as a technically skilled and intellectually engaging lecturer and regularly drew large enrollments for his courses (Bühring, 1996a).

9. Bühring (1996a) states that it was through Stern's initiative that the Breslau Psychological Association would become, 2 years after its founding, the third section (in addition to those at Berlin and Munich) of the German Association for Psychological Research, and these three local organizations would eventually form the core of the Association for Experimental Psychology that would be founded at a congress held in the city of Giessen in April 1904. This latter organization would in turn become, some 25 years later, the German Psychological Association, which exists to this day. Stern would eventually serve as the vice chairman of that association and later would be the organization's duly elected president, only to be stripped of the office in 1933 through "fascist maneuverings" (Bühring, 1996a, p. 40).

10. Due in large part to the efforts of Werner Deutsch, the complete Stern diaries have been transcribed and are available in electronic format at the Max Planck Institute for Psycholinguistics, located in Nijmegen, the Netherlands. So, although

the diaries themselves were never published, a title bibliography of Stern's works compiled by the biographer of Stern, Gerhard Bühring, includes the following entry:

Stern, W., & Stern, C. (1918). *Die Kindertagebücher (1900-1918)*. William Stern Archiv der Jewish National and University Library auf Givat Ram in Jerusalem. (Elektronische Abschrift der unveröffentlichten Tagebücher). Nijmegen: Max-Planck Institut für Psycholinguistik.

11. A portion of the present discussion is adapted from an introductory chapter I authored in collaboration with Werner Deutsch for the volume in which my English translation of *Erinnerung, Aussage, und Lüge in der ersten Kindheit* has been published (Stern & Stern, 1999; see Endnote #2, above). It should also be noted here that although four of the six monographs originally planned by the Sterns never materialized, William Stern did make further use of the diary material in authoring his widely read text, *The Psychology of Early Childhood Up to the Sixth Year of Life* (Stern, 1924a).

12. This trip occurred shortly after the birth of the Sterns' second child, son Günther. According to Bühring (1996a), William Stern was suffering at that time from nervous exhaustion, and he needed some time away from family and professional responsibilities. He traveled by train to Freiburg where he was joined by Cohn, and the two continued on to Interlaken.

13. In 1916, the title of this publication was shortened to *Zeitschrift für angewandte Psychologie (Journal of Applied Psychology)*.

14. Ernst Meumann (1862-1915) was a major contributor to the establishment of educational psychology in Germany (Probst, 1997). In 1911, Meumann assumed a professorship in "philosophy with a concentration in psychology" at what was known then as the Colonial Institute of Hamburg. Due in no small part to the efforts of Stern, who would succeed Meumann in Hamburg following Meumann's death in 1915 (refer below), the Colonial Institute and an entity called the "Hamburg Lecture Program" would become the University of Hamburg in 1919 (Probst, 1997).

15. *"Legt ihr's nicht aus, so legt ihr's unter"* (Stern, 1901, p. 132).

16. In private correspondence with Wilfried Schmidt, Günther Stern indicated that he continued to use the surname "Anders" after adopting it as a pseudonym in writing an essay for which he won a literary prize (see Schmidt, 1991b, p. 128).

17. In his essay, Günther Anders wrote of the fateful role of the pantheistic beliefs he had come to share with his father in the latter's fall from grace in the son's eyes. When he was about 10 years old, Anders wrote, he was in the garden with his father and an aunt. The aunt clipped a flower, held it before young Günther's face, and told him to take it to his mother as an expression of love. Horrified that this flower, a living entity in which God was present, had been decapitated, Günther struck his aunt. Witnessing the event, William Stern swung at Günther, but missed, and had to restrain himself from swinging again. Deriding the father as a "softy" *(Schlappschwanz)*, Günther's aunt took it upon herself to slap the boy about the ears. William Stern then told his son to apologize to the aunt. Günther refused to

do this, protesting that by his father's own pantheistic beliefs, it was the aunt who should apologize for decapitating the flower. Anders wrote in his essay,

> Of course, my aunt dismissed this absurd demand with a scornful laugh, but my father, who remained silent, understood very well what I had meant. As it has ever been through the ages, a rift opened up for the first time between me and my father, who for me up to this moment was always on a pedestal above all criticism, yes on a par with God. He had betrayed our most sacred principles. . . . Saying nothing, I left the garden, and with that, for several years, *him*. Because for years, and not only to my sorrow but probably to his as well, our relationship remained disturbed. Not until 30 years later, across the ocean, when he was approaching death, did he mention the scene in passing. And he did no more than mention it. Because his conscience was no clearer than mine. (Anders, 1971, p. 115)

18.  In a cruel irony, this was the 33rd birthday of the Sterns' first daughter, Hilde.

19.  It appears that at the time, Stern was not fully informed about the cause of either Muchow's or Lipmann's death. In December of 1933, he wrote to Cohn of Lipmann's "swift and peaceful" death due to a heart attack and of Muchow's "tragic death" as "a secret that may well never be explained." (Stern letter to Cohn, December 19, 1933; cf. Lück & Löwisch, 1994, p. 170).

20.  Just at the time Clara had traveled from Switzerland to Hamburg in 1935 to clear out the apartment there, she received word that Hilde had been arrested. Clara and William knew about, and did not approve of, Hilde's affiliation with leftist organizations, and therefore Clara had good reason to believe that there were incriminating materials in Hilde's apartment. At great risk to herself, Clara sneaked into Hilde's apartment the very night that Hilde was being arrested, found such materials, and removed them without being detected.

# Part I

## Historical Beginnings

# Chapter Two

## The Problem of Individuality and the Historical Emergence of a "Differential" Psychology

*Das Besondere unterliegt ewig dem Allgemeinen,*
*Das Allgemeine hat ewig sich mit dem Besonderen zu fügen.*

—Johann Wolfgang von Goethe

*Individuality, problem of the twentieth century!*

With this exhortation, William Stern beckoned readers into his 1900 book, *On the Psychology of Individual Differences (Toward a "Differential Psychology")* (Stern, 1900a). A meticulous scholar, Stern certainly knew that he was not raising questions about individuality for the first time in the history of intellectual discourse. In this instance, however, he was addressing himself to his fellow psychologists and was doing so in the firm belief that even at that very early stage in psychology's life as an experimental discipline certifiably distinct from "armchair" philosophy, the need was pressing for a means of systematically accommodating the facts of human individuality within the discipline, in a manner consonant with the nascent field's explicitly scientific aspirations. (See Figure 2.1.)

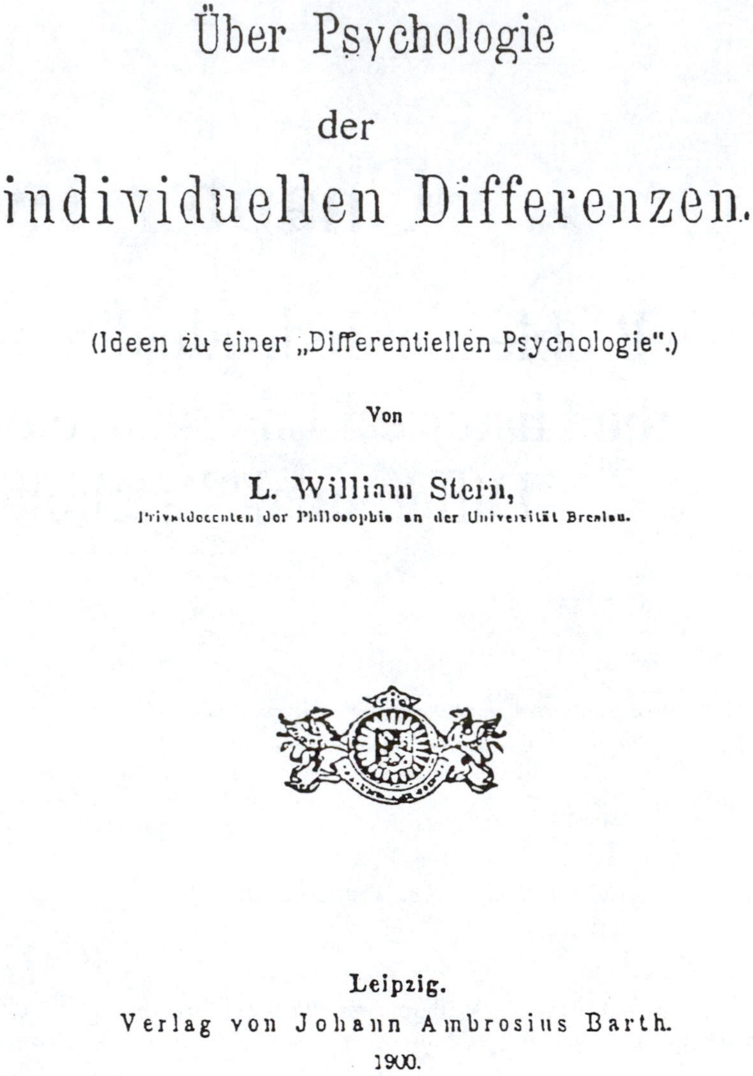

# Über Psychologie

## der

# individuellen Differenzen.

(Ideen zu einer „Differentiellen Psychologie".)

Von

## L. William Stern,

Privatdocenten der Philosophie an der Universität Breslau.

Leipzig.

Verlag von Johann Ambrosius Barth.

1900.

---

**Figure 2.1**    Facsimile of Title Page of Stern's 1900 Book

In his prefatory remarks, Stern noted that even at that time, interest in individual variability in human psychological life was not completely new, and in this connection he directed his readers to the bibliography he had provided at the end of the book. Stern contended, however, that such efforts as had been undertaken up to that point were widely scattered and uncoordinated and had not yet been given a collective identity. He expressed the hope that his book would accomplish this and in the process secure for the new subdiscipline he envisioned, differential psychology, "citizenship in the kingdom of knowledge" (Stern, 1900a, p. v).

Stern's 1900 book may thus properly be regarded as an initial attempt to circumscribe the territory of a differential psychology and to provide at least preliminary guidelines for its scientific agenda. The book's publication gave formal expression for the first time to the view that the systematic study of individual variability within the basic domains of human psychological functioning would help to clear a space within the larger scientific psychology of the day for a viable conception of the distinctly *personal* features of mental life and behavior.

Even as Stern was urging his fellow psychologists to attend to this emerging "problem of individuality," he hastened to emphasize his conviction that a differential psychology should neither be completely isolated from nor in any way undermine the *allgemeine,* or general, psychology of the day. Speaking through Goethe in the epigram used above, Stern advised that "the particular is ever subordinate to the general [even as] the general must ever accommodate the particular." In this spirit, Stern argued that properly understood and prosecuted, a differential psychology would *complement* general psychology and neither oppose nor supplant it.

But what *was* general psychology circa 1900? Why had human individuality become "problematic" vis-à-vis that general psychology? The discussion properly begins with a consideration of these questions, in hopes of clarifying as much as possible Stern's perspective at the time on the "problem" of individuality and on differential psychology and its place within the larger scheme of things.


## *Die allgemeine Psychologie* in Late 19th-Century Germany

Among historians of the field, the birth year of psychology as a distinct scientific discipline is usually fixed at a scant 21 years prior to the appearance of Stern's 1900 book. In 1879, 47-year-old Herr Professor Doktor Wilhelm Wundt (1832-1920), a member of the philosophy faculty at the University of Leipzig, equipped university-held space for the purpose of conducting controlled and systematic experiments on various basic aspects of human mental life. Among lovers of knowledge, of course, interest in understanding human psychological functioning can be traced at least as far back as the pre-Socratics of ancient Greece (Robinson, 1995). This is a fact that Stern's teacher and senior colleague Hermann Ebbinghaus surely had in mind when in 1908, he characterized psychology as a discipline with "a long past but a short history" (Ebbinghaus, 1908, p. 3). Ebbinghaus argued, however, that only in a relatively short time preceding the very work he was writing had there been any appreciable advances in the field beyond what had been achieved by Aristotle (cf. Robinson, 1989). Since the venerable Greek philosopher died in 322 B.C., psychology's wheels, on Ebbinghaus's account, had been spinning in utter futility for roughly two millennia! That psychology had enjoyed relatively recent advances and that it justifiably could look forward to more of same is something Ebbinghaus attributed to "the rise and progress of natural science since the sixteenth century" (Ebbinghaus, 1908, p. 6).

In this respect, Ebbinghaus took his lead from Wundt, who some 35 years earlier as a young physiologist in Heidelberg assisting Hermann Helmholtz (1821-1894) had written as follows:

> [I]t is a doctrine that is impressed on us from every side of the history of the natural sciences, that the progress of each science is tied closely to advances in the methods of investigation. All of modern science has emerged from a revolution of method. (Wundt, 1862, as quoted in Graumann, 1980)[1]

During his years at Heidelberg, from 1858 to 1863, Wundt of course became thoroughly familiar with the central project of a psychophysics, a discipline aimed at empirically establishing the links between variations in the intensity of physical stimuli, on one hand, and concomitant variations in the domain of sensory perception, on the other. Indeed, why wouldn't Wundt have done so? As Graumann (1980) reminds us, the year 1860 hosted the publication of both *Elements of Psychophysics* by Gustav Fechner and the second edition of Helmholtz's *Handbook of Physiological Optics*. A scant 2 years later, in 1862, Wundt's own *Contributions to a Theory of Sense Perception* was published, and the concerted effort to establish a general psychology that would rely primarily on experimental methods modeled after those employed in the natural sciences was unmistakably under way, even if its "official" founding—to the extent that there can be such a thing at all—was still nearly two decades in the future.

Through his various works, including most prominently the pathbreaking *Über das Gedächtnis* (*Memory*; Ebbinghaus, 1885/1964), Ebbinghaus succeeded in persuading many of his contemporaries that contra Wundt, the use of experimental methods need not be restricted to the study of the most elementary psychological processes (sensations and simple feelings), but could in principle be extended to the study of "higher" mental functions as well: memory, to be sure, but also attention, emotion, language, judgment and reason, beliefs, and even the exercise of will. Ebbinghaus (and many others with him) believed that these functions all conformed to certain *general laws,* and in this context, clarity on the meaning of the term *general* is vital.

The German word for general is *allgemein,* and etymologically speaking, this term itself developed as a contracted form of the expression *allen gemein,* meaning "common to all." It is in this light that we must understand the notion carried by scientific psychology's founders of their experimental psychology as an *allgemeine Psychologie,* or *general psychology.* Within the framework of experimental psychology as envisioned by Wundt, Ebbinghaus, and the other "founding fathers" of the discipline, the quest was for knowledge of the general laws, *die allgemeinen Gesetze,* presumed to govern the mental life of the individual. For the early experimentalists, the expression "individual psychology" was synonymous with the expression "general experimental psychology."[2]

Inasmuch as the early experimentalists were seeking general laws in the sense of scientific regularities "common to all," it is easy to see why those investigators conducted their experiments in accordance with what would nowadays be termed an "$N = 1$" approach. Complete experiments were carried out on research "subjects"[3] individually, one at a time, because the phenomena of interest—basic psychological processes—were presumed to be taking place in individual minds.[4] Indeed, the quest for knowledge of general laws governing individual psychological functioning would have been seen not only as *permitting* an "$N = 1$" approach but also as logically *demanding* it, for there would have been no way to determine if a putative law were in fact common to all, *allen gemein, except* by investigating the matter case by case, one research "subject" at a time.

Of course, the early experimentalists appreciated that it would never be possible to investigate every case. But they also understood that to say as much would merely be to point to the limits of induction constraining all scientific inquiry and that any empirically based claim to a lawful regularity in science would necessarily carry with it the implicit caveat "true until further notice." The general-experimental psychologists of 1900 saw (correctly) that in this regard, there was nothing peculiar about psychology as compared with the other more established sciences, and they also saw that when the objective was to establish *general* truths concerning some aspect(s) of *individual* functioning (physical, physiological, mental, behavioral, or any other "-al"), the examination of individual cases was not merely an option, but a requirement.

To the extent that a putative law (such as Ebbinghaus's own famous "forgetting curve") could have been found to hold true in case after individual case, an evidential basis would have accumulated in support of the claim that the law was indeed general in the sense of *allen gemein.* Conversely, to the extent that such evidence failed to materialize (i.e., that empirical findings varied from one case to another), any claim for the generality of some law putatively governing the psychological process in question would have been compromised.[5] Though between-person variation in experimental findings would not have rendered the quest for general laws futile in principle, it most assuredly would have constituted an empirical challenge to any psychology that would overlook or seek to systematically eliminate such variation. Conversely, empirical demonstrations of systematic individual differences in various domains of human psychological functioning would help point to the need for incorporating some conception of individuality into the framework of any viable scientific psychology. This was Stern's point of departure in his call for a "differential psychology."

## The Birth of *die differentielle Psychologie*

### Stern's Vision of the Scope and Mission of Differential Psychology

Stern opened the discussion in Chapter 1 of his 1900 book with an explicit juxtaposition of general and differential psychology:

> One of the few features more or less common to all earlier efforts toward a scientific psychology was that the problem was seen as—and only as—a general one. The investigations were concentrated on the most basic elements out of which all psychological life is built up, on the general laws *(die allgemeinen Gesetze)* according to which mental phenomena occur. In this work, the attempt was made to abstract as much as possible from the unending diversity in which we encounter psychological being and living in different individuals, peoples, social classes, genders, etc.; the objective was precisely to distill from this broad diversity that which is common *(das Gemeinsame),* and the research findings have been related, sometimes justifiably, sometimes not, to mental life, and not to this or that particular instantiation of a psychological event. Abstraction of this sort is justified so long as it emerges from a judicious insight into the limits of our abilities at any given time. But the danger is only too great (and not always avoided) that one forgets that one is dealing with an abstraction and believes that through a general treatment of this sort all problems entailed in psychological investigation can be solved. Fortunately, we are seeing

more and more, in contrast to this view, the emergence of an awareness that the material that has to this point been neglected, specifically the differential peculiarities *(die differentiellen Eigentümlichkeiten)* of the psyche, deserve attention. (Stern, 1900a, pp. 2-3)

From here, Stern went on to specify the major tasks of differential psychology, and he could scarcely have been more explicit. Those tasks, he wrote,

[F]orm a trio, and involve the differences themselves, their causes, and their modes of expression. So the first question is: What are the differences? In what manner do individuals, peoples, etc. distinguish themselves from one another? . . . The second question may be formulated: What causes the differences? Here, inquiry will be focused on the relationship of psychological characteristics to objective factors such as inheritance, climate, social position, rearing, adjustment, etc. . . . Thirdly, one can ask: How are the differences manifested? Here belong those attempts, admittedly unsatisfactory up to now, to infer psychological characteristics from facial marks, handwriting, and other symptoms. In its most general terms, the result of inquiry in this direction would be a psychological symptomatology and diagnostic. (Stern, 1900a, pp. 4-5)

Stern saw the first of these three tasks, that of identifying the basic dimensions of individual differences, as the most fundamental from a scientific standpoint, and he implored his readers to resist the temptation to foreshorten their work on that task in favor of efforts that might seem at first blush to have more immediate practical application. A premature focus on symptomatology and diagnosis, he worried, might wittingly or otherwise reify lay conceptions of individuals' psychological characteristics and, in the process, serve to proliferate without scientific justification certain popular but possibly erroneous notions concerning individual differences. He made clear his view that what was called for would entail the careful, painstaking, and systematic articulation of individual differences concepts within the recognized domains of general psychology.

Stern's firm resolve to link differential psychology "step for step" (Stern, 1900a, p. 8) to general psychology is underscored in Part II of his book. There, Stern discussed in successive chapters "some domains of psychological differentiation and their experimental investigation" (p. 40) and included among these sense receptivity, perception *(Anschauung)*,[6] memory, association, comprehension *(Auffassung)*, attention, combinatorial abilities, judgment, reaction, feelings, psychic "tempo,"[7] and "psychic energy."[8] These were areas of investigation that had become prominent in the experimental psychology of the time, and Stern believed that each offered fertile territory for the investigation of basic individual differences.

That is, he believed that within each of these areas, it would be possible to show that some individuals performed (sensed, perceived, comprehended, felt, reacted, judged, etc.) in ways that would consistently differentiate them from other individuals and that the resulting typologies would ground a differential psychology tied directly, systematically, and effectively to the topics of investigation that were dominating general-experimental-individual psychology.

Underscoring his concern that differential psychologists (a) keep securely tied to the theoretically grounded content domains identified by the general-experimentalists and (b) avoid premature efforts in the direction of practical application, Stern elaborated his thoughts on this matter with an explicit (and rather sharply pointed) reference to the burgeoning efforts of Alfred Binet (1857-1911) in the domain of mental testing:

> [T]here is a new form of experimental procedure already partly headed along a way that is precipitous and that could all too easily lead away from the heights of science. Fortunately, the movement is still quite young; it has existed only for a few years; so we hope that a warning "Halt!" will resonate.
>
> I am speaking here of the so-called "mental tests" *(Seelenprüfungen)*. It is in America and France where this new development has gained the most attention; but too great a concern for the practical, on the one hand, and too much in the way of artistic intuition, on the other, have resulted in the avoidance of many difficult considerations, and this reveals that the theoretical nature of the entire edifice is a house of cards. (Stern, 1900a, p. 34)

Of particular concern to Stern in this context was the suggestion by Binet and Henri[9] that an adequate battery of tests of the "higher" mental functions (memory, imagination, attentiveness, etc.) that could be administered to a child within 90 minutes had been developed and was ready for use in appropriate settings:

> [I]it is difficult to understand how one could claim in all seriousness that such a test of individuality is already possible today, and even practically applicable; yet respected representatives of French scholarship are caught up in this belief. I argued above that at the present time we are not yet up to the task of grasping individuality comprehensively, and this holds especially true for the would-be tests in this area of experimentation. They involve grabbing ten arbitrary points out of one's psychological life, using them sequentially to test an individual in order to see how these ten functions react to certain stimuli, and then claiming from this to have marked out a scheme for individuality: this is the Bertillon-ian system for the examination of criminals by policemen,[10] cloaked in the garb of psychology. (Stern, 1900a, p. 35)

Underscoring his concerns over the premature application of diagnostic instruments and his belief in the importance of theoretically grounded inquiry, Stern proceeded a few pages later as follows:

> Binet and Henri consider that their methods can already today be put to practical use by a teacher or doctor. What an optimistic self-deception! We should only be carrying over into practice such knowledge as has been firmly established, and not vague notions inadequately tied down. If only we would resist believing in the usefulness of material that has been transferred much too prematurely from the domain of theory into that of practice. Practical disappointments and mistakes discredit the entire theoretical foundation, and this danger is something to be avoided. . . . Let us not heed today the calls for practical application that are being made all too prematurely by lay persons, quasi lay persons and also, unfortunately, by scholars. For the time being, let us leave to the graphologists and other "practitioners" the diagnostic forecasts which require less in the way of exactness and reliability than what is required by science. At the present time, considerations of convenience cannot be primary. Ease of use and tractability of a method might perhaps be desired ends, but they can in no way be the beginning of an investigative procedure. . . . If we work restlessly but not in haste on the theoretical problems, then when the time comes practical success will come as ripened fruit falling from the tree: gnosis precedes dia-gnosis and pro-gnosis! (Stern, 1900a, pp. 38-39)

Regarding the pursuit of the requisite gnosis from the standpoint of a differential psychology, the notion of types played a role in Stern's early thinking. The essence of his view was that if basic typologies could be established within the various domains of psychological functioning (e.g., comprehension, perception, memory, association, etc.), the types thus established could in turn be used as the basis for establishing various kinds of type combinations.

In this connection, Stern distinguished between *type complexes* and *complex types*. In the former case, two or more different types are represented in the same person but simply "exist alongside one another" without in any way interacting. A type complex is thus a variation of a *quantitative* sort, and Stern offered as an example of this a person who is a visual perceptual type *and* has a melancholic emotional tone.

In the case of a complex type, however, the two or more different types existing within the same person coalesce in such a way as to differentiate the individual from others not only quantitatively but also *qualitatively*. Stern described an instance, for example,

> [W]here one finds a prevalence of the visual together with a strong aesthetic sense; this is the complex—but closed—type of person that may be described

as highly sensitive to artistic and natural beauty. The picture becomes still more complicated and richer if in addition to the above one finds a tendency toward productivity; we are dealing now with the type of a productive scholar or painter. (Stern, 1900a, p. 12)

Whatever the nature or extent of the complexity under discussion, Stern was firmly of the view that persons could and did differ from one another not only quantitatively but also qualitatively. But beyond this, and in the long run more important, he was also convinced that persons can be understood in typological terms only up to a point. With this latter conviction in mind, he turned his attention directly to his main concern: individuality.

## Stern's Antimechanistic Convictions

In his 1927 intellectual autobiography, Stern wrote that "even then [i.e., in 1900] I could see that true individuality, the understanding of which was my ultimate objective, cannot be grasped through the channels of differential psychology" (Stern, 1927, p. 142). Searching in the 1900 text for evidence that Stern did indeed hold this view "even then," one does not have to look far. In the very first chapter of the work, Stern noted that beyond certain practical constraints on the differential psychologist's ability to do justice to the problem of individuality, there exists also a timeless constraint, owing to the following actuality:

[E]very individual is a singularity, a one-time existing being, nowhere else and never before present. To be sure, certain law-like regularities (Gesetzmäßigkeiten) apply to him, certain types are embodied in him, but the individual is not exhausted by these laws and types; there remains ever something more, through which this individual is distinct from others who conform to the same laws and types. And this last kernel of being, which reveals the individual to be thus and so, distinct from all others, is not expressible in the language of scientific concepts, it is unclassifiable, incommensurable. In this sense, the individual is a limiting concept, toward which theoretical investigation strives but can never reach; it is, one could say, the asymptote of science. (Stern, 1900a, pp. 15-16)

In its spirit, this passage bears a striking resemblance to the following one:

Since there is, therefore, no established end in the general laws to which the causal chain of conditions can be traced back, all subsumption under those laws does not help us to analyze up to its ultimate grounding the single event given in time. There yet remains for us in all historical and individual experiences something left over that is ungraspable, inexpressible, undefinable. So, too, does the ultimate and innermost nature of personality withstand analytic decomposition by means of general categories, and this, unascertainable, appears to our consciousness as the feeling of the causelessness of our nature, that is, individual freedom.

This latter passage comes from a speech titled *"Geschichte und Naturwissenschaft"* ("History and Natural Science"). The speech was delivered in May of 1894 by a German philosopher on the occasion of his assumption of the Rectorship of the University of Strassburg. The philosopher was Wilhelm Windelband (Windelband, 1894/1998, p. 21).

Many readers, though probably not all, will recognize the name Windelband (1848-1915) as one often linked to the "nomothetic versus idiographic" distinction. Invoking Windelband, the American psychologist Gordon W. Allport (1897-1967) drew widespread attention to this distinction in his 1937 text titled *Personality: A Psychological Interpretation* (Allport, 1937a) and in so doing sparked a debate within the field that to this day has not been resolved satisfactorily. In Chapter Four, this matter will be discussed at length. What bears emphasis in the present context is the indication, given by the foregoing juxtaposition of quotations, of metaphysical concerns on Stern's part that extended far beyond experimental psychologists' empirical neglect of individual differences. Given the relevant dates, we can be certain that these concerns were not aspects of Stern's thinking that took shape only later in his career (cf. Allport, 1937a; Holt, 1962; Pawlik, 1994, p. xviii), and there is a wealth of additional evidence pointing in this direction. Some of this evidence comes from Stern's correspondence with his friend and colleague, the Freiburg philosopher Jonas Cohn.

For example, in a 1909 letter to Cohn, Stern alluded to the fact that he had "long since (been) inwardly distanced" from his onetime teacher and senior colleague at Breslau, the aforementioned Hermann Ebbinghaus (refer to Chapter One). Because it was Ebbinghaus who, in full knowledge of Stern's nascent interest in individual differences, had greatly assisted Stern in securing a lectureship at the University of Breslau in 1896 (Bühring, 1996a) and because Ebbinghaus himself had made at least one sojourn into the domain of individual differences research (Ebbinghaus, 1896a), it seems doubtful that the "inward distance" to which Stern alluded could have resulted from any uncompromising opposition on Ebbinghaus's part to the very idea of a differential psychology. On the contrary, the problem for Stern was the mechanistic, and ultimately impersonalistic, conception of human mental life that Ebbinghaus espoused. Windelband, too, had expressed skepticism about the adequacy of precisely this sort of conception, and this is surely one reason that his speech struck such a harmonious chord for Stern.

In a letter to Cohn dated May, 21, 1897, Stern specifically mentioned that he had been reading Windelband. In the same letter, Stern also mentioned having read Ebbinghaus's "Psychology," by which he must have meant the *Foundations of Psychology,* which appeared that year (Ebbinghaus, 1897). The book, Stern confided to Cohn,

> [I]s not to be dismissed so readily as we at first thought. Even if it does not contain any fundamentally new ideas, it is nevertheless an excellent presenta- tion of the current fund of ideas, and it is judgmentally objective and refresh- ing in style. It is very well suited for an orientation in psychology. *Admittedly, I cannot share the associationism he espouses.* (Stern letter to Cohn, May, 21, 1897; Lück & Löwisch, 1994, pp. 21-22; emphasis added)

Still more evidence that Stern's outlook on human nature circa 1900 was already decidedly antimechanistic can be seen in misgivings he expressed about the views of another contemporary, Hugo Münsterberg (1863-1916). In a letter to Cohn dated November, 11, 1900, Stern wrote,

> I am now beginning to read the new work by Münsterberg,[11] which I am sup- posed to review for Ebbinghaus.[12] I find myself very sympathetic toward the seriousness and urgency with which Münsterberg takes up questions of philo- sophical principles. Münsterberg was better than his reputation. Nevertheless, his solution does not satisfy me. He has left us still with the problem of recon- ciling the "two truths." *One cannot without contradiction be an ethical ideal- ist in metaphysics and a mechanist in psychology.* (Stern letter to Cohn, November 11, 1900; Lück & Löwisch, 1994, p. 39; emphasis added)

Stern's sensitivity to the philosophical tension expressed in this last sen- tence is not difficult to understand in light of his intellectual roots. The Kantian-Hegelian idealism Stern took from his studies in philosophy (refer to Chapter One) provided him, in a somewhat modified form, with the core of a *Weltanschauung,* or worldview, that permeated all of his major works. Furthermore, the metaphysical convictions Stern appropriated from this same tradition would fortify him in his opposition to the mechanistic leanings of so many of his contemporaries as these would manifest themselves increasingly during the time period under consideration here.

In this latter connection, it is also helpful to bear in mind the intellectual and cultural turmoil that prevailed in Germany just as Stern was moving into and through the prime of his scholarly life. To Stern as well as to many other thinkers of his time who had been educated in the "Mandarin" tradition (Ringer, 1969), the imposition of the Newtonian science world view on the study of mental life and behavior was generating an utterly *disenchanting* picture of the human condition (Harrington, 1996). From the Newtonian perspective, a person could properly be regarded as nothing more than *matter in motion* (Robinson, 1995), i.e., as an essentially passive entity constituted of distinct parts the coordinated functioning of which could be explained fully in terms of basic biochemical processes and physical forces. This thoroughly mechanistic and reductionistic conception of human nature was entirely devoid of appreciation for organismic wholeness and the role of human values in purposive thought and action, both individual and collective (Ash, 1995, Harrington, 1996). It was the proliferation of this mechanistic worldview within the new experimental psychology, and not the much narrower empirical issue of the discipiline's systematic disinterest in the empirical facts of individual and group differences, that was of greatest concern to Stern.

As this discussion proceeds, further evidence bearing on these contentions will be introduced. For the present, it suffices to say that Stern shared with his colleague and friend Cohn his convictions about the excesses of an impersonalistic, mechanistic psychology quite early on—and rather emphatically. In August of 1900, literally within weeks of the release to the public of differential psychology's "Declaration of Independence,"[13] Stern wrote to Cohn,

> I am gradually moving away from psychology and becoming more and more a philosopher, and am carrying around with me so many ideas which will take me many years to formulate. . . . What we need above all is a comprehensive world view, one that relates the psychological and the physical, that is anti-mechanistic, that is vitalistic-teleological; one in which modern natural science dogma is reduced to its true—that is, relatively inferior—value. This is a huge task, but I will work on it as I can. (Stern letter to Cohn, July 31, 1900; Lück & Löwisch, 1994, p. 33)

Clearly, the "father of differential psychology" did indeed have serious doubts about the adequacy of the subdiscipline vis-à-vis the "problem of individuality" even as he himself was launching the project. To be sure, and to underscore a point made previously: Against the backdrop of a general psychology interested only in knowledge of the laws of mental life "common to all," the empirical documentation of systematic individual differences could help to highlight the need for a conception of human individuality that would somehow have to be accommodated by those general laws. Stern's enthusiastic call in 1900 for programmatic investigations into such differences may be read in this light. However, the evidence considered above also indicates that Stern did not believe that the assessment and study of individual differences could, in and of itself, meet that need as he conceived of it.

Eventually, Stern's accomplishment of the "huge task" he had set for himself would be realized only through the three-volume series entitled *Person and Thing,* a trilogy that would require more than a quarter of a century to complete. As noted in Chapter One, the first volume of the series, *Rationale and Basic Tenets,* was published in 1906 (Stern, 1906) and thus is a work that Stern was almost certainly beginning to formulate even as the 1900 differential psychology book was reaching the shelves of libraries and bookstores.[14] In the 1906 book, Stern wrote,

> A person is an entity which, though consisting of many parts, forms a unique and inherently valuable unity and, as such, constitutes, over and above its functioning parts, a unitary, self-activated, goal-oriented being. . . . A thing is the contradictory opposite of a person. It is an entity that indeed consists of many parts, but these are not fashioned into a real, unique, and inherently valuable whole, and so while a thing functions in accordance with its various parts, it does not constitute a unitary, self-activated and goal-oriented being. (Stern, 1906, p. 16)

Taking his lead from the Kantian distinction between the worth of persons and the price of things (Beck, 1941), the contrast drawn by Stern in this passage was integral to his thinking about the problem of individuality from the very beginning and would remain so throughout his lifelong effort to fashion a system of thought adequate for the conceptual and practical challenges that this problem posed.

## Transitional Summary

In consideration of the foregoing, it becomes apparent that when Stern founded differential psychology in 1900 with the exuberant declaration of individuality as the "problem of the twentieth century," he was a scholar of two rather different minds about the "New Science." On one hand, he was genuinely impressed by what general experimental psychology had accomplished in its short life to that point, and he was characteristically optimistic about the prospects of supplementing those accomplishments through careful and systematic empirical studies of individual variations across the basic domains of human psychological life. This comes through quite clearly in the 1900 book, as I have sought to make clear.

On the other hand, it is also clear that Stern was not in the least enamored—indeed he was somewhat contemptuous—of scientific psychology's penchant for highly mechanistic and hence utterly impersonal accounts of mental life, seeing in all such accounts the eventual reduction of *persons* to mere *things*. This was abhorrent to him, and by 1900, he had already begun to formulate a system of thought, *critical personalism,* that would take as axiomatic the fundamental distinction between persons and things. In this light, it becomes apparent that Stern viewed human individuality as problematic vis-à-vis the prevailing general-experimental psychology not only, or even primarily, because of the discipline's systematic neglect of individual differences, but instead because of its increasingly mechanistic outlook on human nature. Stated otherwise, general psychology was seen by Stern in 1900 not merely as *blind* to the problem of individuality because of its content and methods, but as potentially *destructive* of the very notion of human individuality—with its attendant notions of autonomy, purposivity, free will, and the inherent value of persons—because of its philosophical predilections. These concerns continued to inform Stern's thinking even as his perspective on differential psychology matured and expanded.

## The Personalistic Perspective Within Stern's Broadened Conception of Differential Psychology

Within a few years of the appearance of *Über Psychologie der individuellen Differenzen,* Stern's publisher (the publishing house of Barth, located in Leipzig) was urging him to undertake a second edition of the work. As Stern would later write, however, he regarded such a project as "neither desirable nor possible" (Stern, 1911, p. iii). The field of differential psychology, Stern argued, was developing so quickly that it could no longer be served by a work containing mostly preliminary ideas, suggested directions, and sketches of programmatic research agendas. What was needed, Stern believed, was a set of organizing ideas and procedural principles that would provide differential psychology with a solid foundation as a scientific discipline. To meet this need, Stern offered an altogether new book, appearing in 1911 "in place of"[15] a second edition of the 1900 book, under the new title *Die Differentielle Psychologie in ihren methodischen Grundlagen* (*Methodological Foundations of Differential Psychology;* Stern, 1911; see Figure 2.2).[16]

As its title suggests, this text is essentially a methods handbook. Whereas scarcely 19 of the 132 text pages (discounting the bibliography) of the 1900 book were devoted to a discussion of methods, all of the 378-page 1911 work, save a 28-page introduction, concentrated on questions of research design, data acquisition, and data analysis.[17] Consistent with this overriding concern for questions of method, Stern explicitly relegated his own theoretical interests to a secondary role. Thus, in the foreword to the 1911 book, dated March 7 of that year, he wrote,

# Die

# Differentielle Psychologie

## in ihren methodischen Grundlagen.

Von

### William Stern.

An Stelle einer zweiten Auflage des Buches:
Über Psychologie der individuellen Differenzen
(Ideen zu einer differentiellen Psychologie).

LEIPZIG.
Verlag von Johann Ambrosius Barth.
1911.

**Figure 2.2**    Facsimile of Title Page of Stern's 1911 Book

That my conception of the structure of the human individual and of psychological differentiation is not uninfluenced by my fundamental philosophical convictions is obvious. But since this book is devoted to the founding of an empirical science, I have reduced the philosophical aspects of the work to a minimum. For the justification of ideas many of which are discussed here only too briefly, the reader is referred to my philosophical book.[18] But I hope that the usefulness of the present work is not dependent upon agreement with the author's philosophical assumptions (*which on many points deviate in non-trivial ways from the currently prevailing opinions*). (Stern, 1911, p. v; emphasis added, parentheses in original)

One noteworthy feature of Stern's 1911 book that resonated with, rather than deviated from, the concerns of many of his contemporaries was the emphasis he placed on the possibilities of differential psychology as an applied science. As has been pointed out by several other authors (see Danziger, 1990; Grünwald, 1980; Pekrun, 1996), the early 20th century brought increasing pressure on scientific psychology from sources outside the discipline (e.g., schools, business, industry, the military) to produce knowledge that would be practically useful, and Stern proved to be far from indifferent to these demands. Thus, whereas in the 1900 book he had emphasized the need to tether differential psychology securely to the "basic" (i.e., theoretical) concerns of the general/experimental/individual psychology and so to resist the temptations toward premature applications of research findings, his stance had changed noticeably by 1911. By then, he had pronounced himself to be more of the opinion that "differential psychology's prospects for moving into the phase of steady, progressive development would hinge on its achieving a certain emancipation from the mother discipline of general psychology" (Stern, 1911, p. iv). More than this, he went on to chide a scientific psychology that seemed to him "to have isolated itself on an island and sentenced itself to sterility *(Unfruchtbarkeit)* in relation to socio-cultural issues *(kulturelle Aufgaben)*" (Stern, 1911, p. 6).

Prominent in Stern's thinking about how differential psychology could redress this deficiency were two domains of inquiry he labeled *psychognostics (die Psychognostik)* and *psychotechnics (die Psychotechnik)*. The overriding concern of psychognostics would be *Menschenkenntnis*, or the *understanding* of people through the achievement of scientific insights into basic aspects of human nature. The larger goal of psychotechnics would be *Menschenbehandlung*, or the *treatment* of people—in other words, the realization of certain practical objectives through various combinations of different personal talents, interests, inclinations, and so forth with different programs, assignments, or intervention strategies.

In the next chapter, we will discuss further these two domains of inquiry and their roles in the historical developments we are tracing. For the present, it is important to consider some of the major theoretical points Stern did discuss, however briefly, in the introduction to the 1911 book.

## "Individual" and "Attribute" as Basic Concepts

Stern organized his personalistic conception of differential psychology's various research agendas around the basic concepts of *individual* and *attribute*. With this as his starting point, Stern was then able to articulate the four basic research schemes, or "disciplines," that he took to be proper to differential psychology. He presented these schemes to his readers with the help of a chart like the one shown in Figure 2.3.

The uppercase letters designating the columns in each of these schemes represent individuals, and the lowercase letters designating rows represent attributes. As indicated at the far left of the figure, the first two of these four investigative schemes focus on attributes. In *variation* research, individuals are "placeholders," as it were, and the investigator's objective is to empirically document the manner in which some particular attribute is distributed within—or varies throughout—some population. *Correlational* research incorporates this objective and extends it so as to make possible investigations into the extent of covariation among attributes within populations.

Turning to the third and fourth schemes, or "disciplines," shown in Figure 2.3, the focus shifts from attributes to individuals. In *psychography*, attributes become the "placeholders," and the investigator's objective is to portray or "profile" the salient characteristics of a particular individuality. *Comparative* research incorporates this objective and extends it so as to make possible the profiling of two or more individualities. This, in turn, makes possible systematic analyses of convergences and divergences between two or more individualities.

In a clear reference to the ideas of Windelband (1894/1998), Stern (1911) noted that attribute-centered inquiry "is closer to the nomothetic sciences and hence to general psychology, while individual-centered inquiry is more in line with the concerns of the idiographic sciences and hence with the historical perspective" (p. 19).[19] With specific reference to the concept of individuality, Stern noted further that although he intended that concept to refer "first and foremost to the individual human personality" (p. 19), it might also be used meaningfully to refer to a community of people considered as a collective. In this sense, Stern pointed out, "One could undertake a psychographic investigation of the French people, or of theatrical performers, or one could undertake comparative studies of men vs. women or Aryans vs. Mongolians, etc." (p. 20).

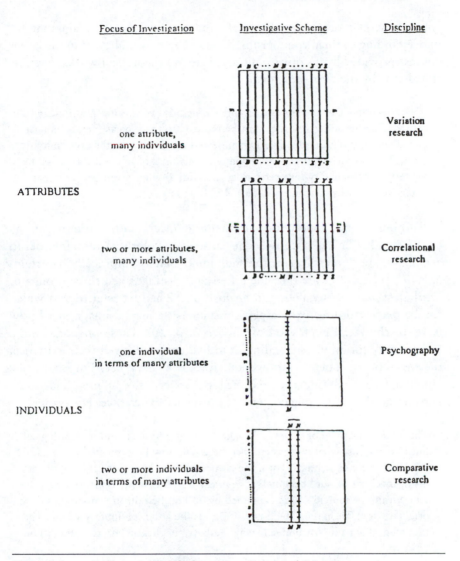

**Figure 2.3**    Differential Psychology as an Empirical Science

SOURCE: Adapted from Stern (1911, p. 18).

Stern also noted here, parenthetically, that the basis on which one might justify the characterization of an entire community of people *(Gemeinschaft)* as if it were a singular personality was a philosophical question.

With all of this as relevant background, Stern moved into a more detailed discussion of the basic concepts of individual and attribute. In doing so, however, he reminded his readers that his treatment of those concepts would necessarily be brief, and he emphasized again that his understanding of them could properly be understood only within the larger context provided by his other philosophical and theoretical works. First, he stated that by the term *individual,*

> We understand a wholeness, which indeed includes within it a multiplicity of components but nevertheless cannot be reduced to these parts (i.e., is indivisible). The unity of an individual is manifested empirically in the continuity of form, the goal-directedness of function, and the unity of self-consciousness. By the term "individuality" we refer to an individual who, as an entirety, manifests a singular distinctiveness. (Stern, 1911, p. 19)

Turning to his conception of *attribute (Merkmal),* Stern began by explaining that he had purposely chosen such a "colorless" term in order to accommodate "everything in the individual that is empirically ascertainable" (1911, p. 20). He then identified and distinguished three groups of attributes: *phenomena, acts,* and *dispositions.* The first refer to that which can be perceived directly by a person, such as "a mental image that I now have, or the facial expression of another" (p. 20). These phenomena are rudimentary for an understanding of individuals, but given their existence, the theoretical problem is to account for their *coherence.* For Stern, this amounted to establishing a relationship between the unitary, individual person and the diverse phenomena of his or her experience. He wrote,

> The individual is more than an aggregate of physical and psychological phenomena; just what more is entailed here will now be expressed in terms of nonphenomenal attributes. Thus, the nature of these hypothetical components is not mechanical but "personal": the many and fragmented phenomena present within the individual are explained by and unified through attributes that originate or reside in the individual, insofar as the latter is a unitary whole. The first step along this (theoretical) way leads from phenomena to acts. (Stern, 1911, p. 22)

It is by virtue of a person's goal-directedness that acts may be said to unify momentary phenomena and thus lend order to what would otherwise be an utterly fragmented and even overwhelmingly chaotic chain of experiences. Though the phenomena unified by an act may be physical or psychological or both, the act itself (e.g., thinking, digestion, sport) cannot properly be said to be either. From Stern's personalistic perspective, there were neither physical acts nor psychological acts, but rather *personal* acts of a purposive, goal-directed individual. In the domain of acts, he argued, "The physical-psychological distinction no longer applies; acts are *psychophysically neutral*"

(Stern, 1911, p. 23). He acknowledged that an act can be oriented more toward physical or psychological ends, but this would not compromise the claim that the act itself is psychophysically neutral.

Stern cited as an example here the act of taking a position *(die Stellung-nahme)*. Position taking, he argued, is an act which realizes one of two opposite possibilities, and this is neither more nor less true of the "fight-or-flight" response than of, for example, answering a question in the negative or voicing one's disapproval of an activity. In either case, the act is an expression of the fact that the person is striving toward some state of affairs that precludes or negates some other state of affairs.[20] The phenomenal material with respect to which a position is being taken might be some physical state of affairs, as in the case of fight-or-flight, or be something of a more psychological nature, as in the case of nay-saying or disapproval, but the act of position taking itself is neither physical nor psychological. It is, in Stern's terminology, "psychophysically neutral."

## The Concept of Dispositions

It stands to reason that just as acts unify phenomena, there must be something that in turn unifies acts. As Stern put it, acts are "temporally acute," meaning that they extend in time but briefly, and there is a manifest coherence in the behavior of individuals that is of a more temporally extended or "chronic" nature. Moreover, Stern argued that in providing any coherent explanation for various "act-ualities," the theorist will necessarily (if not always knowingly or critically) appeal to corresponding "potentialities": "Where acts of a certain kind occur, the prior ability to execute those acts must be postulated. *Actuality presupposes potentiality*" (Stern, 1911, p. 24; emphasis added).

Here, Stern reached the last of the three categories of attributes he had initially mentioned (see above), the category of *dispositions,* and here he also saw differential psychology playing its most prominent role from a genuinely personalistic perspective. But perhaps for precisely this reason, Stern was careful to distinguish his own understanding of the concept of disposition from other already extant views of a distinctly *impersonal* stripe:

> In many contemporary works, there is also talk of "dispositions," but here the meaning of "disposition" is quite different. It refers to the idea that once some or other mental content has occurred, its subsequent recurrence is more likely. In this way, each separate experience results in some corresponding "disposition," the latter being equivalent to a kind of shadow; the individual acquires these dispositions from the outside, but is him/herself passive with respect to them. In contrast, "dispositions" in the sense intended by the differential psychologist refer to the inner, directional effectance capabilities of an individual

as a whole, which might well be prompted by events outside the person but which are never produced by such events. (Stern, 1911, p. 24, footnote)

Unmistakable here is Stern's abiding concern to distance his fundamentally teleological conception of personal dispositions from the mechanistic views of many of his contemporaries. This effort continued into the next passage, where Stern asked rhetorically, "Is our assumption of dispositions not a retreat into the discredited faculty psychology *(Vermögenspsychologie)?*" (p. 25). He immediately answered his own question: "Yes and no," and then elaborated as follows:

Yes, insofar as we are convinced that the mental life of the individual cannot be explained in terms of the mere coming and going and subsequent effects of momentary phenomena and the mechanical laws that govern them; [explanation] requires instead the assumption of capabilities residing within the individual.

No, insofar as we do not conceive of these capabilities as fixed and ultimate special powers which, functioning like independent spirits within the human being, define his/her essence and disrupt his/her unity as an individual. (Stern, 1911, p. 25)

Stern then endeavored to clarify further his understanding of dispositions and their role in the psychological life of the individual. He wanted to convey a conception of dispositions as "the formal capability of an individual to achieve in characteristic ways certain subgoals relevant to the larger purposes of self-maintenance [or survival] *(Selbsterhaltung)* and self-unfolding *(Selbstentfaltung)*" (Stern, 1911, pp. 25-26; emphasis added).

Nearing the conclusion of his theoretical discussion, Stern pointed to one more theoretically important distinction, that between *labile* and *stable* dispositions. The former, Stern argued, are psychological tendencies that have not yet led to a "final and regular" style of individual functioning. Labile dispositions have yet to be elucidated and to mature and hence are highly susceptible to "outer" (i.e., environmental) influences. Stable dispositions, on the other hand, were conceived by Stern as relatively constant forms of behavior that constitute the enduring core of a person's psychological being and, accordingly, are only minimally susceptible to environmental influences. Stern reserved the term *traits (Eigenschaften)* for stable dispositions.

In the nearly apologetic passage from the foreword quoted earlier, we found Stern explicitly stating that his guiding philosophical assumptions about the nature of human individuality deviated "in nontrivial ways from prevailing opinions." Through the various other passages we have just considered, we gain a somewhat clearer sense for what Stern meant by this remark. Of surpassing importance in this regard was Stern's unwavering commitment to a teleological and thoroughly nonmechanistic conception of the individual human person. This commitment was entailed by the very distinction between persons and things on which critical personalism was predicated, and it was punctuated by Stern's understanding of the psychological functioning of the individual as directed toward the goals of self-maintenance and self-development.[21]

These aspects of Stern's 1911 work reinforce a point made earlier in the context of our discussion of his 1900 book: Although Stern's proclamation of individuality as the "problem of the 20th century" was tied to an appreciation of and respect for the empirical facts of individual differences, it was also inspired by and firmly grounded in his essentially philosophical concern to preserve within scientific psychology a genuinely personalistic perspective. Above all, this meant adherence to a nonmechanistic conception of human psychological life. In the next chapter, it will be seen how these concerns were gradually undermined by certain other developments within differential psychology, and how, in light of those developments, Stern became increasingly disenchanted with the field, notwithstanding its relentless attention to the empirical facts of individual differences.

## Summary

At the dawn of the 20th century, the "New Science" of experimental psychology centered on the quest for knowledge of the general laws presumed to regulate various aspects of individual mental life. Because by definition such general laws would capture regularities "common to all," there was little interest in such peculiarities as might surface in observations of one individual as compared with observations of another.

Against this backdrop, in 1900, Stern proclaimed individuality the "problem of the 20th century" and called for the establishment of a *differential* psychology alongside the already existing general-experimental psychology. This differential psychology, Stern proposed, should be dedicated to discovering (a) the fundamental respects in which people differ from one another, (b) the sources of those differences (e.g., in nature and in nurture), and (c) the manifestations of those differences in various domains of practical human activity.

Stern's deepest concern circa 1900 was not that the general-experimental psychology of the day systematically neglected the study of individual differences. Rather, he believed that that psychology was fostering and projecting a far too *mechanistic* conception of human nature. Clearly, he believed early on that a differential psychology could help make salient the *need* for an alternative to this view, but he never believed that a differential psychology would suffice to *realize* the larger objectives of a truly personalistic psychology. Instead, he was convinced that an entire system of thought, a *Weltanschauung,* was required, thoroughly grounded in philosophical as well as psychological considerations. *Critical personalism* is the name Stern gave to that system of thought.

Stern's concerns about scientific psychology's overly mechanistic inclinations, which tended to obscure the distinction between *persons* and *things,* were expressed quite forcefully in his private correspondence with his philosopher friend and colleague Jonas Cohn. But they also found clear, if brief, expression in various places in his 1900 and 1911 differential psychology textbooks. Through a consideration of this material, I have sought to establish in this chapter that in fact the *philosophical tenets of critical personalism*—not the methods of, or any extant empirical discoveries issuing from, differential psychology—grounded Stern's outlook on the problem of individuality from the very beginning of his scholarly life.

# Notes

1.  By no means did Ebbinghaus's thinking follow Wundt's in all respects. See in this connection Danziger (1979), who explains how positivism (which Ebbinghaus, among many others, embraced) served to repudiate Wundt's approach.

2.  See, for example, the Introduction to Wundt's *Outlines of Psychology,* reprinted in Huber, Edwards, and Heining-Boynton (2000). See also the *Einleitung* to Wundt's *Elemente der Völkerpsychologie* (Wundt, 1912). For reasons to be clarified in Chapter Four, this isomorphism between *general* psychology and *individual* psychology is something that would later puzzle Gordon Allport in his own attempt to develop a viable approach to understanding human individuality (cf. Allport, 1937a).

3.  The use of this term is itself a topic of historical interest (see Danziger, 1990).

4.  Indeed, the experimentalists of the time were, on occasion, themselves the individual subjects they were studying. This was famously true of Ebbinghaus, and it was less famously true of Stern himself, in at least one instance. The study (Stern, 1894) concerned variations in the acuity of perception of moving or stationary objects as a function of stimulation in various areas of the retina. In his discussion of this work, Stern's biographer Bühring (1996a) correctly notes that Stern's practice of using himself as his research subject would by modern standards be highly questionable.

5.  Because it underscores the logic of this point, it is interesting to note that Stern's first empirical contribution to differential psychology, an article he entitled "A Contribution to the Differential Psychology of Judgment," was based on an

experimental investigation of but *two* research subjects (Stern, 1899). The study involved the perception of tones varied systematically in pitch and tempo, and Stern's findings indicated that whereas one of the subjects, "K.," listened patiently to the tones and judged that they had changed only when he was certain, "R.," in contrast, was impatient and reacted impulsively before he could be sure of himself.

6. The reference here was to individual differences in reliance on visual, auditory, or motoric experiences.

7. Stern had in mind here individual differences in what might be described as the "pace" of psychological life.

8. Here, Stern was interested partly in variations within a person over the course of a day in his or her energy level and partly in between-person distinctions such as those commonly made nowadays between "morning" persons and "evening" or "night" persons.

9. The reference Stern gave here was to Binet and Henri (1896).

10. The allusion here was to the French investigator Alphonse Bertillon (1853-1914), who advocated an anthropometric approach to the identification of criminals that included the recording of height as well as the lengths of a foot, arm, and finger. Bertillon's system also called for photographs of the right ear. Hacking (1990) has noted that it was from the work of Bertillon that the practice developed in the United States of photographing immigrants facing left, with the right ear clearly visible.

11. This would have been the first edition of Münsterberg's basic text, like Ebbinghaus's also entitled *Foundations of Psychology* (Münsterberg, 1900).

12. Stern was referring here to the task of writing a review of Münsterberg's book for publication in the journal Ebbinghaus was editing, the *Journal for Psychology and the Physiology of Sense Organs*.

13. I mean, here, the 1900 book. As it turned out, Stern would provide differential psychology's "Constitution" as well, in the form of his 1911 book *Methodological Foundations of Differential Psychology*. This work will be discussed further, below.

14. By Stern's own account, he had authored in 1901 a work setting forth some of the key ideas of critical personalism, even though that work, titled *Vorgedanken zur Weltanschauung (Preliminary Considerations for a Worldview)*, was not published until 1915 (Stern, 1915).

15. Stern's own expression, appearing on the title page of the 1911 book.

16. Another unrevised edition of the text was published in Leipzig (Barth) in 1921. Much more recently, in 1994, a memorial edition of the 1911 book was published in Göttingen (Hans-Huber), on the initiative of Professor Dr. Kurt Pawlik, of the University of Hamburg. This republication was timed to coincide with the 75th anniversary of the founding of the University of Hamburg, an event in which Stern had played an important role (refer to Chapter One).

17. Excluded from this count is Part IV of the book, which contains about 125 pages of bibliography, appendices, and a name index.

18. I take Stern to have been referring here to his 1906 book, the first volume of *Person und Sache* (Stern, 1906).

19.  Elsewhere (e.g., Lamiell, 1981, 1987), I have argued against the thesis that attribute-centered inquiry is compatible with the objectives of a nomothetic science of personality, and later in this work I am going to reiterate and extend that argument. On this specific point, then, I believe that Stern (1911) was in error.

20.  There is a striking resemblance between Stern's thinking about position taking and the notion of *affective assessment* central to Rychlak's (1988) more contemporary logical learning theory, and it is noteworthy that, as did Stern, Rychlak has firmly defended a teleological conception of human behavior and psychological functioning (Rychlak, 1981, 1997). More on this point will be said in Chapter Ten.

21.  Lest these terms be misconstrued, it should be noted here that critical personalism was anything but a mere "psychology of the self." Indeed, Stern was as wary of an unbridled preoccupation with "self" as he was of attempts to account for behavior and personality in strictly mechanistic terms. This point will be developed further in Chapter Ten.

# Chapter Three

## The Narrowing of Perspective in the Proliferation of Standardized Testing and Correlational Research

In the previous chapter, passing mention was made of Stern's view that as a practical discipline, differential psychology would have two closely related, yet nevertheless distinguishable, agendas. The first (and more important) of these he termed *psychognostics (die Psychognostik)*, the goal of which was to be *Menschenkenntnis,* or an understanding of the fundamentals of human nature. The realization of this goal would entail, among other things, a determination of the most basic attributes by which to characterize persons. An additional requirement would be the development of practically viable procedures for measuring those attributes, so as to be able to specify with some scientific precision the standing of any given individual with respect to those standards.

The other of differential psychology's two broad agendas, according to Stern (1911), would be what he termed *psychotechnics (die Psychotechnik).* Its proper concern, as noted earlier, would be *Menschenbehandlung,* or the realization of certain scientifically ascertainable practical objectives through various combinations of persons having different characteristics with alternative treatments, programs, assignments, or intervention strategies. In modern parlance, one would include among the objectives of psychotechnics the deployment of "human resources."

It was clear to Stern that in certain respects, both psychognostics and psychotechnics could be well served by scientifically viable mental tests, and in his 1911 *Methodological Foundations* text, Stern gave full voice to his conviction that meeting this objective would in turn require sustained, programmatic inquiry within the discipline he had designated as *correlational* research (see Figure 2.3, previous chapter). However, during the first 25 years following the publication of *Methodological Foundations,* differential psychologists' perspectives on human individuality would come to be dominated by the measurement and statistical techniques proper to that discipline. As this trend gained momentum—above Stern's repeated cautions and ever more pointed objections—those same techniques came to be seen not merely as components of a subdiscipline of scientific psychology respectful of human individuality and accommodating of individual (and group) differences (as Stern himself viewed those techniques), but as methods necessary and altogether sufficient both for the purposes of psychognostics and those of psychotechnics. The eventual consequence of this would be the ascendance, by the late 1930s, of a differential psychology tethered almost exclusively to the methods of standardized testing and correlational research. Within the emergent field of *personality psychology,* this framework would be adopted by the majority as one equally serviceable both for the purposes of *Menschenkenntnis* and of *Menschenbehandlung,* and whatever could not be captured by or rendered conformable to this framework would come to be regarded by most as falling outside the boundaries of a properly scientific approach to the problem of individuality.

In this chapter, we will begin to examine these developments, highlighting for consideration some especially revealing contributions by E. L. Thorndike (1874-1949) and Hugo Münsterberg (1863-1916) and paying close attention to Stern's view of matters as they unfolded. The picture that will take shape is one of Stern's ever-growing disenchantment as differential psychologists themselves came to embrace an increasingly impersonal perspective on human individuality.

## Stern's Understanding of the Role of Standardized Testing in Differential Psychology

From the outset, it is well to keep in mind the enthusiasm Stern showed early on for the practical turn being taken within scientific psychology by many of his contemporaries. In Chapter Two, we considered some of the evidence for this enthusiasm that is found in *Methodological Foundations*. More of the same is found in an article Stern published 3 years after the appearance of the 1911 book (Stern, 1914c), in which he described differential psychology's still relatively new place within the overall scheme of the "New Science." After pointing with approval to the fact that Wundt's *Völkerpsychologie* had emerged alongside the older experimental psychology—and in the process strengthened psychology's relationship to the humanities—Stern (1914c) made explicit his view that "this Wundtian bifurcation of method—experiment on the one side, psychological anthropology on the other" (p. 416) was no longer adequate for psychology. Whereas that bifurcation entailed a distinction between experimental methods and nonexperimental/observational methods of the *Völkerpsychologie,* Stern pointed with obvious pleasure to a third alternative, a new kind of experimental procedure involving tests. This new procedure, Stern noted, could be used to investigate individual differences not only with respect to intelligence but also with respect to other attributes in terms of which psychologically consequential differences between individuals can be ascertained: demographic factors, to be sure, but also temperament, character, and specific abilities. Moreover, in these domains, the erstwhile common experimental procedure of investigating individual subjects one at a time, sequentially (the "$N = 1$" approach discussed in Chapter Two), was being replaced by an approach involving the simultaneous investigation of large numbers of subjects. This new procedure, Stern announced, "has meant that statistical methods have made their way into our discipline" (Stern, 1914c, p. 416).

This was quite consistent with the perspective Stern had laid out 3 years previously. Chapter VI of *Methodological Foundations* is titled *Das Prüfungsexperiment (Der Test),* and Stern devoted it to a discussion of the method, then still new, he called the "test experiment." In that context, he noted with approval the advances that had been made in psychological testing during the first decade of the century, including not only improvements in the test instruments themselves but also insights into the kinds of correlational analyses necessary to establish the scientific adequacy of those instruments. For example, Stern noted (1911, pp. 95-96), that the proper standardization or "calibration" *(Eichung)* of testing instruments requires that the measures obtained with them be compared systematically with (i.e., correlated with) measures of the same persons derived independently of the tests in question. These latter measures might be scores obtained on other tests (resulting in "test-test comparisons"), or they might be indices obtained nonexperimentally, such as age, school performance (grades), or indicators of overall psychological condition *(Geisteszustand).*

Elaborating on these ideas, Stern drew particular attention to research showing that a composite index of intelligence compiled out of subjects' performances on a series of tests[1] would correlate more highly with a criterion such as school achievement than would performance on any single test considered alone. From the practical standpoint of psychotechnics, this was an encouraging sign in light of the disappointing results that had been obtained some years previously by Wissler (1901) with a battery of would-be tests of intelligence suggested by James McKeen Cattell (1890; see below). Stern (1911) also cited approvingly—albeit in a tone that can fairly be described as "guarded"—the work of Charles Spearman (1863-1945) and Felix Krueger (1874-1948) in developing the correlation-based statistical technique of factor analysis.[2] Noteworthy as well in this context is Stern's argument at the conclusion of Chapter VI that a well-developed test would, among other things, (a) permit the accurate group classification or rank ordering of tested individuals with respect to the tested attribute(s) and (b) have maximum possible applicability to different persons or groups tested under comparable conditions.

This material clearly documents Stern's appreciation for the important role that standardized psychological tests and the discipline of correlational research could play in a well-rounded differential psychology, and in light of these considerations, it is not difficult to find warrant for the praise that H.J. Eysenck (1990) would, years later, bestow on Stern:

> [He] may be credited with originating the concept of differential psychology, and laying down some of the rules which should govern its methodology. He clearly argued for an empirical and statistical approach and for a separation from orthodox experimental psychology. He anticipated many modern developments, and ranks among the founders of our science. (p. 249)

But as was emphasized in the previous chapter, Stern's outlook on differential psychology and the "problem of individuality" was considerably broader than what is revealed by the foregoing considerations alone, and far more nuanced than Eysenck's remarks would suggest.[3] For this reason, we do well to more closely examine Stern's views regarding standardized tests of intelligence and other aspects of mental functioning as the sole method for investigating individualities.

## Stern's Views on the Limits of Standardized Psychological Testing

As has been well documented elsewhere (see Fancher, 1985; Sokal, 1990), a major impetus to the experiments entailing psychological tests discussed by Stern in his various works was provided by James McKeen Cattell (1860-1944). After completing his doctoral studies under Wundt in Leipzig in 1886, Cattell spent 2 years in England pursuing research modeled on the anthropometric investigations being carried out by Francis Galton (1822-1911). This work both reflected and fueled Cattell's long-standing interest in the study of individual differences—an interest that Wundt is said to have dismissed as *ganz amerikanisch,* or "thoroughly American"—and soon after Cattell returned to the United States, his article titled "Mental Tests and Measurements" appeared in the journal *Mind* (Cattell, 1890).

In *Methodological Foundations,* Stern (1911) took explicit note of this publication by Cattell, mentioning 9 of the 10 basic tests Cattell had described: (1) dynamometric pressure, (2) maximal speed of arm movement, (3) two-point differentiation threshold for touch, (4) pain threshold for pressure, (5) difference threshold for weights, (6) reaction time for colors, (7) visual bisection of a length, (8) reproduction of a 10-second interval, and (9) number of letters that could be correctly repeated after one hearing (cf. Fancher, 1985).[4] Stern then commented as follows:

> Of course it is possible that studying an individual through the administration of such a battery of tests can yield material that will be valuable for many purposes of comparative research. But for the specific goal of fashioning a comprehensive characterization of the psychological functioning of an individual, precious little is to be gained in this way. One can determine how the tested person behaves at a particular time with respect to ten or twenty functions, but this momentary behavior permits no conclusions whatsoever concerning any lasting trends in the tested functions, and offers even less by way of knowledge about the characteristic functioning of the person in other areas. And it is precisely the most characteristic traits that lie furthest from the more peripheral performances examined in these tests. Naturally, one can increase the number of such tests, and sequence them as one will. How little is to be achieved in this way is demonstrated by the studies of Emile Zola and [Henri] Poincaré carried out by Toulouse.[5] He went to great effort to have his heroes submit to a large number of various tests (including tests of the senses), but in this way was scarcely able to achieve insight into the essential nature of either of the two individualities. (Stern, 1911, p. 90)

Stern's position here on the limits of what could be achieved through reliance on standardized mental tests was a *principled* one. That is, although problems might indeed have accrued to flaws in the specific tests Cattell used, Stern believed there were fundamental deficiencies in the approach that could never be remediated by technical improvements in the devices themselves. For one thing, standardized tests would by definition fail to capture qualitative aspects of a person's psychological functioning that might be peculiar to that individual alone. Moreover, and in any case, the inherently "snapshot" nature of testing per se (and not the specific limitations or deficiencies of this or that particular test or battery of tests) would ever preclude gaining sufficient depth of insight into persons' individualities through tests alone. With this in mind, even within the context of the generally positive discussion of mental testing given in Chapter VI of *Methodological Foundations,* Stern saw fit to conclude that chapter as follows:

> The test is only *a*—and not *the*—method for examining individuality. By no means does it render nonexperimental methods of investigation superfluous. To be sure, tests can supplement such methods. But tests are also supplemented by such methods, are dependent upon such methods for the confirmation and elaboration of what they reveal, and in many cases must give way to what is revealed by the other methods. Psychological testing *per se* is to be regarded as a "psychographic minimum"; it serves as a stopgap measure *(Notbehelf)* when time constraints or other circumstances will not admit of supplemental methods. It also serves as a method of preliminary investigation for the purpose of selecting from a large group some particular individual as a subject of further and more detailed psychographic investigation. (Stern, 1911, p. 106; emphasis added)

Alas, no rational critique of mental testing along the lines taken by Stern could have persuaded one of such positivistic and empiricistic sensibilities as Cattell (cf. Sokal, 1990) to abandon his efforts. Decisive in this regard, however, was hard empirical evidence generated through correlational studies carried out by one of Cattell's own students, Clark Wissler (1901). Proceeding in logical accordance with one of Cattell's key assumptions, Wissler reasoned that if the different tests employed by Cattell could in fact be regarded as alternative indicators of intelligence, then within a large sample of subjects, relative performances on any one of those tests should correlate substantially both with relative performances by the same subjects on the other tests and with some independent indicator of intellectual performance, such as grades in school.

As Fancher (1985) put it, the results Wissler (1901) obtained in his study were "devastating" for the particular collection of mental tests assembled by Cattell. With a sample size of around 300 college students, Wissler found that Cattell's mental tests evinced vanishingly small—and sometimes even negative—intercorrelations, and none was found to correlate higher than $r = + .16$ with academic achievement. On the other hand, Wissler did find some substantial intercorrelations between grades in different academic subjects. For example, grades in Latin and Greek correlated $r = + .75$.[6] Considered altogether, Wissler's findings gave reason to believe that there might well be something like "general intellectual ability," but if so, this was a dimension of individual differences that could not be tapped in any scientifically precise way by tests tied as closely as were Cattell's to sensory physiology.

The lesson here was one that Alfred Binet (1857-1911) had seen some years earlier. Already by 1896, Binet had recorded his conviction that to be practically useful with children, mental tests should be oriented around "higher" mental functions such as memory, imagination, attention, and suggestibility (Binet & Henri, 1896), and this is the thinking that informed the scales Binet devised with Theodore Simon (1873-1961) in 1905, 1908, and 1911 (Fancher, 1985). With the translation of these latter two instruments into English by H.H. Goddard (1866-1957) and the subsequent revision of the translated scales by Lewis Terman (1877-1956), the IQ testing movement in the United States was off and running (Samelson, 1979).

Stern was by no means merely a distant, critical observer of this movement. To be sure, as we saw in Chapter Two, he had taken Binet and Henri to task in 1900 for what he perceived to be precipitous practical applications of instruments the scientific adequacy of which was far from established. But a decade later, Stern's concerns in this regard had been substantially allayed. Indeed, soon after the publication of the 1911 book, he was addressing himself to the question of how best to quantitatively index a child's performance on such tests (Stern, 1912) and in this regard suggested that the arithmetic difference between mental age (*MA*) and chronological age (*CA*) be abandoned in favor of the ratio of the two (cf. Schmidt, 1994). With this, the concept of the intelligence quotient was born, carving Stern's niche in psychology's history as "the inventor of the IQ" (Lamiell, 1996).

Yet even in this context, in which Stern was specifically concerned with a technical problem central to the task of measuring a particular psychological attribute, he was careful to remind his readers of the limits *in principle* of any such procedure for getting at the individuality of some aspect of psychological life. In a follow-up to the above-cited 1912 work, Stern (1916) once again discussed the advantages of the intelligence quotient as a quantitative index of a child's level of intellectual functioning. To this argument, however, he added a warning very much in the spirit of the personalistic outlook that, it is to be hoped, is becoming familiar to the reader as characteristic of Stern's thinking:

In [some] respects, feeblemindedness is a qualitatively distinct kind of intellectual development. One must resist the temptation to equate the psychological constitution of a 15-year-old feebleminded youth having a mental age of 9 with a 9-year-old of normal intelligence. . . . The Binet-Simon test has only a limited significance for purposes of determining feeblemindedness. Obviously, the volitional and emotional changes that are of some importance in all kinds of feeblemindedness and are in some cases quite prominent, are not touched upon at all by the test. But even within the domain of intellectual life, genuinely qualitative particularities remain unexamined by the test. Indeed, they ought to remain unexamined if the test is to do its job properly. Just as is true of normal children, where the investigation of intelligence types has its own significance over and above the investigation of intelligence level, so also is it necessary with children who are not normal to take into account qualitative abnormalities alongside the quantitative subnormalities, and to ascertain the former through special methods of investigation. *The current inclination, prominent in America, to see in the test a single, comprehensive, and universally valid method is to be steadfastly opposed.* (Stern, 1916, pp. 16-17; emphasis added)

Here again, we find Stern pointing to the need to consider more than merely intelligence in attempts to gain insight into human individuality: Volition (will) and emotional factors are also highly relevant. But the mere application of standardized tests of these additional functions, however good those tests might be, would still not solve the problem completely, for here again, we find Stern emphasizing that individuals differ from one another not only quantitatively but also *qualitatively*. This latter fact, in Stern's view, pointed up the need for "special methods of investigation" beyond standardized testing.

## Investigating Individualities

As he moved from his discussion of variation studies and correlational research in Part II of *Methodological Foundations* to the topic of studying individualities in Part III, Stern opened the discussion as follows:

However divergent the problems of differential psychology discussed to this point may have been, they all had one thing in common: *the object of investigation was the attribute in its distribution across individuals; the individuals were merely the means of the research by virtue of their status as carriers of the attribute(s) to be studied.*

But now the direction of inquiry must swing 90 degrees (see the diagrams on pp. 17-18).[7] The object of research now becomes not the horizontal distribution of an attribute across many individuals but instead the vertical structure of an individual in terms of many attributes. We confront here the problem of psychography, the empirical psychological designation of individuality. (Stern, 1911, p. 318; emphasis added)

Recalling the discussion of Figure 2.3 in Chapter Two, a *psychographic* investigation entails the construction of a multiattribute profile of a particular individuality. Following Stern's terminology, such a profile would be called a *psychogram,* and two or more psychograms would enable further studies of a comparative nature.

A difficult but vitally important question becomes apparent at this point: What are the attributes with respect to which the psychogram of a particular individual is to be constructed? To follow one of Stern's own examples, we may ask this question: Just what should attributes, *a, b, c, d,* and so on, be for purposes of constructing a psychogram of Goethe? What should the attributes be in the case of Schiller? What should they be for any specific individual we might wish to study and understand?

In the face of these questions, one possibility would be to select some common set of attributes, *a, b, c, d,* and so on, as the basis for constructing any given psychogram. Obviously, this approach would well serve the additional research objective of comparing psychograms. Moreover, were the attributes comprising the set selected to coincide with those that had also been systematically investigated in variation and covariation (correlational) studies, a means would have been found for systematically coordinating all four investigative disciplines set forth by Stern as proper to differential psychology.

Stern was not blind to these possibilities. Indeed, he pointed out that if many psychograms were constructed using methods that allowed for their direct comparison, an investigator would have not only the wherewithal for comparative studies but also, de facto, "the most ideal material imaginable for addressing all of the problems of (between-person) variation studies and correlational research" (Stern, 1911, p. 328).

In a fashion wholly consistent with his overall outlook as we have exposed it to this point, Stern was nevertheless wary of the requirements of method gaining priority over considerations of knowledge objectives and fidelity to the subject matter: individuality. He reminded his readers that the objective of a psychographic investigation would be to achieve a faithful, multifaceted characterization of the individual and that "every method-imposed constraint leads to the exclusion of features *(Gesichtspunkten)* that are part of the overall structure of an individuality" (Stern, 1911, p. 332). Similarly, blind insistence on some common framework for profiling all individualities would in many individual cases require the consideration of irrelevant attributes. Accordingly, Stern believed that nothing could substitute completely for inquiry of an essentially biographical nature, and he left no room for doubt about how he viewed the relationship between psychography and biography:

> To avoid a possible misunderstanding from the very beginning, it must be
> emphasized that psychography can never substitute for biography. On the

contrary, the biographer of the future will be able to make use of a psychographic scheme, or perhaps an already completed psychogram, as preliminary material for the project. But it is only through an artistic, empathic synthesis of this material that a genuine biography emerges. (Stern, 1911, p. 329)

With this passage, we come full circle to a point noted early in Chapter Two concerning Stern's conviction that knowledge of the sort Windelband (1894/1998) had termed *idiographic* would be essential to an understanding of human individuality. We see also that, in Stern's view, however *helpful* psychographic and comparative studies might be in this regard, they would not *suffice* to meet idiographic objectives. Despite the views of differential psychology's founder on these matters, however, the field was even then moving decidedly in directions inhospitable to his convictions. Investigators were increasingly gravitating toward standardized testing procedures. Psychography would survive only as means of profiling individuals on sets of attributes presumed applicable to "people in general," and comparison research would be undertaken almost exclusively for purposes of differentiating groups of individuals—collectives—according to those putatively common attributes. Neither biography nor any other special methods of idiographic inquiry would play any prominent role at all.

## The Ascendance of Standardized Methods in Psychognostics and Psychotechnics

We saw in Chapter One that during his years in Hamburg, which extended from 1916 until Hitler's accession to power in 1933, Stern devoted a great deal of time and effort to the direction of, and often firsthand participation in, large-scale research projects of an applied nature. A great many of those projects were tied in some way to the practical concern, important from both a social and a pedagogical standpoint, of identifying highly gifted and talented children and adolescents (Feger, 1991). In this context (and some others as well, such as research on occupational aptitudes and further investigations in the domain of intelligence testing; Bühring, 1996a), Stern relied extensively on the methods of "test experiments" and correlational research. Beyond its reflection of the formal suitability of such methods for addressing certain practical problems arising in schools, industry, and the military, Stern's sustained engagement in such work is a clear reflection of his responsiveness to calls from many quarters outside psychology for these types of efforts (Danziger, 1990; Grünwald, 1980; Pekrun, 1996).

As will become apparent below, however, Stern never allowed his thinking about psychological issues to be dominated by the standardized methods of "test experiments," either as a basis for psychognostics/*Menschenkenntnis* or as a basis for psychotechnics/*Menschenbehandlung*. Alas, the same could not be said of some of his more prominent and influential contemporaries, and therein lay the root of a very far-reaching problem.

## Edward L. Thorndike's Reformulation of the Problem of Individuality

In 1911, the year in which Stern's *Methodological Foundations* was published, there also appeared a small monograph by Edward L. Thorndike (1874-1949) titled, of all things, *Individuality*. At the very outset of the work, the author made clear his basic approach to the topic:

> We may study a human being in respect to his common humanity, or in respect to his individuality. In other words, we may study the features of intellect and character which are common to all men, to man as a species; or we may study the differences in intellect and character which distinguish individual men. (Thorndike, 1911, p. 2)

Prominent enough in this passage is Thorndike's view, consonant with Stern's, that an understanding of individuality would require the consideration not just of intelligence, but of attributes of character as well. From this point on, however, Thorndike's perspective took leave of Stern's in two fundamentally important ways. The first lay in Thorndike's conviction that scientific inquiry into human individuality is *equivalent to*—not merely *served* in some way(s) *by*—the systematic assessment and study of individual differences. The second was Thorndike's call for an abandonment of the distinction between quantitative and qualitative differences. He argued as follows:

> [A] quantitative difference exists when the individuals have different amounts of the same trait. . . . A qualitative difference exists when some quality or trait possessed by one individual is lacking in the other. . . . *A qualitative difference in intellect or character is thus really a quantitative difference wherein one term is zero, or a compound of two or more quantitative differences.* (Thorndike, 1911, pp. 4-5; emphasis added)

Using this argument as the basis for his claim that *all* individual differences are quantitative and not qualitative in nature, in other words, that this is true not only of intelligence but of "all of the tendencies which the psychologist calls abilities, interests, habits, qualities of mind, or mental traits" (Thorndike, 1911, p. 3), Thorndike was setting up his further and more comprehensive claim:

> The difference between any two individuals, if describable at all, is described by comparing the amounts which A possesses of various traits with the amounts which B possesses of the same traits. In intellect and character, differences of kind between one individual and another turn out to be definable, if defined at all, as compound differences of degree. (Thorndike, 1911, p. 5)

As to how one would go about actually quantifying these "differences of degree," Thorndike made clear his investment in the notion that because most, if not all, traits of interest to psychologists would be found to be distributed more or less normally in the population, any given individual's standing on some particular trait could be indexed as his or her position along or within such a distribution.[8]

With this as his basic rationale, Thorndike then illustrated with various diagrams what multitrait profiles of individuals, and types of individuals, might look like. Figure 3.1 below juxtaposes two of Thorndike's figures (specifically, his Figures 5 and 6, from pp. 16 and 20, respectively, of the 1911 monograph) in such a way as to reflect the essence of his views on the measurement problem.

The horizontal line near the middle of the figure, marked off with the numerals 0 through 5 spaced so as to be equidistant from one another, was used by Thorndike to represent varying amounts or degrees of traits, and Figure 3.1 was constructed so as to show how, conceptually, these different degrees would "map into" the normal curve. Referring then to what is shown here in the lower portion of Figure 3.1, Thorndike explained (1911, p. 20) that the five-trait profiles of three hypothetical individuals, W. Roberts, John Smith, and H. Thomas, had been depicted as curves $R$, $S$, and $T$, and hence these three individuals could be represented by the following equations:

$$\text{W. Roberts} = 2a + 2b + 5c + 3d + 3e$$

$$\text{John Smith} = 1a + 4b + 2c + 5d + 1e$$

$$\text{H. Thomas} = 4a + 1b + 1c + 2d + 3e$$

On one level, this scheme for representing individualities is quite compatible with the schemes for psychography and comparison research laid

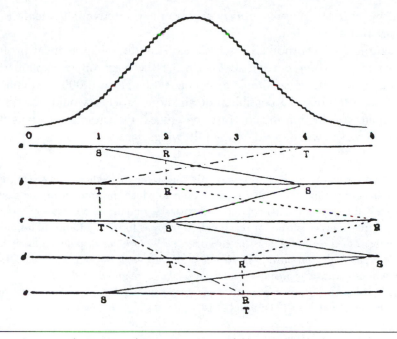

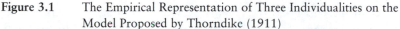

**Figure 3.1**    The Empirical Representation of Three Individualities on the Model Proposed by Thorndike (1911)

NOTE: The upper and lower portions of this figure juxtapose Figures 5 and 6, from pages 16 and 20, respectively, of Thorndike's monograph.

out by Stern (1911) in *Methodological Foundations* (see Figure 2.4). Bearing in mind the immediately preceding discussion, however, we must not allow superficial similarities to conceal deeper differences. Stern believed that persons can differ from one another not only quantitatively, that is, with respect to the amounts or degrees of putatively common attributes, but also qualitatively—and hence with respect to the attributes that are relevant to a characterization of a given individual in the first place. In his view, therefore, common-attribute profiles of the sort advocated by Thorndike (1911) could not possibly in a satisfactory manner capture the individuality of any of the individuals so represented.

Because Thorndike placed no credence in the quantitative-qualitative distinction to begin with, it is the case on his account that *all relevant attributes are perforce relevant in some degree to all persons*. As a result, once those relevant attributes had been properly determined, it would always be possible to undertake meaningful comparisons of two or more individuals on that basis; and each of the profiles considered in isolation could, in principle at least, *comprehensively* capture the respective individualities of the persons represented.[9]

Returning to Thorndike's discussion of the three hypothetical profiles shown in the lower portion of Figure 3.1, he went on to explain that although within even so simple a scheme as this, over 3,000 "varieties of men" (p. 19) would be possible, not all those varieties would necessarily obtain empirically. On the contrary, he argued, the varieties or kinds that can in fact exist will depend on the following:

> [T]he relations, or, as they are commonly called, the *correlations,* betweeen the amounts of the five traits, that is, the extent to which the amount of one trait possessed by an individual is bound up with the amount he possesses of some other trait. This is as true for five hundred traits as for five, and for an infinite number of degrees of each as for five degrees. *What kinds of individuals there will be, and what proportion there will be of each kind, is a result of the distribution of individuals in single traits and of the correlations of the traits.* . . . A type [of human nature] represents some particular combination of amounts of the list of human traits. (Thorndike, 1911, pp. 21-22; emphasis in original)

In effect, what Thorndike sketched in his 1911 monograph was a thoroughly empiricistic approach to the problem of individuality. In his view, any given individuality could properly be regarded simply as an empirical instantiation of a *type* of individuality, meaning that in principle, any given person could properly be regarded as intersubstitutable for any other person instantiating the same type. At best, this approach would accommodate Stern's notion of a "type complex," but not his notion of a "complex type" (refer to discussion of these concepts in Chapter Two). Moreover, on Thorndike's account, there would never arise any need to supplement the approach he advocated with biographical inquiry or any other "special methods of investigation." Because any and all strictly qualitative aspects of individuality were "defined away" from the start as being merely special instances of quantitative differences, nothing beyond the methods suitable for capturing "differences of degree" would be required for purposes of a scientific understanding of individuality.

If these utterly impersonalistic notions within the domain of psychognostics/*Menschenkenntnis*, springing up from within the ranks of differential psychologists, greatly troubled Stern, so, too, would developments in the domain of psychotechnics/*Menschenbehandlung* being spearheaded at about the same time by his erstwhile countryman, Hugo Münsterberg (1863-1916).

# Hugo Münsterberg's Identification of Applied Psychology With Psychotechnics

Along with Stern and many other psychologists of the era, Münsterberg was eager to respond to pressures impinging on the discipline from without to produce knowledge that would be practically useful to workers in education, the military, business and industry, and so on (Danziger, 1990). In his highly influential *Psychology and Industrial Efficiency,* published in 1913,[10] Münsterberg made clear his belief that differential psychology was crucially important in this regard:

> As long as experimental psychology remained essentially a science of the mental laws, common to all human beings, an adjustment to the practical demands of daily life could hardly come into question. With such general laws we could never have mastered the concrete situations of society, because we should have had to leave out of view the fact that there are gifted and ungifted, intelligent and stupid, sensitive and obtuse, quick and slow, energetic and weak individuals (Münsterberg, 1913, pp. 9-10).

Referring specifically to Stern's 1911 book, Münsterberg (1913) went on to state approvingly that "today we have a psychology of individual variations from the point of view of the psychological laboratory" (p. 10), advising his readers that although "the study of individual differences itself is not applied psychology . . . it is the presupposition without which applied psychology would have remained a phantom" (p. 10).

In further agreement with Stern and many other differential psychologists of the time (including Thorndike, as we have just seen), Münsterberg believed that differential psychology would have to take into consideration many factors beyond intelligence to be effective as an applied science. Of interest to him were any and all potentially relevant variations in "qualities of men . . . [those of] will and feeling, of perception and thought, of attention and emotion, [and] of memory and imagination" (Münsterberg, 1913, pp. 27-28).

But *to what end* were investigations into these variations in "qualities of men" of interest to Münsterberg? Here, we find his views diverging from Stern's in ways that proved troubling from the perspective of the latter's fundamental distinction between persons and things.

After further discussing the need for an applied psychology in a brief chapter titled "The Demands of Practical Life," Münsterberg (1913) went on in his third chapter to address himself to the question of "means and ends" (p. 17). In this context, he identified applied psychology as a technical science and took pains to point out that therefore, it was not for the practitioners of applied psychology to decide whether some or another end *should* be pursued, but only *how* it should be pursued if, on some other grounds, that had been deemed desirable. Münsterberg then pointed out that the psychotechnician can view the relevant means-ends relationships in one of two ways: either "from the point of view of the psychological laboratory," the perspective characteristic of the differential psychology for which he credited Stern, or from the point of view of those turning to psychologists from outside the discipline. As he put it:

> Either we might start from the various mental processes and ask for what end each mental factor can be practically useful and important, or we can begin with studying what significant ends are acknowledged in our society and then we can seek the various psychological facts which are needed as means for the realization of these ends. The first way offers many conveniences. . . . Nevertheless, the opposite way which starts from the tasks to be fulfilled seems more helpful and more fundamentally significant. The question, then, is what mental processes become important for the tasks of education, what for the hospital, what for the church, what for politics, and so on. (Münsterberg, 1913, pp. 21-22)

Quite obviously, Münsterberg's main concern in his 1913 book was the application of psychology to problems in business and industry, and with specific reference to that context, he was able to specify the "chief ends" of psychotechnics quite succinctly. They were (a) finding the "best possible man" (person) for particular kinds of work, (b) determining how to get the "best possible work" from persons of varying psychological makeup under various working conditions, and (c) learning how to secure the "best possible effects" on different people through various marketing strategies and advertising techniques (Münsterberg, 1913, p. 23-24).

As the passage quoted above makes clear, Münsterberg regarded the approach he was advocating for industrial/organizational psychology as a model for other applied endeavors as well. More generally, applied psychology would *be* psychotechnics. This meant that the essential business of applied psychology would be that of *Menschenbehandlung*—including what we now call the deployment of human resources—and the procedural principles would be the same, regardless of the particular domain of application. Following Münsterberg, the psychotechnician would start with the specification by the client of the specific ends to be achieved and then "work backward," employing empirical indicators of demonstrably important individual differences variables in the process to find out how best to select and/or treat different people *as instruments of those ends*. No "special methods of investigation," biographical or otherwise, for achieving a deeper understanding of individual cases would be called for here, because the objective was not *Menschenkenntnis* to begin with. The applied psychologist's proper objective, according to Münsterberg, was not to *understand* individualities, but to determine empirically how best to *treat* (handle, deploy) various kinds of people so as to maximize over the long run the realization of certain economic objectives specified by a client.

# The Growing Disenchantment
# of a Critical Personalist

Given Stern's personalistic convictions, neither Münsterberg's vision of psychotechnics nor Thorndike's vision of psychognostics could possibly have been acceptable to him. For his entire professional life, Stern remained convinced of the limitations of standardized testing and correlational research methods with respect to both *Menschenkenntnis* and *Menschenbehandlung*, and of the untoward consequences of an overreliance on those methods, both for applied differential psychology and the persons who would be the subjects of its inquiries. From various of Stern's published works over the ensuing two decades, we gain a clear sense for the depth of his convictions in this regard as well as his growing dissatisfaction with the direction in which differential psychology was heading.

One relevant commentary came in the context of a presentation made at the Seventh Congress for Experimental Psychology, held in Marburg in April of 1921. In that forum, Stern expressed his concern that in their effort to meet the rapidly mounting demands being made on them by the larger society, applied psychologists might be enticed into exaggerating what they could achieve. More specifically, he feared that the growing preference for standardized tests that could be administered quickly would lead psychometricians to neglect other forms of inquiry—most notably, methods of "direct observation" so necessary for a thorough understanding of the individual case. Stern argued his point as follows:

> Many psychologists and virtually all of the general public view psychotechnical methods as consisting of psychological tests and nothing else. In contrast to this, we at the Hamburg Institute have been emphasizing from the very beginning that diagnoses based on tests alone are limited not only in fact but in principle, and hence require without exception supplementation through methods of direct observation. (Stern, 1921, p. 3)

Stern argued that in the first place, tests by their very nature provide only a "momentary snapshot" of performance capabilities of the examinee. He added that because tests require the examinee to react, they merely capture reactive behaviors and preclude the possibility of learning something about the examinee that might only be revealed by spontaneous expressions of interests and inclinations, or through play or artistic activities. To tap these sources of insight into an individual's psychological functioning, Stern argued, would require "the observations by sensitive persons who have spent some extended time with the person whose psychological profile is being constructed" (Stern, 1921, p. 3). Continuing this line of argument, Stern noted,

> For the examinee in question, tests yield a number on the basis of which that examinee can be located somewhere along a quantitative scale, but which obscure things qualitatively peculiar to that individual. The results of direct observation cannot be quantified, but make possible a qualitative refinement of the psychological profile. For all of these reasons, the methods of direct observation of an examinee must always be used to supplement the test methods, and the former must be developed and refined with the same care as the latter. (Stern, 1921, pp. 3-4)

Here, we find reiterated many of the same themes Stern emphasized fully a decade earlier in *Methodological Foundations*. He insisted yet again that tests are limited not only in fact but also in principle, and this in part because they provide only a "momentary snapshot" of a person's performance capabilities. In addition, Stern pointed to the inherently reactive nature of the testing process, a fact that mitigates against the expression by the examinee of spontaneous, but possibly very revealing, interests, inclinations, and so on. These were crucial to an understanding of individuality, in Stern's view, and could be captured only through the exercise of careful attention by "sensitive persons who have spent some extended time" with the examinee.

This latter requirement of "extended time" obviously points in the direction of the "special methods of observation" that Stern consistently advocated, and we saw, above, how in Thorndike's view, the need for recourse to such methods was defined away by collapsing the distinction between qualitative and quantitative differences. However, an additional point warranting our attention here follows from Stern's mention of the importance of a *sensitive observer*. This, too, is something that was being rapidly undermined by the ascendant perspectives both in psychognostics and in psychotechnics. In both domains, extensive—indeed, virtually complete—reliance on the kind of knowledge produced by statistical analyses of large data sets was becoming the rule, and as Gigerenzer (1987) has effectively argued, a large part of the attractiveness of statistical methods lay in the scientific objectivity they seemed to promise. This was a discipline still struggling to become (and to be recognized from without as having become) a genuine science. The fight against subjectivity had to be won, and this would not be facilitated by the widespread admission of investigative procedures calling for observations by "sensitive observers" who had "spent some time" with the examinee.[11]

Still, Stern not only continued to urge others to incorporate such observations into their investigations, but as Schmidt (1994) points out, he also made observational methods an integral component of his own research program at the Hamburg institute. Schmidt explains that part of that research program entailed training teachers in the administration of psychological tests to the students. For those teachers, it was compulsory to participate in a semester-long training course in which they were familiarized with the test instruments at a level that made it possible for them not merely to administer the tests in an essentially mechanical fashion but also to participate meaningfully in the interpretation of the results. In connection with this point, Stern wrote,

> The tests were not designed simply to enable the teachers to generate some number with which to label the psychological performance of the children, but instead to prompt the testers to look into the basic attentional, memoric, understanding, critical, and combinatorial capabilities that were the basis of the performance. Accordingly, we only made our test materials available to those teams of testers whose members had participated in this preparatory course. (Stern, 1925b, p. 293; original German quoted in Schmidt, 1994, p. 15)

Beyond practicing what he preached, Stern also criticized others who did not practice what he preached. Of particular concern to him were researchers in Berlin who were doing similar work but who, in the interest of increasing the level of cooperation among Berlin school teachers, had simplified the tests and the preadministration teacher training programs so as to reduce the amount of time that the teachers would have to invest in testing and in scoring (Schmidt, 1994). Stern took pains to warn against this. Commenting with some disdain on the procedures being used in Berlin, he noted that the scoring of test results had been so schematized that a teacher or other test administrator could tabulate the results quickly and easily without any special psychological training or preparation whatsoever. "The approach," Stern wrote, again scarcely bothering to disguise his disdain, "bears a striking resemblance to the American model—just put up a number instead of any genuine psychological analysis and interpretation of the results" (Stern, 1925b, p. 452; original German quoted in Schmidt, 1994, p. 15).

Two years later, and by then markedly alarmed by the increasing identification of applied psychology with psychotechnics on the model that had been advocated by Münsterberg (see above), Stern used the occasion of the Fourth International Congress for Psychotechnics, held in Paris in October of 1927, to lecture on "Personality Research and Test Methods." In that lecture (published 2 years later), Stern began by stating that "though our conference is supposed to be devoted to applied psychology, it would be wrong to neglect theory entirely" (Stern, 1929, p. 63). He then moved quickly into a discussion of his central point, which again had to do with the danger of the belief that human individuality could be captured or faithfully represented by standardized psychological tests. In an emphatic rejection of the approach to individuality illustrated by the work of Thorndike (1911) discussed above, one notices that Stern's language was becoming increasingly pointed:

> The person is a unified whole, and has depth. . . . A human being is not a mosaic, and therefore cannot be described as a mosaic. *All attempts to represent a person simply in terms of a sequence of test scores are fundamentally false.* (Stern, 1929, pp. 63-64; emphasis added)

He continued: "By dissecting the person in accordance with elementary tests applied in isolation, we do not get closer to the essence of the personality. On the contrary, we move further away from it" (p. 65). Stern went on from here to make an urgent call for the development of *personalistic methods of interpretation.* He acknowledged that "it will require decades to develop these methods" (p. 69), but insisted,

> The effort must begin immediately. If up to now we have been concentrating our efforts on the perspective afforded by correlational research, in which we look horizontally at the relationship between the different existing individual attributes, we must now look vertically at the individual, in a way that leads beyond the surface into the depth, and from the depth then again outward. (Stern, 1929, p. 69)[12]

Quite obviously, the years between 1911 and 1927 had not witnessed any significant advances in this direction. Staeuble (1983) has speculated that when Stern tried to conceptualize personality dimensions on the basis of his personalistic assumptions but in a fashion not tied to the common-attribute model, he got "stuck," as she put it, in ideas "to which there were no corresponding methods of investigation" (p. 11). There is merit in this view.

In Chapter VI of *The Human Personality,* a chapter he titled "Principles of Personality Measurement," Stern (1918a) discussed at length his theoretical understanding of the measurement issues involved. Here, he once again and quite explicitly took his distance from the approach advocated by Thorndike (1911; see above), arguing that "the comparison of many personalities" to one another would be beside the point, "since the problem at hand pertains specifically to the relationship between the person and his/her world" (pp. 186-187) rather than to the position of one person relative to others in a large group along some dimension(s) necessarily presumed common to all.

Stern then discussed at some length a measurement logic in terms of which the person-world relationship could theoretically be represented. Clearly, he had a vision of what would have to be accomplished in the domain of measurement to faithfully reflect his personalistic outlook. Near the end of this discussion, however, he reminded his readers that logical "measurement principles must be clearly distinguished from empirical application and actual mathematical computation. In practice, the greatest of difficulties would be encountered" if one attempted to actually apply the ideas being discussed, and so in this context, "the methodological and empirical difficulties are left undiscussed, so that the basic principles, which are themselves difficult enough to formulate, can be worked out" (Stern, 1918a, p. 210).[13]

Unfortunately for Stern, practical empirical application, not conceptual analysis of "basic principles," was of surpassing interest to most of his contemporaries; and for the former purposes, the "horizontal" perspective proper to standardized testing and correlational research had something to offer that other perspectives did not, at least not at the time and perhaps not ever. Nevertheless, toward the end of his speech, Stern once again admonished the gathering at the Paris congress:

> Psychotechnicians using their test results for various selection purposes must remember that they are not dealing with machines or materials, whose quality and economic significance for the company is in fact expressible through test scores, but rather with human beings, whose occupation is a part—and indeed a very essential part—of their entire personal life. (Stern, 1929, p. 72)

Reflecting the convictions on which he had based critical personalism, Stern's concern that the methods of standardized testing were nurturing a view of persons as things is here fully visible. The concern is one he would soon voice again, and even more emphatically. The venue this next time was Moscow, and the occasion was the Seventh International Conference for Psychotechnics, held in 1931 (again, the text of the lecture was published 2 years later):

[I]n contrast to a chemist or an economist, the psychotechnician does not work with machines, or with wares, or, in short, with things, but rather with human beings. Under all conditions, human beings are and remain the centers of their own psychological life and their own worth. In other words, *they remain persons, even when they are studied and treated from an external perspective and with respect to others' goals.* Much more comparable to the psychotechnician would be doctors and hygienists, because these professionals, too, work with people. And to these researchers and practitioners, it is obvious that in their work—even in those cases where it is "transpersonal" in the sense of being devoted to the public health, or to the finding of a new cure for a disease, or to the prevention of an epidemic—they must nevertheless take into consideration the well-being and pain, the health or healing of the individuals whom they are treating. Working "on" a human being must always entail working "for" a human being. (Stern, 1933, pp. 54-55; emphasis added)

Stern proceeded from here to the following admonition:

The psychotechnician has every good reason to take these considerations seriously. Because if there are places today where the term "psychotechnician" is uttered with something of a disdainful tone, that is due to the implicit or explicit belief that psycho-technicians not only intercede but interfere in the lives and rights of the individuals they deal with. The feeling is that psychotechnicians degrade persons by using them as a means to others' ends. (Stern, 1933, p. 55)

It is highly significant that the concerns Stern was voicing here were not merely of an empirical nature. That is, he was not simply worried that the facticity of statements about persons was being compromised by the narrowness of prevailing research practices. In his view, the *treatment* of persons encouraged by those very practices was morally worrisome. This is altogether consistent with the central position assigned to considerations of human values within critical personalism as a system of thought. *Because persons are not things, they ought not be treated as things.* A differential psychology that could not or would not honor this principle was thus, from Stern's personalistic perspective, inevitably and necessarily problematic.

Turning his critical gaze once again away from psychotechnics and back to psychognostics, and in the process leaving no doubt about his disenchantment with developments in this domain as well, Stern went on to criticize attempts to represent individuals' personalities in terms of "polysymptomatic" profiles as might be constructed on the basis of some or other series of standardized trait measurements. As he put it, such an approach leads "to an array of multifaceted empirical findings, which are then combined in summary fashion into a profile or a listing of traits. This is now widely regarded as 'personality research,' and this is especially true in America" (Stern, 1933, pp. 60-61).

Whereas in previous works, Stern seems to have been trying to rein in his colleagues and to persuade them to think more broadly—more personalistically—about their testing procedures and about differential psychology overall, it appears that by the 1931 Moscow meetings, he had altered his sights. In the contribution under discussion here, he called for the explicit recognition of a distinction between psychotechnics, as it had come to be understood to that point, and "practical psychology": a new subdiscipline that would be defined as "the practical science of understanding human characteristics, behaviors and modes of experience from the standpoint of their mutual interactions and across various domains of life" (Stern, 1933, pp. 56-57).

A few pages later, Stern concluded his lecture, in typically modest fashion, as follows:

> I come to the end. As a conclusion, it is perhaps not idle to point out once again that the theme of my lecture has not been "psychotechnics" in its full breadth, but rather the "personal factor" within psychotechnics. For me, the question has simply been: What does psychotechnics, and practical psychology, mean for the individual person who is subjected to the methods of those disciplines? It is because this question is usually pushed to the background in discussions of the nature and significance of psychotechnics that I thought I should give it special attention. (Stern, 1933, p. 63)

Without doubt, the applied differential psychology Stern was so enthusiastically advocating in the 1911 *Methodological Foundations* book was to be a discipline in which knowledge of basic aspects of human nature would be won and then put to practical use in various domains of human life. But by 1933, the quest for *Menschenkenntnis* within the scientific mainstream of the discipline had been almost completely co-opted by the vision Thorndike had set forth in 1911 (cf. Danziger, 1990), and in Stern's view, the methods proper to that vision were not and could never be entirely adequate as a foundation for psychognostics. Compounding matters, psychotechnics had also come to be dominated by the same methods and, furthermore, by an orientation that regarded persons as the instruments of others' ends. Thus, Stern proposed a new subdiscipline, "practical psychology," distinct from psychotechnics as it had developed to that point and also committed to the pursuit of psychognostics tied to a vision of human individuality decidedly broader and more nuanced, or personalistic, than that which could be accommodated within the framework provided by Thorndike. In effect,

Stern was trying to "reinvent" applied differential psychology along lines more consonant with his initial vision.

There can be no doubt as to where Stern intended to direct his efforts from that point on. Alas, he could not have imagined in 1933 that so little time would be left to him to direct his efforts anywhere at all. As noted in Chapter One, Stern was summarily dismissed from his academic offices at the University of Hamburg on April 7 of that year, only weeks after Hitler and the Nazis had seized power—and with that, his productive intellectual life was virtually ended. With his death in 1938, prospects for his personalistic perspective on the "problem of individuality," a view so drastically at odds with the empiricism that had by then taken firm root within differential psychology, were greatly dimmed.

## Summary

Consistent with the tenor of the times, William Stern promoted differential psychology early in the 20th century as a field suited to the generation of scientific knowledge that would be of practical utility outside the laboratory, in schools, in health care settings, in business and industry, and in the military. One branch of such a psychology would be concerned with *Menschen-kenntnis,* or with advances in the understanding of human nature. A second branch of the discipline would be concerned with *Menschenbehandlung,* or the treatment of people and the handling of human resources in a way consistent with particular practical objectives. Stern saw that within both subdisciplines, the need would exist for systematic studies of individual differences in various psychological functions (intelligence, perception, judgment, memory, etc.) in accordance with the methods and psychometric principles of that research scheme within differential psychology he called correlational inquiry, and he was a significant contributor to this effort.

Stern never allowed his conception of the problem of individuality within scientific psychology to be dominated by mental testing or, more generally, by the technical concepts and research methods of correlational inquiry. On the contrary, from the outset and throughout his career, Stern regarded psychological tests and correlational research to be of limited value in the quest for an understanding of the individual human person and, as ever, in need of supplementation by methods respectful of the fact that persons differ from one another not only quantitatively, but qualitatively as well.

Many of Stern's contemporaries did not see matters as he did, however, and other views gradually came to dominate within the field. Concerning *Menschenkenntnis,* Edward L. Thorndike urged in his 1911 book,

*Individuality,* that the distinction between qualitative and quantitative between-person differences be abandoned in favor of a perspective from which all such differences would be regarded as quantitative in nature. From this perspective, any given individual's personality could be specified scientifically as his or her standing relative to others along certain specified attribute (trait) dimensions that could be regarded as common to all.

Concerning *Menschenbehandlung,* in his 1913 book, *Psychology and Industrial Efficiency,* Hugo Münsterberg called for an applied differential psychology in which research would be guided not by psychology's theoretical concerns at all, but by the organizational objectives of those outside the discipline who would be turning to psychologists for practical advice. The psychologist's job would be to show organizational leaders how to maximize their desired outcomes given (a) the kinds of assignments or activities involved and (b) the kinds of persons available.

Neither of these developments could possibly have been acceptable to Stern given his personalistic outlook on the problem of individuality. Contrary to the view espoused by Thorndike, Stern steadfastly insisted that individual *persons* could not be adequately understood simply as mere instances of *person categories,* and contrary to the practices advocated by Münsterberg, Stern could not possibly have embraced an applied psychology that would entail treating persons as mere things: that is, simply as commodities to be deployed in the service of others' ends.

In the years following the publication of his *Methodological Foundations of Differential Psychology* and continuing until his ouster from the University of Hamburg by the Nazis in 1933, Stern repeatedly and ever more pointedly expressed his misgivings about the above-mentioned developments in differential psychology. In numerous articles and conference presentations, he argued that the knowledge yielded by mental tests and common trait personality profiles is *in principle* insufficient for purposes of grasping human individualities, and he also drew attention to the morally questionable practice of regarding persons as means to others' ends. By the time of his death in 1938, differential psychology had moved quite some distance in a direction Stern neither intended nor endorsed, and the prospects within the mainstream for that larger system of thought he called critical personalism were already fading rapidly.

# Notes

1.   In the time period under discussion here, the term *test* was used to indicate what is today referred to as a test *item.* In Stern's time, a collection of "tests" would

be used to form a "scale," whereas in contemporary parlance, a collection of "items" is said to comprise a "test."

2. In this connection, Stern cited works by Spearman (1904) and by Krueger and Spearman (1906). With particular reference to the former, Stern wrote, "In this way [i.e., through factor analysis], Spearman believes, he can arrive with a relatively small number of principle tests at a measure of 'general intelligence.' However, the empirical basis here is still too thin, and the computational methods still too controversial, to admit of a final judgment about this approach to scaling" (Stern, 1911, p. 96).

3. Nor was this imbalance redressed anywhere else in Eysenck's (1990) regrettably one-sided and self-serving article.

4. For some reason, Stern did not mention in this passage a 10th measure employed by Cattell, reaction time for sound.

5. Here, Stern referenced two works published in French by E. Toulouse. The first of these is titled *A Medical-Psychological Study of the Relationship Between Superior Intellect and Abnormality. I. General Introduction* (Toulouse, 1896). The second work is titled *A Medical-Psychological Study of Superior Intelligence: Henri Poincaré* (Toulouse, 1910).

6. For the benefit of readers not familiar with this statistic, the nature and meaning of that coefficient of correlation commonly designated $r$, the Pearson product-moment correlation coefficient, will be discussed in some detail in Chapter Five. Suffice it for the present to say that this statistic can range in absolute value from a low of zero (0.00) to a high of one (1.00). An $r$ of .16 is thus quite low, and an $r$ of .75 is rather high.

7. Stern refers to the pages of the original 1911 text on which the figure reproduced in Chapter Two (see Figure 2.3) were printed.

8. With specific reference to "school marks" (grades), Thorndike also advised that records be kept of a student's standing at a given time relative to his or her standing at some previous point in time. Thorndike's views thus did admit of a form of measurement R. B. Cattell (1944) would later call *ipsative*. In subsequent chapters of this work, issues pertaining to measurement will be considered in detail (see also Lamiell, 1987).

9. Readers familiar with the contemporary literature of personality psychology will recognize this view as precisely the one that continues to dominate the field. This point will be discussed at length in Chapter Six.

10. In a prefatory note to this work, Münsterberg stated that it could not be regarded simply as a translation of the German version of the same work that had been published some months previously under the title *Psychologie und Wirtschaftsleben: Ein Beitrag zur angewandten Experimental-Psycholgie (Psychology and Economic Life: A Contribution to Applied Experimental Psychology)*, because parts of the German volume had been abbreviated or omitted entirely and other parts had been enlarged and supplemented. "Yet," Münsterberg said, "the essential substance of the two books is identical."

11. Gigerenzer (1987) developed his point with specific reference to "probabilistic" thinking in experimental psychology from the late 1920s until around

1950, noting the widespread investment in the interpretation of treatment group *means* and the dismissal of between-person variance as *error*. But the ideals of determinism and objectivity that Gigerenzer cites as central to these developments were widely prevalent among differential psychologists and other statistically minded social scientists, too (cf. Danziger, 1990, esp. Chapter 9; see also Porter, 1986). Moreover, the statistic in which those investigators would invest so heavily as a means of revealing the order in between-person variation, the Pearson product-moment correlation coefficient, is itself a *group mean,* though the fact and profound implications of this matter seem to have been lost on most 20th-century differential psychologists (see Lamiell, 1990a, 1997, 2000). Here, too, we touch on an issue to be discussed at much greater length in Chapter Seven.

12.   Once again, these references to looking "horizontally" and "vertically" relate to Stern's depiction of the various research schemes displayed in Figure 2.3.

13.   In Chapter Nine, I will return to Stern's nascent ideas on the matter of measurement from a personalistic perspective and attempt to advance further with them.

# Chapter Four

## The Entrenchment of a "Common Trait" Perspective on Human Individuality

Among prominent psychologists in America (and after World War II, psychologists in America were the ones who would matter the most), no one concerned with questions about individuality was both more familiar with and sympathetic to Stern's thinking than Gordon W. Allport (1897-1967). In fact, Allport had spent part of 1923 with Stern at the University of Hamburg, and during his months there had even rented a room in the Sterns' home (Bühring, 1996a). So, partly because of the direct personal and professional connections between the two, but also partly because Allport's own work has been so pivotal in the field, the path of our study of developments in psychologists' thinking about the problem of individuality during the years after Stern's death necessarily leads through a discussion of Allport's key ideas and arguments.

The previous chapter treated at some length of Stern's steadfast resistance to the increasingly restrictive preference of differential psychologists for empirical inquiry tied to the methods of standardized testing, and it was thanks mostly to Allport that a "minority resistance" to that trend continued after Stern's death. As we will see, however, the resistance ultimately withered, and it is arguable that to an appreciable extent, the last best hope for Stern's critical personalism withered then, too. This is by no means to say that Stern and Allport held identical views. On the contrary, critical personalism is a much more comprehensive and philosophically sophisticated system of thought than Allport's trait theory of personality. Because of their differences, I also do not wish to suggest that critical personalism would necessarily have flourished if only Allport's views had won wider favor.

Nevertheless, for the most part, Stern's ideas were set forth in a language that few—and with each passing year ever fewer—American psychologists could (or would bother to) read, and of course not all of them were interested in the "problem of individuality," anyway. To be sure, many American psychologists were interested in intelligence and other forms of mental testing, and in these circles "the IQ guy" was relatively well-known (Lamiell, 1996). But as should now be abundantly clear from the first three chapters of this work, knowing Stern "the IQ guy" did not then (and does not now) provide much insight into Stern the critical personalist. As a consequence, it is surely the case that most of what (little) American psychologists came to know about critical personalism was learned through Allport.[1] To this extent, Allport's own retreat from the center stage of the discipline he helped define as "the psychology of personality" (see below) undoubtedly made familiarity with Stern's thinking seem less necessary to, and as a result less widespread among, scholars within the field than it otherwise would have been.

In any case, with Allport effectively dispatched, adherents of a perspective on the problem of individuality, which both Allport and Stern before him had persistently criticized as too limited and/or simply off the mark, could get on with their work, largely if not entirely unopposed. Certainly, other dissenting voices were raised from time to time (e.g., Carlson, 1971; Lamiell, 1981, 1987; Rosenzweig, 1958; Runyan, 1982; Tyler, 1959, 1978; cf. Alexander, 1993), but to date, these efforts have had little sustained impact on work being done within the mainstream of the field. Something of a crisis of confidence within that mainstream did arise in the late 1960s, touched off by the publication of Walter Mischel's *Personality and Assessment* (Mischel, 1968); but defenders of the traditional view, which Mischel (1968) had questioned on empirical grounds, eventually met his challenge in kind (at least to their own satisfaction; cf. Epstein, 1977, 1979, 1980; Pawlik, 1992), and business as usual proceeded with renewed vigor.[2] At present, thinking about the "problem of individuality" within the mainstream of scientific psychology remains dominated as much as ever by the *common trait* view of personality Allport so roundly criticized and by the measurement procedures and statistical analysis methods to which that view is so splendidly tailored.[3]

The present chapter will focus on the basis for and nature of Allport's opposition to mainstream views and on the reception of Allport's ideas among his contemporaries. How did Allport's approach to the problem of individuality differ from Stern's? What were the key ideas underlying Allport's approach? What arguments did he mount in favor of that approach? On what grounds were Allport's arguments resisted? Consideration of these questions yields further insight into the historical developments that have culminated in the trait psychology that currently dominates mainstream conceptions of human individuality.

## Gordon W. Allport's Efforts Toward a "Psychology of Personality"

With respect to our concerns in this book, the year 1937 was something of a watershed. One noteworthy publication was an article written by Allport for the journal *Character and Personality*,[4] titled "The Personalistic Psychology of William Stern" (Allport, 1937b). This article gave a critical review of Stern's last major work, a general psychology text (refer to discussion in Chapter One[5]), and it stands today as one of the most accessible, concise treatments of Stern's thinking that is available in the English literature.[6]

Of course, Allport very much shared Stern's concern for the "problem of individuality" within scientific psychology, and by 1937, the inadequacies of *differential* psychology in this regard—inadequacies that as we have seen, Stern himself anticipated—seemed altogether manifest to Allport. Not surprisingly, therefore, Allport's review of Stern's 1935 book was decidedly positive, and he concluded his commentary by suggesting how Stern's ideas would challenge prevailing views:

> [Stern's book] will, of course, offend the dignity of those who have sacrosanct ideas of what constitutes "scientific" psychology. The same psychologists who shun the deeper problems of emotion lest they seem emotional, and who over-look the whole field of sentiment lest they appear sentimental, will now avoid the person lest they become personal. But should they dip into this book and observe the immense range of problems they have left out of their own systems, it will be some time before they can rationalize their way back into a comfort-able *impersonal* equilibrium. (Allport, 1937b, p. 246; emphasis in original)

So congenial did he find Stern's thinking to his own that Allport made a condensed version of his review of Stern's book part of the concluding chapter of his own book, which also appeared in 1937, titled *Personality: A Psychological Interpretation* (Allport, 1937a). In this latter context, how-ever, Allport took pains to distinguish Stern's *personalistic* psychology from the discipline he himself wished to represent as *the psychology of personality*. In this connection, Allport stated that personalistic thought posits,

> [T]he individual person as a many-sided unity must serve as the center of gravity for each and every investigation and formulation of theory undertaken by psychology. The intention is to rewrite the science of mental life entirely around this new center of emphasis. Note well: the goal is not merely to free the study of personality from over-rigid conceptual barriers drawn by general psychology, but to demolish and reconstruct the entire edifice of general psychology from the ground up. In this respect personalistic psychology is more extreme than the psychology of personality which is content to play its role *within* the many-sided science of psychology. (Allport, 1937a, p. 550; emphasis in original)

Clearly, then, Allport was of the view that Stern's critical personalism entailed a more radical stance vis-à-vis mainstream scientific psychology than he (Allport) himself wished to adopt. But what, then, was Allport's own position, and how did it differ from Stern's?

## Circumscribing the Discipline

"As a rule," wrote Allport in the opening line of the preface to the 1937 book, "science regards the individual as a mere bothersome accident" (p. vii). Against this view, he went on to note, a "new movement" within psychology had gradually grown up and had progressed significantly within the preceding 15 years. Allport noted that in America, this movement had come to be known as "the *psychology of personality*" (p. vii; emphasis in original), and it is by this name that most psychologists since have referred to that subdiscipline of scientific psychology concerned with questions of individuality. Allport's expressed purpose in his book was to provide a text that would "*define* the new field of study" (p. vii; emphasis in original).

To define something is to set limits about it and in the process make clear, or at least as clear as possible, what it entails or includes, and by implication what it does not entail or specifically excludes. If by his own account, Allport wanted to be as inclusive as possible in his circumscription of the discipline for which he was intending to write the definitive text, he also made it quite clear that certain approaches to the psychology of personality extant at the time seemed to him inadequate, if not altogether untenable. Allport regarded psychoanalysis, for example, as too limited for the narrowness of its "monosymptomatic bias" (p. vii), and he categorically rejected the social-psychological view of personality as nothing more than an individual's "stimulus value" to others.[7] He anticipated being taken to task for deemphasizing the relationship between personality and culture but sought refuge in the argument that "the interest of psychology is not in the factors *shaping* personality (but) in personality *itself* as a developing structure. . . . Culture is relevant only when it has become interiorized within the person as a set of personal ideals, attitudes, and traits" (p. vii; emphasis in original).[8] In addition to these points, Allport made his doubts clear as to the adequacy of statistical approaches to understanding personality, stating of those approaches that "sometimes they are useful; but many times they are not" (p. vii).

With these preliminary considerations out of the way, Allport went on to tackle his major problem head-on, which was essentially the same problem Stern had defined nearly four decades earlier: how to reconcile a concern for human individuality with the aspirations of a scientific psychology. Stern's ultimate answer to this question was critical personalism—*not* differential psychology[9]—and though Allport acknowledged in the first chapter of his 1937 book that "the logical culmination of interest in the individual is the creation of a personalistic psychology" (p. 18), we have already seen that Allport viewed personalism as a system more antagonistically disposed toward mainstream thinking than he himself was at the time. Allport decided to take a somewhat different (albeit largely compatible) approach to the problem, and later in the book he would cast the difference as follows:

> The swiftly rising tide of interest in the systematic study of personality carries with it a denial of the traditional belief that individuality is beyond the limit of science, or at least beyond the limit of psychological science. . . . This modern revolt has two distinguishable fronts. The first is the aggressive doctrine usually known as *personalistic psychology*. The second front of attack is the *psychology of personality,* as represented in the present volume. The shafts of the former are heavily supplied with metaphysical barbs; the weapon of the latter is empirical necessity. Though the two lines of attack have something in common—namely, their insistence that the person be given more adequate recognition in psychology—it is well to consider them separately, and to mark their differences. (Allport, 1937a, pp. 549-550; emphasis in original)

Hence, in contrast to a comprehensive, philosophically grounded system of thought for conceiving of human persons and their interrelationships, the *Weltanschauung* Stern called critical personalism, Allport's preferred approach to the problem of individuality was by his own account a decidedly less "aggressive" and rather more empirically inspired psychology of personality. The conceptual pillars of his framework would be (a) the notion of *traits* as the basic structural elements of personality and (b) the distinction between *nomothetic* and *idiographic* investigative methods made in the service of a further distinction he would draw between common traits and individual traits. In this latter connection, Allport borrowed terms that had been introduced to scholarly discourse many decades earlier by Windelband (1894/1998). Let us examine Allport's foundational ideas more closely.

## Common Traits and Individual Traits as Structural Elements of Personality

Allport devoted Part III of his 1937 book to a discussion of the structure of personality, and he adopted the view that traits would be the appropriate structural elements for a science of personality. He proposed to understand these as biophysical characteristics *"really there"* in the individual (1937a, p. 289; emphasis in original) and not merely cognitive constructions of one sort or another ("biosocial" characteristics) existing only in the "eyes of the beholder."[10]

From here, Allport (1937a) went on to discuss certain conceptual distinctions he believed needed to be drawn between traits and, respectively, determining tendencies, habits, attitudes, and types. With regard to the distinction between traits and types, Allport pointed out that "unlike traits, types always have a biosocial reference" (p. 295). Hence, Allport argued that whereas a person could be said to *have* a trait (traits are not biosocial, but *biophysical*), a person cannot *have* a type. A person can only *fit* a type.

Allport went on to draw the further distinction between common traits and individual traits. His sense of the need for this distinction was tied closely to his conviction that in the final analysis, every individual person is *unique*. It followed from this, Allport believed, that any psychology that would prove true to the nature of human individuality would have to bring this uniqueness to light.

*Common traits* were widely understood as dimensions of psychological functioning, such as intelligence, introversion-extraversion, or high versus low achievement motivation, along which individuals could be compared with one another in terms of amount or degree. This understanding accorded fully with the view that had been advanced by Thorndike (1911; refer to Chapter Three). Though Allport found no need to deny a place within the psychology of personality for concepts referring to such dimensions, he did pause briefly over the question of whether such dimensions were properly called traits. In this connection, he pointed to the potential for confusion in using the term to refer, on one hand, to dispositions having real neuropsychological existence *within* individuals (his own understanding of what a trait actually is) and, on the other hand, to "empirical continua" realized through "abstractive analysis" of differences for purposes of making comparisons *between* individuals (see Allport, 1937a, p. 299). Still, bowing to conventional usage of the term trait as well as research practices that by then had already become customary, Allport recommended that the expression "common traits" be retained as a way of referring to such empirical continua.

As we have already seen, the concept of common traits can be made serviceable within all four research schemes or "disciplines" identified by Stern in the 1911 *Methodological Foundations* text. They are of course the *focus* in variation studies and correlational research, but they can also serve as the *basis* for psychographic investigations and comparative research. As had Stern before him, however, Allport expressed doubts that a person's individuality could ever be fully captured in terms of common traits alone. For Allport, the solution to this problem would require the consideration of *individual* traits; as far as he was concerned, such traits could not possibly be represented quantitatively in a way that would make them commensurate with common traits.[11] Nevertheless, Allport argued, individual traits do exist and can be detected empirically, and for clear evidence of this, he advised, one need look no further than to the work that clinicians, counselors, and therapists were carrying out daily. Allport believed that the intuitive judgments on which such workers based the characterizations of their patients/clients were very often, if not always, grounded in essentially idiographic considerations of each person individually. For the more formal purposes of empirical research, Allport argued, this "clinical method" could be and should be supplemented both by experimental methods and observer ratings, with the understanding that the relevant data, whether experimental or nonexperimental in nature, would be based on extensive observations made of individual persons over time.

Worthy of mention here in relationship to our previous discussion of Stern's views is that Allport's interests were situated squarely within the investigative domain Stern had termed *psychognostics,* though Allport did not employ that expression.[12] Clearly, Allport's main concern was not with how to apply knowledge about individuals' personalities for the purpose of achieving certain practical objectives set by others (the province of *psychotechnics,* at least as it had been redefined by Münsterberg; cf. discussion in Chapter Three); he was more concerned with the sort of knowledge about individuals that is necessary to gain true insights into their psychological functioning as human beings. Apart from his appreciation for the work of clinicians and other psychologists working in applied settings, Allport's questions were not those of *Menschenbehandlung,* the treatment of people, but rather those of *Menschenkenntnis,* the understanding of human nature. For this purpose, he believed, knowledge of individual traits would be indispensable supplements to knowledge of common traits, and if prevailing methods for measuring the latter were not suited to the requirements of the former, then methods that answered the need would have to be invented.[13] The goal of one's empirical investigations should dictate the methods, and not vice versa, Allport believed. In this connection, he found the distinction between nomothetic and idiographic knowledge formulated by Windelband (1894/1998) to be very useful.

## The Call to Supplement Nomothetic
## With Idiographic Inquiry in Personality Studies

The terms nomothetic and idiographic were invented by Windelband to refer to two distinct kinds of knowledge. Nomothetic knowledge, Windelband argued, is knowledge of the sort contained in the general laws formulated in the natural sciences *(die Naturwissenschaften)*. The defining characteristic of a general law is that it reflects "what always is" *(was immer ist)* within some explicitly circumscribed domain of empirical events covered by the law.[14]

Idiographic knowledge, by contrast, is knowledge of an essentially historical or biographical sort. Its defining characteristic is its reflection of *"what once was" (was einmal war)*, and so idiographic knowledge is precisely that sort of knowledge needed to understand some unique entity or event. Idiographic knowledge, on Windelband's account, is knowledge of the kind sought in the *Geisteswissenschaften*, or what would be referred to in English as the *moral sciences* or *human sciences* or, most commonly, the *humanities*.

Windelband's nomothetic versus idiographic distinction seemed to Allport to conform quite well to the idea that within a viable psychology of personality, there would be a need both for knowledge of common traits and for knowledge of strictly individual traits. The former kind of knowledge would, Allport believed, provide the proper empirical basis for claims about *people in general* and hence would win for personality psychology the kind of knowledge, nomothetic, that would be needed to warrant the discipline as scientific on the model of the *natural* sciences.

On the other hand, and without in any way prejudicing the above, knowledge about personalities gained through procedures appropriate for the empirical investigation of individual traits—procedures other than and quite possibly incommensurable with those appropriate for the common trait approach—would, Allport believed, provide needed additional knowledge of specific *people in particular*. Such procedures would win for the psychology of personality the kind of knowledge, idiographic, appropriate to the *human* sciences. In the view of Allport (also Stern and a relative handful of others down through the years), such knowledge would be necessary to do justice to the focal subject matter, human individuality, whatever the status of such knowledge might be according to the canons of natural science. Allport believed that only in this way, that is, only within an investigative paradigm in which nomothetic knowledge is supplemented by idiographic knowledge, could any psychology of personality worthy of the name thrive.

To underscore the importance of these distinctions, Allport drew attention to their implications for interpreting the findings of the widely known studies of character carried out by Hartshorne, May, and Shuttleworth during the late 1920s, under the auspices of the *Character Education Inquiry* (CEI; Hartshorne & May, 1928, 1929; Hartshorne, May, & Shuttleworth, 1930). Across a wide variety of tasks and settings, those authors had found that the intercorrelations between different manifestations of the same supposed trait were so consistently low as to render doubtful the very existence of such traits.

For example, in a large sample of school children, Hartshorne and May (1928) had found a correlation of only $r = +.132$ between measures of stealing and lying,[15] and this finding was seen by the investigators to call into question the assumption of the existence of some underlying, unitary trait of "dishonesty." The evidence, Hartshorne and May (1928) argued, pointed instead to the conclusion that alleged traits such as dishonesty (and helpfulness, persistence, self-control, etc.) are more properly regarded as groups of specific learned *habits*.

Allport's argument in this connection was that the low correlations reported by Hartshorne, May, and Shuttleworth proved "only that children are not consistent *in the same way*, not that they are inconsistent with *themselves*. This," Allport added gravely, "is an exceedingly important discovery" (Allport, 1937a, p. 250; emphasis in original).

Allport sought to illustrate his point with the aid of the diagram reproduced here in Figure 4.1. Whereas Hartshorne and May (1928) had investigated stealing and lying as alternative behavioral expressions of the presumed common trait of dishonesty, Allport argued that each of those behaviors might in fact be expressions not of some common trait at all, but rather of a variety of quite different individual traits that the researchers had overlooked entirely:

It may be that child A steals pennies because he has a consistent personal trait of *bravado* based upon his admiration for the gangsters he reads about in

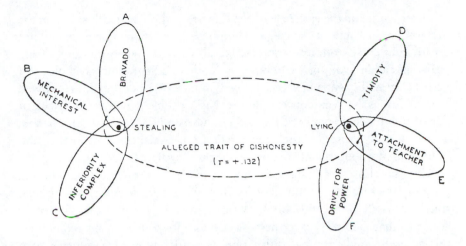

**Figure 4.1**    Critique of One Statistical Conception of Trait

NOTE: Dotted ellipse represents the trait as conceived by investigators in the Character Education Inquiry; solid ellipses represent possible personal traits overlooked by them).

SOURCE: Adapted from Allport (1937a, p. 251).

the tabloids and sees on the screen; child B steals because he has a persistent *interest in tools and mechanics* that drives him to buy more equipment than he can honestly afford; child C, suffering from a gnawing *feeling of social inferiority,* steals pennies to purchase candy to buy his way into favor with his classmates. Child D does not steal pennies, but he lies about his cheating, not because he has a general trait of dishonesty, but because he has a general trait of *timidity* (fear of consequences); child E lies because he is afraid of hurting the feelings of the teacher whom he adores; child F lies because he is *greedy for praise.* Each of these children behaved as he did toward these tests, not because he had specific habits, but because he had some deep-lying and characteristic trait. All that the C.E.I. discovered was that the particular trait of honesty as defined in the usual ethical terms and tested in various conventional situations, was not one of which the children possessed constant individual degrees. . . . The children did not all have the *same* trait, but they had nevertheless their own traits. (Allport, 1937a, pp. 251-252; emphasis in original)[16]

These, then, were the sorts of considerations central to Allport's steadfast conviction that "nothing is more essential in the entire field of personality than an adequate recognition of individual traits" (1937a, p. 302).

Roughly a quarter of a century after the publication of his 1937 text, Allport published another major work titled *Pattern and Growth in Personality* (Allport, 1961). As one would expect, there are many differences between this later work and the earlier one. Nevertheless, Allport himself stated in the preface that in "outlook, scope, and emphasis," the two volumes were "not greatly" different from one another. He also noted that in the intervening years, his call in 1937 for a combined nomothetic-idiographic psychology of personality had been subjected to "lively attacks." Undaunted, he avowed that as far as he was concerned, the basic problem within the field of personality psychology in 1961 was the same as it had been in 1937. It was, as he put it, "to discover the proper balance between uniform factors and individual morphogenic factors in personality" (Allport, 1961, p. x).

The two classes of "factors" referred to here were for all intents and purposes the respective equivalents of the common traits and the individual traits discussed in the 1937 book. A further examination of the later book confirms that with respect to these basic concepts, as well as his reliance on the nomothetic-idiographic distinction he had discussed a quarter of a century earlier, Allport's convictions about the psychology of personality in 1961 remained what they had been in 1937.

One thing *had* changed rather dramatically in the intervening years: the profile of William Stern and critical personalism in Allport's work. The name index of the 1937 book shows 32 page citations following Stern's name, and ideas central to critical personalism per se are discussed at some length (see Allport, 1937a, pp. 552-557). In the 1961 book, the comparable number of page citations is 10, and very few of the substantive references pertain to critical personalism per se. So, even in Allport's eyes, it appears, the "star" that had once shone so brightly for psychologists interested in the problem of individuality had become, by 1961, scarcely more than a faint glimmer. In the meantime, Allport himself was locked in a losing battle posterity would christen the "nomothetic versus idiographic controversy." We now turn to a consideration of the major contours of this controversy.

# Major Contours of the Nomothetic-Idiographic Debate

We should recall here that unlike Stern, Allport's perspective on the problem of individuality was, by his own account, guided far more by empirical than by philosophical considerations. In research findings such as those that had been reported by Hartshorne, May, and Shuttleworth (refer above), Allport saw unambiguous evidence of the *need* for incorporating individual traits into accounts of personality; and in the practical activities of clinicians and counselors faced daily with the task of formulating coherent impressions of unique personalities, he saw tangible evidence of the *possibility* of meaningful and enlightening characterizations of an essentially idiographic nature. Most of Allport's most influential contemporaries, however, were inclined to view the same evidence rather differently.

In his discussion of the issues, for example, McClelland (1951) pointed to a variety of possible explanations for the apparent failure of some general nomothetic law to hold in many specific individual cases. The possibility must be considered, McClelland argued, that the law in question had not been tested properly, that is, tested under conditions actually conforming to those in which the law was supposed to hold. Or perhaps there was more than one general law determining the behavior in question, and the researcher had failed to take the additional laws into account. Or again, perhaps the putative general law had not been formulated properly to begin with, and a reformulated law, corrected on the basis of new research findings, might improve the scientist's ability to account for individual behavior. In short, McClellend (1951) recognized many possible interpretations of low correlations such as those reported by Hartshorne, May, and Shuttleworth, and though he was appropriately circumspect in his analysis of the alternatives, he also left little doubt of his conviction that through a sharpening of the trait concept and the further refinement of measurement *methods,* a psychology of personality tied predominantly to the common trait approach would prove most theoretically enlightening and empirically fruitful.

Swift and emphatic opposition developed to Allport's notion that clinically formulated personality impressions, and predictions based on them, were somehow intrinsically idiographic and hence different in some logically fundamental way from the formal personality characterizations and actuarially based predictions issuing from the nomothetic, common trait perspective. An article by Lundberg published just 4 years after Allport's 1937 text had appeared is illustrative in this regard (Lundberg, 1941). In opposition to Allport's contention, quoted by Lundberg (1941, p. 383), that "the only way in which we can predict the chances [*sic*] that a given individual has of behaving in a certain way is to study him as an individual and especially his subjective mental processes with the aid of subjective categories," Lundberg replied,

> Study, if you will, a given individual as thoroughly as can be imagined, including his most subjective or subconscious mental processes, with the aid of as many subjective categories as anyone desires. What possible basis for prediction does all this material provide *except a basis for classifying the case as more or less like other cases with which the analyst has had experience* (directly or indirectly . . . ) all of which represent a formal or informal actuarial basis of

*every* prediction regarding "the chances that a given individual has of behaving in a certain way"? What possible basis of prediction could the most intimate knowledge of a case provide . . . unless the predicter [*sic*] can interpret this knowledge in terms of knowledge of other cases and how they behaved? . . . *To the degree that [clinical] methods achieve reliable prediction, analysis of the procedures involved will show that they are of the same basic character as those employed by the statistician.* (Lundberg, 1941, p. 383; former emphasis in original, latter added)

Three years later, Sarbin (1944) would articulate a rather more extensive and thoroughgoing argument consistent with Lundberg's, and in the course of so doing conclude that in the domain of person characterization and behavioral prediction, only one model is worthy of scientific consideration:

The operations of those who reject the statistical method of prediction and substitute for it a "dynamic" clinical or individual prediction, may be described in one of two ways: *Either they are making statistical predictions in an informal, subjective, and uncontrolled way, or else they are performing purely verbal manipulations which are unverifiable and akin to magic.* (Sarbin, 1944, p. 214; emphasis added)

For Sarbin (and Lundberg, and virtually all others who were or would become interested in the matter), the real question was not *whether* clinical judgments and predictions of the sort Allport regarded as idiographic were grounded in the same logical structure as formal trait measurements after all, that is, in considerations of a putatively nomothetic nature. Of course they were. The only real question was whether predictions based on informal and subjective but *implicitly* nomothetic judgments could empirically outperform predictions based on the formal, objective, and hence *explicitly* nomothetic procedures underlying the common trait approach to personality measurement (and clinical diagnosis). The debate over the relative merits of clinical versus statistical prediction continued for some time (see, e.g., Wiggins, 1973), but Allport's suggestion that there might be a coherent logic for person characterization at once suitable for science and fundamentally different from that underlying the logic of the nomothetic methods of standardized testing would gain little further support.[17]

In the eyes of most of Allport's contemporaries, then, the empirically based arguments he mounted in favor of admitting idiographic procedures into the discipline's methodological arsenal simply were not convincing. The manifest weaknesses of the common trait approach would properly be remediated not by abandoning or supplementing that approach, but by refining it. Furthermore, the idea that informal, clinical judgments were grounded in idiographic considerations that were somehow fundamentally different from and irreconcilable with the nomothetic logic of the common trait approach was dismissed out of hand as nonsensical.

Beyond these considerations, a good deal of the opposition to Allport's views also reflected the concern that to admit idiographic methods and knowledge objectives into the psychology of personality would be to compromise the scientific status of the discipline. One expression of this concern came from E.B. Skaggs in an article titled "Personalistic Psychology as Science" (Skaggs, 1945).

Against the background of the observation that "science, as we know it today, searches for general laws and principles" and with an eye toward the distinction between nomothetic and ideographic[18] knowledge Allport (1937a) had borrowed from Windelband, Skaggs stated,

> Allport takes a bold stand for the broadening of the concept of science. This may be the proper progressive stand to take, but we doubt that our fellow scientists in physics, chemistry, geology, or astronomy will be very receptive to the idea. Perhaps we, as psychologists, could attain a more satisfactory adjustment to the order of things by saying that some of our content or knowledge *is science* while other content or knowledge *is non science*. (Skaggs, 1945, p. 234)

For Skaggs, the hallmarks of scientific knowledge were the temporal durability and generality (or universality) of phenomena, and of course these criteria corresponded perfectly with the defining characteristic of nomothetic knowledge specified by Windelband. Such knowledge, Windelband said, is knowledge of "what always is," and this is the sort of knowledge sought within the natural sciences. Noting that knowledge of what is temporary, peculiar, or unique to isolated individual cases fails by definition to meet the criteria of durability and generality/universality and hence could not possibly be regarded as scientific knowledge "in the eyes of our colleagues in physics, chemistry and astronomy" (Skaggs, 1945, p. 237), Skaggs wondered whether perhaps it might not be better to resist Allport's call for an expansion of our understanding of what constitutes scientific knowledge. Because "we all want to bask in the light of the great Sun-God Science," Skaggs wrote (p. 238), ought we perhaps, instead of heeding Allport,

> [M]ake another category of knowledge, call it by any other name than science, and leave the basic restricted concept [of science] as it is? Why not admit that much of that which is studied in psychology and sociology is simply not science? (Skaggs, 1945, p. 238)

In his reply to Skaggs, Allport (1946) found it necessary to begin by clearing up some confusions that he feared Skaggs's article had unwittingly created. First, Allport noted, one should not equate personalistic psychology with the idiographic outlook. Allport noted that a reading of Stern's *General Psychology From the Personalistic Standpoint* (by this time available in the English translation by Spoerl published in 1938) would reveal any number of concepts referring to aspects of psychological functioning presumed ever and everywhere true of human persons. Hence, at least in terms of its long-range theoretical objectives, personalistic psychology aspired toward Skaggs's nomothetic criteria of durability and generality.

This much said, Allport added that his own views could not properly be called personalistic, anyway. Referring to his 1937 text in which, as we have already seen, he had taken explicit note of various differences between his own views and those of Stern, he wrote,

> If [Skaggs] wishes to label my own views "personalistic" I cannot prevent him, but because of the many differences between Stern's "system" and my own, I myself would hesitate to accept the label. Stern has prior rights to it. (Allport, 1946, p. 133)

Having (again) distanced himself from Stern, Allport addressed himself directly to Skaggs's misgivings about making idiographic methods, and idiographic knowledge, a legitimate part of the psychology of personality. In this connection, Allport (1946) questioned Skaggs's specification of durability and generality as the defining characteristics of science, and he argued that the more customary view pointed to the definition of scientific knowledge as that which "enhances our *understanding, prediction,* and *control* of phenomena above the level achieved by unaided common sense" (p. 185; emphasis in original). With these as the criteria, Allport reemphasized his conviction that idiographic approaches should supplement the common trait (nomothetic) approach and not replace it, toward the end of ensuring that a judiciously broadened psychology of personality would "do a better job than it has traditionally done in handling the phenomenon of individuality" (p. 184). In the face of the danger seen by Skaggs that to admit idiographic methods and knowledge into personality psychology, even as a supplement to the nomothetic, would be to risk compromising the scientific status of the discipline, Allport did not cower:

> This logic of appeasement has little attractiveness for me. Prestige for psychology will scarcely be won by aping those who, at this particular moment in the world's history, enjoy exalted status. Rather, when psychology has ripe wisdom to

offer concerning the development of human personality, whether it offers it in a nomothetic or idiographic manner (or both), it will then merit the high position which Dr. Skaggs covets for it. (Allport, 1946, p. 186)

In the disciplinary climate of the time, the zeitgeist, few were willing to be as cavalier as Allport about reconciling idiographic knowledge objectives with the aspirations of a discipline seeking to achieve and maintain status as a science on the model of the natural sciences. Because Windelband had defined idiographic knowledge as a kind of knowledge other than that sought within the natural sciences, the question among those otherwise sympathetic to Allport's views was this: How would the necessary reconciliation be accomplished? One attempt along these lines was made by S.J. Beck (1953) in an article titled with the question: "The Science of Personality: Nomothetic or Idiographic?" This article would promptly be rejoined by H.J. Eysenck (1954) in a work he titled with an emphatic answer: "The Science of Personality: Nomothetic!"

In his article, Beck argued that the answer to the question posed in his title should be "Both!" He made clear his full appreciation for the importance of traditional nomothetic investigations carried out in accordance with the *attribute-focused* disciplines Stern had called "variation studies" and "correlational research" (though Beck did not specifically mention Stern). He then went on, however, to argue that to accomplish scientific studies of personality, an investigator must go beyond research focused on discrete attributes and extend inquiry into studies of the patterning and dynamics of the various attributes in specific individual cases:

> To the student of the personality as a whole, the deficit in the nomothetic technique is that . . . (attribute) variables are observed one by one. (Beck, 1953, p. 355)

> The essence of the idiographic method is that it focuses its glass on the universe of behavior traits co-functioning as a universe. This is the individual. (Beck, 1953, p. 356)

> A universe of traits, variables in mutual interplay, affecting one another, these are the individual. This is the task which the idiographic method undertakes. (Beck, 1953, p. 357)

To realize idiographic objectives empirically, Beck advocated the use of a kind of obverse factor-analytic procedure that Stephenson (1952) had called the "Q-technique." The essence of this approach is that starting with an attributes-by-persons matrix of trait measurements (organized in accordance with the scheme for correlational research shown in Figure 2.3, in

Chapter Two), one can (a) intercorrelate persons across attributes (instead of attributes across persons, as in the more common factor-analytic procedure) and (b) analyze those intercorrelations toward the end of identifying clusters of individuals displaying similar attribute profiles. Thus, where conventional analyses aim at identifying underlying *attribute factors*,[19] Q-technique analyses are aimed at identifying underlying *person types* and as such are essentially a form of what Stern (1911) called "comparison" research (see Figure 2.3). Having used the Q-technique in studies of schizophrenics, Beck wrote that the results enabled him to identify "the kind of whole person" who, under certain specified conditions, "is likely to have hallucinations" (Beck, 1953, pp. 358-359).

Beck recognized that to apply the "Q-technique" (or any other form of factor analysis), one must have an attributes-by-persons matrix of measurements to start with, and it was at least partly in recognition of this point that his answer to the question he had posed in the title of his article was "Both!" Stated otherwise, on this basic point, Beck embraced the widely accepted view that it is impossible to study persons "idiographically" (in his sense of the term) "until we have criteria obtained by measuring each variable as distributed within a population. This is to fall back on the nomothetic approach. That is a first step. It must precede the idiographic" (Beck, 1953, p. 356).

Eysenck (1954) opened his commentary on Beck's (1953) article by acknowledging,

> [T]he cleavage (or perhaps cleft would be a less emotionally charged term) between the nomothetic and idiographic approaches to the study of personality is indeed, as Beck has pointed out in his recent paper on this subject "a principal and vigorously debated issue before psychology today." (Eysenck, 1954, p. 339)

This is as positive as Eysenck's commentary on Beck's arguments would get, and if the playfulness of the parenthetical remark in this opening quotation is any guide, Eysenck must have delighted at the ease of the challenge with which Beck had left him.

Eysenck (1954) began by questioning Beck's use of the term idiographic. For Windelband, Eysenck reminded, idiographic knowledge referred to that kind of knowledge proper to humanistic disciplines, such as history, biography, and literature. One of the defining characteristics of such knowledge is that it is not the sort of knowledge sought within (natural) science. Continuing with his mildly suggestive wordplay, Eysenck noted that "literature, even if called a 'science' by Allport . . . does not lie down easily with psychometrics" (p. 339). So, from Eysenck's perspective, the first problem with Beck's analysis was that he had "emptied the term [idiographic] from its usual, and very useful meaning" (p. 339). This done, Eysenck argued, Beck proceeded to invest the term idiographic with a new meaning that, on close examination, revealed itself to be . . . *nomothetic!*

> As far as can be deduced from (Beck's) paper, it would appear that the measurement of isolated traits . . . is to be regarded as nomothetic; it becomes idiographic when we ask about any person how much does he have (of each of the traits) that fuse into character. Nothing here of the complete and total rejection of such nomothetic concepts as traits, which is the main characteristic of the traditional idiographic attitude;[20] instead we find that when we study traits in combination, we are no longer doing nomothetic research, but idiographic! (Eysenck, 1954, p. 340)

Given the approach to the scientific study of personality that Eysenck had long since embraced and advocated (e.g., Eysenck, 1952), there is no possibility whatsoever that Beck's article could in any way have furthered the cause of idiography in Eysenck's eyes. For years, Eysenck had been extensively engaged in factor analytic work intended to uncover the basic underlying dimensions of the human personality, and this work by definition entailed looking at more than "one variable at a time," as Beck had characterized the nomothetic approach in writing of its fundamental limitation. So, from Eysenck's perspective (as well as that of numerous of his factor-analytically oriented contemporaries, including R. B. Cattell, 1950, 1957; Guilford, 1954, 1959; and McClelland, 1951), the arguments developed by Beck in his article were not only misguided or ill advised, but simply wrong. In the event, Eysenck did not miss the opportunity to remind his readers of the nature of his own credentials as a card-carrying "nomothetical psychologist" and, in the process, to jest at Beck's expense:

> Having throughout his professional life studied traits in combination, having always paid particular attention to the ways in which they interact, modify each other, and, through their interaction, "[bring] about the total behavior which we identify as a particular personality,"[21] the present writer notes with surprise that instead of being a hard-bitten nomothetical psychologist, he has in fact always acted on idiographic principles. The reader may recall Molière's *Monsieur Jourdain,* who discovered late in life that he had always been speaking prose! (Eysenck, 1954, p. 340)

Eysenck followed these remarks with a brief critique of Beck's endorsement of Q-technique factor analysis. Eysenck noted in passing that several other investigators, including Stern (1911), had formulated the central ideas of the technique prior to Stephenson (1952) and that, in any case, empirical work by Burt (1937) and R.B. Cattell (1952) appeared to leave "no doubt that, statistically, factors derived from the intercorrelations between persons (Q-technique) are transposable from factors derived from intercorrelations between tests (R-technique)" (Eysenck, 1954, p. 340). So, although one could undertake factor analyses of the sort Beck had described (without becoming an "idiographist" and in the process compromising one's credentials as a "hard-bitten nomothetical psychologist"), the evidence available at the time suggested that there was no particular reason to do so, because the results would inevitably conform to those that emerged from the more traditional (R-technique) analyses, anyway.

With the foregoing considerations in mind, Eysenck argued as follows:

> [T]he only valid conclusion to be drawn from Beck's paper and his implicit withdrawal from the idiographic position [as that position had been originally articulated by Windelband and endorsed by Allport] is that suggested in the title of this article: *the science of personality must by its very nature be nomothetic.* This is the conclusion to which the writer was led after an extensive examination of the arguments adduced by many writers in this field,[22] and Beck's contribution has strengthened, rather than weakened, belief in the essential correctness of this view. (Eysenck, 1954, p. 341; emphasis in original)

Quite in the spirit of Eysenck's (1954) scathing critique of Beck (1953), Holt (1962) did his utmost in his own signal contribution to the Great Debate to resurrect the original meaning of idiographic intended by Windelband.[23] That is, Holt sought to restore an understanding of that term as a referent for a kind of knowledge characteristic of humanistic disciplines, hence distinctly and irreconcilably unlike the kind of knowledge that would properly be sought within a psychology of personality fashioned on the model of natural science. Holt thus emphatically rejected the very notion that there could be any coherent "idiographic *science*" of personality.

Holt (1962) positioned the interest in idiographic knowledge shown by some "personologists," specifically mentioning Stern and Allport in this connection, as being recent incarnations of the "romantic movement in science" (p. 378) historically characteristic of Kantian and neo-Kantian thinkers such as Windelband, Dilthey, Rickert, and Spranger.[24] The objective of such thinkers, Holt argued, was/is a *verstehende* psychology, one that produces a kind of empathic *understanding* of human life, rather than an *erklärende* psychology, one that enlightens through *explanations* of psychological phenomena on the model of natural science. The following quotation conveys the full essence of Holt's position on this matter:

> The goal of those who profess an idiographic point of view is not anything so antiseptic and inhuman as a family of curves; it is *understanding*. That conception [of understanding in the sense of *verstehen*] is an empathic, intuitive *feeling* of knowing a phenomenon from the inside, as it were. . . . [This] feeling of understanding is a subjective effect aimed at by artists, not scientists. In science, when we say we understand something, we mean that we can predict and control it, but such aims are foreign to the romantic viewpoint. . . . Here we see the issues drawn clearly. Is personology to be an art, devoted to word portraits that seek to evoke in the reader the thrill of recognition, the gratifying (if perhaps illusory) feeling of understanding unique individuals? Or is it to be a science, which enables us to study these same persons in all their uniqueness and to derive from such study general propositions about the structure, development, and other significant aspects of personality? If we elect for a science, we must abandon art whenever it takes us in a different direction than the one demanded by the scientific method, and we must recognize that the ideal of an idiographic science is a will-o'-the-wisp, an artistic and not a scientific goal. (Holt, 1962, pp. 388-390; emphasis in original)

In further developing his arguments against any and all concessions to the "romantic" view within a scientific psychology of personality, Holt (1962) addressed himself in turn to a number of specific issues that had been raised in the Great Debate as it had unfolded to that point. These included the deemphasis on quantification in personological inquiry; the alleged importance of individualized knowledge and the putative hazards of scientific generalizations; the avowed preference of idiographists for "structural" (concrete, as opposed to highly abstract) accounts of psychological phenomena; the challenge to the notion of general laws posed by considerations of chance and free will in the affairs of individuals; and the impossibility of finding general laws that give adequate due to the uniqueness of individuals. In every case, Holt's strategy was to show that the idiographic ("romantic") perspective either (a) really *is* a non- or antiscientific view and hence one that disqualifies itself from a properly and decidedly preferable scientific psychology of personality or (b) is only *apparently* different from or incompatible with the traditional nomothetic view, but in that case not truly a call for an "idiographic science" after all.

Because for Holt, the expression "idiographic science of personality" was oxymoronic, it followed that the expression "nomothetic science of personality" was redundant. He was thus led to conclude that the ill-advised séance with Windelband's "Teutonic ghost" (Holt, 1962, p. 377) was only haunting personality psychology, visiting much trouble upon but bringing nothing of positive value to the discipline. "In the end," Holt concluded,

> [W]e see that there is no need for a special type of science to be applied to individual personalities, and that the attempt to promulgate such a science fell into hopeless contradictions and absurdities. Today, Windelband's terms continue to appear in psychological writing but largely as pretentious jargon, mouth-filling polysyllables to awe the uninitiated, but never as essential concepts to make any scientifically vital point. Let us simply drop them from our vocabularies and let them die quietly. (Holt, 1962, p. 402)

As if on cue, Allport suggested in an article directly following Holt's in the same issue of the *Journal of Personality*,[25] that the term "idiographic" be dropped as a referent for his views and the term "morphogenic" be used in its place. For even if he intended to continue to argue along the same general lines, Allport conceded,

> [It] would serve no good purpose here to review the longstanding debate between partisans of the nomothetic and idiographic methods, between champions of explanation and understanding. Indeed, to insure more rapid progress I think it best to avoid traditional terms altogether. For the purposes of our present discussion I shall speak of "dimensional" and "morphogenic" procedures. (Allport, 1962, p. 409)

By "dimensional procedures," Allport meant nothing other than what he had previously referred to as the common trait approach. In elaborating on the term "morphogenic," Allport explained that he had borrowed it from the discipline of molecular biology. The scientific challenge to the biologist, Allport noted, was to account for the "morphogenesis," or *distinct patterning,* in the characteristics of individual organisms despite the fact that the fundamental building blocks of life, vegetable and animal, "turn out to be strikingly uniform in terms of nucleic acids, protein molecules, and enzymatic reactions" (Allport, 1962, p. 409). And so, Allport suggested, the scientific challenge to the "morphogenic psychologist" is that of accounting for the distinct patterning of individual personalities over and above their common fundament.

One year previously, in the discussion of the same point in his 1961 text, Allport had implored his readers as follows:

[Bear] in mind that we are not condemning the common trait approach. . . . We are simply saying that there is a second, more accurate way of viewing personality: namely, the internal patterning (the morphogenesis) of the life considered as a unique product of nature and society. . . . Personality exists only at a postelementary state . . . only when the common features of human nature have already interacted with one another and produced unique, self-continuing and evolving systems. This is not to say that the search for common elements or common human functions is undesirable. For the most part the science of psychology does this and nothing else. I insist only that if we are interested in *personality* we must go beyond the elementaristic and reach into the morphogenic realm. (Allport, 1961, pp. 360-361; emphasis in original)

Why the new terminology? It is not apparent that the substance of Allport's views had changed in any significant way since his articulation through the earlier terminology. Indeed, by his own account in the preface to the 1961 book, there had been no such change. What purpose, then, was to be served by abandoning references to "common traits" and "idioigraphic" studies in favor of discussions of the "dimensional approach" and "morphogenic" inquiry? For his own part, Allport (1962) offered only that he found the term morphogenic "better than 'idiographic,' which so many students of personality misuse and misspell" (Allport, 1962, p. 421).

The new language never caught on. In any case, perhaps by 1962, Allport was rather more chastened than he had been earlier in his career (e.g., in his 1937 review of Stern's general psychology text or in his 1946 reply to Skaggs) by his contemporaries' perception of him as an advocate for a non- or perhaps even antiscientific point of view. Perhaps he had decided that his theoretical objectives would be served better by a term borrowed from the scientifically respectable discipline of biology than by a term borrowed from philosophy. Perhaps he was simply reemphasizing the conviction he had expressed in his 1937 text that the psychology of personality he envisioned would play its role within the established parameters of the psychology viewed as science. Perhaps he came to the conclusion that his views were not as distant from, or antagonistic to, those of the nomotheticists as he had previously thought. After all, the latter had no principled reason to argue with the proposition that a developed science of personality should explore the ways in which the *common elements* of personality combine "morphogenically" to determine, in accordance with general laws, individual persons' very possibly *unique* personalities. If this is what the debate had been about all along, as Holt had suggested, then indeed, it might just as well never have happened!

Commenting on Allport's efforts over many years to clear a place within the mainstream of personality psychology for idiographic inquiry, Sanford (1963) observed,

> By and large, psychologists seem to have been rather unimpressed by Allport's argument and plea. Many have taken the trouble to answer him by pointing out that every entity in nature—each part or feature of a person, each event—is unique and that science can proceed only by noting uniformities; that all laws of nature are essentially of a statistical character, being statements about the average of a number of events; that if we can average the responses of a single individual we may do the same with the responses of many individuals; that the uniqueness of a given personality may be set forth by specifying his position with respect to a number—and not necessarily a very large number—of nomothetic variables. (Sanford, 1963, p. 547)

In a direct reference to Sanford's comments, Allport concluded his final article on this topic gracefully. He advised his readers that throughout the article, titled "Traits Revisited," he had intentionally avoided

> [H]ammering on the distinction between common (dimensional, nomothetic) traits such as we find in any standard profile, and individual traits (personal dispositions) such as we find in single lives. . . . Nevitt Sanford (1963) has written that by and large psychologists are "unimpressed" by my insisting on this distinction. Well, if this is so in spite of 4 decades of labor on my part, and in spite of my efforts in the present paper—I suppose I should in all decency cry "uncle" and retire to my corner. (Allport, 1966, p. 10)

Within a year of this public retreat by Allport, there appeared a textbook titled *Psychometric Theory,* by Jum C. Nunnally (1967), containing the following observation:

> The idiographists may be entirely correct, but if they are, it is a sad day for psychology. Idiography is an antiscience point of view: it discourages the search for general laws and instead encourages the description of particular phenomena (people). . . . Efforts to measure personality traits are based on the hypothesis that the idiographists are not entirely correct, that there are some general traits of human personality. The nomothetic point of view should be tested to the limit; otherwise, to accept an idiographic point of view in advance is to postulate that only chaos prevails in the description of human personalities. (Nunnally, 1967, p. 472)

Allport may or may not have suffered the harshness of Nunnally's words firsthand. Either way, those words quite vividly underscore the views of Sanford (1963): In the eyes of the vast majority of Allport's contemporaries (and, as it happens, his successors as well), calls for an idiographic psychology of personality to supplement the predominant nomothetic approach were at best uncompelling, and at worst a veritable impediment to the progress of the discipline. In principle, according to the prevailing view, convictions about individual uniqueness *can* be reconciled with the nomothetic approach in just the way Sanford (1963) had indicated; and whatever else there might be about the "problem of individuality" that *cannot* be captured in terms of the concepts and methods of that approach has no proper place within a *scientific* personality psychology, anyway. As most saw things, then, the challenge was not to replace or augment the nomothetic approach, but to develop it, refine it further, and pursue it relentlessly, and this is precisely what the vast majority of mainstream personality psychologists has been doing over the past several decades.

## Summary

Among prominent psychologists in the English-speaking world, no one was at once more familiar with and sympathetic toward Stern's thinking than Gordon W. Allport (1897-1967). For some months in 1923, Allport studied with, even lived with, Stern in Hamburg, and this contact certainly nourished Allport's concern for what Stern had identified in 1900 as the "problem of individuality" within scientific psychology.

Allport's perspective was by no means identical to Stern's. Most important, Allport's views were, by his own account, guided primarily by empirical considerations, whereas Stern's thinking was based much more on considerations of a philosophical nature. Be this as it may, Allport fully shared Stern's conviction that human individuality could not be adequately grasped within an investigative paradigm tied too exclusively to the methods of standardized testing and correlational research. Both thinkers were convinced that inquiry of a more idiographic nature would be necessary, and following Stern's death in 1938, Allport became the most prominent advocate of this view throughout the middle portion of the 20th century.

Allport's theoretical conception of personality was based on the concept of the personality *trait*. He allowed that there could be *common* traits, that is, dimensions of individual differences with reference to which any given individual could meaningfully be said to have some particular location or position. He insisted, however, that there are also *unique* traits present within each personality, that is, attributes or characteristics peculiar to the specific individual in question and hence, by definition, *not* common. Allport conceded that the measurement methods and statistical analysis procedures proper to what Stern had called *correlational* inquiry were logically adequate to the task of investigating common traits but would necessarily fail in the face of the challenge to identify unique traits.

Borrowing the terms *nomothetic* and *idiographic* from the 19th-century philosopher Wilhelm Windelband (1848-1915), who had used those terms to distinguish the kinds of knowledge sought within the natural sciences and the humanities, respectively, Allport urged that personality investigators supplement the nomothetic methods of common trait inquiry with idiographic methods that would be suitable for uncovering the unique aspects of individual cases. Allport's conviction that it should be possible to develop such methods was buttressed in part by his belief that counselors and clinicians were daily faced with the task of making meaningful judgments about their clients in an essentially idiographic fashion.

Allport's pleas for more idiographic inquiry in personality studies were greeted less than enthusiastically, and at times quite harshly, by the majority within the mainstream. One of his suggestions, summarily dismissed as nonsensical, was that subjective or intuitive personality judgments by counselors and clinicians might be grounded in intuitive considerations whose basic logic was somehow fundamentally different from the logic guiding the conventional nomothetic approach to the measurement of common traits. Furthermore, his call for the pursuit of a kind of knowledge other than that sought within the natural sciences was branded widely as non- or even antiscientific.

Shortly prior to his death in 1967, Allport felt compelled to concede defeat in the "Great Nomothetic-Idiographic Debate." Since then, the common trait conception of personality widely endorsed within the mainstream survived a crisis of confidence occasioned by Mischel's (1968) empirically based critique of the assumption of transsituational consistency in behavior, and today, it is widely hailed as demonstrably adequate for scientifically addressing the problem of human individuality.

# Notes

1. According to a title bibliography compiled in 1996 by Stern's biographer, Gerhard Bühring (Bühring, 1996b), there have been very few English language

treatments of critical personalism apart from one well-known article (Allport, 1937b; see below). Immediately following Stern's death, several English language obituaries appeared, authored by Allport (1938), MacLeod (1938), and Spoerl (1938), plus an anonymously authored obituary published in the *British Journal of Psychology* in 1939. Beyond these, Bühring's bibliography includes references to articles by Sanborn (1939), Werner (1939), Beck (1941), Hanfmann (1952), Brand-Auraban (1972), and Hardesty (1976, 1977). Most recently, an article appeared by Lamiell and Deutsch (2000).

2.  For a more detailed discussion of these developments, see Lamiell (1987).

3.  See, for example, the recent *Handbook of Personality Psychology*, edited by Hogan, Johnson, and Briggs (1997).

4.  This journal was founded in 1932. In 1946, the word *character* was dropped from the title, and the publication was renamed the *Journal of Personality*. The publication is known by this name today.

5.  By 1937, Allport's graduate student H.D. Spoerl had significantly advanced with his English translation of Stern's book, though the translation would not actually appear in print until the following year.

6.  See also Allport (1968).

7.  This is a view Allport (1937a) attributed to M.A. May, articulated in a work titled "The Foundations of Personality" (May, 1932) and published as a chapter in a volume published in 1932 by A.S. Achilles, titled *Psychology at Work* (Achilles, 1932).

8.  In a similar vein, Stern had written in *Methodological Foundations* that although "culture is in fact the very embodiment of general values, norms, and ideals, culture is *realized* only in the phenomenal experiences, acts, and capabilities of the individual" (Stern, 1911, p. 319; emphasis added). Unlike Allport, Stern certainly did not contend that personality psychology has no interest in culture as one of the factors shaping personality.

9.  In this connection, Allport made the following observation in the first chapter of his 1937 book:

It is an interesting fact that the most prominent representative of personalistic psychology, William Stern, was in past years the leading figure in the study of differential psychology. It was in fact his perception of the limitations of the psychology of individual differences, based upon long experience, that led him to attempt a more adequate formulation of the psychology of individuality (p. 18).

But as we know from the material introduced in the first three chapters of this work, this characterization by Allport of the course of Stern's thinking is not at all accurate. Stern was beginning to formulate critical personalism *at least* as early as he was writing anything in differential psychology. Moreover, his appreciation for the "limitations of the psychology of individual differences" vis-à-vis the "problem of individuality" was clearly stated in the 1900 book, and so can hardly be regarded as an insight achieved only through "long experience" in the psychology of individual differences. Unfortunately, Allport's mischaracterization of Stern's thinking was picked up and passed along by subsequent authors (see, e.g., Ash, 1995, p. 44; Holt, 1962, pp. 383-384, discussed below; see also Hothersall, 1995, p. 408 Pawlik, 1994, p. xviii).

10.   This latter view leads to the conception of personality as an individual's social stimulus value, and this is a view that, as noted earlier, Allport rejected from the very outset.

11.   This is not to say that Allport saw no prospects whatsoever for quantifying individual traits. On the contrary, he would later recommend what is essentially an *ipsative* form of measurement for this purpose (see, e.g., Allport, 1961, pp. 455-456). These and other important points having specifically to do with questions of measurement will be discussed more fully in Chapter Nine.

12.   There are several places in Allport's 1937 text where he discussed *psycho-diagnostics,* but that concept is by no means equivalent to Stern's *psychognostics,* the superficial similarity between the two words notwithstanding. *Gnosis,* as Stern wrote in 1900, precedes both "dia-gnosis" and "pro-gnosis."

13.   The compatibility of Allport's ideas here with Stern's repeatedly expressed conviction concerning the need for "special methods of investigation" as supplements for—and even, at times, as alternatives to—standardized testing procedures is both clear and, of course, entirely nonaccidental.

14.   The expression "domain of empirical events" is important here, because Windelband did not intend the notion of nomothetic laws to be applied to universal truths of a purely logical or mathematical (i.e., nonempirical) nature. The distinction being drawn here parallels that drawn by Kant between *analytic* or logical truths, and *synthetic* or empirical truths.

15.   The concept of correlation and the method of its computation will be discussed thoroughly in the following chapter.

16.   In connection with his allusion here to the definition of honesty "in the usual ethical terms," Allport (1937a) elaborated by explaining that the methods used by Hartshorne and May "were not devised from the point of view of child psychology, but from the point of view of society and its conduct values" (p. 252). Allport voiced misgivings about such an approach, stating that "a study of *good* qualities and *bad* qualities is not the same as a study of natural qualities. The study of personality is difficult enough without complicating it at the beginning with ethical evaluation" (p. 252). This passage reflects another—and ultimately very important—way in which Allport's outlook differed from Stern's. Specifically, Allport's notion that there is a categorical distinction to be drawn between *ethical* qualities and *natural* qualities, as if the former somehow were not part of the latter, is entirely foreign to critical personalism. Here again, we touch on an important topic, further discussion of which must be deferred to a later chapter.

17.   In a more recent incarnation of the arguments by Lundberg (1941) and Sarbin (1944) discussed here, Epstein (1983) proclaimed that "while some may deny

it, it is meaningless to [subjectively] interpret the behavior of an individual without a frame of reference of others' behavior" (p. 381). This long-standing truism will be examined closely in Chapters Nine and Ten, and it will be found wanting.

18. This misspelling of the word *idiographic* is something Allport would encounter often enough over the ensuing years to warrant specific mention by him in his 1961 text. In a footnote that appears on p. 9 of that text, Allport wrote,

> The reader's attention is called to the spelling of *idiographic*. Its origin lies in the Greek *idios* (meaning one's own). The same root is found in *idiom, idiosyncrasy*. It should not be confused with *ideographic*, which, like *ideology*, derives from [the Greek] *idea* (that which is seen, a semblance). The term *nomothetic* is from [the Greek] *nomothetikos* (the giving or enacting of laws).

19. Of course, the very existence of these conventional methods belied Beck's claim that nomothetic methods focused exclusively on only one attribute at a time, and this point would not be lost on Eysenck (1954) in his critique of Beck's article (see below).

20. Eysenck provided no citations in connection with this remark, so it is difficult to know the basis for his claim here concerning "the usual idiographic attitude." Allport certainly did not hold this attitude, and for reasons to be discussed in Chapter Seven, it simply would not have occurred to Windelband to embrace *or* reject "nomothetic trait concepts."

21. In this phrase, Eysenck was quoting Beck (1953, p. 254).

22. Here Eysenck (1954) again cited his 1952 text.

23. As regards the term nomothetic, Holt (1962) mentioned in a footnote (p. 378) that Egon Brunswik (1943) had embraced an understanding of that term that did not conform to the usage that by then had become customary. On Brunswik's (1943) account, Holt stated, nomothetic knowledge referred to knowledge in the form of "exact laws expressible as functions or equations," and by this definition, knowledge in the form of statistical generalizations such as those produced by the correlational research methods of a common trait psychology of personality would not qualify. However, Holt made it clear that he did not endorse Brunswik's view and held instead to the more widely shared view that such statistical generalizations do qualify as nomothetic knowledge. Holt's critique of Allport proceeded on this basis.

24. Of Stern in particular, Holt (1962) wrote,

> William Stern, a man of some influence in psychology, must be at least briefly mentioned even though he began in intelligence testing and his work converged only rather late with the main line of developments traced above. . . . The nomothetic-idiographic distinction played no part in his writings (p. 383; emphasis added).

Later in the same article, Holt wrote that Stern's "personology *grew out of* differential psychology, the psychology of individual differences" (p. 387; emphasis added). Perhaps here Holt was following the mistaken lead of Allport (see Endnote #9, above). In any case, this passage strongly suggests that Holt wrote it without benefit of any firsthand familiarity with Stern's work.

25.    An editorial note in the issue in which the articles by Holt and by Allport appeared advised that though the articles had been prepared independently of one another, their simultaneous publication afforded readers a fortuitous opportunity to consider the two lines of argument in convenient juxtaposition.

# Part Two

## Statistical Thinking in Post-Wundtian Psychology

# Chapter Five

## The Emergence of a "Neo-Galtonian" Framework for Psychological Research:

### *A Historical Sketch*

The role that statistical thinking came to play throughout scientific psychology was of surpassing importance as an undercurrent of the historical developments traced thus far. Stern himself originally welcomed the introduction of statistical methods into the discipline, seeing in them a viable means of broadening psychology's investigative horizons as they appeared early in the 20th century. He also insisted throughout his career, however, that the value of statistical methods vis-à-vis the "problem of individuality" was limited, and he repeatedly warned against overreliance on those methods to the exclusion of other approaches. Of course, Allport was in full agreement with Stern on this point. Statistical methods were (and are) the very basis of the *common trait* approach to personality studies Allport called *nomothetic,* and he devoted much of his career to arguing that a satisfactory understanding of individual personalities, or individualities, could never be achieved on that basis alone.

As seen through the discussion in the previous two chapters, differential psychology as a discipline parted company with Stern and Allport on this matter. Statistical knowledge came to bear more and more of the epistemic burden within the field as investigators focused their attention ever more exclusively on population means, variances, and covariances (intercorrelations) of dimensional and categorical variables representing individual and group differences. As it happens, differential psychologists were not alone in this regard. To the contrary, and as paradoxical as it may seem at first blush, the general/experimental psychologists whose work differential psychology was supposed to augment were themselves embracing in ever increasing numbers the same statistical concepts as the fundament of their own accounts of human behavior.

In the present chapter, the historical background of this profoundly important epistemic turn within scientific psychology will be examined further. How did statistical thinking make its way into the discipline? Whence came statistical thinking in the first place? On what grounds did such thinking come to be regarded as appropriate for advancing scientific accounts both of human behavior generally *and* of human individuality more specifically? What epistemic and metaphysical commitments accompanied the investment in such thinking as the basis for a scientific psychology? These are the central questions to be taken up in the present chapter.

## The Restructuring of Scientific Psychology's "Two Disciplines"

In an important contribution, Danziger (1987) shed very helpful light on some of the historical developments relevant to these questions. Noting that modern investigative practices in scientific psychology have their origins in two vastly different research models, Danziger began his analysis by describing the essential features of those models and then discussed historical factors leading to the disappearance of one and the transformation of the other. Guided in part by Danziger's analysis, some insight can be gained here into the nature of the "two disciplines of scientific psychology" that Lee J. Cronbach would famously celebrate in his 1957 "Presidential Address to the American Psychological Association" (Cronbach, 1957).

### In the Beginning . . .

Of the two models discussed by Danziger (1987), he named the first the "Wundtian" model. The name is an obvious reference to the approach to experimentation adopted at Leipzig[1] and in other laboratories of the day, according to which investigations were carried out on individual research participants,[2] one at a time. In modern parlance, such investigations would be referred to as "$N = 1$" experiments, and as noted when this topic was mentioned in Chapter Two, this approach was altogether consistent with—indeed, it was logically mandated by—the concern to discover *general* laws governing *individual* mental life. That is, inasmuch as the phenomena of interest (in Wundt's specific case, the elements of consciousness) were presumed to transpire in individual human minds, it was clear to the founders of experimental psychology that it would be necessary to look for scientific evidence of the presumed causal regularities in the laboratory performances of individual subjects.

Without question, statistical methods of data analysis were known to and used by adherents of the Wundtian model. This fact is amply reflected in the methodological and conceptual room that was made, under the terms of that model, for Fechnerian psychophysics (Danziger, 1987), and it is also apparent in Ebbinghaus's famous studies of memory (Ebbinghaus, 1885/1964). However, in these and other uses to which statistics were put in this research tradition, the computations were executed on multiple observations made of the same individual research subject. Logically, the generality sought within this tradition would accrue to empirical demonstrations that the regularities uncovered through the analysis of data obtained from one subject could repeatedly be discerned in parallel analyses of data obtained from additional subjects, each of whom would be studied individually. This is why one properly understands experimental psychology on the Wundtian model as both an individual psychology and a general psychology.[3]

The second of the two historic research models within scientific psychology identified by Danziger (1987) is one he called the "Galtonian" model. This model was quite different from the Wundtian model, both in its nature and in its uses.

Regarding *uses*, it might fairly be said that the most fundamental difference between the Wundtian and Galtonian models is that the latter model seemed to have some, whereas the former did not! In Chapter Two, mention was made of the fact that by the early 1900s, increasing pressure was already being brought to bear on scientific psychology to produce knowledge that would have some immediate practical relevance to problems and challenges being faced by persons outside the laboratory, in education, health services, industry, and the military. The Wundtian experimental psychology was proving itself sterile in this regard;[4] however, work undertaken in accordance with the methodological principles of the Galtonian model, most notably research in the domain of mental testing (Samelson, 1977), clearly illustrated the practical uses to which that model could be put.

The Galtonian and Wundtian models differed not only in practical usefulness but also in kind. It has already been noted that although research within the Wundtian model occasionally entailed the use of statistical procedures, it was not fundamentally statistical in nature. The Galtonian model, however, was inherently statistical in that it was tied inextricably to the systematic analysis of aggregated, group level data.

The linchpin of the Galtonian model was that statistical index named after Galton's student, protégé, and eventual biographer, Karl Pearson.[5] Building on the insights of his mentor, Pearson succeeded in devising a very useful numerical index of the extent to which within some population of research subjects considered as a whole, the relative standings of individuals with respect to some particular variable X matched their respective relative standings on some other variable Y. This index, known to this day as the *Pearson product-moment correlation coefficient,* was defined as the average of the cross-products of the standardized scores (*z* scores) associated with each of a number of observed cases with respect to the two variables being correlated. Given the enormous epistemic burden borne by the correlation coefficient in 20th-century scientific psychology generally and in the emergent nomothetic psychology of personality in particular, it is worthwhile to examine a bit further the nature and intellectual background of this familiar and ubiquitous, yet widely misunderstood, statistic.

## Briefly on the Nature and Provenance of the Pearson *r*

Commonly symbolized *r*, the Pearson product-moment coefficient of correlation between two variables, X and Y, is defined mathematically as follows:

$$r_{X,Y} = \sum ((Z_{k,X})(Z_{k,Y})) / N \qquad [5.1]$$

where

$r_{X,Y}$ represents the coefficient of correlation between variables X and Y,

$Z_{k,X}$ represents the standard score on variable X associated with observational case $k$,

$Z_{k,Y}$ represents the standard score on variable Y associated with that same observational case $k$, and

$\sum$ represents the operation of summing the indicated $(Z_{k,X})(Z_{k,Y})$ cross-products across the N cases of observation.

The standard score for a given case, $k$, with respect to a particular variable is defined by computing the arithmetic difference between the "raw score" for that case on that variable and the average raw score among all

$N$ cases on that variable, and then dividing that difference by the standard deviation of those same $N$ raw scores. This latter value, the standard deviation, is defined as the square root of the average among all $N$ cases of the squared differences between the respective raw scores and the group mean. The standard deviation thus indexes the extent to which within a set of scores considered as such, individual scores "spread out" from or *vary* around their arithmetic center.

Among mathematicians, a standard $z$ score is regarded as the *first moment* about the mean of a variable (with $z^2$ being the *second moment,* $z^3$ the *third moment,* and so on). The computational "core" of the Pearson $r$ thus consists of the cross-*products* of (first) *moments* about the respective means of the two variables being correlated, hence the *product-moment* coefficient of correlation. It serves as a numerical indicator of the degree to which two variables *covary* in linear fashion within some set of pair-wise observations.

Numerically, the Pearson $r$ can range in value from $-1$ ($r = -1.00$), indicating a perfect negative linear relationship between two variables, through zero ($r = 0.00$), indicating the total absence of a systematic linear relationship, to $+1$ ($r = +1.00$), indicating a perfect positive linear relationship. It is instructive to reflect briefly on the empirical eventualities that could generate these different values.

A perfect positive correlation between two variables $X$ and $Y$ is realized empirically if and only if the value of $Z_{k,X}$ is identical both in sign and in magnitude to the value of $Z_{k,Y}$ for all $N$ of the $(Z_{k,X})(Z_{k,Y})$ pairs considered. Inversely, if for all $N$ of the $(Z_{k,X})(Z_{k,Y})$ pairs considered, the value of $Z_{k,X}$ is identical in magnitude but opposite in sign from the corresponding value of $Z_{k,Y}$, the resulting correlation is perfectly negative.

Neither of these limiting outcomes is ever realized in actual practice. However, to the extent that it is the case within the sample as a whole that positive $z$ scores on one variable are with appreciable regularity paired with positive $z$ scores on the other variable, and, likewise, negative $z$ scores on one variable are regularly paired with negative $z$ scores on the other variable, the signs of the $z$ score cross-products symbolized in Equation 5.1 will, with commensurate regularity, be positive. Consequently, the average of those cross-products, $r$, will deviate from zero in the direction of $+1.00$. Inversely, to the extent that it is the case within the sample as a whole that positive $z$ scores on one variable are with appreciable regularity paired with negative $z$ scores on the other variable and vice versa, the signs of the $z$ score cross-products symbolized in Equation 5.1 will, with commensurate regularity, be negative. Consequently, the average of those cross-products, $r$, will deviate from zero in the direction of $-1.00$.

Finally, it is possible that within the sample as a whole, positive $z$ scores on one variable will sometimes be paired with positive but also often with negative $z$ scores on the other variable, and negative $z$ scores on the one variable will sometimes be paired with negative but also often with positive $z$ scores on the other variable. Under these conditions, the signs of the $z$ score cross-products will throughout the sample as a whole sometimes be positive but also often be negative, and substantially, if not entirely, cancel each other in the summation operation used to determine the numerator of $r$. The obvious consequence is that $r$ itself will decline toward zero.

The need for a statistical index of precisely the sort developed by Galton and Pearson grew directly out of their shared interest in the demographics of human intelligence. More specifically, their overarching scientific objective was to explain interindividual differences in intelligence through analyses of the systematic covariation between measures of those differences and other individual/group difference variables such as race, gender, socioeconomic status, and so forth. For these investigative purposes, *aggregates* of individuals were necessarily the units of analysis because they are the smallest units for which interindividual differences can be brought into existence as objects of scientific investigation.

It is useful to bear in mind in this connection that neither Galton nor Pearson was primarily a psychologist. Neither was greatly concerned with scientific psychology's theoretical problems generally or, more specifically, with anything remotely like Stern's "problem of individuality." The scientific interests of Galton and Pearson were grounded more in evolutionary biology, and as their commitment to eugenics attests, their major concerns were population level rather than individual level. In their view, the interindividual variations in intelligence (and, by extension, character) that so preoccupied them[6] had emerged in *homo sapiens* according to the principles of natural selection set forth in the theory of evolution formulated by Galton's cousin, Charles Darwin (1809-1882). This is the conceptual backdrop for Pearson's observation:

> It is almost impossible to study any type of life without being impressed by the small importance of the individual. . . . Evolution must depend upon substantial changes in considerable numbers and its theory therefore belongs to that class of phenomena which statisticians have grown accustomed to refer to as mass phenomena. (Pearson, 1901-1902, p. 3)

It is surely one of the great ironies of 20th century scientific psychology that the statistic named for the author of this passage would become the "sacred coin of the realm" (Bem & Allen, 1974, p. 512) within that subdiscipline of the field specifically devoted to an understanding of individuality. One of the major burdens of this discussion is to provide some insight into this historic irony and the enormous implications it has carried for our understanding of what it means to scientifically address the "problem of individuality."

Part of the story that is relevant here has already been told, for it was shown in Chapter Three that the Galtonian model was assigned an important niche in Stern's early, but broad, vision of differential psychology. Specifically, Stern proposed in his 1911 *Methodological Foundations* text that the measurement and statistical analysis procedures proper to the Galtonian model should guide those subdisciplines of differential psychology devoted to the study of *attributes* in terms of their variation and covariation (correlation) across persons within populations. It was also shown in Chapter Three that the widespread favor that this research model came to enjoy among Stern's contemporaries had much to do with its suitability for addressing a great variety of practical concerns preeminent in the branch of applied psychology that Stern (and Münsterberg after him) called *psychotechnics*. After all, knowledge about patterns of intercorrelation between selected individual and group difference variables, on the one hand, and various performance measures, on the other, can be very useful for guiding decisions concerning the deployment of organizational personnel, advertising strategies, medical treatment plans, the assignment of students to educational programs, and so forth.

There is much more to the story than this, however, because the correlational research methods that literally define the Galtonian model have long been, and continue to be, favored by their adherents not only for the applied purposes of psychotechnics (for a current representation of this position, see Hogan, Hogan, & Roberts, 1996) but also for the more theoretical purposes of psychognostics (see, e.g., Johnson, 1997; McCrae & Costa, 1995). Stated otherwise, the Galtonian research model has seemed to provide a sound scientific basis both for research relevant to questions concerning how best, in the long run, to treat or handle people *(Menschenbehandlung)* and for studies intended to yield insights into various fundamental truths about human nature *(Menschenkenntnis)*. To account for the establishment and enduring hegemony of this vision requires discussion extending well beyond the reach of our considerations up to this point.

## Redressing the Deficiencies of the Galtonian Model

Although by the criterion of practical usefulness, the Wundtian model proved manifestly inferior to the Galtonian model, the latter nevertheless had two major deficiencies not shared by the former (Danziger, 1987). One of these may be termed *metaphysical,* because it had to do with the problem of drawing inferences concerning cause and effect. The other may be termed *epistemic,* because it had to do with bridging the gap between the knowledge supplied by aggregate level empirical findings and the knowledge needed to address individual level theoretical questions. Each of these issues will be discussed in turn.

### Solving the Metaphysical Problem: From Natural Categories to "Treatment Groups"

Wundtian experimentation entailed making observations about changes in specific aspects of an individual subject's mental state (as reflected in that subject's perceptions, judgments, etc.) following the systematic manipulation of carefully specified antecedent conditions. The formal suitability of this model of experimentation for drawing cause-effect inferences was widely acknowledged (Danziger, 1987) even if the phenomena actually investigated were not regarded as intrinsically interesting or as having great practical import in the world outside of the laboratory. In contrast, the Galtonian model was by its very (correlational) nature ill suited to the objective of gaining knowledge of cause-effect relationships. As students of research methods in psychology are still taught very early on, the empirical determination of a correlation between two variables, $X$ and $Y$, does not settle any questions concerning causation. It could be that $X$ causes $Y$, but it could also be that $Y$ causes $X$, or that both $X$ and $Y$ are caused by some third variable, $Z$, that has not even been investigated.

Within the domain of psychotechnics, the problem of drawing causal inferences could readily be finessed. So long as appreciably strong and reliable correlations could be established between predictor variables and performance criterion variables, the strictly practical, predictive objectives of *Menschenbehandlung* could be realized in total ignorance of cause-effect relationships.[7]

With respect to the *Menschenkenntnis* objectives of psychognostics, however, the problem of making causal inferences was acute, for such inferences would clearly be central to any claims to *scientific* understanding of some given aspect(s) of human nature. As things turned out, investigators found the key to a solution for this metaphysical problem in the Galtonian model itself.

Danziger (1987) has explained that much of the early research carried out within the Galtonian model entailed statistical comparisons between *naturally* constituted groups. In terms of intelligence, for example, children of one age could be compared statistically with those of another, men could be compared with women, people of various nationalities and ethnic backgrounds could be compared with each other, and so forth. Such studies were obviously correlational,[8] but soon enough, investigators would come to appreciate that the statistical analysis procedures used in those studies could just as well be employed to analyze data generated in studies comparing the performances of groups that had been *deliberately* constituted, by exposing research subjects to different treatments. These investigations brought into existence what Danziger (1987) described as "a fundamentally new entity in psychological research, namely, the *treatment group*" (p. 41). In the following passage, the historical significance of this development is made clear:

> The invention of the treatment group provided a way of dealing with problems in drawing causal conclusions from correlational data in natural human populations. Psychologists, who had been taught to appreciate the value of laboratory methods by Wundt and his pupils, were able to see that the source of the trouble lay in the absence of controlled conditions that could be systematically varied in an experiment. They therefore modified the original Galtonian model by applying it, not to natural groups, but to deliberately constituted experimental groups. Because these groups had been created by the manipulations of the experimenter, it was assumed that any relevant differences in their attributes could be seen as the effects of these manipulations. There emerged a style of research that is a hybrid product of the Wundtian and the Galtonian models. One may call it the *neo-Galtonian* model because the Galtonian component is the dominant one. (Danziger, 1987, p. 42; emphasis in original)

According to Danziger (1987), the widespread adoption of this "neo-Galtonian" model during the first quarter of the 20th century rendered later experimental psychologists particularly receptive to the analysis-of-variance (ANOVA) techniques pioneered by R.A. Fisher (Rucci & Tweney, 1980). In turn, the fact that ANOVA techniques had achieved such widespread use by the early 1950s paved the way for Cronbach (1957) to argue so effectively for the unification of psychology's "two disciplines"; for the version of experimental psychology of which Cronbach wrote was by no means the original Wundtian model but instead the post-Wundtian, hybrid, neo-Galtonian model described by Danziger (1987). Cronbach saw, and was able to help many others to see, that with the sole exception of differences in the ways in which comparison groups were constituted—whether non-experimentally, through consideration of naturally given factors such as age, gender, and race, or experimentally, through the creation of different treatment conditions established by an investigator—there was no fundamental distinction to be drawn between (Galtonian) correlational psychology and (neo-Galtonian) experimental psychology. Investigators in both disciplines were routinely pursuing exactly the same goal: explaining between-person variance in some criterion or dependent variable(s) in terms of between-person variance (whether naturally occurring or deliberately produced) in one or more predictor or independent variables.[9]

Undoubtedly, part of what continued to separate workers in these respective disciplines was the fact that neo-Galtonian experimentalists commonly employed ANOVA techniques to analyze their data statistically, whereas the Galtonian correlationists were, in keeping with their traditions, examining Pearson $r$'s and the parameters of their associated regression equations.[10] These two sets of procedures are really just superficially different versions of the same thing,[11] however, and Cronbach (1957) was therefore altogether correct in his insight that no technical obstacle stood in the way of a full merger of psychology's two disciplines into a unified science. In this hybrid psychology, investigators could regularly incorporate into their research designs both experimentally created between-person variables made possible by the introduction of different treatments and the non-experimentally available between-person variables served up by "nature herself" (cf. Cronbach, 1957). The result, Cronbach argued, could only be a psychology capable of providing richer and more complete explanations of behavior than could be achieved within either of the field's two scientific disciplines separately.

### Solving the Epistemic Problem: Statistical Patterns in Aggregate Data as Grounds for Generalizations About Individual Level Phenomena

It will be recalled that the problem here arose from the conceptual gap that seemed to exist between knowledge of aggregates yielded by the statistical methods of the Galtonian model, on one side, and the need for theoretically grounded insights into the behavior/psychological functioning of individuals, on the other.

As was true of the metaphysical question just discussed, this knowledge gap was much more problematic in the domain of psychognostics than in the domain of psychotechnics. In the latter domain, it was widely understood that when based on the findings of studies conducted according to Galtonian/neo-Galtonian principles, all answers to questions concerning the "best possible person/work/effect" (Münsterberg, 1913) meant "best" on average, and from the perspective of those to whom psychotechnicians were lending (or selling) their expertise.[12] Stated otherwise, when the problem concerned the handling or treatment of people (including the deployment of human resources), the task was to scientifically determine what would prove most efficacious (expedient, economical, productive, profitable, etc.) in the long run for the organization within which that deployment was being undertaken. In this context, the applied psychologist could not afford to be, and so should not be, concerned about an outcome in this, that, or any specific individual case considered in isolation.[13]

Again, however, when the research objective was psychognostic and the goal of empirical inquiry was to advance the scientific understanding of human nature, the strict maintenance of an aggregate level perspective and an indifference to individual level realities would hardly suffice. How could one possibly lay claim to genuine knowledge about some psychological phenomenon and at the same time disclaim all knowledge of that phenomenon's structure and/or dynamics within the mental life and/or behavior of individuals? Clearly, the objectives of *Menschenkenntnis* demanded of theoretically oriented psychologists a solution to the epistemic problem presented by the Galtonian model, even if the requirements of *Menschenbehandlung* would permit the applied psychotechnician to sidestep the problem or ignore it altogether.

As Danziger (1987) instructs, E.L. Thorndike once again pointed the way out of the dilemma. In a psychophysical study of 37 research subjects, Thorndike (1909) found great interindividual variability and, following the thinking of most experimentalists of his day, might have viewed that variability as evidence of "measurement error" in the experimental attempt to establish the true value of some underlying parameter. This is not the conclusion to which Thorndike was drawn, however. He argued that what exists is not a single psychophysical law that except for measurement error, holds generally in the sense of being "common to all" (*allen gemein;* see discussion in Chapter Two), but instead a host of response tendencies residing within individual subjects and varying in strength from one subject to the next. The aggregate level variability manifested by the *set of 37 subjects regarded as one unit* was thus used by Thorndike (1909) as a platform on which to mount inferences about the psychological functioning of *individual subjects regarded as 37 separate units.*

Perhaps even more instructive in this connection is a statement from Thorndike's 1911 monograph, *Individuality,* which was discussed in Chapter Three. In that work, Thorndike wrote of the correlation between measures of two traits in a group of individuals as indicating "the extent to which the amount of one trait possessed by an individual is bound up with the amount he possesses of some other trait" (p. 21).

Given his quantitative sophistication, Thorndike certainly would have known that intertrait correlations of the specific sort he was discussing were not defined for any particular research subject. In that context, each individual is represented by one pair of $z$ scores, and as Equation 5.1 makes perfectly clear, $r$ is defined not by any single $z$ score cross-product, but only by the average of a set of such cross-products. Nevertheless, Thorndike's own words make clear his belief that such correlations could be interpreted at the level of the individual subject. Here, just as in his 1909 psychophysical research, the aggregate level reality was taken as a "window" onto some corresponding individual level reality.

Despite the internal contradiction just noted, this view of statistical knowledge gained widespread favor among psychologists during the first quarter of the 20th century and finally assured what Danziger (1990) termed "the triumph of the aggregate" in psychological research. With this triumph, it appeared that the gap between aggregate level empirical evidence and individual level theoretical questions could be closed after all. The epistemic deficiency of the Galtonian model thus seemed to have been eliminated, and with that accomplished, the neo-Galtonian model appeared perfectly adequate for the purposes of a unified scientific psychology. This psychology would effectively merge the "old" population level correlational methods with the "new" treatment group experimental methods and would be suited as well, in elegantly symmetric fashion, to the knowledge objectives of psychognostics as to those of psychotechnics.

As widespread and long-standing as the endorsement of this outlook has been among 20th-century research psychologists, one easily imagines that there is nothing particularly controversial or conceptually problematic about it. But in light of the contradiction just noted in connection with Thorndike's reasoning in his 1911 *Individuality,* the critical reader will at least be prepared to entertain some doubt on this issue—nor, as it happens, would such skepticism be unprecedented. On the contrary, scholars have not always been in such widespread agreement on the matter, and so it is instructive to take a brief glance a bit further back into the history of the ideas out of which the currently received view has emerged.

# An Overview of Some Major Developments in the History of Statistical Thinking

## From Political Arithmetic to Social Physics

Persons not familiar with the history of statistical thinking[14] are often surprised to learn that at its inception as an identifiable discipline, such thinking did not emerge as a branch of theoretical mathematics. On the contrary, many mathematicians at first kept their distance from the exercises that as early as the 1680s, William Petty had called "political arithmetic" (Hacking, 1990; Porter, 1986). Although this expression might sound pejorative to the modern ear, such was not its intention in its original historical context. The label simply referred to the gathering and systematic tabulation of information about various aspects of society that would be of use to government leaders in formulating social and economic policies.

This early and direct tie to civic concerns is further reflected by the term that eventually replaced "political arithmetic" as the name of the discipline. Porter (1986) notes that the German *Statistik* was first used in 1749 by a professor at the University of Göttingen named Gottfried Achenwall. This expression was descriptive of the view (which would come to be widely shared among scholars by early in the 19th century) that the discipline in question was "a science concerned with *states,* or at least with those matters that ought to be known to the *'statist'*" (Porter, 1986, pp. 23-24; emphasis added).[15]

The Scotsman John Sinclair (1754-1835) anglicized Achenwall's expression, and in so doing noted the following:

Many people were at first surprised at my using the words *Statistics* and *Statistical.* . . . In the course of a very extensive tour, through the northern parts of Europe, which I happened to take in 1786, I found that in Germany they were engaged in a species of political inquiry to which they had given the name *Statistics.* By statistical is meant in Germany an inquiry for the purpose of ascertaining the political strength of a country, or questions concerning matters of state; whereas the idea I annexed to the term is an inquiry into the state of a country, for the purpose of *ascertaining the quantum of happiness enjoyed by its inhabitants and the means of future improvement.* (Sinclair, 1798, quoted in Hacking, 1990, p. 16; emphasis in original)

Porter (1986) notes that although statistics was not at first a specifically quantitative discipline, the transition in this direction was steady, if slow and subtle, and seems to have been largely effected throughout Western Europe by the 1820s. This development itself was tied closely to socioeconomic/political concerns:

The "era of enthusiasm" in statistics was thus inspired by a new sense of the power and dynamism of society. Society was regarded both as a source of progress, revealed by the beginnings of industrialization, and as a cause of instability, typified by the French Revolution and by continuing unrest in Great Britain as well as France. Statistical investigation was not the product of sociological fatalism, however, but of cautious hopefulness for improvement. . . . The statists sought to bring a measure of expertise to social questions, to replace the contradictory preconceptions of the interested parties by the certainty of careful empirical observation. They believed that the confusion of politics could be replaced by an orderly reign of facts. (Porter, 1986, p. 27)

With statistical thinking thus established as a feature of the intellectual landscape, the Belgian scholar Adolphe Quetelet (1796-1874) gave impetus to the next development, so decisive for modern social science generally and for scientific psychology in particular. Bearing in mind that the relevant history here is far more multifaceted and nuanced than can be conveyed through the present discussion, a condensed version may be given as follows.[16]

Quetelet was trained in astronomy and so was thoroughly conversant with the "law of errors" that by the beginning of the 19th century had been established for that scientific discipline (and others; cf. Hacking, 1990). Knowledge of this law emerged from investigations into the source of discrepancies among the records provided by multiple observers telescopically tracking the movements of celestial bodies. It was learned that these discrepancies were not (as had previously been suspected) the result of varying degrees of carelessness on the part of observers, but instead reflected the basic reality that human beings are imperfect recording devices.

Happily, the observed discrepancies were not altogether chaotic. On the contrary, given a sufficiently high number of observations, it could regularly be shown that the discrepancies would take on a pattern well described by what is familiar to scholars today as the *bell-shaped curve*. Thus, a frequency distribution of a large set of observations would peak at the arithmetic mean of those observations and would show deviations from that mean, the frequencies of which decreased symmetrically with increasing distance in either direction from the mean. On the reasonable assumption that there was in fact a correct or true value pertaining to the movement of the celestial body under observation (e.g., the time actually required for that body to appear to traverse a specified distance across the sky), these discrepancies could be seen as measurement error, and the average of a large set of observations could be regarded as the best possible estimate of the true value.

Though Quetelet's appetite for statistical thinking was whetted by his work in astronomy, his intellectual interests ranged well beyond that discipline and extended into theoretical mathematics, philosophy, and, most important for present considerations, disciplines known at the time as the "moral" (today "social") sciences.

The confluence of these interests inclined Quetelet toward his investigations during the 1830s into the statistical properties of measures of various physical characteristics of human beings, such as height, weight, head circumference, chest size, and so forth. He found when he examined frequency distributions for large sets of such measures that they regularly took on the same formal properties as the astronomical measurement errors just discussed. For Quetelet, the parallels were too striking to be ignored, and they formed the basis for the notion he introduced of *l'homme moyen,* or the *average man.* The essence of Quetelet's idea was that just as isolated observations concerning the movement of a planet could be expected to contain an element of error, obscuring to some extent the actual or true value, so apparently could isolated measures of, say, the heights of various individuals be viewed as containing an element of error, obscuring to some extent the naturally "proper" or "correct" height for a hypothetically perfect representative of the population. On the (far from trivial or incontestable) assumption that such a value in fact exists, Quetelet held that it is best estimated as the average within some specified population of measures of the heights of many individuals. For him, that average represented *nature's ideal* for the population in question, and the deviation of any given individual's height (weight, chest size, etc.) from that ideal would then properly be regarded as *nature's error* in that specific case.

In his thinking about *l'homme moyen,* Quetelet assumed (a) that if the frequency distribution within a population of measures of some physical characteristic takes on a shape identical (or nearly so) to frequency distributions regularly obtained in records of the movements of celestial bodies, then the former affords a picture of some sort of "error" no less than do the latter and (b) that the particular kind of "error" embedded in measures of people's physical characteristics (i.e., nature's error in the production of human beings), is properly estimated not by taking multiple measures of one individual, but by taking a single measure of each of many individuals. Both of these assumptions were again invoked by Quetelet as he extended his treatment of *l'homme moyen physique,* or the "average (hu)man" considered in terms of physical characteristics, to his analysis of *l'homme moyen moral,* or the "average (hu)man" considered in terms of psychosocial, or "moral" attributes. Of interest in this latter domain would be characterological features such as courage, criminality, or affection.

Porter (1986) has well described how Quetelet proceeded. He notes that, in contrast to the calculation of *l'homme moyen physique,* the intent to calculate *l'homme moyen moral* presented Quetelet with a problem:

> [H]uman individuals do not present themselves to the scientist endowed with measurable quantities of courage, criminality, or affection. In this respect, the average man was a far more tractable problem than the concrete individual. In principle, wrote Quetelet, the courage or criminality of a real person could be established if that person were placed in a great number of experimental

situations, and a record kept of the number of courageous or criminal acts elicited. *This would be interesting, but it was wholly unnecessary for social physics.* Instead, the physicist need only arrange that courageous and criminal acts be recorded throughout society, as the latter already were, and then the average man could be assigned a "penchant for crime" equal to the number of criminal acts committed divided by the population. In this way, a set of discrete acts by distinct individuals was transformed into a continuous magnitude, the penchant, which was an attribute of the average man. (Porter, 1986, p. 53; emphasis added)

Clearly, one finds here, in that system of thought Quetelet called "social physics," a nascent form of the notion that knowledge of empirical continua within populations may properly serve as a basis for inferences about psychological inclinations, tendencies, or penchants in an individual, or the "average man." This was not yet a finished foundation for modern trait psychology, partly because this "average man" was merely an abstract individual, but also because Quetelet's interest as a moral scientist was restricted to population mean values and did not extend to a systematic consideration of the differential degrees of variation of individuals around those mean values. Indeed, it has just been explained that in Quetelet's view, the examination of concrete individual cases would amount to nothing more than a study of "nature's errors." This conviction was the basis for his 1835 observation:

If one seeks to establish, in some way, the basis of a social physics, it is he *(l'homme moyen)* whom one should consider, without disturbing oneself with particular cases or anomalies, and without studying whether some given individual can undergo a greater or lesser development in one of his faculties. (Quetelet, 1835, quoted in Porter, 1986, pp. 52-53)

It would remain for Francis Galton, taking his lead from cousin Charles Darwin, to awaken widespread interest in the individual deviations around *l'homme moyen* as phenomena warranting more than dismissal as "nature's error." As noted previously, this was the development that, extended by the insights of Pearson, would effectively complete the foundation on which the correlational research methods of contemporary "nomothetic" personality research have been built. The proverbial circle of this exposition does not yet close with this observation, however, for it was also noted previously that strictly speaking, neither Galton's nor Pearson's scientific interests were any more focused on individuals than were Quetelet's.[17] So, important questions beg concerning conceptual developments that attended and succeeded the idea of social physics.

## From Social Physics to Laws Governing
## Individual Psychological Functioning

For Quetelet, the very idea of a social physics was grounded in the notion, seemingly confirmed by countless exercises in the erstwhile "political arithmetic," that there is a remarkable order in a great many aspects of human affairs—births and deaths, marriages and divorces, crimes and acts of courageous altruism—that can be discerned, provided that one is willing to bow to the "law of large numbers" and view matters statistically, that is, in the aggregate. Capitalizing on the regularities revealed by quantitative representations of *l'homme moyen*, Quetelet seems to have believed that it should be possible, at least in principle, to ascertain general laws governing the development of a society by tracking the "average human" over time and relating this course to forces variously prevalent within that society. Extrapolating from such knowledge, it should then have been possible to predict at least some significant aspects of that society's future. This, then, would be the long-term project of social physics.

However, noting that "not a single trajectory calculation is to be found in all of Quetelet's works," Porter (1986, p. 55) has argued that social physics was influential more as a metaphor than as a vital discipline in any practically consequential sense. Through that metaphor, Quetelet was able to recruit many thinkers of his time to the notion that quantitative, objective, and empirically testable insights into human affairs could best be pursued by abandoning attempts to explain and understand individuals' actions and focusing instead on statistical summaries of behavior within populations. As Porter (1986) put it,

> [Quetelet's] metaphorical science of social physics . . . seemed to reveal plainly that statistical laws can prevail for a mass even when the constituent individuals are too numerous or too inscrutable for their actions to be understood in any detail. (p. 55)

So, through social physics, the view ascended among mid-19th-century thinkers that scientifically worthy accounts of human behavior could indeed be formulated, provided that the laws constituting such accounts were understood to apply to humans en masse and not to any particular human. The invitation to the moral scientists of the day was to see society as "an entity in its own right, *independent of the whims and idiosyncracies of its constituent individuals*" (Porter, 1986, p. 51; emphasis added).

This exclusion of concern for individual level phenomena would not long prevail, however. In his 1857 *History of Civilization in England* (second edition printed posthumously in 1898), Henry Thomas Buckle (1821-1862) challenged the view that aggregate level order is uninformative about individual level lawfulness. In the course of arguing for a view of history as science (and in the process adopting a position quite at odds with the one that nearly 40 years later, Windelband (1894/1998) would defend in articulating the distinction between nomothetic and idiographic knowledge; refer to discussion in Chapter Four), Buckle (1857/1898) expressed the central problematic of his work as follows:

> We shall thus be led to one vast question, which indeed lies at the root of the whole subject, and is simply this: Are the actions of men, and therefore of societies, governed by fixed laws, or are they the result either of chance or of supernatural interference? (p. 6)

By no means was Buckle blind to the logical possibility of attributing the "actions of men"—by which he clearly meant the actions of *individual* human beings—neither to chance nor to divine intervention, but instead to an element of capriciousness commonly referred to as "free will." Indeed, much of the discussion in the introductory chapter of *History of Civilization in England* was devoted to precisely this point; and within the context of Buckle's treatment of the issue, he revealed his position regarding the relevance of aggregate statistical knowledge to an understanding of individual level psychological phenomena.

Rejecting what he termed the metaphysical dogma of free will on the grounds that it is at best empirically unverified, and at worst empirically refuted,[18] Buckle (1857/1898) argued,

> [W]e are driven to the conclusion that the actions of men, being determined solely by their antecedents, must have a character of uniformity, that is to say, must, under precisely the same circumstances, always issue in precisely the same results. And as all antecedents are either in the mind or out of it, we clearly see that all the variations in the results—in other words, all the changes of which history is full, all the vicissitudes of the human race, their progress and their decay, their happiness or their misery—must be the fruit of a double action; an action of external phenomena upon the mind, and another action of the mind upon the phenomena.
>
> These are the materials out of which a philosophic history can alone be constructed. On the one hand, we have the human mind obeying the laws of its own existence, and, when uncontrolled by external agents, developing itself according to the conditions of its organization. On the other hand, we have what is called Nature, obeying likewise its laws; but incessantly coming into contact with the minds of men, exciting their passions, stimulating their intellect, and therefore

giving to their actions a direction which they would not have taken without such disturbance. Thus we have man modifying nature, and nature modifying man; while out of this reciprocal modification all events must necessarily spring. (pp. 14-15)

This passage leaves little doubt that in Buckle's view, a scientific account of human affairs, up through and including all of history, would be one that incorporated not only the laws of nature revealed by the physical sciences but also the laws governing the mental life of individual human beings. Furthermore, Buckle did not temper the expression of his faith in the formal appropriateness of large-scale statistical investigations, patterned on the model of Quetelet's social physics,[19] for revealing the laws of the "double modification" described in the foregoing passage. Referring to the orderliness revealed by Quetelet's and others' investigations, Buckle (1857/1898) argued,

Such is the regularity we expect to find, if the actions of men are governed by the state of the society in which they occur; while, on the other hand, if we can find no such regularity, we may believe that their actions depend on some capricious and personal principle peculiar to each man, as free will or the like. It becomes, therefore, in the highest degree important to ascertain whether or not there exists a regularity in the entire moral conduct of a given society; and this is precisely one of those questions for the decision of which statistics supply us with materials of immense value. . . . [From carefully compiled statistical facts], *more may be learned [about] the moral nature of Man than can be gathered from all the accumulated experiences of the preceding ages.* (p. 17; parentheses and italics added)

There followed in Buckle's text further discussion of numerous additional empirical findings issuing from various statistical investigations, all pointing toward the conclusion he wished to highlight, namely, that "the moral actions of men are the product not of their volition, but of their antecedents" (p. 22). Illustrative in this regard is his discussion of suicide, by definition an individual act:

All of the [statistical] evidence we possess respecting it points to one great conclusion, and can leave no doubt on our minds that suicide is merely the product of the general condition of society, and that the individual felon only carries into effect what is a necessary consequence of preceding circumstances. In a given state of society, a certain number of persons must put an end to their own life. This is the general law; and the special question as to who shall commit the crime depends of course upon special laws; which, however, in their total action, must obey the large social law to which they are all subordinate. (p. 20)

Two pages after this passage, Buckle reemphasized to his readers that the proofs of his argument "have been derived from statistics" (p. 24). He then boldly delivered himself of the opinion that the discipline of statistics constituted "a branch of knowledge which, though still in its infancy, has already thrown more light on the study of human nature than all the sciences put together" (pp. 24-25).

In Buckle's work, then, there is a clear and forceful defense of a position on two points of fundamental and enduring relevance to 20th-century scientific psychology. Here again, one of these points may be identified as metaphysical, the other as epistemic. Regarding the first, Buckle's view was that in principle, a full understanding of all human actions can be achieved through causal explanations modeled on (and indeed fused with) those developed within the physical sciences. These explanations would be articulated in the laws governing mental life, on one hand, and the laws governing events in the world external to the mind, on the other, and they would not appeal in any way at all to the role of "personal capriciousness" or free will.

On the epistemic point, Buckle defends the view that empirical knowledge relevant to an articulation of the laws governing the nature and functioning not only of population aggregates but also of individual minds—and hence the actions of individual persons—had been and would continue to be advanced through large-scale statistical investigations conducted on the model of Quetelet's social physics. So, unlike Quetelet himself, who was content to view the social order revealed by statistical methods as strictly an aggregate level phenomenon, Buckle regarded that same order as a "window" onto individual level lawfulness.

## Disagreements in Late-19th-Century Thought Over the Proper Understanding of Statistical Knowledge

As the foregoing quotations of Buckle (1857/1898) suggest, the epistemic issue here is not altogether separate from the metaphysical one. If, as Buckle's argument implies, the aggregate lawfulness revealed by large-scale statistical investigations indeed reflects some corresponding individual level lawfulness, then, Quetelet notwithstanding, the findings unearthed by social physics would have to be seen as challenging assumptions about the role of free will in human affairs, both collective and individual. On the other hand, if aggregate lawfulness is actually silent regarding the determinants of individual actions, then it could not properly be seen as challenging the notion of individual free will as one of those determinants. So, a great deal of consequence for the moral sciences, including an understanding of the extent to which, if at all, individuals could be regarded as responsible for their actions, hinged significantly on which view of statistical knowledge prevailed. The importance of this matter was not overlooked at the time. On the contrary, Porter (1986) remarked that in comparison with debates over this issue during the 1860s and 1870s, "It is far from clear that Darwin or Comte was discussed with greater urgency" (p. 164).

Some thinkers were inclined toward agreement with views expressed by, for example, M.W. Drobisch (1802-1896). In 1867, he published a treatise titled *Die moralische Statistik und die menschliche Willensfreiheit: Eine Untersuchung (A Study of Moral Statistics and Human Free Will)*. In this work, he argued that it is "only through a great failure of understanding [that] the mathematical fiction of an average man . . . [can] be elaborated as if all individuals . . . possess a real part of whatever obtains for this average person" (Drobisch, 1867; quoted in Porter, 1986, p. 171).

Clearly, Drobisch believed that Buckle's understanding had failed him and hence that Buckle's entire project was founded on a mistake. But others disagreed. For example, in 1864, 3 years earlier, Adolph Wagner (1835-1917) had published *Die Gesetzmäßigkeit in den scheinbar willkürlichen menschlichen Handlungen vom Standpunkt der Statistik (The Lawfulness in Deceptively Arbitrary Human Actions From the Standpoint of Statistics)* and through this work made clear his enthusiasm for the views put forth by Buckle. Porter (1986) stated that Wagner stopped short of adopting a settled position on the metaphysical question of free will, but nevertheless was persuaded that "mass regularity indicated the existence of genuine laws *acting on every individual*. . . . [Wagner] accounted for [the] failure [of those laws] to express themselves uniformly by pointing to the disturbing forces which often cancel their effects" (Porter, 1986, p. 169). In this view, behavioral unpredictability signals neither mere "measurement error variance" nor causes of human action lying in principle beyond the reach of determinants revealed by statistical laws. Such unpredictability signals only that, in fact, a complete accounting of behavior in some specified domain requires more and/or more refined laws of the same basic sort. When all population level variance has been accounted for and "error variance" thus reduced to zero, the quantitative expressions (e.g., multiple regression equations; cf. Endnote #10) through which this empirical state of affairs has been realized will define the laws that can fully explain the behavior/psychological functioning of every individual within that population.[20]

In the English language literature, Cambridge University Fellow and Lecturer in the Moral Sciences John Venn (1834-1923) was one of the most prominent 19th-century spokespersons for a view of statistical knowledge fundamentally at odds with that propounded by Buckle. In his *The Logic of Chance,* Venn (1888) resolutely defended the thesis that probability statements of the form endemic to statistical treatments of phenomena are inextricably embedded within, and hence dependent for their very sensibility on, the consideration of a *series*. To say, for example, that the probability is .50 that a particular flip of a coin will come up heads is to say precisely and only that in a sufficiently lengthy series of (fair) coin flips, heads will come up on half the flips.

In Venn's view, the notion of probability (as opposed to certainty) cannot coherently be said to apply at all to any single coin flip. To be sure, the strength of a coin-flipper's confidence or belief about the outcome of a single flip might sensibly be conveyed by an expression such as "I'm about half sure that the next flip will come up heads," but this is a statement about the subjective state of the person flipping the coin, not a statement about some sort of objective force operating on or within the coin being flipped so as to bring about a particular outcome. To confuse these issues, Venn argued, is to flirt with an epistemic position under the terms of which one's claims to scientific knowledge would always be false. Continuing with his simple coin-flipping example, Venn elaborated his point as follows:

> I am about to toss (a coin) up, and I therefore half believe, to adopt the current language, that it will give head. Now it seems to be overlooked that if we appeal to the event, . . . our belief must inevitably be wrong. . . . For the thing must either happen or not happen: i.e. in this case the penny must either give head, or not give it; there is no third alternative. But whichever way it occurs, our half-belief, so far as such a state of mind admits of interpretation, must be wrong. If head does come, I am wrong in not having expected it enough; for I only half believed in its occurrence. If it does not happen, I am equally wrong in having expected it too much; for I half believed in its occurrence, when in fact it did not occur at all.
>
> *The same difficulty will occur in every case in which we attempt to justify our state of partial belief in a single contingent event.* (Venn, 1888, p. 141; emphasis added)

In light of the inherently probabilistic nature of claims to partial or incomplete knowledge about individuals' thoughts or actions based on group level statistical findings, the last statement of this quotation clearly reflects Venn's conviction that the logic of his analysis would apply no less to such claims than to those concerning coin flips. The lesson in the case of coin flips is that despite our knowledge that in a sufficiently lengthy series of flips, heads will come up on half of them, uncertainty regarding the outcome of some particular flip remains complete until *after* the flip has been executed, at which point the uncertainty vanishes instantly and entirely.

By the very same token, Venn's argument requires us to appreciate that even if statistical findings reveal that, say, 80 of 100 students entering the university with SAT scores of 1200 finally graduate with grade point averages between 3.25 and 3.75 on a 4.00 scale, uncertainty regarding the final grade point average of some particular entering student with an SAT score of 1200 nevertheless remains complete until his or her final record is in. Then, and only then, does the uncertainty vanish instantly and entirely. Suppose an admissions officer claims on the basis of available statistical evidence that "there is an 80% chance that if admitted, this applicant with an SAT score of 1200 will graduate with a grade point average between 3.25 and 3.75." The assertion might be permitted to stand as an imprecisely phrased expression of subjective belief on the part of the admissions officer—that is, as a statement the admissible meaning of which is "I, the admissions officer, am about 80% sure that such will occur." From Venn's perspective, however, the above claim could not be permitted to stand as a scientifically proven claim to objective knowledge about the applicant, for example, as an empirically verified finding concerning the strength of some propensity or force residing within or acting on the individual in question.

In conclusion, it is clear that well before the turn of the 20th century, an intellectual line had been drawn separating opposing views on the use of aggregate statistical knowledge as an empirical basis for drawing inferences concerning individual level phenomena. Some thinkers believed, in basic agreement with Venn (1888), that such knowledge is not properly used for these purposes. Other thinkers sided with Buckle (1857/1898) in believing that aggregate level order could scarcely exist apart from some corresponding individual level order and hence that the former may properly be taken as a "window" onto the latter.

Seen in the light of the preceding discussion of the "neo-Galtonian" research model identified by Danziger (1987), it should now be apparent that Buckle's position on the nature and proper interpretation of aggregate statistical knowledge is embedded within Thorndike's (1909, 1911) solution to the epistemic problem left to scientific psychology by the original Galtonian model for empirical research. Accordingly, through their subsequent endorsement of what I shall henceforth refer to as the "Thorndike maneuver," most mainstream scientific psychologists throughout the "two disciplines" of the field discussed by Cronbach (1957) wittingly or otherwise embraced Buckle's view of statistical knowledge, and in so doing rejected the views of Venn. In the next chapter, we examine the consequences of this epistemic commitment for modern understandings of nomothetic personality research.

# Summary

Statistical thinking played an enormously important role in the restructuring of scientific psychology that took place during the first third of the 20th century. Committed as Wundtian-style experimenters were to the study of the single case, statistical methods played only a secondary role within experimental psychology at its outset. However, such experimentation was also proving rather impotent in the face of pressures on the discipline from outside to produce knowledge that would be of practical use in various settings such as health care, education, business and industry, government, and the military. In this regard, the correlational research methods that were being deployed with apparent success in connection with mental testing seemed to hold much greater promise, and those methods were, of course, inherently statistical.

Yet for all the practical advantages that correlational methods seemed to offer relative to Wundtian-style experimentation, the former also had some serious drawbacks. For one thing, the lack of experimental control created a metaphysical problem insofar as it undermined the search for knowledge of cause-effect relationships. For another, reliance on aggregated research findings created an epistemic problem insofar as it compromised the quest for individual level understanding.

The metaphysical problem was resolved to the satisfaction of most by the invention of the concept of *treatment groups*. In the development of this approach to research, statistical methods would be used to compare averages obtained in two or more groups of subjects—defined not by "natural" categories such as age, sex, or race, as was true of original Galtonian style inquiry, but instead through the random assignment of different research subjects to different treatment conditions created by the experimenter. The epistemic problem was resolved to the satisfaction of most by embracing the view that aggregate level patterns in data are properly regarded as a kind of "window," limited in practice perhaps, but not in principle, onto individual level phenomena. These two developments in the thinking of mainstream research psychologists were fundamental to the emergence of the neo-Galtonian framework for psychological research, the logic of which centers both "basic" and "applied" investigative efforts within the discipline to this day.

With specific reference to the epistemic problem just named, the solution entailed by neo-Galtonian thinking about psychological research has been so long and so widely accepted that the impression is easily gained that there is nothing especially controversial or conceptually problematic about it. However, consensus on this matter has not always been so widespread.

On the contrary, the nature and proper uses of statistical knowledge was widely debated during the second half of the 19th century.

Some scholars favored the view championed most prominently by the historian Henry Thomas Buckle, according to which aggregate level order *must* reflect some corresponding individual level order. In this view, sample or population statistics are regarded as informative about the individuals constituting those samples or populations. In opposition to this view, Buckle's contemporary John Venn, a logician, argued resolutely that aggregate level order is utterly silent in the face of what is going on at the level of the individual event or entity and that this is no less true in the case of the behavior of a particular human being than it is in the case of the outcome of some particular flip of a coin.

As statistical thinking made its way into scientific psychology through mental testing and correlational research, the majority of investigators embraced, with E.L. Thorndike, an understanding of aggregate level data consistent with that represented by Buckle. In the course of this development, the views of Venn were, wittingly or otherwise, rejected.

# Notes

1.  In a later work, Danziger (1990) would refer to this model as the "Leipzig model."

2.  See Endnote #4, Chapter Two.

3.  To say that Wundt's psychology was an individual psychology is not to claim that it was a personal psychology. Unlike Stern (1900a), Allport (1937a) failed to fully grasp this distinction, which is why he erroneously criticized as "inappropriate" Wundt's own characterization of his general-experimental psychology as an individual psychology (e.g., Wundt, 1912; cf. Allport, 1937a, p. 7).

4.  Indeed, citing Wundt's 1913 *Die Psychologie im Kampf ums Dasein* (*Psychology's Struggle for Existence;* Wundt, 1913), Danziger (1987) noted that Wundt "actually opposed . . . the application of scientific psychology to real life problems" (p. 39).

5.  Danziger (1987) noted that strictly speaking, the "Galtonian" model should be named the "Galton-Pearson" model, because it was Pearson who refined the approach that Galton had inspired. Nevertheless, Danziger opted for the expression "Galtonian," though in so doing emphasized the importance of recognizing this name as a kind of convenient historical shorthand. I will follow Danziger's lead in this, and continue to refer to the Galtonian model.

6.  See, for example, Galton's 1865 essay "Hereditary Talent and Character" and Pearson's 1903 essay "On Breeding Good Stock." Excerpts of both essays

highlighting sections of special relevance to the present considerations can be found in a volume edited by Jacoby and Glauberman (1995).

7. An insurance company executive does not, after all, have to know or care *why* gender is correlated with automobile accident frequency to know that annual premiums for male clients must be higher than those for their same-aged female counterparts if the company is to show an overall annual profit within that client group. The executive's objective, after all, is not to understand behavior, but to make money.

8. To say, for example, that, on average, blacks and whites differ with respect to some psychological characteristic is equivalent to saying that race is correlated with measures of that characteristic. The reverse, of course, is equally true.

9. In time, some experimental psychologists wedded to ANOVA procedures would also come to employ "within-person" experimental designs, in which each subject is exposed to more than one level of one or more treatment variable(s). Such experimental designs cannot properly be regarded as straightforward extensions of the original Galtonian model of investigation. In fact, completely within-subject designs are much closer in nature to the original Wundtian style of experimentation. However, such designs are also, by definition, no better suited to the assessment and study of *individual and group differences* than was the original Wundtian model. For precisely this reason, they have not played, and still do not play, any significant role in the work of contemporary mainstream personality investigators. Accordingly, "within-subject" ANOVA designs fall outside the boundaries of the present discussion.

10. For any given $r_{Y,X}$ specifying the correlation between some criterion variable Y and some predictor variable X, a regression equation can be written specifying the algorithm to be followed in order to generate, on the basis of that correlation, the best (least squares) estimate of Y in some particular case, k, given a knowledge of X in that same case k and the value of $r_{Y,X}$. This equation has the general form $\hat{Y}_k = a + b_{Y,X}(X_k)$, where $\hat{Y}_k$ is the best (least squares) estimate of the criterion variable score associated with case k; $X_k$ is the actual value of variable X in case k; $b_{Y,X}$ is the slope of the line defined by the regression equation; and $a$ is the Y-intercept of that line. The value of $b_{Y,X}$ is determined as $r_{Y,X}((SD_y/SD_x))$ and the value of $a$ is determined as $\bar{Y} - b_{Y,X}(\bar{X})$, where $\bar{Y}$ and $\bar{X}$ symbolize, respectively, the means of the criterion and predictor variables. The reader will note that if the standard deviations of the criterion and predictor variables are equal, then $b_{Y,X} = r_{Y,X}$.

11. By far the most thorough and readable exposition of this point known to me is the 1974 edition of the text authored by Kerlinger and Pedhazur, *Multiple Regression in Behavioral Research* (Kerlinger & Pedhazur, 1974). See also Cohen (1968) and Darlington (1968).

12. Münsterberg (1913) himself was quite clear on this point (see esp. Chapter XII, titled "Individuals and Groups.")

13. It will be recalled from the discussion in Chapter Three that from his personalistic perspective, Stern had—and repeatedly voiced—serious misgivings about this attitude.

14. My discussion in this section draws extensively on, and hence owes much to, a highly instructive work by the historian Theodore M. Porter (1986) titled *The Rise of Statistical Thinking: 1820-1900*.

15. The German term for "the state" is *der Staat*.

16. The reader wishing to explore this history further is urged to consult, in addition to the aforementioned work by Porter (1986), that same author's *Trust in Numbers* (Porter, 1995) as well as works by Daston (1988), Hacking (1990), and Stigler (1986).

17. This point is consistent with, and further underscored by, the fact that populations variances and covariances (in which Galton and Pearson were vitally interested) are themselves group means (cf. discussion of computational procedures in following chapter).

18. Buckle also rejected the theological doctrine of predestination on the grounds that appealing as it does to a Divine (supernatural) Providence, it is not empirically testable.

19. On page 18 of the book under discussion here, Buckle (1857/1898) specifically referred to the large body of researches by Quetelet.

20. The German statistician Gustav Rümelin (1815-1889) was one of many other 19th-century scholars identified by Porter (1986), who, with Drobisch (1867), doubted the appropriateness of population level statistical findings as an epistemic basis for claims to knowledge about individual psychological states. Rümelin set forth his views in a work entitled *Über den Begriff eines sozialen Gesetzes (On the Concept of a Social Law)*, published in 1875 as part of a collection of "Speeches and Essays."

# Chapter Six

## Contemporary "Nomotheticism" Within the Framework of Neo-Galtonian Inquiry

### *A Methodological Primer*

With the demise of the resistance movement Gordon Allport had so energetically but futilely championed following Stern's death in 1938 (see Chapter Four), the majority within the mainstream of scientific personality psychology could renew its collective (if not always entirely univocal) pursuit of an exclusively "nomothetic" discipline. Within this framework, the primary challenge became that of identifying the most rudimentary common attributes of "the" human personality, those presumably fundamental empirical continua with respect to which human beings "in general" could be said to differ from one another, and through which, consequently, the basic features of any given individual's personality—his or her individuality—could be articulated. Once scientific research had accomplished this, and in the process filled out something that could pass muster as a kind of "periodic table of personality elements" (Lamiell, 2000), programmatic inquiry could be directed in turn to identifying (a) the sources or causes of such individual differences as they might be located in "nature" or "nurture" or some combination of the two and (b) the consequences or effects of those differences in various domains of human behavior. Research in this latter direction would establish empirically the sought-after

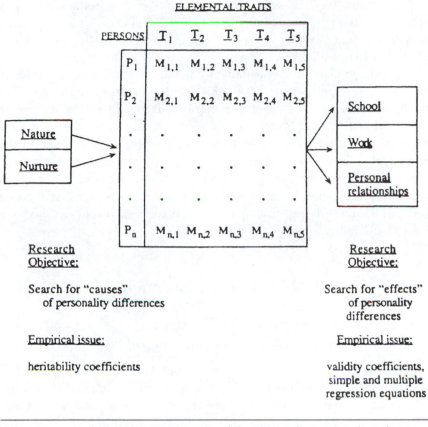

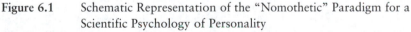

**Figure 6.1**    Schematic Representation of the "Nomothetic" Paradigm for a
Scientific Psychology of Personality

SOURCE: Adapted from Lamiell (2000).

"nomothetic" laws of personality functioning. Figure 6.1 schematizes the
essential components of this scientific agenda.[1]

The central purpose of the present chapter is to make clear how the
scientific agenda just sketched has been, and continues to be, prosecuted as
part of the more general "neo-Galtonian" paradigm for psychological
research discussed in Chapter Five. To this end, the discussion begins by
considering a simple (and hypothetical) treatment group comparison study
illustrating the basics of neo-Galtonian *experimentation*. Once in place, this
example is then easily expanded to show how the paradigm incorporates
*correlational* inquiry and thus accommodates the interests of investigators
concerned primarily with individual and group differences (Cronbach,

1957). In this way, the status of contemporary "nomotheticism" as a species of neo-Galtonian inquiry can be made manifest, and with this, a proper foundation will be laid for the critique of modern "nomotheticism" offered in Chapter Seven.

The present chapter is essentially a "method-ology," that is, a study of methods. More precisely, it is a (highly condensed) study of the statistical methods proper to neo-Galtonian inquiry. To facilitate the discussion, Table 6.1 defines and shows computational formulas for the most rudimentary statistics involved. For readers with no prior background in this subject, the illustrative exercises to be discussed presently may serve as a kind of primer in the exercise of these methods. For readers with prior training in this subject, the exercises may nevertheless serve, at the very least, as a kind of refresher course, one that for some may even shed new light on a familiar topic.

# The Rudiments of Neo-Galtonian Inquiry

## The Statistical Comparison of Treatment Groups in Neo-Galtonian Experimentation

For starters, then, let us suppose a neo-Galtonian (as opposed to Wundtian) experiment with 20 fourth-grade school children, in which the goal of the experiment was to examine the effects of two alternative teaching methods on spelling performance. In this hypothetical experiment, 10 pupils were assigned at random to a class employing Method 1 ($m_1$), emphasizing formal drill, while random assignment placed 10 other pupils in a class employing Method 2 ($m_2$), emphasizing silent reading of meaningful prose featuring the words to be learned. At the end of the school term, a 20-item spelling test designed to measure the pupils' mastery of the target words was administered, with scores on this test serving as the experiment's dependent variable. The results of this hypothetical experiment are displayed in Table 6.2.[2]

Examining Table 6.2, it is clear that the average number of words correctly spelled is higher among the pupils exposed to Method 2 ($\bar{m}_2 = 12.20$) than among those exposed to Method 1 ($\bar{m}_1 = 9.60$). The question is this: Is there any scientific basis for inferring that Method 2 would be better than Method 1 among fourth-grade pupils "generally"? Stated more technically, can the difference between the treatment group means displayed in Table 6.2 be regarded as statistically significant and hence inferentially attributable to some lawful regularity governing the effects of the different methods of instruction, rather than to chance and/or some other unknown factor(s)?

**Table 6.1**    Definitions and Computational Formulas for Statistical Indices Fundamental to Correlational/Regression Analyses in Neo-Galtonian Inquiry

| Statistics | Definition | Computation | Equation Number |
|---|---|---|---|
| Mean, X, of variable $\overline{X}$ | Sum over N cases of scores on variable X divided by number of scores, N | $\overline{X} = (\Sigma X_p) / N$ | [6.1] |
| Variance of variable X, $v_x$ | Average over N cases of squared deviations of scores around their means | $v_x = (\Sigma(X_p - \overline{X})^2) / N$ | [6.2] |
| Standard deviation of variable X, $sd_x$ | Square root of variance | $sd_x = [(\Sigma(X_p - \overline{X})^2) / N]^{1/2}$ | [6.3] |
| Standard score $Z_{p,x}$ of case p on variable X | Difference between $X_p$ and $\overline{X}$ divided by $sd_x$ | $Z_{p,x} = (X_p - \overline{X}) / sd_x$ | [6.4] |
| Coefficient of correlation, $r_{y,x}$ between criterion variable Y and predictor variable X | Average over N cases of cross products of standard scores on criterion variable Y and predictor variable X | $r_{y,x} = \Sigma((Z_{p,y} Z_{p,x})) / N$ | [6.5] |
| Coefficient of regression, $b_{y,x}$ | Slope of line defining the regression of criterion variable Y onto predictor variable X | $b_{y,x} = r_{y,x} (sd_y / sd_x)$ | [6.6] |
| Additive constant of regression, a | Difference between the mean of Y, i.e., $\overline{Y}$, and the product of the coefficient of regression $b_{y,x}$ and the mean of X, i.e., $\overline{X}$ | $a = \overline{Y} - b_{y,x}(\overline{X})$ | [6.7] |

Though this question could readily be addressed through a *t* test for the difference between independent means or, alternatively, a simple one-way analysis of variance (ANOVA), entirely equivalent results can also be achieved through correlational/regression analysis.[3] Set up as a correlation/

**Table 6.2**    Hypothetical Data Illustrating a "Neo-Galtonian" Experiment
Involving the Comparison of Two Treatment Groups

| | | | |
|---|---|---|---|
| | *Method of Instruction (M)* | | |
| *$m_1$: Formal Drill* | | | *$m_2$: Silent Reading* |
| $P_1$ | 6 | $P_{11}$ | 12 |
| $P_2$ | 9 | $P_{12}$ | 15 |
| $P_3$ | 7 | $P_{13}$ | 11 |
| $P_4$ | 9 | $P_{14}$ | 13 |
| $P_5$ | 5 | $P_{15}$ | 11 |
| $P_6$ | 11 | $P_{16}$ | 12 |
| $P_7$ | 13 | $P_{17}$ | 13 |
| $P_8$ | 11 | $P_{18}$ | 11 |
| $P_9$ | 16 | $P_{19}$ | 15 |
| $P_{10}$ | 9 | $P_{20}$ | 9 |
| $\bar{m}_1 = 9.60$ | | $\bar{m}_2 = 12.20$ | |

Overall Mean = 10.90

NOTE: Each P in the table represents an individual pupil, and each numerical value indicates the number of correctly spelled words on the 20-item test used as the dependent variable in the experiment.

regression problem, the hypothetical experiment depicted in Table 6.2 is framed as one involving a "criterion" or "dependent" variable, Y, and a single "predictor" or "independent" variable defined by method of instruction *(M)*. Using what Kerlinger and Pedhazur (1974) call the "effect coding" procedure for representing a two-category predictor variable of this sort, the data can be represented as shown in Table 6.3. There, the independent variable *method of instruction (M)* has been defined for analysis through an arbitrary coding procedure according to which the 10 subjects exposed to the formal drill treatment ($m_1$) have been coded −1, while the 10 exposed to the silent reading treatment ($m_2$) have been coded +1.[4]

In accordance with the mathematical definition of the Pearson *r* given by Equation 6.5 in Table 6.1 (see also discussion in previous chapter), the analysis of these data using correlational statistics requires the redefinition of each of the two variables involved, Y and M, in terms of *z* scores, or standard scores.[5] As Equation 6.4 in Table 6.1 indicates, however, the transformation of Y and M into standard-score form in turn requires knowledge of the means and standard deviations of each of the two variables. These are determined according to Equations 6.1 and 6.3 in Table 6.1, and the obtained values are shown at the bottom of Table 6.3.

Table 6.3        Hypothetical Data of Table 6.2 Arranged for Simple
Correlation/Regression Analysis

|  | Criterion $Y$ | | Predictor $M$ |
|---|---|---|---|
| $P_1$ | 6 | (−1.71) | −1 |
| $P_2$ | 9 | (−0.66) | −1 |
| $P_3$ | 7 | (−1.36) | −1 |
| $P_4$ | 9 | (−0.66) | −1 |
| $P_5$ | 5 | (−2.06) | −1 |
| $P_6$ | 11 | (+0.03) | −1 |
| $P_7$ | 13 | (+0.73) | −1 |
| $P_8$ | 11 | (+0.03) | −1 |
| $P_9$ | 16 | (+1.78) | −1 |
| $P_{10}$ | 9 | (−0.66) | −1 |
| $P_{11}$ | 12 | (+0.38) | +1 |
| $P_{12}$ | 15 | (+1.43) | +1 |
| $P_{13}$ | 11 | (+0.03) | +1 |
| $P_{14}$ | 13 | (+0.73) | +1 |
| $P_{15}$ | 11 | (+0.03) | +1 |
| $P_{16}$ | 12 | (+0.38) | +1 |
| $P_{17}$ | 13 | (+0.73) | +1 |
| $P_{18}$ | 11 | (+0.03) | +1 |
| $P_{19}$ | 15 | (+1.43) | +1 |
| $P_{20}$ | 9 | (−0.66) | +1 |
| Mean | 10.90 | 0.00 | 0.00 |
| sd | 2.86 | 1.00 | 1.00 |

NOTE: Values shown in parentheses are criterion variable z scores. See text for explanation.

Obtaining the requisite $Z_{pY}$ scores is then a simple matter of subtracting the mean of variable Y, 10.90, from each "raw score" in the *Criterion* column of Table 6.3 and then, in accordance with Equation 6.4, dividing each difference thus obtained by 2.86. The results are given by the values shown in parentheses after each "raw" Y score in Table 6.3.

Following the same procedures for computing the needed $Z_{pM}$ values, that is, the standard scores for the predictor variable *M*, one discovers that the resulting numerical values are identical to those with which the computations begin. The principle here, which might be less than obvious to readers not already thoroughly familiar with these procedures, is that any arbitrary but systematically executed procedure for numerically coding subjects with respect to the independent variable *M* would, if the data were converted to $z$ scores in accordance with the logic of Equation 6.4, result in quantities identical to those already shown for $M$ in Table 6.3. That is, any arbitrary (but systematically executed) coding procedure would result in each subject being represented as standing either exactly 1 standard deviation below the mean (where $Z = -1.00$) or exactly 1 standard deviation above the mean (where $Z = +1.00$) on a two-category variable representing experimental treatment conditions. So by "effect coding" variable $M$ in the manner shown, that variable has merely been defined from the start as it must inevitably be defined anyway for purposes of statistical analysis.

The data of the hypothetical experiment are thus fully configured for correlational analysis. In accordance with Equation 6.5, the reader can verify that for these hypothetical data, the simple correlation between the criterion variable, $Y$, and the predictor variable, $M$, is $r_{Y,M} = +.45$. Because it happens that the square of a Pearson $r$, that is the quantity $r^2$, indexes the percentage of variance in one of two correlated variables that can be explained in terms of the other, it may be said in this instance that the independent variable, method of instruction, accounts for $.45^2$, or slightly more than 20% of the total between-pupil variance in performance on the spelling test used to define the dependent variable $Y$.

It happens that in a sample comprising 20 subjects, a correlation of magnitude $r = .45$ will occur by chance alone less than 5 times in 100, and it thus meets the standard commonly used by research psychologists for establishing statistical significance.[6] The inference that would be drawn in an actual study of this sort, therefore, is that the statistical relationship between the dependent and independent variables discovered in the experiment is systematic rather than "random" or "chance," and understandable as a reflection of the real effect of instructional method on the spelling performance of fourth graders.

Though the point is not often made explicitly in the contemporary research literature, it is the case that what is finally being sought is a kind of knowledge that, when pared to its essentials, can be "packaged" in an expression having the following general form:

$$\hat{Y}_p = a + b_{Y,X} (X_p) \tag{6.8}$$

where

$\hat{Y}_p$ represents the statistically estimated standing of person $p$ with respect to some specified criterion or "dependent" variable, $Y$,

$b_{Y,X}$ represents, in a geometric two-space, the slope of a line representing the empirically discovered correlation between the criterion or "dependent" variable, $Y$, and some selected predictor or "independent" variable, $X$, and *a* represents, in the same geometric two-space, the "Y-axis intercept" of that so-called regression line.

   In the case of the present example, the parameters of the equation expressing the empirically discovered relationship between variables $Y$ and $M$ are easily specified. Here, the regression coefficient $b_{Y,M}$ indicates the slope of the line geometrically describing the statistical relationship, that is, the linear correlation, between $Y$ and $M$. As can be seen by Equation 6.6 in Table 6.1, $b_{Y,M}$ would literally equal the correlation between $Y$ and $M$, $r_{Y,M}$, if the standard deviations of the two variables were numerically identical. Such is not the case here, however. As already noted, the standard deviation of variable $Y$ is 2.86. Because, as just explained, variable $M$ is by default a set of standard scores, its standard deviation is by definition 1.00. Following Equation 6.6, then, we have $b_{Y,M} = .45\ ((2.86/1.00)) = 1.3$ (rounded to nearest tenth).

   The "additive constant" $a$ of Equation 6.8 above is the so-called Y-intercept of the regression line describing the relationship between variables $Y$ and $M$. In effect, this constant is defined so as to assure that the value of $\hat{Y}_p$ generated by the final regression equation will equal the actual mean of the criterion variable, $\bar{Y}$, in that case where the value of the predictor variable is equal to its actual mean. In this example, however, the arithmetic mean of the predictor variable, $\bar{M}$, is obviously zero (0.00). Hence, by Equation 6.7 in Table 6.1, it is determined that $a = 10.90 - (1.3)(0.00) = 10.90$.

   The final regression equation describing the relationship between $Y$ and $M$ for this set of hypothetical data is thus:

$$\hat{Y}_p = 10.90 + 1.3(M) \tag{6.9}$$

   By now working backward, so to speak, and inserting possible values of $M$ (i.e., $-1$ or $+1$) into Equation 6.9, values of $\hat{Y}_p$ can be generated for each of the 20 subjects in the experiment. These values are thus recursive estimates or "retrodictions" of individual subjects' dependent variable scores, given knowledge of (a) the treatment condition to which each was exposed and (b) the (now known) correlation between the variables $Y$ and $M$. These retrodictions are shown in Table 6.4, arrayed between the actual criterion values for each subject and a set of residuals, defined by calculating $(Y_p - \hat{Y}_p)$ for each subject. These latter values thus indicate the difference between a given subject's actual criterion score and the score retrodicted for that subject on the basis of the empirical regularity discovered through the research investigation. There are several noteworthy points to be made in connection with Table 6.4.

**Table 6.4**    Actual and Retrodicted Criterion Scores of Twenty Pupils in
Hypothetical Neo-Galtonian Experiment

*Regression Equation:*

$$\hat{Y}_p = 10.90 + 1.30(M)$$

| Pupils | Actual Criterion Scores, Y | Retrodicted Criterion Scores, $\hat{Y}$ | Residuals $(Y - \hat{Y})$ |
|---|---|---|---|
| $P_1$ | 6 | 9.60 | −3.60 |
| $P_2$ | 9 | 9.60 | −0.60 |
| $P_3$ | 7 | 9.60 | −2.60 |
| $P_4$ | 9 | 9.60 | −0.60 |
| $P_5$ | 5 | 9.60 | −4.60 |
| $P_6$ | 11 | 9.60 | +1.40 |
| $P_7$ | 13 | 9.60 | +3.40 |
| $P_8$ | 11 | 9.60 | +1.40 |
| $P_9$ | 16 | 9.60 | +6.40 |
| $P_{10}$ | 9 | 9.60 | −0.60 |
| $P_{11}$ | 12 | 12.20 | −0.20 |
| $P_{12}$ | 15 | 12.20 | +2.80 |
| $P_{13}$ | 11 | 12.20 | −1.20 |
| $P_{14}$ | 13 | 12.20 | +0.80 |
| $P_{15}$ | 11 | 12.20 | −1.20 |
| $P_{16}$ | 12 | 12.20 | −0.20 |
| $P_{17}$ | 13 | 12.20 | +0.80 |
| $P_{18}$ | 11 | 12.20 | −1.20 |
| $P_{19}$ | 15 | 12.20 | +2.80 |
| $P_{20}$ | 9 | 12.20 | −3.20 |
| Mean | 10.90 | 10.90 | 0.00 |
| Var. | 8.19 | 1.69 | 6.50 |

First of all, it is to be seen that the only two discrete values of $\hat{Y}_p$ generated by Equation 6.9 are in fact the treatment group means shown in Table 6.2. The lawful regularity uncovered through the statistical analysis thus holds that the best regression-based estimate of the performance of any given pupil just is the mean, or average score, achieved within that treatment group of which the individual in question was a member. These estimates are "best" in the *least squares* sense, meaning that the sum of the squares of the residual values shown in the far right column of Table 6.4 is less than it would be following any other algorithm for generating values of $\hat{Y}_p$.

A second point to be noted in connection with the data shown in Table 6.4 concerns the variances shown at the bottom of the display. As determined in accordance with Equation 6.2 in Table 6.1, the total variance in the criterion scores, $V_Y$, is 8.19, while the variance in the statistically retrodicted criterion scores, $V_{\hat{Y}}$, is 1.69. It is not mere coincidence that the ratio of this latter value to the former, that is, 1.69/8.19 or .206, is identical (within rounding error) to the previously determined value of $r_{Y,M}^2$, that is, $.45^2$ or .202. Both computations yield the percentage of total variance in $Y$ that can now be said to be explainable in terms of, or predictable on the basis of, $M$. Nor is it mere coincidence that the difference between the *total* variance in $Y$, 8.19, and the *predictable* variance in $Y$, 1.69, is equal (again within slight rounding discrepancies) to the variance of the $(Y - \hat{Y})$ values, that is, the *residual* variance, 6.50. Indeed, taking note of this equivalence helps to draw attention to the central objective of neo-Galtonian inquiry: to partition variance into the components *systematic* and *error*. Systematic variance is variance for which some explanation can be given (e.g., in terms of experimental treatments, as in the present example). Error variance is variance that within the context of a particular research study remains unexplained, that is, cannot be attributed to any identifiable source(s).

The third point to be made here follows directly from the second: The fact that at the conclusion of any particular investigation, some of the criterion variance will inevitably be left unexplained does not mean that that variance is in principle unexplainable. Indeed, the goal of programmatic inquiry within the neo-Galtonian framework, grounded as it is in a way of thinking traced to the mid-19th century writings of Henry Thomas Buckle (refer to the previous chapter), is to eventually explain *all* the variance. As Cronbach (1957) pointed out, researchers working within what he called the "correlational" tradition (i.e., the original Galtonian framework), long maintained that substantial portions, if not all, of the variance left unexplained by the neo-Galtonian experimentalists' treatment variables could regularly be found attributable to factors corresponding to nonexperimentally created individual (e.g., personality) and group (e.g., demographic) differences. By systematically extending the example begun above, these ideas can be illustrated.

## Extending the Research Design to Incorporate a Group Difference Variable

Let us suppose that in the study just described, half the pupils randomly assigned to each of the two experimental treatment conditions were boys, and half were girls. Table 6.5 reconfigures the original data to accommodate this design modification, and Table 6.6 displays the same data in a form suitable for correlation/regression analysis.

**Table 6.5**      Extension of Original Design to Include Gender as a
Nonexperimental Group Difference Factor

|  | Method of Instruction (M) | | | | |
|---|---|---|---|---|---|
|  | $m_1$: Formal Drill | | | $m_2$: Silent Reading | |
| $g_1$: Boys | $P_1$     6 |  |  | $P_{11}$     12 |  |
|  | $P_2$     9 |  |  | $P_{12}$     15 |  |
|  | $P_3$     7 | $g_1m_1 =$ 7.20 | $g_1m_2 =$ 12.40 | $P_{13}$     11 | $\bar{g}_1 =$ 9.80 |
|  | $P_4$     9 |  |  | $P_{14}$     13 |  |
|  | $P_5$     5 |  |  | $P_{15}$     11 |  |
| Gender (G) |  |  |  |  |  |
| $g_2$: Girls | $P_6$     11 |  |  | $P_{16}$     12 |  |
|  | $P_7$     13 |  |  | $P_{17}$     13 |  |
|  | $P_8$     11 | $g_2m_1 =$ 12.00 | $g_2m_2 =$ 12.00 | $P_{18}$     11 | $\bar{g}_2 =$ 12.00 |
|  | $P_9$     16 |  |  | $P_{19}$     15 |  |
|  | $P_{10}$     9 |  |  | $P_{20}$     9 |  |
|  | $\bar{m}_1 = 9.60$ |  |  | $\bar{m}_2 = 12.20$ |  |

Grand Mean = 10.90

In Table 6.6, the data displayed in columns $Y$ and $M$ are of course identical to those shown in Table 6.3. Column $G$ shows the arbitrary numerical codes used to represent the group difference variable gender $(G)$: boy pupils have been coded $-1$, and girl pupils have been coded $+1$. The far-right column in Table 6.6 shows numerical codes to be used to assess the possible joint effects of method of instruction and gender on criterion performance (exactly as one would by examining an interaction term in ANOVA). Each numerical value in this column is determined simply as the cross-product of the corresponding $M$ and $G$ codes (cf. Kerlinger & Pedhazur, 1974).

Guided by the previous discussion of the simpler design and making use of the formulas in Table 6.1, the reader can verify that in addition to the previously determined correlation $r_{Y,M} = +.45$ between the criterion variable, $Y$, and the experimental treatment variable, $M$, the simple correlations between $Y$ and, respectively, the group difference factor, $G$, and the interaction factor, symbolized by $M \times G$, are $r_{Y,G} = +.38$ and $r_{Y,M \times G} = -.45$.[7] Because in this particular example, the three predictor variables, $M$, $G$, and $M \times G$ are themselves uncorrelated, the total percentage of the variance in $Y$ that can be accounted for by the combination of the three predictor variables is given by

Table 6.6    Hypothetical Data of Extended Design, "Effect" Coded for Correlation/Regression Analysis

| | Criterion | | Predictors | | |
|---|---|---|---|---|---|
| | Y | | M | G | M × G Interaction |
| $P_1$ | 6 | (−1.71) | −1 | −1 | +1 |
| $P_2$ | 9 | (−0.66) | −1 | −1 | +1 |
| $P_3$ | 7 | (−1.36) | −1 | −1 | +1 |
| $P_4$ | 9 | (−0.66) | −1 | −1 | +1 |
| $P_5$ | 5 | (−2.06) | −1 | −1 | +1 |
| $P_6$ | 11 | (+0.03) | −1 | +1 | −1 |
| $P_7$ | 13 | (+0.73) | −1 | +1 | −1 |
| $P_8$ | 11 | (+0.03) | −1 | +1 | −1 |
| $P_9$ | 16 | (+1.78) | −1 | +1 | −1 |
| $P_{10}$ | 9 | (−0.66) | −1 | +1 | −1 |
| $P_{11}$ | 12 | (+0.38) | +1 | −1 | −1 |
| $P_{12}$ | 15 | (+1.43) | +1 | −1 | −1 |
| $P_{13}$ | 11 | (+0.03) | +1 | −1 | −1 |
| $P_{14}$ | 13 | (+0.73) | +1 | −1 | −1 |
| $P_{15}$ | 11 | (+0.03) | +1 | −1 | −1 |
| $P_{16}$ | 12 | (+0.38) | +1 | +1 | +1 |
| $P_{17}$ | 13 | (+0.73) | +1 | +1 | +1 |
| $P_{18}$ | 11 | (+0.03) | +1 | +1 | +1 |
| $P_{19}$ | 15 | (+1.43) | +1 | +1 | +1 |
| $P_{20}$ | 9 | (−0.66) | +1 | +1 | +1 |
| Mean | 10.90 | 0.00 | 0.00 | 0.00 | 0.00 |
| sd | 2.68 | 1.00 | 1.00 | 1.00 | 1.00 |

NOTE: Values shown in parentheses are criterion variable $z$ scores. See text for details.

the sum of the squares of the three simple correlations.[8] In this hypothetical case, therefore, the square of the multiple correlation, $R$, between the criterion, $Y$, and the combination of the three predictor variables, $M$, $G$, and $M \times G$ (i.e., the value $R^2$), is determined as $r^2_{Y,M} + r^2_{Y,G} + r^2_{Y,M \times G} = .45^2 + .38^2 + (-.45)^2 = .55$ (rounded) or 55%. So, if it was found previously that roughly 20% of the criterion variance could be explained in terms of the treatment variable alone, we now find that by also considering both the effects of gender as such and the joint effects of specific gender/treatment combinations, it is possible to increase by 35% the total percentage of explainable criterion variance.

The nature of the gender and gender-by-treatment interaction effects is most easily seen by examining the relevant means in Table 6.5. Looking first at the simple effect for gender, it can be seen that, on average, the girls did better ($\bar{g}_2 = 12.00$) than did the boys ($\bar{g}_1 = 9.80$). However, this gender difference was much more pronounced under (teaching) Method 1 than under Method 2. In the former case, girls averaged 12.00 correctly spelled words in comparison with the average of 7.20 for boys; in the latter case, the girls again averaged 12.00 correctly spelled words, whereas the boys' average performance rose to a level even slightly above that, 12.40. Hence, although method of instruction had no effect on the average performance of the girl pupils, it had a rather large effect on the average performance of the boys. We may say, therefore, that the effect of one factor itself varied across categories of the other factor, and this is what *interaction* in the statistical sense means.

The multiple regression equation needed to describe the results obtained in this expanded research design has the following form:

$$\hat{Y}_p = a + b_{Y,M}(M) + b_{Y,G}(G) + b_{Y,M \times G}(M \times G) \quad\quad [6.10]$$

Referring to the data given at the bottom of Table 6.6 and making use of the appropriate equations in Table 6.1, the reader can verify (allowing, as always, for rounding discrepancies) that the three regression coefficients of this equation are $b_{Y,M} = 1.3$ (as determined previously), $b_{Y,G} = 1.1$, and $b_{Y,M \times G} = -1.3$. Technically, $a$ in this case is determined as $a = \bar{Y} - b_{Y,M}(\bar{M}) - b_{Y,G}(\bar{G}) + b_{Y,M \times G}(\overline{M \times G})$, but of course the values of $\bar{M}$, $\bar{G}$, and $\overline{M \times G}$ are all zero, meaning that here, as before, $a = 10.90$. The final multiple regression equation in this case is thus:

$$\hat{Y}_p = 10.90 + 1.3(M) + 1.1(G) - 1.3(M \times G) \quad\quad [6.11]$$

If for each of the 20 subjects, in turn, the "effect" codes displayed in Table 6.6 are inserted into this equation, the reader can verify that the resulting values of $\hat{Y}_p$ are as displayed in Table 6.7. Following the format of Table 6.4, these $\hat{Y}_p$ values have been arrayed between the actual criterion scores of the subjects and residual values indicating, as before, the arithmetic difference between the actual $Y$ scores and the new statistically estimated retrodictions for each pupil.

The first noteworthy feature of the data in this table is the fact that the statistically estimated retrodictions now include four discrete values rather than the two generated by the previous equation. In this sense, it can be said that by expanding the research design to take into consideration not only the differential treatment of subjects but also the gender differences between them and possible joint effects, finer empirical discriminations between the research subjects have been made possible.

**Table 6.7**    Actual and Retrodicted Criterion Scores, and Residuals, of Twenty Pupils in Extended Hypothetical Experiment

Regression Equation:

$$\hat{Y}_p = 10.90 + 1.30(M) + 1.10(G) - 1.30(M \times G)$$

| Pupils | Actual Criterion Scores, Y | Retrodicted Criterion Scores, $\hat{Y}$ | Residuals $(Y - \hat{Y})$ |
|---|---|---|---|
| $P_1$ | 6 | 7.20 | −1.20 |
| $P_2$ | 9 | 7.20 | +1.80 |
| $P_3$ | 7 | 7.20 | −0.20 |
| $P_4$ | 9 | 7.20 | +1.80 |
| $P_5$ | 5 | 7.20 | −2.20 |
| $P_6$ | 11 | 12.00 | −1.00 |
| $P_7$ | 13 | 12.00 | +1.00 |
| $P_8$ | 11 | 12.00 | −1.00 |
| $P_9$ | 16 | 12.00 | +4.00 |
| $P_{10}$ | 9 | 12.00 | −3.00 |
| $P_{11}$ | 12 | 12.40 | −0.40 |
| $P_{12}$ | 15 | 12.40 | +2.60 |
| $P_{13}$ | 11 | 12.40 | −1.40 |
| $P_{14}$ | 13 | 12.40 | +0.60 |
| $P_{15}$ | 11 | 12.40 | +1.40 |
| $P_{16}$ | 12 | 12.00 | 0.00 |
| $P_{17}$ | 13 | 12.00 | +1.00 |
| $P_{18}$ | 11 | 12.00 | −1.00 |
| $P_{19}$ | 15 | 12.00 | +3.00 |
| $P_{20}$ | 9 | 12.00 | −3.00 |
| Mean* | 10.90 | 10.90 | 0.00 |
| Var. | 8.19 | 4.59 | 3.60 |

NOTE: Figures given for means and variances are computer generated. Hand calculations might differ slightly due to rounding.

The second point to be made here is that, as was the case previously and as the reader can now see by comparing Tables 6.7 and 6.5, the four discrete statistically estimated retrodictions generated by Equation 6.11 are identical to the group means of the four gender/treatment combination as shown in Table 6.5. The underlying statistical principle here thus remains exactly what it was in the case of the previous, simpler research design: the *best estimate* (in the least squares sense) of any given subject's criterion performance is the *average actual* criterion performance among subjects of the same gender/treatment classification as the subject in question.

Third, we find again in Table 6.7 the same additivity of variance components noted in the discussion of Table 6.5. The total variance in the actual criterion scores, 8.19, of course remains what it was. However, as a reflection of the fact that the consideration of gender and the treatment-by-gender interaction has made it possible to increase the proportion of that total variance that can be explained or accounted for, we see that the variance of the statistically estimated criterion scores has increased from the previous figure of 1.69 to the new figure of 4.59. This increase of 2.90 is balanced by a decrease of the same amount in the variance of the residuals, from the previous figure of 6.50 to the new figure of 3.60. Furthermore, the ratio of predictable criterion variance, 4.59, to total criterion variance, 8.19, yields a figure for the total percent variance accounted for, .56, that is identical (within rounding, as always) to the value of the squared multiple correlation, $R^2$, discussed above. Again, none of these convergences is accidental, and taking note of them should serve to deepen one's understanding of what is meant by references to *variance partitioning* in neo-Galtonian inquiry.

Finally, in this connection, explicit mention is made of the fact that even after expanding the hypothetical research design in the way discussed, unexplained criterion variance remains: The column of residuals in Table 6.7 has not yet been reduced to an exceptionless array of zeros. We can therefore extend the design yet again and in the process show how measures of individual differences of the sort of the sort commonly employed in contemporary "nomothetic" personality studies fit into the larger picture framed by the neo-Galtonian paradigm for psychological research.

## Extending the Research Design Further to Include an Individual Differences Variable

Let us suppose that the design of the hypothetical study we have been discussing had been guided from the start by the foresight to administer to each of the 20 research subjects a personality questionnaire known to yield reliable and valid measures of achievement motivation in elementary school children. Let us suppose further that the raw score assessments generated by this test can range in value from zero to 100 and that the scores for the 20 pupils serving as subjects in the experiment are as shown outside parentheses in the far right panel of Table 6.8.

Given that these raw scores have a mean of 50 and a standard deviation of 14.14, their corresponding $z$ scores, as computed by Equation 6.4 in Table 6.1, are as shown inside parentheses. Using Equation 6.5, the reader can verify that

Table 6.8    Hypothetical Data of Two-Factor Experiment, "Effect" Coded for Correlation/Regression Analysis and Extended to Include Achievement Motivation as a Personality Variable

| | Criterion | | Predictors | | | |
|---|---|---|---|---|---|---|
| | Y | | M | G | $M \times G$ | Ach. Mot. |
| $P_1$ | 6 | (−1.71) | −1 | −1 | +1 | 30 (−1.41) |
| $P_2$ | 9 | (−0.66) | −1 | −1 | +1 | 60 (+0.71) |
| $P_3$ | 7 | (−1.36) | −1 | −1 | +1 | 40 (−0.71) |
| $P_4$ | 9 | (−0.66) | −1 | −1 | +1 | 70 (+1.41) |
| $P_5$ | 5 | (−2.06) | −1 | −1 | +1 | 50 (0.00) |
| $P_6$ | 11 | (+0.03) | −1 | +1 | −1 | 50 (0.00) |
| $P_7$ | 13 | (+0.73) | −1 | +1 | −1 | 60 (+0.71) |
| $P_8$ | 11 | (+0.03) | −1 | +1 | −1 | 40 (−0.71) |
| $P_9$ | 15 | (+1.78) | −1 | +1 | −1 | 70 (+1.41) |
| $P_{10}$ | 9 | (−0.66) | −1 | +1 | −1 | 30 (−1.41) |
| $P_{11}$ | 12 | (+0.38) | +1 | −1 | −1 | 40 (−0.71) |
| $P_{12}$ | 15 | (+1.43) | +1 | −1 | −1 | 60 (+0.71) |
| $P_{13}$ | 11 | (+0.03) | +1 | −1 | −1 | 30 (−1.41) |
| $P_{14}$ | 13 | (+0.73) | +1 | −1 | −1 | 70 (+1.41) |
| $P_{15}$ | 11 | (+0.03) | +1 | −1 | −1 | 50 (0.00) |
| $P_{16}$ | 12 | (+0.38) | +1 | +1 | +1 | 50 (0.00) |
| $P_{17}$ | 13 | (+0.73) | +1 | +1 | +1 | 60 (+0.71) |
| $P_{18}$ | 11 | (+0.03) | +1 | +1 | +1 | 30 (−1.41) |
| $P_{19}$ | 15 | (+1.43) | +1 | +1 | +1 | 70 (+1.41) |
| $P_{20}$ | 9 | (−0.66) | +1 | +1 | +1 | 40 (−0.71) |
| Mean | 10.90 | 0.00 | 0.00 | 0.00 | 0.00 | 50   0.00 |
| sd | 2.86 | 1.00 | 1.00 | 1.00 | 1.00 | 14.14 1.00 |

NOTE: Values shown in parentheses are $z$ scores. See text for details.

the simple correlation between the criterion scores and the achievement motivation *(AM)* scores is $r_{Y,AM} = +.53$. Once again, the design of this example is such that the achievement motivation scores do *not* correlate (i.e., correlate zero) with the other predictor variables $M$, $G$, and $M \times G$, meaning that the value $r^2_{Y,AM} = +.53^2 = .28$ can be added to the squares of the three previously determined simple correlations to determine the revised value of $R^2$. Because the previously determined value of $R^2$ was .55, the new value of $R^2$ equals .55 + .28 = .83. The multiple correlation, $R$, between the criterion variable, $Y$, and the combination of $M$, $G$, $M \times G$, and $AM$ is thus equal to the square root of .83. That is, $R_{Y,(M, G, M \times G, AM)} = .83^{1/2} = .91$.

The (further revised) regression equation needed to take into account this additional empirical finding is a straightforward extension of Equation 6.10 (just as Equation 6.10 was a straightforward extension of Equation 6.8) and has this general form:

$$\hat{Y}_p = a + b_{Y,M}(M) + b_{Y,G}(G) + b_{Y,M\times G}(M \times G) + b_{Y,AM} (AM) \quad [6.12]$$

Due once again to the fact that the predictor variables in this hypothetical study are completely uncorrelated with one another, the values of $b_{Y,M}$, $b_{Y,G}$, and $b_{Y,M\times G}$ remain as specified in Equation 6.11. Applying Equation 6.6 to the requisite data reported above, the value of $b_{Y,AM}$ is computed as $b_{Y,AM} = .53((2.86/14.14)) = .107$. Following Equation 6.7, the value of $a$ in Equation 6.12 is thus determined as $a = 10.90 - (.107)(50) = 5.525$.[9] The newly revised regression equation is thus:

$$\hat{Y}_p = 5.525 + 1.3(M) + 1.1(G) - 1.3(M \times G) + .107(AM) \quad [6.13]$$

Repeating the by now familiar procedure of inserting into this equation the values of the predictor variables for each subject, retrodictions of the criterion scores of individual subjects can be generated. Consistent with the format established in Tables 6.4 and 6.7, these newly generated values of $\hat{Y}_p$ are displayed in Table 6.9 between the actual criterion scores to the left and the residuals to the right.

Note should be taken first of all of the further refinement in the values of $\hat{Y}_p$ generated by the new regression equation. Whereas under the previous statistical law, the value of $\hat{Y}_p$ generated for a given subject was identical with that generated for at least 4 other subjects and in the case of the girls, with that of 9 others, it is now the case that among boys, the values of $\hat{Y}_p$ generated by Equation 6.13 are unique, and among girls, no particular value of $\hat{Y}_p$ occurs more than twice. As the statistical analysis becomes more extended and nuanced, it would seem that the individuality of the separate cases can be brought into ever sharper focus.

The second point to be noted here concerns, once again, the additivity of the variance components. Obviously, the variance of the actual criterion scores remains 8.19. However, we have just seen that above and beyond the portions of that variance attributable to $M$, $G$, and $M \times G$, an additional 28% is attributable to the individual differences variable, $AM$. Twenty-eight percent of 8.19 is approximately 2.30, and this is why the variance of the $\hat{Y}_p$ values in Table 6.9 (i.e., the value 6.91), is greater by 2.30 (allowing for rounding discrepancy) than the variance of the $\hat{Y}_p$ values shown in Table 6.7.

Table 6.9    Actual and Retrodicted Criterion Scores, and Residuals, 20 Pupils
in a Hypothetical Experiment Based on a Revised Model
Illustrating the Incorporation of a Personality Variable

*Revised Regression Equation:*

$$\hat{Y}_p = 5.525 + 1.30(M) + 1.10(G) - 1.10(M \times G) + .107(AM)$$

| Pupils | Actual Criterion Scores, Y | Retrodicted Criterion Scores, $\hat{Y}$ | Residuals $(Y - \hat{Y})$ |
|---|---|---|---|
| $P_1$ | 6 | 5.05 | +0.95 |
| $P_2$ | 9 | 8.27 | +0.73 |
| $P_3$ | 7 | 6.12 | +0.88 |
| $P_4$ | 9 | 9.35 | −0.35 |
| $P_5$ | 5 | 7.20 | −2.20 |
| $P_6$ | 11 | 12.00 | −1.00 |
| $P_7$ | 13 | 13.08 | −0.08 |
| $P_8$ | 11 | 10.92 | +0.08 |
| $P_9$ | 16 | 14.15 | +1.85 |
| $P_{10}$ | 9 | 9.85 | −0.85 |
| $P_{11}$ | 12 | 11.32 | +0.68 |
| $P_{12}$ | 15 | 13.48 | +1.52 |
| $P_{13}$ | 11 | 10.25 | +0.75 |
| $P_{14}$ | 13 | 14.55 | −1.55 |
| $P_{15}$ | 11 | 12.40 | −1.40 |
| $P_{16}$ | 12 | 12.00 | 0.00 |
| $P_{17}$ | 13 | 13.08 | −0.08 |
| $P_{18}$ | 11 | 9.85 | +1.15 |
| $P_{19}$ | 15 | 14.15 | +0.85 |
| $P_{20}$ | 9 | 10.92 | −1.92 |
| Mean | 10.90 | 10.90 | 0.00 |
| Var. | 8.19 | 6.91 | 1.28 |

Commensurately, the variance of the residuals shown in Table 6.9 is lower
by 2.30 (again allowing for rounding discrepancy) than the variance of the
residuals shown in Table 6.7. "Error" variance has still not yet been reduced
to zero, but this example illustrates how the consideration of individual differences can facilitate the pursuit of the objective of specifying empirical laws
of ever greater comprehensiveness: The ratio of the predictable criterion
variance, 6.91, to the total criterion variance, 8.19, now equals .83 (note
again that this value is identical, within rounding, to the value of $R^2$

computed above), considerably higher than the value of .56 achieved without taking the personality variable into account.

Considered within the context of all that has gone before it, this last example should suffice to illustrate how "nomothetic" personality studies are incorporated into the dominant neo-Galtonian paradigm for psychological research and thus how modern scientific personality psychology "works." Clearly, the examples could be extended endlessly to include more variables representing further experimental treatments; additional non-experimental group variables, such as race, age, or ethnicity; and/or other personality factors, such as one or more of the so-called Big Five (see Endnote #1). Moreover, with any and all such extensions, the possibilities for examining interactions in the sense illustrated above increase geometrically. So to be sure, from a *substantive* standpoint, research considerably more elaborate than the examples provided here is possible, and computations commensurately more complex than those illustrated here can be employed.

However, no substantive extensions of the examples, however many or complex, would alter in any fundamental way the basic logic of the investigative approach as it has been illustrated to this point. In any domain of human behavior/psychological functioning singled out for investigation within a neo-Galtonian framework, the basic problem is structured as one of *accounting for between-person variation*. The working hypothesis is always that basic dimensions of individual differences represented by "common traits" (e.g., achievement motivation in the last example above, or the "Big Five," as discussed below) have an important role to play in this scientific enterprise, whether alone, in (additive) combination, or in (multiplicative) interaction with other nonpersonality variables (e.g., group difference variables such as gender, ethnicity, etc.). The basic assumption guiding this entire approach to psychological research is that through cumulative successes in accounting for ever more between-person variation in measures of theoretical or practical interest, scientific accounts of the behavior/psychological functioning of individual persons in terms of statistical laws of the sort illustrated will become commensurately more refined. On such convictions has the entrenched "nomothetic" framework for scientific personality studies been constructed.

In Chapter Seven, a close critical examination of this approach to what Stern identified over a century ago as the "problem of individuality" will be undertaken. Beforehand, however, we consider briefly the provenance of the particular framework that in recent years has gained widespread acceptance among contemporary "nomotheticists" as a universal scheme for representing the basic attribute dimensions of "the" human personality.

# The Establishment of Contemporary "Nomotheticism's" Periodic Table of Elements

In an article revealingly titled "The Structure of Phenotypic Personality Traits," Goldberg (1993) delivered himself as follows:

> Once upon a time we had no personalities (Mischel, 1968).[10] Fortunately times change, and the past decade has witnessed an electrifying burst of interest in the most fundamental problem of the field—the search for a scientifically compelling taxonomy of personality traits. More importantly, the beginning of a consensus is emerging about the general framework of such a taxonomic representation. As a consequence, the scientific study of personality dispositions, which had been cast into the doldrums in the 1970s, is again an intellectually vigorous enterprise poised on the brink of a solution to a scientific problem whose roots extend back at least to Aristotle. (Goldberg, 1993, p. 26; parentheses added)

Whether or not the establishment of a trait-variable taxonomy ought truly to be regarded as personality psychology's most fundamental problem—more fundamental than, say, achieving a philosophically sound and theoretically coherent conception of those entities we call *persons*—is dubious at best, and the very idea that such might be the case reflects the empiricism that has taken deep root within the field over the years. Nevertheless, Goldberg's claim concerning an emergent consensus within the field on the content of such a taxonomy does seem valid. Indeed, numerous contributions to the literature published during the past 15 years or so have explicitly and enthusiastically endorsed the proposition that human personalities vary along five basic and largely independent dimensions of individual differences. These are (for now said to be): *neuroticism, extraversion, openness, agreeableness,* and *conscientiousness* (see, e.g., Angleitner, 1991; Digman, 1989, 1990; John & Robins, 1993; McCrae & Costa, 1986, 1987; Wiggins & Trapnell, 1997), and *en ensemble,* this quintet is now widely referred to as "the Big Five." As to their scientific importance, McCrae and Costa (1986) have ventured so far as to assert that these five attribute dimensions offer "a universal and comprehensive framework for the description of individual differences in personality" (p. 1001).

This claim of universality and comprehensiveness is a heady one indeed, and faith in its essential validity has doubtless energized many of those contemporary researchers now sailing confidently into the 21st century on waves of enthusiasm over the prospects of discovering the underlying causes and manifest effects of these putatively basic human differences (cf. Figure 6.1). So, prior to critiquing mainstream "nomotheticism," it is appropriate to discuss the evidential basis on which this disciplinary investment in the "Big Five" has been constructed.

## The "Lexical Hypothesis" and Its Systematic Investigation Through Factor Analysis

As Goldberg (1993) explained, the investigative effort that has culminated in the postulation of the "Big Five," an effort that has spanned several decades, has proceeded from the "lexical hypothesis." According to this hypothesis, the dimensions of individual differences most important or salient within a given culture should be mirrored in the language of that culture. Consequently, analyses of trait-descriptive terms within a given language should yield important clues regarding basic personality structure; and to the extent that the findings of such analyses can be replicated across different languages, evidence accumulates in favor of the hypothesis that the identified structure is indeed suitable for characterizing personality differences among human beings generally (McCrae, 2000).

But what form should analyses of trait-descriptive language take? By what methods should investigation proceed? Paradoxically, adherents of the lexical hypothesis within the mainstream of scientific personality psychology owe much to the seminal contributions of none other than Gordon Allport. For together with Henry S. Odbert, Allport long ago undertook a "psycho-lexical study" of the English language, and in the course of that study identified 17,953 terms in *Webster's New International Dictionary* that could be used "to distinguish the behavior of one human being from that of another" (Allport & Odbert, 1936, p. 24).[11] Obviously, no lexicon of such size could without reduction be made practicable for the scientific purposes of a common trait psychology of personality. Investigation had to begin somewhere, however, and thanks to the statistical technique known as *factor analysis*, researchers found themselves able to proceed on the basis of Allport and Odbert's (1936) contribution with some real hope of reducing the vast domain those investigators had identified to a manageable number of basic *dimensions of meaning*.[12]

Other authors (e.g., Digman, 1989, 1990; Goldberg, 1993; McCrae & Costa, 1987; Wiggins & Trapnell, 1997) have discussed various aspects of the research done over the ensuing years following this beginning, and readers interested in more of the details of the story are referred to those works. The objective here, being methodological, is simply to describe the conceptual basics of the factor analytic work that has been so central to this endeavor and to point to the main empirical findings that have issued to date from that work.

To this end, it may be supposed that the extensive lexicon assembled by Allport and Odbert (1936) has been sampled broadly, and that on this basis, a smaller set of adjective pairs (say, 80 or so pairs) has been identified to investigate a wide variety of personality differences. Examples of such adjective pairs would be calm versus worrying; retiring versus sociable; unadventurous versus daring; callous versus sympathetic, and lazy versus hard-working (cf. McCrae & Costa, 1987). It may further be supposed that each of a large number of research subjects recruited to an investigation has been asked to make numerical ratings describing several of his or her peers in terms of each of these 80 or so adjective pairs. A subject might be asked, for example, to make each rating on a 7-point scale, in which a rating of 1 would indicate that the first-named adjective in each pair is highly descriptive of the target and a rating of 7 would indicate that the opposite adjective in each pair is highly descriptive of the target. Integer ratings between 1 and 7 would be used to indicate different degrees of applicability of one adjective versus its opposite in a given pair.

With data of this sort, it would be possible to compute Pearson product-moment correlations between ratings of the targets on any one item and ratings of the same targets on each of the other items. For example, one could determine the extent to which ratings of 30 targets on the item *calm versus worrying* correlated with ratings of the same 30 targets on the item *retiring versus sociable*. Under the logic of the statistical procedure being described here, this correlation would be interpreted to reflect the extent to which one adjective pair taps a dimension of meaning in common with the other. Hence, were a high correlation to be obtained between the item *calm versus worrying* and, say, *patient versus impatient,* the interpretation would be that the two items are reflective of some common underlying dimension of meaning, such as (low vs. high) neuroticism. On the other hand, were one to obtain a low or, in the limiting case, zero, correlation between two items, such as between *calm versus worrying* and *submissive versus dominant,* the interpretation would be that the two items tap different underlying dimensions of meaning (e.g., low vs. high neuroticism in the case of *calm versus worrying* and introversion vs. extraversion in the case of *submissive versus dominant*)[13]

In its application in this context, the goal of factor analysis, the complex statistical procedure used to analyze large sets of intercorrelations of the sort just described, has been to represent with as few dimensions as possible, but no fewer than necessary, the entire set of item intercorrelations.[14] To the degree that the adjectives used to constitute the items have been

**Table 6.10**    Hypothetical Intercorrelation Matrix Illustrating the Presence of Two Underlying Factors

|           | Variables | | | | | | |
| Variables | 1 | 2 | 3 | 4 | 5 | 6 | 7 |
|---|---|---|---|---|---|---|---|
| 1 | — | | | | | | |
| 2 | .80 | — | | | | | |
| 3 | .85 | .83 | — | | | | |
| 4 | .10 | .21 | .09 | — | | | |
| 5 | .06 | .01 | .07 | .91 | — | | |
| 6 | .15 | .05 | .10 | .79 | .88 | — | |
| 7 | .12 | .11 | .22 | .87 | .86 | .79 | — |

sampled representatively from the larger pool identified for the language in question, the factors emerging from such an analysis should, it is thought, accurately represent the basic dimensions of personality expressible in that language.

Table 6.10 displays hypothetical intercorrelations among seven variables and provides a schematic and highly simplified illustration of the general idea underlying factor analysis (cf. Nunnally, 1967). Note that in these hypothetical data, Variables 1, 2, and 3 all correlate highly among themselves, and none correlates substantially with any of Variables 4 through 7. On the other hand, these latter four variables all correlate highly among themselves. A factor analysis of these data would yield two factors: one defined or "marked" by whatever it is that Variables 1 through 3 could be discerned to share in common and the other defined or "marked" by whatever it is that Variables 4 through 7 could be discerned to share in common.[15]

The quest for a "periodic table of personality elements" has of course involved many more than seven variables and, hence, correlation matrices having considerably more than 21 entries. But the underlying logic of the analyses has always been as just described. The empirical findings issuing from many such analyses conducted over the years have pointed decisively toward the conclusion that the number of factors both necessary and sufficient to account for the obtained patterns of item intercorrelations is five and that these five factors will bear interpretation as the aforementioned "Big Five" (Angleitner, 1991). Statistically speaking, then, it appears that the basic dimensions of meaning underlying the great multiplicity of terms used in a variety of languages by people to describe their own and others' personality characteristics are the empirical continua of (high vs. low) neuroticism, extraversion, openness, agreeableness, and conscientiousness.

**Table 6.11**    Hypothetical 15-Item Inventory for Assessing "Big Five" Personality Characteristics

---

1. I do not often fret about things.
2. My attitude toward new acquaintances is usually positive.
3. I am blessed with a lively imagination.
4. I am generally wary about the hidden agendas of people I meet.
5. Most people regard me as sensible in day-to-day affairs.
6. I scare easily.
7. I do not eagerly engage in small talk or chit-chat.
8. My thinking is down-to-earth; no unrealistic imaginings.
9. I think the best of people until they prove me otherwise.
10. I'm pretty indifferent about community issues.
11. Seldom am I anxious or fearful.
12. I'm widely regarded as welcoming and socially pleasant.
13. I am blessed with a lively fantasy life.
14. If you are not careful, others will exploit you.
15. I take in lots of information and so am usually well informed.

---

## Convergent and Discriminant Validity of the Five-Factor Model

Complementing the empirical evidence just described are additional research findings based on subjects' responses to questionnaire items designed to tap the same five factors using another method. To illustrate this work, we may consider the 15 statements shown in Table 6.11 as items on a hypothetical personality assessment inventory. Both in their form and in their content, these 15 items are similar to (but not identical with) 15 actual items on the *NEO Personality Inventory* (Costa & McCrae, 1992), a questionnaire instrument that is now widely used by personality investigators for purposes of measuring the "Big Five" personality characteristics.

In responding to the items on that inventory (and so likewise to those shown for illustrative purposes in Table 6.11), the individual whose personality is being assessed[16] would be asked to "speak" through the language of a five-category response rubric offering the following possibilities: *strongly disagree, disagree, neutral, agree,* and *strongly agree.*

To assess someone's personality by means of such an inventory, his or her responses to each item would be coded numerically on a 5-point scale that (following the procedure actually used with the *NEO Inventory*) might be specified arbitrarily to range over the consecutive integers zero through 4. Whether these numerical values would be aligned with the response alternatives "left to right" (i.e., with zero corresponding to *strongly disagree* and 4 corresponding to *strongly agree*) or "right to left" (i.e., with zero corresponding to *strongly agree* and 4 corresponding to *strongly disagree*) would depend on the content and wording of a particular item. To illustrate with a reference to three of the items shown in Table 6.11, let us say that Items 2, 7, and 12 are intended to assess extraversion and that the scoring convention has been adopted according to which relatively higher total scores on the inventory will be taken to indicate comparatively higher levels of extraversion. Under these conditions and on the basis of a theoretical conception of extraversion according to which the trait would be signaled by a *strongly agree* response to Item 2, a *strongly disagree* response to Item 7, and in turn a *strongly agree* response to Item 12, it follows that Item 7 would have to be scored in the direction opposite the scoring of Items 2 and 12 to ensure the conceptual integrity of the operation of summing the numerically coded responses to the three items into a total extraversion raw score.[17] In this hypothetical case, therefore, the zero-to-4 response scoring scheme would have to be aligned with the response rubric in the "left-to-right" direction for Items 2 and 12, but in the "right-to-left" direction for Item 7. Following this logic, the reader can deduce its application, in turn, to the item triads [1, 6, and 11], [3, 8, and 13], [4, 9, and 14], and [5, 10, and 15], where, again, each of these latter 4-item triads is here intended to mimic the *NEO Personality Inventory* items that are actually used to assess respondents on neuroticism, openness, agreeableness, and conscientiousness, respectively.

Suppose now for further illustrative purposes that a subject has responded as shown in parentheses in Table 6.12 below to each of the 15 statements of our hypothetical inventory and that in accordance with the scoring rationale elaborated above, these responses have been coded numerically (i.e., "scored") as shown in the right-hand panel of the table. What results is the following: *neuroticism* (the sum of scored responses to Items 1, 6, and 11) = 6; *extraversion* (the sum of scored responses to Items 2, 7, and 12) = 6; *openness* (the sum of scored responses to Items 3, 8, and 13) = 5; *agreeableness* (the sum of scored responses to Items 4, 9, and 14) = 8; and *conscientiousness* (the sum of scored responses to Items 5, 10, and 15) = 9.

In an actual study, the scoring of *NEO Personality Inventory* protocols would be carried out in formal accordance with this procedure, the only substantive difference being that the actual *Inventory* contains 240 items rather than just 15.[18] Supposing now that such a study had been carried out with, say, several hundred research subjects, a factor analysis of the responses could be undertaken following the very same principles as those sketched above. That is, correlations could be computed across respondents for all possible item pairs, and the resulting matrix of item intercorrelations, which would be identical in its basic structure to (albeit much larger than)

**Table 6.12**    Scored Responses of Hypothetical Subject's Answers to Items of a Hypothetical 15-Item Personality Assessment Inventory

| | SD | D | N | A | SA |
|---|---|---|---|---|---|
| 1. I do not often fret about things. ("disagree") | 4 | **3** | 2 | 1 | 0 |
| 2. My attitude toward new acquaintances is usually positive. ("neutral") | 0 | 1 | **2** | 3 | 4 |
| 3. I am blessed with a lively imagination. ("disagree") | 0 | **1** | 2 | 3 | 4 |
| 4. I am generally wary about the hidden agendas of people I meet. ("disagree") | 4 | **3** | 2 | 1 | 0 |
| 5. Most people regard me as sensible in day-today affairs. ("strongly agree") | 0 | 1 | 2 | 3 | **4** |
| 6. I scare easily. ("strongly agree") | **0** | 1 | 2 | 3 | 4 |
| 7. I do not eagerly engage in small talk or chit-chat. ("agree") | 4 | 3 | 2 | **1** | 0 |
| 8. My thinking is down-to-earth; no unrealistic imaginings. ("disagree") | 4 | **3** | 2 | 1 | 0 |
| 9. I think the best of people until they prove me otherwise. ("agree") | 0 | 1 | 2 | **3** | 4 |
| 10. I'm pretty indifferent about community issues. ("disagree") | 4 | **3** | 2 | 1 | 0 |
| 11. Seldom am I anxious or fearful. ("disagree") | 4 | **3** | 2 | 1 | 0 |
| 12. I'm widely regarded as welcoming and socially pleasant. ("agree") | 0 | 1 | 2 | **3** | 4 |
| 13. I am blessed with a lively fantasy life. ("disagree") | 0 | **1** | 2 | 3 | 4 |
| 14. If you are not careful, others will exploit you. ("neutral") | 4 | 3 | **2** | 1 | 0 |
| 15. I take in lots of information and so am usually well informed. ("neutral") | 0 | 1 | **2** | 3 | 4 |

NOTE: The hypothetical subject's response to each item is shown in parentheses following each item. The scoring of the response is indicated by the bold numeral in the array of numerals displayed to the right of each item.

the matrix shown in Table 6.10, could be analyzed for its underlying factor structure. Here again, the results of many studies conducted along these general lines have led most contemporary personality investigators to the conclusion (a) that five factors are both necessary and sufficient to account for intercorrelations among responses to the items of the *NEO Personality Inventory* (thus confirming that the *Inventory* functions as it was designed to function) and (b) that these five factors closely correspond with the five independently identified in the research with trait adjectives described previously. Table 6.13 displays some key data relevant to this latter point, published by McCrae and Costa (1987).

Several features of Table 6.13 warrant comment here. To be noted first of all is that the correlations shown in the body of the table are based on data emanating from four different sources: Subjects have both *described themselves* and *been described by peers,* and they have done so both in terms of five factors derived, through factor analysis, from bipolar adjective rating data of the sort discussed previously, and in terms of factors found, also through factor analysis, to underlie the items of the *NEO Personality Inventory.*[19] Hence, through the data displayed in Table 6.13, McCrae and Costa (1987) have offered empirical evidence crucial to what Cronbach and Meehl (1955) called "construct validity," and they have done so following principles set forth more than 40 years ago by Campbell and Fiske (1959) for establishing *convergent* and *discriminant* validity by means of the *multitrait-multimethod* matrix.

As its name indicates, a multitrait-multimethod investigation entails the measurement of at least two traits by at least two operationally independent methods. Clearly, these conditions were met by McCrae and Costa (1987) inasmuch as Table 6.13 displays data based on research involving five traits, each of which has been measured four ways.

The essence of the aforementioned concepts of convergent and discriminant validity is simply that intercorrelations between alternative and operationally independent measures of the same putative trait should be relatively high, whereas intercorrelations between measures of putatively different and psychologically distinct traits should be relatively low, or even zero. The data displayed in Table 6.13 give impressive evidence that with alternative measures of the "Big Five," both of these psychometric desiderata have been met. Consider, for example, the intercorrelations in the upper-left quadrant of the table. If one examines the five intercorrelations shown beneath $N$ for self-report/adjective factor data, one sees that those measures correlated $r = +.50$ with the measures of $N$ obtained from peer rating/adjective factor data. This is evidence of convergent validity. Moreover, the four correlations displayed directly below this one, the $r$ values $+.19, +.01, -.05,$ and $-.09,$ indicate that the neuroticism measures based on self-report/adjective factor data did not correlate to any appreciable extent with measures of any of the remaining four traits obtained from the peer rating/adjective factor data. Here is evidence of discriminant validity.

Moving one column over in the upper-left quadrant of Table 6.13, the extraversion data can be examined in similar fashion, and it can be seen that the same pattern just described for neuroticism holds here as well. That is, the self-report/adjective factor measures of extraversion correlate substantially ($r = +.48$) with the peer rating/adjective factor measures of extraversion (convergent validity) but not appreciably ($r$ values of .00, −.01,

Table 6.13 Intercorrelations Among Adjective Factors and Questionnaire Scales in Both Self-Report Data and Peer-Rating Data

| | Self-Reports | | | | | | | | | |
| | Adjective Factors | | | | | NEO Personality Inventory | | | | |
| Mean Peer Rating | N | E | O | A | C | N | E | O | A | C |
|---|---|---|---|---|---|---|---|---|---|---|
| **Adjective Factors** | | | | | | | | | | |
| N | **50***** | 00 | 02 | 05 | -10 | **38***** | 06 | 08 | 01 | -09 |
| E | 19** | **48***** | 01 | 09 | -07 | 08 | **40***** | 16* | 04 | -03 |
| O | 01 | -01 | **49***** | -01 | -08 | 02 | 11 | **43***** | -06 | -11 |
| A | -05 | -14 | -18** | **49***** | -20*** | -08 | -26*** | -02 | **28***** | -19** |
| C | -09 | -08 | -12* | -08 | **40***** | -11 | -02 | -09 | 11 | **40***** |
| **NEO Personality Inventory** | | | | | | | | | | |
| N | **44***** | -03 | 00 | -03 | -15* | **42***** | 02 | 02 | -11 | -14* |
| E | 06 | **45***** | 16** | 00 | 06 | -04 | **47***** | 25*** | 02 | 02 |
| O | 07 | 08 | **45***** | 13* | -07 | 03 | 13* | **57***** | 02 | -13* |
| A | -06 | -11 | -15* | **45***** | -10 | -12 | -25*** | -02 | **30***** | -12 |
| C | -11 | -05 | -10 | -09 | **39***** | -14* | -02 | -08 | 08 | **43***** |

SOURCE: Adapted with permission from McCrae & Costa (1987, p. 87); see text for discussion.

NOTE: N = Neuroticism, E = Extroversion, O = Openness, A = Agreeableness, C = Conscientiousness. $N = 255$-267. Convergent correlations are shown in boldface. Decimal points are omitted.

$*p < .05. **p < .01. ***p < .001.$

−.14, and −.08) with any of the other peer rating/adjective factor measures (discriminant validity). Continuing in this fashion, the reader can see that throughout Table 6.13, evidence of both convergent and discriminant validity abounds: By and large, measures that in theory should intercorrelate do so, and measures that in theory should not intercorrelate do not.[20]

To sum up, by the statistical criteria generally regarded within the mainstream as appropriate for establishing the scientific validity of a taxonomy of fundamental dimensions of individual differences, the currently available evidence acquits the "Big Five" framework handsomely. The results of factor analyses carried out on adjective rating data have consistently pointed to the presence of five underlying factors. Moreover, a questionnaire instrument, the *NEO Personality Inventory*, has been constructed and proven useful for tapping the same five underlying factors. This body of evidence, then, constitutes a great deal of the empirical ground on which contemporary personality investigators have staked their endorsement of and enthusiasm for the "Big Five" as a kind of "periodic table of elements" for a scientific personality psychology. With this as a foundation, research into the sources and manifestations of personality differences can proceed systematically. We turn here to a brief discussion of these lines of contemporary inquiry.

## In Search of the Sources of Personality Differences and the Laws Governing Their Behavioral Manifestations

### Isolating the Relative Effects of Nature Versus Nurture as Causes of Personality Differences

Inasmuch as the founder of Galtonian inquiry was himself vitally interested in the problem of understanding the sources of individual differences in intelligence and character, it is scarcely surprising that this question has remained a focal one among contemporary personality investigators working within the neo-Galtonian research framework. To be sure, attention to the so-called nature versus nurture issue waned in several decades of the 20th century during which behavioristic thinking dominated scientific psychology (Kimble, 1993), but the demise of that school of thought in the latter third of the century opened space for renewed interest in the question. Hence, considerable effort has been devoted in the relatively recent past to empirically discovering the genetic basis of between-person variability with respect to a wide variety of psychological characteristics, including (but not limited to) characteristics of infant temperament and adult personality traits (see, e.g., Plomin, 1993).

As indicated at the outset of this chapter in Figure 6.1, the primary empirical issue of research along these lines is a statistic known as the *coefficient of heritability*. Commonly symbolized $h^2$, this statistic indexes the proportion of total (phenotypic) variation of an attribute or characteristic within a specified population that can be attributed to, or explained strictly in terms of, the genetic variation between individuals within that population. There is a wide variety of research designs for investigating questions of heritability, and there is also a variety of methods for calculating $h^2$, the method of choice depending on the exact version of the question an investigator is seeking to answer and on the constraints imposed by a particular research design. A full treatment of the complexities and subtleties encountered in this line of research would be well beyond the scope of this discussion (see Plomin, 1994). As in the above discussion of factor analysis, our objective here is simply to sketch the main contours of research in this domain and, most important, to take note of the pivotal role that correlational considerations play in inquiry of this sort.

By way of one illustration, we may consider a study by Saudino and Eaton (1991) undertaken to investigate the heritability of the childhood temperamental characteristic *activity* (plausibly an early precursor to the adult trait of extraversion). In that study, the investigators attached infants (mean age 8 months) to an "actometer," a mechanical device that records bodily movements. Among the infants studied were 39 pairs of monozygotic (MZ) twins and 21 pairs of same-sex dizygotic (DZ) twins. Data were gathered over a 2-day period, and as reported by Rowe (1997), the co-twin correlations for composite actometer activity measures were $r_{MZ} = +.76$ and $r_{DZ} = +.56$. Using one widely accepted method for computing the coefficient of heritability in studies of this sort, according to which $h^2 = 2(r_{MZ} - r_{DZ})$, Saudino and Eaton were thus able to estimate that $2(.76 - .56) = .40$, or 40% of the total between-infant variance in the activity levels of 8-month-olds was attributable to or explainable in terms of genetic factors, or "nature," leaving 60% of the variation attributable to other factors (i.e., shared and nonshared environmental factors).

Turning to research specifically focused on the "Big Five" personality characteristics, Rowe (1997) included in his recent discussion of this literature a summary of findings adduced by Loehlin (1992). Compiling results obtained in numerous previous studies worldwide, Loehlin reported that when computed in a way that takes into account the possibility of complex gene-gene interactions, correlation-based model-fitting estimates of the heritability of basic personality characteristics ranged from a low of .35 for agreeableness to a high of .49 for extraversion. For the other three of the "Big Five" dimensions, conscientiousness, emotional stability (neuroticism) and culture/openness, the estimated heritability coefficients were, respectively, .38, .41, and .45. In addition to these results, Loehlin also reported estimates of the proportions of between-person variance in the "Big Five" personality characteristics that could be attributed to shared environmental factors, or part of what would make up the "nurture" component of personality development.[21] These estimates were .02 for extraversion, .11 for agreeableness, .07 for conscientiousness, .07 for emotional stability, and .08 for culture/openness. Clearly, Loehlin's findings suggest that individual differences in those personality characteristics now widely presumed to be basic to human nature are rooted much more in variations of "nature" than in those of "nurture."

Concluding his discussion of this topic with a commentary on their implications for future research, Rowe (1997) stated,

> Despite scientific progress, many interesting and unresolved questions remain to complete a general theory of personality. Some fundamental questions are: Why do family environments have so little effect on personality development? What maintains genetic variability in personality over many generations? Is genetic variation related to human adaptive traits, or is it merely genetic "junk"? How does environmental transmission occur? Can the specific environmental causes of "non-shared" environmental variation be found? (p. 384)

Rowe (1997) advised his readers that further inquiry along the general lines sketched above, aimed at the questions posed in the quoted passage, "should occupy the next generation of social scientists concerned with trait variation" (p. 384). It seems not unreasonable to expect that this is precisely what will happen.

## Discovering the Lawful Regularities Governing the Behavioral Manifestations of Personality Traits

However interesting and important knowledge about the sources of personality differences may be, knowledge concerning the manifestations of those differences in various domains of human endeavor has long been seen to be of considerable consequence in its own right. Such knowledge, it is held, can be of importance with respect to the basic scientific objectives of what Stern long ago called *psychognostics,* but for obvious reasons can be seen as especially important for the practical purposes of what used to be known as *psychotechnics*.

Referring once again to the recently published *Handbook of Personality Psychology,* a voluminous work produced through the editorship of Hogan, Johnson, and Briggs (1997), the reader can find numerous examples of current research and theorizing along these lines. In the wake of a broad-based discussion by Wiggins and Trapnell (1997) of the "Big Five" as an overall framework for personality research, the Hogan et al. volume offers separate chapters devoted to extensive and empirically detailed discussions of "extraversion and its positive emotional core" (Watson & Clark, 1997, p. 767); "agreeableness [as a] dimension of personality" (Graziano & Eisenberg, 1997, p. 795); "conceptions and correlates of openness to experience" (McCrae & Costa, 1997, p. 826); and "conscientiousness and integrity at work" (Hogan & Ones, 1997, p. 849). In each of these pieces, the authors explore in some depth correlations between alternative measures of individual differences in the trait under consideration and various other measures of individual differences that on theoretical or conceptual grounds would be expected to covary with that particular trait.[22]

This work proceeds in fundamental accordance with the principles of neo-Galtonian inquiry as discussed earlier in this chapter. Whether these studies are regarded as, in and of themselves, revealing of empirical regularities of a lawful nature or whether they are regarded more cautiously simply as part of the scientific basis for such knowledge as it will one day be more fully articulated (cf. Buss & Craik, 1983; Ozer, 1990), they are in either case the very model of contemporary "nomothetic" personality studies. Having now considered the methods by which such inquiry is conducted, we are well positioned to probe its limitations as an approach to understanding human individuality.

# Summary

Having met successfully, at least to its own satisfaction, the challenge to "nomothetic" hegemony represented by the views of Gordon Allport and his (relatively few) sympathizers, the majority within the mainstream of scientific personality psychology has, for several decades now, been able to pursue the agenda of the "nomothetic" approach largely unopposed. That agenda has entailed identifying those fundamental, and presumably few, empirical continua by which human beings "in general" can be distinguished from one another and then empirically discovering (a) the sources or causes, in nature and/or nurture, of such individual differences and

(b) the consequences or effects of those differences in various domains of human behavior. The present chapter has been devoted to a discussion of research methods by means of which this agenda has been, and continues to be, pursued and of the major findings that have issued from this approach to date.

Through the use of concrete, albeit simple and hypothetical, research examples, I have sought to make clear in the present chapter how empirical research within the mainstream of contemporary personality psychology has proceeded within the larger framework of the neo-Galtonian paradigm for psychological research discussed in Chapter Five. The exposition thus began with a discussion of a simple neo-Galtonian experiment involving the random assignment of each of 20 research subjects to one of two experimental treatment conditions. The hypothetical research findings considered in this context indicated that approximately 20% of the total variance in the dependent variable could be accounted for or explained by the experimental treatment variable.

Following this, a group difference variable, gender, was added to the research design, with results indicating that by considering not only treatment differences but also gender differences and the treatment-by-gender interaction, fully 56% of the total variance in the dependent variable could be accounted for or explained.

As a final step in the expansion of this hypothetical study, individual differences in achievement motivation were taken into consideration, thus illustrating how personality factors (as traditionally understood within the "nomothetic" framework) are readily incorporated into neo-Galtonian inquiry. In the example discussed in the text, taking achievement motivation into account increased to 83% the proportion of total criterion variance that could be explained.

Highlighting what Danziger (1987) properly called the "primarily Galtonian" nature of neo-Galtonian inquiry, the discussion of these research examples was couched in terms of the concepts and methods of correlation and regression data analysis procedures, with notice being taken of the logical equivalence of those procedures to the $t$ test and/or ANOVA methods more familiar to most contemporary experimentalists.

In the latter portion of this chapter, some discussion was devoted to the nature of the empirical evidence accepted as warranting the currently widespread consensus among mainstream personality investigators that the "Big Five" trait dimensions of neuroticism, extraversion, openness, agreeableness, and conscientiousness may be regarded as providing a "universal and comprehensive" framework for personality measurement (McCrae & Costa, 1986). The chapter concluded with a brief discussion of current work aimed at identifying the sources, in nature and nurture, of individual differences along these five dimensions and the manifestations of those differences in various behavioral domains. A major objective of this discussion has been to set the stage for the critique of conventional "nomotheticism" that ensues in the following chapter.

# Notes

1.   The fact that the elemental traits are depicted in Figure 6.1 as five in number is not entirely fanciful. On the contrary, it mimics the number chosen by Thorndike (1911) to illustrate his conception of scientific studies of individuality (refer to Chapter Three, especially to Figure 3.1), and it also reflects the widespread consensus that has emerged among contemporary personality investigators holding that in general, human personalities are to be understood in terms of five basic dimensions. The empirical basis for this emergent view will be considered later in this chapter.

2.   Here and throughout this discussion, the hypothetical data sets will be kept small, and the numerical values will be kept both simple and "tidy," so as to highlight the computational methods that are of central interest. No suggestion is hereby intended that actual research would typically entail such small sample sizes, simple measures, or "tidy" data. By the same token, however, it should be emphasized that the concessions to simplicity made here in no way compromise the integrity of the examples as instruments for illustrating the methods in question.

3.   The computation of such statistics in data analysis does not, of course, turn a neo-Galtonian experiment into a correlational study. This latter distinction hinges on the way in which the status of research subjects with respect to the independent/predictor variable(s) is determined, not on the computational procedures used to analyze the data. For a thorough treatment of the quantitative equivalence between ANOVA and correlation/regression, the reader is once again referred to Kerlinger and Pedhazur (1974).

4.   The "effect coding" procedure described here is also readily applicable to variables constituted of more than two categories. However, the coding schemes do become somewhat unwieldy and the computations rather more tedious in such designs, and because nothing of fundamental conceptual significance changes when such designs are adopted, no illustration of them will be undertaken here. The interested reader is referred to Kerlinger and Pedhazur's (1974) superb text for a thorough discussion of the relevant material.

5.   Of course, raw score computational formulas exist for determining $r$. But any such formula is necessarily mathematically equivalent to computing the average of the cross products of $z$ scores, because that is what the Pearson $r$ literally is. To actually go through the computational steps required to transform raw scores into standard scores prior to computing the correlation, therefore, is only to make explicit what otherwise happens "by default," as it were.

6. There are 18 degrees of freedom associated with a correlation based on 20 pairs of observations, and the so-called critical value of $r$ at alpha = .05 with 18 degrees of freedom (i.e., the value that must be exceeded to infer the statistical significance of the empirical relationship under discussion here) is $r = .378$.

7. Each of these simple correlations is statistically significant by commonly accepted criteria. Also, no importance attaches to the fact that the correlation between $Y$ and $M \times G$, $r_{Y,M\times G} = -.45$, is the inverse of the correlation between $Y$ and $M$, $r_{Y,M} = +.45$. This just happens to be how the results worked out in this particular example.

8. In a great many, perhaps most, instances in which nonexperimental individual and group differences are being examined, the predictor variables are themselves intercorrelated, at least to some degree. Under these conditions, simple $r^2$ values do not sum to $R^2$, a squared multiple correlation. This circumstance complicates computational procedures but in no way alters the essential conceptual points under development here.

9. Once again, the number given here is a computer-generated value in which base figures are extended to 7 decimal places, not the truncated values given in the text. As a result, hand calculation using the latter values will result in slight discrepancies.

10. Goldberg's allusion here was to the crisis of confidence in trait-based approaches to the study of personality sparked by Walter Mischel's highly influential 1968 book, *Personality and Assessment*. An extended treatment of this epoch in the 20th-century history of scientific personality psychology can be found in Lamiell (1987).

11. I do not claim here to have counted the terms in Allport and Odbert's (1936) list, but report instead the figure they themselves gave (p. 18).

12. Of course, Allport would eventually be harshly critical of exclusive reliance on such a scheme for scientific personality studies (refer to discussion in Chapter Four). There is a very real sense, therefore, in which Allport can be regarded as both "father" to and critic of the "Big Five," a point that has been nicely illuminated by John and Robins (1993).

13. In analyses of the sort being discussed here, only the absolute magnitude of the correlations is relevant. The signs are in this instance irrelevant because they can be reversed simply by reversing the arbitrary first-versus-second listing of the adjectives in a given item pair. To illustrate: If ratings of target peers on the pair *calm* (1) *versus worrying* (7) correlate $r = -.80$ with ratings on the pair *nervous* (1) *versus at-ease* (7), this correlation could be reversed, to the value $r = +.80$, simply by reversing the (arbitrary) scoring on one of the pairs so that, for example, the second pair is redefined to be *at-ease* (1) *versus nervous* (7).

14. Note that the number of intercorrelations in the set could be quite large. In the hypothetical study described here, for example, in which subjects would be rating peers with reference to 80 item pairs, there would be $(80^2 - 80)/2 = 380$ nonredundant pairwise item intercorrelations.

15. Note that factor analysis does not bear the burden of interpreting the factors that are statistically isolated. This is something that requires rational

considerations on the part of the investigator(s). So, for example, the results of a factor analysis might signal that statistically speaking, Variables 1, 2, and 3 have "something" in common. The task of specifying just what that "something" is falls to the investigator(s) or, speaking more broadly, the scientific community.

16.   Form S of the actual *NEO Personality Inventory* contains items worded in the first person, as are those in Table 6.11. In responding to the items, the "target" individual is thus characterizing him- or herself. There is also a Form R of the *Inventory*, in which the same items are worded in the third person, and thus with this form of the inventory, the "target individual" is being characterized by someone else. The items in Table 6.11 thus mimic items on Form S of the actual *NEO Personality Inventory*, and in all references to that inventory which follow, Form S is meant unless otherwise indicated. However, it should be emphasized that all conceptual and technical points being developed in this chapter would apply equally to Form R data.

17.   The technique of wording items in opposite "directions" is often used in the construction of personality assessment devices as a procedural hedge against the possibility that the target might respond thoughtlessly by simply marking, say, *agree*, to all items. Where item wording has been manipulated in the way described, such a consistent response pattern would reflect a markedly inconsistent psychological pattern and thus be "flagged" as untrustworthy. See in this regard the discussion by Wiggins (1973) of "response sets" and "response styles."

18.   Within each of the "Big Five" categories, called "domains," six subcategories, called "facets," are assessed. On the actual *NEO Personality Inventory*, each facet is assessed by 8 items. Hence, each of the "Big Five" domains is assessed by 48 items, resulting in a grand total for the entire *NEO Inventory* of 240 items.

19.   The reader should recall here that there are two forms of the *NEO Personality Inventory*, as mentioned in Endnote #16.

20.   For readers who might desire it, a far more extensive discussion of the voluminous evidence bearing on the convergent and discriminant validity of the five-factor model and the *NEO Personality Inventory* has been provided by Wiggins and Trapnell (1997).

21.   The other part would be *nonshared environmental factors*, itself said to comprise "the lasting consequences of experiences uniquely changing each person" and "measurement error" (Rowe, 1997, p. 380).

22.   To cite just a few of the many available examples, in Watson and Clark (1997) see Table VI, p. 785; in Graziano and Eisenberg (1997) see pp. 804 and 807, as well as the discussion on p. 809 in which the authors consider evidence pertaining to the heritability of agreeableness; in McCrae and Costa (1997), see Table I, p. 829; in Hogan and Ones (1997), see discussion on pp. 857-858.

# Chapter Seven

## Contemporary "Nomotheticism" in Critical Perspective

Some 65 years have now passed since Gordon Allport sought to highlight the importance in a psychology of personality of the epistemic distinction that the German philosopher Wilhelm Windelband had termed *nomothetic* and *idiographic* in 1894 (Allport, 1937a). The controversy Allport thereby touched off was discussed in Chapter Four. There, it was seen that at virtually every turn, debate has led to an emphatic rejection by the majority within the mainstream of calls for a "more idiographic" psychology of personality and to an equally decisive affirmation of the appropriateness of, indeed necessity for, a "strictly nomothetic" pursuit of the discipline's scientific objectives. Most centrally, this endeavor would entail systematic, statistical studies of individual and group differences. Chapter Six was devoted to a discussion of what this paradigmatic commitment has meant methodologically and where it has led investigators empirically as of the conclusion of the 20th century.

Throughout the course of these historic developments, the understanding of the meanings of the expressions nomothetic and idiographic that has prevailed among personality investigators is well captured by the following:

> Personality traits and types allow us to compare one person with another. This is the usual approach in personality research, the *nomothetic* approach. Groups of individuals are studied, and the people are compared by applying the same concepts (usually traits) to each person. . . . Alternatively, some psychologists study personality without focusing on individual differences. The

*idiographic* approach studies individuals one at a time, without making comparisons with other people. (Cloninger, 1996, p. 5; emphasis in original)[1]

As long-standing and widely shared as these conceptions of idiographic and nomothetic are, they bear only a tenuous relationship to the meanings of the terms as Windelband himself originally understood them (Lamiell, 1998). As far as it goes, the definition of idiographic given above is consistent with Windelband's conception, but that definition is also much narrower in scope than the meaning that the philosopher first intended. What is vastly more problematic is the fact that the definition of nomothetic given above articulates not at all with Windelband's understanding as it would properly be applied to the knowledge objectives of a psychology of personality.

This latter point is of surpassing importance and one that, fatefully, critics of "mainstream nomotheticism," including but not limited to Allport, consistently have either failed to fully appreciate or decided to overlook. The problem is that in referring to the doctrinaire *common trait* psychology of personality as a "nomothetic" approach, critics of that approach have only encouraged its practitioners to believe that it is, in fact, precisely what they have always most wanted it to be: nomothetic on the model of the natural sciences, and so in precisely the sense intended by Windelband. Branding adherents of the common trait approach as "nomotheticists" thus has been tantamount to throwing them into the proverbial briar patch. Deep within the tangles of that rhetorical thicket, the prized but ill-begotten label "nomothetic" is easily defended, and the conviction is merely fortified that statistical knowledge about individual and group differences constitutes knowledge of general laws governing the behavior or psychological functioning of individuals. The purpose of the present chapter is to clarify that view and explain why it is untenable.

## *Geschichte und Naturwissenschaft:* A Brief Look at Windelband's (1894) History and Natural Science

*Hochansehnliche Versammlung! Es ist ein wertvolles Vorrecht des Rektors, daß er am Stiftungsfest der Universität das Ohr ihrer Gäste und ihrer Mitglieder für einen Gegenstand aus der von ihm vertretenen Wissenschaft in Anspruch nehmen darf.*[2]

Thus began Windelband the speech he delivered on May 1, 1894. The occasion was his assumption of the Rectorship of the University of Strasburg on the 273rd anniversary of that university's founding. The text Windelband

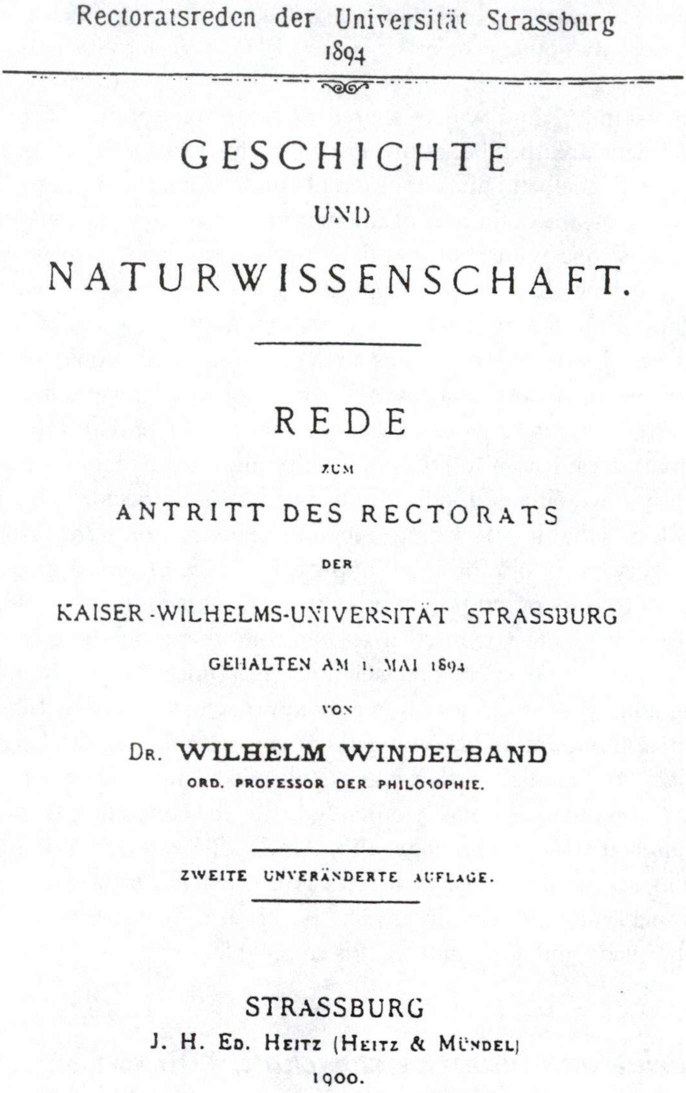

Rectoratsreden der Universität Strassburg
1894

# GESCHICHTE

UND

# NATURWISSENSCHAFT.

## REDE

ZUM

### ANTRITT DES RECTORATS

DER

#### KAISER-WILHELMS-UNIVERSITÄT STRASSBURG

GEHALTEN AM 1. MAI 1894

VON

### Dr. WILHELM WINDELBAND

ORD. PROFESSOR DER PHILOSOPHIE.

ZWEITE UNVERÄNDERTE AUFLAGE.

## STRASSBURG

J. H. Ed. Heitz (Heitz & Mündel)

1900.

Figure 7.1    Facsimile of Title Page From the Second Unrevised Edition of
Windelband's 1894 Speech: History and Natural Science

had prepared for the event was entitled *Geschichte und Naturwissenschaft
(History and Natural Science),* and in the course of that speech, he introduced
the neologisms nomothetic and idiographic. Given the problem presented by
the rhetorical thicket mentioned above, it is most worthwhile to begin the
discussion with a consideration of what Windelband himself actually said in
his speech, viewed within its own historical context.

## Minting the Expressions: Nomothetic and Idiographic

One of the first distinctions drawn by Windelband was that between the nonempirical or *rational* sciences *(die rationalen Wissenschaften)*, logic and mathematics, and the *empirical* sciences *(die Erfahrungswissenschaften)*, disciplines engaged in some way or another with the task of gaining knowledge about the experienced world. Within the latter category, Windelband drew the further distinction between the *natural* sciences *(die Naturwissenschaften)* and the *sciences of the spirit (die Geisteswissenschaften)*, or what would commonly be referred to in English as the *moral sciences* or *humanities*. Windelband introduced this distinction within the context of a discussion of the division of labor that had arisen within the German academy in the latter part of the 19th century. He questioned the advisability of such intellectual compartmentalization and, significantly for our purposes here, did so partly on the grounds that no strict division between the natural sciences and the humanities could do justice to the emerging discipline of psychology. Windelband said,

> [A]n empirical discipline of such significance as psychology is not to be accommodated by the categories of the natural sciences and the humanities; to judge by its subject, it can only be characterized as a humanity, and in a certain sense as the foundation of all of the others; but its entire procedure, its methodological arsenal, is from beginning to end that of the natural sciences. For this reason, psychology has had to allow itself to be characterized at times as the "natural science of inner sense" or even as "the natural science of the mental" *(geistige Naturwissenschaft)*. (Windelband, 1894/1998, p. 11)

Windelband then asked rhetorically: "In what, then, does the methodological relationship of psychology to the natural sciences consist?" and he answered his own question as follows:

> Obviously, in the fact that, like the natural sciences, psychology identifies, gathers and analyzes its facts only from the standpoint, and toward the end, of thereby understanding the general lawfulness [*die allgemeine Gesetzmäßigkeit*] to which these facts submit. (Windelband, 1894/1998, p. 12)

Windelband juxtaposed these remarks with the following:

> In contrast to the foregoing, the many empirical disciplines which one otherwise properly labels as humanities are directed decidedly to the complete and exhaustive portrayal of a particular, more or less protracted occurrence of a unique, temporally circumscribed reality. On this side, too, the subjects, and the special concepts through which one secures their understanding, are of

great variety. One deals here with an isolated event or an interconnected
sequence of acts and fates, with the peculiarity and development of a language,
religion or legal system, of a product of literature, of art or of science.
(Windelband, 1894/1998, p. 12)

Having in this way distinguished the overriding knowledge objectives of
the natural sciences from those of the humanities, Windelband underscored
his point by drawing attention to the following:

The principle of classification is the formal character of the sought-after knowledge. Some [disciplines] seek general laws, the other [disciplines seek] special
historical facts. . . . Thus is this difference connected to every important and
decisive relationship in human understanding that has been recognized from the
time of Socrates as the fundamental relationship of all scientific thought: the
relationship of the general to the particular. (Windelband, 1894/1998, p. 12)

Windelband continued:

So we may say that the empirical sciences seek in the knowledge of reality
either the general in the form of the natural law or the particular in the historically determined form *[Gestalt]*. They consider in one part the ever-enduring
form, in the other part the unique content, determined within itself, of an
actual happening. The one comprise sciences of law, the other sciences of
events; the former teach us what always is *[was immer ist]*, the latter what once
was *[was einmal war]*. If one may resort to neologisms, it can be said that
*scientific thought is in the one case nomothetic, in the other idiographic.*
(Windelband, 1894/1998, p. 13; emphasis added)

## Probing Windelband's Meanings

In light of modern understanding of the terms nomothetic and idiographic,
as reflected, for example, in the above quotation of Cloninger (1996), there
are several points warranting amplification here. The first has to do with
the honorific terms *science* and *scientific*.

The German term for science is *Wissenschaft,* a term with roots referring to
a *body of knowledge.* Some disciplines have as their objective the accumulation of a body of nomothetic knowledge, whereas the goal of other disciplines
is a body of idiographic knowledge. In German, both categories of disciplines
are understood to be empirical, and both are referred to as sciences: *die
Erfahrungs-wissenschaften* are comprised of *die Natur-wissenschaften* and *die
Geistes-wissenschaften.*

In English, however, the favored expression for the latter group of disciplines, humanities, not only makes no reference to science but is also often used in ways that emphasize a contrast with science (as, for example, when one asks whether another has a greater interest in the sciences or the humanities).[3] One can only speculate on the role played by this linguistic difference in the gradual ascendance among personality investigators of the view that the quest for idiographic knowledge is a non- and perhaps even antiscientific undertaking. In any case, the following may be stated with confidence: First, this is *not* a view that Windelband can be said to have shared, for he did not equate nomothetic knowledge with scientific knowledge. He did link nomothetic knowledge with the natural sciences, but he spoke of idiographic knowledge as a kind of knowledge sought within another category of disciplines that also qualified as empirical *Wissenschaften*.

Second, and Windelband's view notwithstanding, we saw in Chapter Four that the equation of nomothetic knowledge with science and idiographic knowledge with non- or even antiscience *is* a view that came to dominate personality psychologists' understanding of the terms.

Third, within the context of a psychology feverishly concerned to be widely recognized within the scholarly community as having achieved, and as maintaining, the status of a science on the model of the natural sciences, the pursuit of (allegedly) non- or even antiscientific knowledge would not qualify as a worthy undertaking (refer again to Chapter Four of this volume, and especially to the discussion of the works by Eysenck, 1954; Holt, 1962; Nunnally, 1967; Sanford, 1963; and Skaggs, 1945).

An additional point to be made here is that, in Windelband's view, idiographic inquiry would not necessarily entail the study of individual persons. Without question, such could be the case, and this is why it is not inappropriate to regard Cloninger's (1996) description of idiographic as consistent with Windelband's usage. For Windelband, however, idiographic inquiry was a much more inclusive category, in which the decisive question was not one of level of analysis but instead one of *knowledge objectives*. When the goal of an investigation, whatever its specific subject matter, is to gain knowledge of "what once was" *(was einmal war)*, then from the perspective adopted by Windelband, the objectives of that investigation would qualify as idiographic in nature. The level-of-analysis question is left open. Investigation might indeed be focused on "a single man," but it might just as well be trained on "an entire folk," perhaps emphasizing historical developments in a people's language, cultural customs, religious practices, or legal codes.[4]

All this concerning Windelband's understanding of idiography aside, our primary concern in this chapter really has much more to do with a proper understanding of the term nomothetic. We have seen that Windelband explicitly defined nomothetic knowledge as knowledge of "what always is" *(was immer ist)* and that he regarded such knowledge as just the sort captured by and hence expressible in terms of general laws. As was the case when we considered the understanding the early "Wundtian" experimentalists had of their discipline as a "general psychology," in Chapter Two, clarity on the meaning of the term *general* is crucial here.

It was explained in the previous discussion of this point that the German term for general, *allgemein*, developed as a contracted form of the expression *allen gemein*, meaning "common to all." Writing in 1894, this is without doubt the meaning of general that Windelband intended in his references to "general laws" *(allgemeine Gesetze)*. In his view, a general law governing the behavior of falling bodies (for example) would be a law common to all falling bodies and, as such, one that would hold for, or apply to, *each particular one of many discrete instances of falling bodies*. If the law did not hold in just this way, then the validity of the claim that the law could be generalized over instances of falling bodies (i.e., that the law captured something common to all instances of falling bodies) would be cast into doubt. For science to progress, that doubt would have to be resolved, either by convincingly explaining away those particular instances in which the law did not hold as merely apparent failures attributable to some sort of procedural error (e.g., in observation or measurement) or by reformulating the law so that those particular instances in which the law had failed were now either accounted for or explicitly acknowledged as falling outside the domain of instances over which the generality of the law would henceforth be asserted.

It is precisely the fact that a general law applies to—indeed, governs— individual cases that makes it a general law in the sense of *allen gemein*. Stated otherwise, the fact that such a law covers any given particular instance of the phenomenon it is said to cover enables one to know, through that law, what is common to all those particular instances. It follows that to achieve nomothetic knowledge in the sense intended by Windelband, it is necessary to (among other things) (a) specify the events or entities over which a putatively general law should generalize and (b) devise and execute some means of checking to see whether or not, empirically, the law does in fact hold for each of those many individual events or entities. If it does not, then it cannot be said to constitute knowledge of "what always is" within the domain of those particular events or entities; it does not establish something common to all of those events or entities; it is not a general law covering those events/entities; and it does not embody nomothetic knowledge of those events/entities in the sense of nomothetic intended by Windelband (1894).[5]

The brand of psychology known to Windelband was the experimental psychology of the original Wundtian model. As noted previously, that psychology was a discipline seeking, through the systematic investigation of individual cases, knowledge of the general laws presumed to govern the mental life of individual beings. In other words, the discipline Wundt himself called, properly, an *individual* psychology was one in which both its knowledge objectives and its corresponding "N = 1" methods were thoroughly nomothetic in precisely the sense of that term meant by Windelband.

The discipline that by 1937 would be accepted widely as a nomothetic approach to the scientific study of personality was radically different from Wundtian experimental psychology. In fact, the common trait psychology that Allport (1937a) found so limited as a framework within which to grasp human individuality was housed within the neo-Galtonian model for psychological research that had long since replaced—even *dis*placed—the Wundtian model (Danziger, 1987, 1990). In the course of this development, the statistical way of thinking about psychological phenomena that was so tangential to Wundtian experimentation but so very essential to neo-Galtonian inquiry had fundamentally altered psychologists' understanding of "general."

To speak statistically of some empirical state of affairs as holding true "in general" is to speak about what is found to be the case *on average*. Conceptually, this is vastly different from speaking about what holds true in general in the above-noted sense of "common to all": Something that holds true on average need not be, and typically will not be, true of all of the entities or events over which that average has been compiled and, indeed, might very well not be true of any of them. There exists, then, a significant epistemic gap between statements about what is generally true in the sense of "common to all" proper to Wundt's general/experimental/individual psychology, and statements about what is generally true in the sense of "on average" proper to Galtonian and neo-Galtonian investigations of aggregates. Whereas Windelband attached the nomothetic *concept* to the former meaning of general, personality investigators on both sides of the nomothetic-idiographic debate were by 1937 pinning the *nomothetic label* onto the latter meaning of general.

Even at the time, prominent figures within psychology questioned this usage of the term nomothetic. Kurt Lewin (1890-1947), for example, emphatically rejected the notion that statistical regularities gleaned from aggregate data could be regarded as constituting nomothetic laws of behavior or human psychological life (Lewin, 1935). Egon Brunswik (1903-1955) explicitly agreed with Lewin on this point (Brunswik, 1943). Both scholars understood "nomothetic" in the sense that according to my thesis above,

Windelband meant it.[6] In contrast, Holt (1962) made brief mention of Brunswik's understanding of nomothetic, but then, as noted in Chapter Four, summarily rejected Brunswik's view in favor of the one that by 1962 was almost universally accepted among investigators who regarded themselves as "personality psychologists."

The two meanings of general, and hence of nomothetic, that became confounded as neo-Galtonian thinking became paradigmatic for psychological research can be made to seem compatible with one another only by the dubious grace of what was christened in Chapter Five the "Thorndike maneuver." That maneuver, it will be recalled, entails an acceptance of the view that the aggregate statistical findings issuing from studies of variables marking differences between individuals provide scientific warrant for knowledge claims concerning the behavior/psychological functioning of individuals. As explained in Chapter Five, this conceptual maneuver accords with a view of statistical knowledge that had been championed in the mid-19th century by the historian Henry Thomas Buckle, but rejected by his contemporary John Venn. Moreover, that was the maneuver that made the neo-Galtonian model for psychological research seem so suited, in perfectly symmetrical fashion, to the basic theoretical purposes of psychognostics as well as to the practical, applied purposes of psychotechnics.

Under the terms of the "Thorndike maneuver," a maneuver Allport himself implicitly endorsed the moment he accepted the "empirical continua" constituted of dimensions of individual differences as legitimate components of a trait psychology of personality (refer to discussion of this point in Chapter Four), the confound identified above concerning the meanings of general and nomothetic becomes essentially invisible. The reason for this is that from the perspective imposed by that maneuver, the study of many individuals simultaneously through large-scale statistical investigations on the neo-Galtonian model appears simply as an alternative, but enticingly more practical and efficient, means to the same knowledge ends as the study of many individuals, one by one, in the original Wundtian model. The problem before us, then, is to critically appraise the long-presumed conceptual integrity of this view.

## Method as Metaphysics in the
## Explanatory Pretensions of Neo-Galtonian Inquiry

The previous chapter sketched the methods through which knowledge of the lawful regularities presumed to govern individual behavior is sought within the neo-Galtonian research paradigm. In that context, three hypothetical investigations were discussed in order of increasing complexity, so as to illustrate the statistical analysis procedures that not only drive such inquiry but also structure the explanations that such inquiry is widely, but mistakenly, seen to entitle. It is to a closer analysis of this matter of *explanation* that we turn our attention here.

It will be recalled that the three hypothetical studies discussed in Chapter Six were variations on a simple experiment in which each of 20 children was assigned at random to one of two spelling classes employing different instructional methods. At the conclusion of the school term, a spelling test was administered to all 20 pupils, with scores on the test defining the dependent (criterion) variable *(Y)*. The first hypothetical study investigated only the relationship between criterion performance and method of instruction *(M)*. The second study included an investigation of gender *(G)* as an independent factor in criterion performance and thus also allowed the investigation of an instructional method-by-gender interaction *(M × G)*. Finally, a third hypothetical study incorporated, in addition to the above, an investigation of the role of individual differences in achievement motivation *(AM)*. The statistical relationships uncovered in these three hypothetical studies were defined by Equations 6.9, 6.11, and 6.13, reproduced here for the reader's convenience (along with the simple/multiple correlations respectively associated with each).

$$\hat{Y}_p = 10.90 + 1.3(M_p) \quad (r = .45) \tag{6.9}$$

$$\hat{Y}_p = 10.90 + 1.3(M_p) + 1.1(G_p) \\ - 1.3(M_p \times G_p) \quad (R = .74) \tag{6.11}$$

$$\hat{Y}_p = 5.525 + 1.3(M_p) + 1.1(G_p) - 1.3(M_p \times G_p) \\ + .107(AM_p) \quad (R = .91) \tag{6.13}$$

The question central to our present concerns is this: How is knowledge of the sort conveyed by these expressions translated into explanations for the behavior (criterion performance) of individual pupils?

To answer this question, it is first necessary to grasp that the sought-after explanations always and necessarily take as their point of departure the overall (or "grand") mean of the dependent variable within a given study. This follows from the fact that what is actually analyzed through the statistical techniques proper to neo-Galtonian inquiry (i.e., the data analysis procedures issuing in the putatively explanatory models) is variation around that overall mean. Logically, there is nothing in a correlation/regression analysis per se or in its ANOVA (analysis of variance) equivalent from which to fashion an explanation for the finding that (to abide by the illustrative example under present consideration) the average number of words on a 20-item exam correctly spelled by 20 fourth graders was 10.90 instead of, say, 9.26 or 13.71 or some other value. On the contrary, the analytic procedure begins at the grand mean, that is, with the empirical fact that that mean "just is" whatever it has been found to be within a particular study, and analysis proceeds from that point.[7] It follows from these considerations that insofar as the results of such analyses may rightly be said to "explain" anything at all about individual behavior—and this is the idea that is under critical examination here—that which is explained could not possibly be the individual's behavior as such, but instead could merely be, at best, the deviation of that behavior from the overall mean. To be consistent with the logic of traditional statistical analyses, therefore, discussion of the individual case must begin at the grand mean and proceed from there, moving along the scale of criterion measurement away from that fixed value and then, perhaps, back toward it again, in accordance with the dictates of the empirical law(s) in terms of which the sought-after explanation is being articulated. A concrete illustration of this point will serve to clarify matters.

Let us view Equation 6.9 as an empirical law through which one might seek to explain the respective relative performances of individual pupils in the first of the three hypothetical experiments. Knowing that that overall mean was 10.90 and proceeding in accordance with the above considerations, this law would be seen to entitle the inference that the effect of exposure to the "formal drill" method of instruction was to drive the respective relative performances of each of the 10 students exposed to that treatment 1.3 units downward from the overall mean along the criterion scale of measurement, to the value 9.60. Similarly, the same law would be seen as evidence that the effect of exposure to the "silent reading" method of instruction was to drive the respective relative performances of each of the 10 students exposed to that treatment 1.3 units upward from the overall mean along the criterion scale of measurement, to the value 12.20.[8]

Entailed in the foregoing is the notion that were the law represented by Equation 6.9 fully explanatory of the respective relative performances of the 20 individual pupils, then the criterion score of each of the 10 who had been exposed to the formal drill method of instruction would have been precisely 9.60 and that of each of the 10 who had been exposed to the silent reading method of instruction would have been precisely 12.20. The fact that these theoretical expectations were not empirically realized in any one case would not be seen as evidence contraindicating the relevance of the law represented by Equation 6.9 to understanding the behavior of each of the

20 individual pupils studied. On the contrary, this empirical state of affairs would be taken to indicate that additional factors must have been at work in determining individual pupils' respective relative performances above, beyond, and possibly even counter to—*but not instead of*—the influence of method of instruction. In this hypothetical case, then, the scientific challenge would be seen as that of searching for additional lawful regularities that would extend the partial explanation seen to have been achieved through Equation 6.9.

Progress in this regard might be achieved through a study incorporating gender as a factor contributing to relative performance, as in the second of the three hypothetical studies described in Chapter Six. The results of that hypothetical study are represented by Equation 6.11 above, and considering that equation, we may see how it would be taken to improve on the explanatory achievements of Equation 6.9.

Starting again at the grand mean, Equation 6.11 retains the notion that the effect of exposure to the formal drill method of instruction was to drive the respective relative performances of each of the 10 students exposed to that treatment 1.3 units downward along the criterion scale of measurement, to the value 9.60, whereas the effect of exposure to the silent reading method of instruction was to drive the respective relative performances of each of the 10 students exposed to that treatment 1.3 units in the opposite direction along the same scale, to the value 12.20. However, the lawful regularity seen to be revealed by Equation 6.11 stipulates further that in and of itself, being female drove the relative performance of each girl 1.1 scale units upward along the criterion scale of measurement, whereas being male drove the relative performance of each boy an equivalent amount (1.1 scale units) downward along that scale. Further refining the explanation for individual pupils' performances, Equation 6.11 stipulates that over and above the separate effects of instructional method and gender, the joint effect of being a boy taught by formal drill or a girl taught by the silent reading method was to drive the relative performance of each of those five boys and five girls 1.3 units downward along the criterion scale of measurement, whereas the joint effect of being a boy taught by the silent reading method or a girl taught by formal drill was to drive the relative performance of each of those five boys and five girls 1.3 units upward along that scale.

The above, then, articulates the dynamics specified by Equation 6.11 when that equation is viewed as a law applicable to an explanation for the respective relative criterion performances of each of the 20 individual pupils. Here, again, the notion is that if that law were fully explanatory in this respect, then the criterion score of each boy pupil exposed to the formal drill method of instruction would have been precisely 7.20 (bearing in mind the simplifying disclaimer stated in Endnote #8), that of each boy pupil exposed to the silent reading method 12.40, and that of each girl pupil 12.00. The fact that the actual scores of 18 of the 20 pupils deviated to one degree or another from these expectations would not be taken as evidence against the validity of partially explaining each individual case in the manner described. Instead, and just as before, this fact would be taken to indicate that there must have been some additional factor(s) determinative of individual pupils' respective relative performances apart from and possibly counter to, *but not instead of,* those stipulated by Equation 6.11.

The third of the three hypothetical experiments discussed in Chapter Six illustrates one possibility here, namely, that a personality variable such as achievement motivation *(AM)* could be found to "have an effect" on each child's relative criterion performance over, above, and possibly counter to the "effects" revealed through the less comprehensive laws represented by Equations 6.9 and 6.11. Equation 6.13 represents the results of a study designed to investigate this possibility and stipulates how the "effect" of achievement motivation would be incorporated into an explanation for any given individual pupil's relative criterion performance.[9]

To illustrate, let us consider the case of Pupil 1, a boy with an *AM* score of 30 exposed to the formal drill method of instruction. Incorporating the previously discussed findings, Equation 6.13 again specifies the "effect" of formal drill as a movement of 1.3 criterion scale units downward along the scale of criterion measurement, from a starting position of 5.525 to the value 4.225.[10] The "effect" of being a boy is again indexed as movement another 1.1 units downward on the criterion scale, from 4.225 to 3.125, and the joint "effect" of these two factors is indexed as movement of an additional 1.3 units downward on the criterion scale, to 1.825. Finally, the "effect" of having a level of achievement motivation commensurate with an *AM* score of 30 is indexed as movement of $(.107) \times (30) = 3.21$ criterion scale units *upward* from 1.825, to a value of 5.035.[11]

Here again, the discrepancy between the value 5.035 and the criterion score of 6 actually obtained by Pupil 1 would not be regarded as in any way contradictory of the relevance of Equation 6.13 to an explanation of Pupil 1's relative criterion performance. Instead, this discrepancy would be seen as yet another reflection of the incompleteness of the law expressed by that equation, that is, as an indication that one or more factors beyond those incorporated into Equation 6.13 must have been influential.[12]

In Chapter Six, mention was made of the ease with which this approach to empirical investigation can be expanded to accommodate the consideration of additional variables—including but not limited to personality variables such as one (or some, or even all) of the "Big Five." But however complex or expansive the content of the investigation might become, the basic objective and the means to its realization would remain the same. Put simply, the objective is always to explain individuals' respective relative positions on criterion variables taken to index behaviors of theoretical and/or practical interest, and the explanation that is sought is one that can be articulated in terms of the "effects" of individual and/or group difference factors, whether considered alone or in combination with each other and/or "situational" or experimental treatment variables. Inherent in neo-Galtonian inquiry as a basis for articulating scientific explanations for individual behavior/ psychological functioning—and it must be kept firmly in mind that the manner in which neo-Galtonian inquiry is seen to serve this objective is what is under critical examination here—is the notion that the degree or magnitude of the statistical relationship between some criterion/dependent variable and some predictor/independent variable(s) indexes the "effect(s)" or "influence(s)" of the latter on the former. In neo-Galtonian psychological investigation, method and metaphysics fuse.

If a search of the literature of contemporary trait psychology for a discussion of explanation expressly aligned with the foregoing would prove futile, that is only because adherents of the received view have themselves been less than entirely clear on the epistemic and metaphysical implications of their own empirical practices.[13] What is beyond doubt is the paradigmatic commitment within the mainstream to the notions that (a) individual and group difference factors, including but not limited to personality traits, do exert causal influences in the production of individual behavior (cf. McCrae & Costa, 1995) and that (b) the statistical findings of neo-Galtonian inquiry bear directly on this conviction by empirically reflecting the nature and extent of those presumed influences. It is difficult to see how any thoroughgoing elucidation of these dual notions could lead to a conception of behavioral explanation within the dominant paradigm that would differ in any significant way from what has been described above.

On this understanding, individuals are essentially congeries of "basic tendencies" and conduits of external influences.[14] The assumption is that in various (and doubtless highly complex) combinations, these tendencies and influences are wholly determinative of individual behavior, and the task of a science of human individuality is to discover the specifics of these determinations. The entire enterprise is predicated on the assumption that "in the moral [i.e., human psycho-social] world, as in the physical . . . all is order, symmetry, and law" (Buckle, 1857/1898; quoted in Porter, 1986, p. 61).

Nor is this assumption tempered in any way by disavowals of claims to precise knowledge of the underlying processes presumed to be the actual determinants of behavior. Invoking Newton's famed *"Hypotheses non fingo!"* for example, McCrae and Costa (1995) argued that *"explanations need not specify causal mechanisms"* (p. 246, emphasis in original). Nevertheless, those authors made clear their adherence to the assumptions that (a) such causal mechanisms do exist, (b) they are determinative of individual behavior, (c) they are, at least in principle, empirically specifiable, and (d) the quest for knowledge of them is entirely consistent with the mission of a scientific personality psychology.

It is noteworthy that in their discussion of this issue, McCrae and Costa (1995) embraced a view strikingly similar to that adopted more than a century ago by Ebbinghaus (1896b) in his harsh critique of the call by Wilhelm Dilthey (1833-1911) in 1894 for an *understanding* psychology *(eine verstehende Psychologie)* as an alternative to the *explanatory* psychology *(die erklärende Psychologie)* that was already dominating mainstream thinking. Dilthey (1894) had seen in the latter psychology a clear commitment to an essentially mechanistic conception of human mental life and behavior, a conception of psychological science patterned after the matter-in-motion model of Newtonian physics. He was convinced that such a psychology would never be able to construct satisfactory accounts of the meanings that human beings invest in their actions and in the actions of their fellow human beings.

Ebbinghaus (1896b) argued that the psychology Dilthey had attacked was a "straw man," and in elaborating this point, he implored his readers,

> [R]ecall the writings of [the physicist and philosopher] E. Mach, who never tired in his [defense of the view that] *the mechanical explanation of things is not a necessary component of genuine and truly scientific investigations of nature.* Rather, when such occurs at all, it is a supererogatory matter, so to say. To see this [in psychology], one need look no further than to the law of association. Psychologists see a causal relationship in the co-occurrence of two sensations based on the fact that, over a series of instances, the mental image of one produces the other. *No one claims on the basis of such a relationship [to be able to specify the underlying mechanics of the empirical relationship].* (Ebbinghaus, 1896b, p. 186; translation mine, emphasis added)

Whether or not McCrae and Costa (1995) intended to style themselves as modern-day Machian/Ebbinghausian positivists in their own treatment of "mechanism and the chains of causality" (pp. 245-246), this is, in effect, exactly what they did, and their posture in this matter is entirely consonant with the zeitgeist of contemporary trait psychology (cf. Pervin, 1994).[15]

For reasons to be elaborated presently, however, the epistemic props of this entire approach to explaining (and, presumably, understanding) individual behavior and psychological functioning cannot withstand the weight of close and careful scrutiny. To the extent that any explanatory power at all attaches to expressions like Equations 6.9, 6.11, and 6.13—or their proxies in ANOVA or other aggregate statistical techniques, however sophisticated they might be—that power is strictly limited to discussions of *proportions of total between-person variance* (Lamiell, 1990a). Because no coherent articulation of the notion of between-person variance is possible at the level of the individual, it follows that there is no real basis on which to claim that knowledge of the kind conveyed by, say, Equation 6.13 above explains anything at all about any pupil's behavior. Least of all is there any genuine scientific warrant for "seeing" in the arithmetic of such an expression the play of forces somehow emanating from variables $M$, $G$, $M \times G$, and $AM$ and exerting determinative "effects" on individual pupils' respective relative criterion performances.

The issue of crucial relevance here is one touched on briefly by Bakan (1966) in his landmark critical analysis of the test of significance in psychological research. In that work, Bakan noted the importance of distinguishing between, on one hand, knowledge of the general in the sense of "common to all" and, on the other hand, knowledge of the aggregate, properly using this latter term to refer to general in the sense of "on average." Perhaps one reason that within the mainstream of 20th-century scientific psychology, this distinction has been all but completely obliterated is to be found in the fact that logically, there is a specifiable point of convergence between these two kinds of knowledge. That is, there are conceivable, albeit highly restrictive, and rarely, if ever, realized empirical circumstances under which knowledge of what holds true for an aggregate of individuals is at once and perforce knowledge of what holds true in general for the individuals within that aggregate. The problem is that contemporary "nomotheticism" requires for its metaphysical and epistemic coherence the assumption that this is always true, in other words, that whatever is true in the aggregate is inevitably at least a partial "window" onto individual level phenomena. Without this assumption, "nomotheticism" cannot possibly work as an approach to understanding individuals except under conditions never realized empirically. It happens, however, that this critical assumption is false, and therein lies the fatal problem.

# The Epistemic Limits of Neo-Galtonian Inquiry and "Nomothetic" Laws of Personality Functioning

## On Prediction

Perhaps no single idea is more fundamental to the presumed adequacy of neo-Galtonian inquiry as a framework within which to discover general laws of human psychological functioning than the notion that based on statistical knowledge of the sort generated through such inquiry, individual behavior can be rendered, to some specified degree, *predictable*. Manifestly, claims in this regard are central to actuarial endeavors in the domain of psychotechnics, the aim of which, it will be recalled, is *Menschenbehandlung,* or the deployment of individuals as "human resources" in such a way as to maximize some desired practical outcome in the long run (see discussion of psychotechnics in Chapter Three). But the issue of prediction is also epistemically crucial in the domain of psychognostics, the aim of which is *Menschenkenntnis,* or the understanding of human nature. Evidence that individual behavior has been rendered predictable is necessary to underwrite explanatory claims of just the sort discussed above, and on the positivist-empiricist model of psychological science that continues to dominate within the mainstream, it is law-grounded explanation that provides genuine scientific understanding.

Accordingly, a close examination of what sort of claims concerning prediction are actually entitled by the empirical findings issuing from neo-Galtonian studies is needed here. To this end, it will be useful to refer once again to the illustrative research examples introduced in Chapter Six and discussed further above.

Let us assume for the sake of discussion that all questions pertaining to the adequacy of research design and replicability of empirical findings have been settled to the satisfaction of everyone concerned, so that any of the three expressions defined by Equations 6.9, 6.11, and 6.13 could be said to qualify as an *empirical law,* or "law-like empirical regularity," of precisely the sort that is sought within, and that is in principle discoverable through, neo-Galtonian inquiry. The question is this: How (if at all) could any of these laws or lawlike empirical regularities properly be said to have rendered individual behavior predictable—and hence, presumably, explainable and understandable? Table 7.1 helps point the way toward an answer to this question.

Shown in Table 7.1 are three sets of "residual values." Moving in order from left to right, Column *A* displays the values of $(Y_p - \hat{Y}_p)$ resulting from the recursive application of Equation 6.9 to the data of the first hypothetical experiment discussed in Chapter Six (cf. Table 6.4). Similarly, Columns *B* and *C* in Table 7.1 display the values of $(Y_p - \hat{Y}_p)$ resulting from recursive applications of Equation 6.11 and 6.13, respectively (cf. Tables 6.7 and 6.9).

Two features of the data shown in Table 7.1 are decisive with respect to questions concerning the "retrodictability" (or recursive "predictability") of individual criterion scores. One of these features is to be seen by examining the entries in Table 7.1 "top to bottom," noticing that in each of the

**Table 7.1**    Residual Values Issuing From Three Statistical Laws Derived From the Hypothetical Experiments of Chapter Six

| Pupils | A<br>Equation 6.9<br>Residual Values | B<br>Equation 6.11<br>Residual Values | C<br>Equation 6.13<br>Residual Values |
|---|---|---|---|
| $P_1$ | −3.60 | −1.20 | +0.95 |
| $P_2$ | −0.60 | +1.80 | +0.73 |
| $P_3$ | −2.60 | −0.20 | +0.88 |
| $P_4$ | −0.60 | +1.80 | −0.35 |
| $P_5$ | −4.60 | −2.20 | −2.20 |
| $P_6$ | +1.40 | −1.00 | −1.00 |
| $P_7$ | +3.40 | +1.00 | −0.08 |
| $P_8$ | +1.40 | −1.00 | +0.08 |
| $P_9$ | +6.40 | +4.00 | +1.85 |
| $P_{10}$ | −0.60 | −3.00 | −0.85 |
| $P_{11}$ | −0.20 | −0.40 | +0.68 |
| $P_{12}$ | +2.80 | +2.60 | +1.52 |
| $P_{13}$ | −1.20 | −1.40 | +0.75 |
| $P_{14}$ | +0.80 | +0.60 | −1.55 |
| $P_{15}$ | −1.20 | −1.40 | −1.40 |
| $P_{16}$ | −0.20 | 0.00 | 0.00 |
| $P_{17}$ | +0.80 | +1.00 | −0.08 |
| $P_{18}$ | −1.20 | −1.00 | +1.15 |
| $P_{19}$ | +2.80 | +3.00 | +0.85 |
| $P_{20}$ | −3.20 | −3.00 | −1.92 |
| Residual Variation | 6.55 | 3.68 | 1.47 |
| % Criterion Variation | 80% | 45% | 17% |

three columns, the $(Y_p - \hat{Y}_p)$ residual values vary in magnitude from one individual pupil to the next. The second important feature of these data is to be seen by examining them "left to right," noticing that although residual variance (and hence its proportion of total criterion variance) decreases steadily and substantially in accordance with "movement" from Equation 6.9 through Equation 6.11 to Equation 6.13, the residual values associated with individual cases do not necessarily conform to this pattern. The significance of these two observations can be elaborated as follows.

First, it must be understood that it is the value of $(Y_p - \hat{Y}_p)$ in any specific case that empirically marks the degree to which the statistical law used to generate a particular value of $\hat{Y}_p$ has "held true" or "worked" in that particular case, and hence the extent to which that law can be said to explain the criterion outcome in that case. In any instance where the value of $(Y_p - \hat{Y}_p)$ is zero, the retrodicted criterion score generated by the equation expressing the law in question has corresponded perfectly with the actual criterion score in that case. Note that if the correlation serving as the basis of such retrodictions is perfect, then, by definition, the value of $(Y_p - \hat{Y}_p)$ will be zero in every case, meaning that residual variance within the sample will also be zero. This hypothetical state of affairs specifies the previously referred to point of convergence between the aggregate and the general, that is, the logically conceivable but never actually realized circumstance in which what is true of an aggregate of individuals considered as such (i.e., perfect retrodictability of criterion scores) is by definition also common to all of the individuals within that aggregate (likewise perfect retrodictability of criterion scores) and hence properly regarded as true of those individuals not only on average but also in general.

Under empirical circumstances in which the statistical basis of retrodiction is a correlation that is less than unity, however (i.e., under all circumstances actually realized in neo-Galtonian/"nomothetic" inquiry), what is true about retrodictive accuracy in the aggregate cannot be said to be true about retrodictive accuracy in general. For when a less-than-perfect correlation is serving as the basis for criterion score retrodiction, it is necessarily true that the value of $(Y_p - \hat{Y}_p)$ will vary from case to case in just the fashion illustrated in Table 7.1, and it is not possible to know what the value is in any individual case without examining that individual case. *That is the problem.*

The extent to which a lawful regularity such as that captured by, say, Equation 6.9 has "held true" in the case of any given one of the 20 individual pupils is unknown, given only knowledge of that law and of the experimental treatment to which that pupil was exposed. A pupil identified only as one who was exposed to the silent reading method of instruction, for example, might be Pupil 11, in which case we could discover post hoc, by examining in Table 7.1 the data for that individual, that the law turned out to have "held" quite well; but on the other hand, the pupil so identified might very well not be Pupil 11 at all but instead, Pupil 12. In that case, we would be forced to say—but again only on the basis of a post hoc inspection of the results for that individual case—that the law did not "hold" so well in that instance. The point is that knowledge of the law itself (and its statistical basis) entitles no claim at all to knowledge of the extent to which it has held true in *any* particular case. All that can be known given a law based on a less-than-perfect correlation is that that law did not hold equally true in all cases, and this simply means that no statement concerning the degree of correspondence between $Y_p$ and $\hat{Y}_p$ can properly be regarded as generalizable over individual cases. Hence, however stable (and thus replicable) such an empirical regularity might be found to be at the aggregate level, it does not and cannot possibly qualify as a general law of individual behavior in the nomothetic sense of general, or "common to all," originally intended by Windelband.

Clearly, the point just made holds not only for the empirical law represented by Equation 6.9 but also, and for exactly the same reasons, for the laws represented by Equations 6.11 and 6.13. Dispository in this regard is the stark and stubborn fact that in both Columns $B$ and $C$ of Table 7.1, the values of $(Y_p - \hat{Y}_p)$ still vary from one individual case to the next. The total amount of between-person variance in these residual values is indeed smaller in the case of Equation 6.11 than in the case of Equation 6.9, and smaller still in the case of Equation 6.13. (More on these facts and their implications will be discussed below.) So long as that variance has not been reduced to zero, however—and this cannot be said to happen unless the correlational basis for the retrodictions is perfect—knowledge of the value of $(Y_p - \hat{Y}_p)$ in any individual case and hence in each and every individual case considered as such is not merely "attenuated" or "compromised to some degree," but negated altogether. Stated otherwise, the value of $(Y_p - \hat{Y}_p)$ resulting from the recursive application of some statistical law is neither known nor knowable for any individual case on the basis of the statistical law itself. Note that to claim otherwise would be to claim that the degree of inaccuracy or "error" in the retrodiction of individual criterion scores could somehow be known without examining actual outcomes in specific cases. Were this true, research psychologists should never find it necessary to suffer predictive error! For it would then always be possible to adjust in advance for such error and thereby eliminate it altogether (effectively achieving the single point of convergence between the aggregate and the general explained above).

The temptation must be resisted to find warrant in the foregoing for concluding that the aggregate statistical regularities captured by Equations 6.9, 6.11, and 6.13 at least rendered the criterion performances of "some" of the 20 individual pupils recursively predictable. In fact, the epistemic burden of the "Thorndike maneuver" is rather heavier than this, and if at first blush matters seem otherwise, that is only because the *dis*-aggregation operation that was necessary to construct Table 7.1 in the first place has already negated the opacity of Equations 6.9, 6.11, and 6.13 regarding the question of individual predictability.

The central thesis of the "Thorndike maneuver" is that aggregate level statistical knowledge is already a "window" onto individual level phenomena. This being so, that thesis cannot properly be critically appraised simply by singling out certain individuals post hoc, on some basis other than aggregate statistical knowledge, whose behavior turns out to match abstract assertions about "some" individuals formulated on the basis of the aggregate knowledge. On the contrary, the test question mandated by the "Thorndike maneuver" is this: Given a statistical law of the sort exemplified by any one of the expressions specified above (implying, of course, knowledge of the magnitude of the aggregate correlation, simple or multiple, that underlies that expression), what can be said to be known about the degree of correspondence between the actual criterion performance, $Y_p$, of any specific one of the 20 pupils who served as subjects in the experiment and the performance retrodicted for that pupil on the basis of the statistical law, $\hat{Y}_p$? For reasons that should be clear at this point, the answer to this question under any circumstances in which the absolute value of $r$ or $R$ is less 1.00 can only be "Nothing at all can be said to be known in this regard." It is vital to see that this is the only correct answer not just for "some" of the 20 individuals but for each and every one of the 20 considered individually. Hence, far from constituting knowledge about the predictability of "all of the people" (Epstein, 1979) or even just "some of the people" (Bem & Allen, 1974), the aggregate statistical relationships gleaned from neo-Galtonian/"nomothetic" inquiry—including but not limited to personality studies—actually deliver knowledge of the predictability of none of the people—quite literally, of *no one*. Any other interpretation of such statistical relationships is false and betrays a fundamental misunderstanding of their nature.

Against the notion that increases in aggregate level accuracy in the retrodiction of criterion scores must perforce signal some sort of "improvement" in this regard at the level of the individual even if the precise level of accuracy in individual cases still cannot be specified (cf. Dar & Serlin, 1990), there are, once again, the data in Table 7.1 to consider. In this context, the residual values shown there should be examined in "left to right" fashion.

The bottom two rows of the table document the reductions in aggregate residual variance across the three hypothetical experiments. The first experiment, issuing in Equation 6.9, may be said to have reduced unexplained variance by 20%, that is, from the 100% that may be said to have prevailed prior to any investigation at all to the 80% remaining after the consideration of the relationship between criterion performance and method of instruction *(M)*. The first extension of the basic experiment, involving the consideration of gender *(G)* and enabling an investigation of the $M \times G$ interaction, issued in Equation 6.11, resulting in a reduction of residual variance from 80% to 45% of the total criterion variance. The final extension of the design, bringing into consideration achievement motivation *(AM)* as an individual differences variable, issued in Equation 6.13 and led to a further reduction of residual variance to a mere 17% of the total criterion variance.

Examining individual rows of Table 7.1, it can easily be seen that the steady reduction in aggregate residual variance just described is not mirrored in any consistent way by corresponding decreases in the values of $(Y_p - \hat{Y}_p)$ associated with specific pupils. Among the 20 subjects in this hypothetical study, such a steady decrease did occur in six individual cases, those of Pupils 1, 7, 8, 9, 12, and 20. However, in eight cases (Pupils 2, 4, 10, 11, 13, 15, 17, and 19), the value of $(Y_p - \hat{Y}_p)$ was actually greater under Equation 6.11 than under Equation 6.9, the 35% reduction in aggregate error variance achieved under Equation 6.11 notwithstanding. Similarly, in seven cases (Pupils 3, 5, 6, 11, 14, 15, and 18), residual values obtained under Equation 6.13 were either equal to or greater than those obtained under Equation 6.11, the additional 28% reduction in aggregate error variance achieved under Equation 6.13 notwithstanding.[16] In five cases (Pupils 2, 10, 11, 14, and 15), residual values obtained under Equation 6.13 were either equal to or greater than those obtained under Equation 6.9, regardless of the fact that the law expressed by Equation 6.13 accounted for 63% more of the criterion variance than that expressed by Equation 6.9. In three cases (Pupils 11, 14, and 15), recursive predictive error under Equation 6.13 was equal to or greater than that which ensued under either of the other two statistically inferior laws, and there was even one case, that of Pupil 11, in which the magnitude of $(Y_p - \hat{Y}_p)$ steadily *increased* from Equation 6.9 through Equation 6.11 to Equation 6.13, following a course directly *opposite* to that traced by the respective residual variances.

It should be emphasized that there is no feature of the examples constructed for purposes of this illustration that would somehow place neo-Galtonian inquiry in an unfairly or peculiarly disadvantageous light. In fact, the empirical laws illustrated by Equations 6.11 and 6.13 express correlational relationships of magnitudes that far exceed the degrees of statistical regularity found in actual studies incorporating individual and group difference variables. Nevertheless, empirical eventualities of the sort just identified are to be seen even here (for another example, see Lamiell, 1990a). Eventualities of this sort are endemic to the statistical way of thinking that forms the very foundation for *so-called* nomothetic personality studies within the neo-Galtonian framework, and this is what makes such studies so ill suited in principle to the search for *genuinely* nomothetic laws of human behavior and personality functioning.

## On the Empirical Discovery of "Basic Human Tendencies"

A slightly different angle of regard from which to appreciate the fundamental epistemic problem just identified can be gained by critically examining the basis for claims made by contemporary "nomotheticists" that they are advancing the scientific understanding of individuals' behavioral and psychological *tendencies*. Wiggins (1979), for example, identified "the principle goal of personality study" as that of providing "a systematic account of individual differences in *human tendencies* (proclivities, propensities, dispositions, inclinations) to act or not to act in certain ways on certain occasions" (p. 395; emphasis in original). McCrae and Costa explicitly identify the "Big Five" as "basic tendencies" in their "model of the person" (1995, Figure 1, p. 237).

To illustrate the epistemic difficulty that inevitably arises when claims to knowledge about the tendencies of persons are mounted on the empirical findings of neo-Galtonian investigations, we may consider Figure 7.2, in which are plotted the data underlying one of the statistical relationships discussed in the previous chapter.

The statistical analysis conducted on these data revealed a significant correlation of $r_{Y,G} = +.38$ between spelling performance *(Y)* and gender *(G)*, such that the average performance achieved among the girls, 12.00, exceeded that achieved among the boys, 9.80. Under a commonly accepted way of speaking about data of this sort, it would be said that they show that the girls "had a tendency" to score higher than the boys. In fact, however, such data would not and could not possibly reveal anything at all about the behavioral or psychological tendencies of any girl (or, for that matter, any boy) investigated in such a study. To be sure, it would be accurate to say of findings such as these that "there was a tendency for girls to score higher than boys," but the reason that this latter phrasing says what the data actually show is that it explicitly locates the "tendency" as being "there" in the data array.

The phrasing "The girls had a tendency," or any locutionary equivalent of it, does something quite different: It invites an understanding of the "tendency" under discussion as being one that has been discovered empirically to be "there" in those research subjects who are girls. The illegitimacy of this view is easily seen by considering Figure 7.3. In each of the four panels of that figure, a single data point has been plotted indicating everything about an individual subject that is also represented in the composite array shown in Figure 7.2. The data point in Panel A, for example, represents a girl subject who scored 11 on the test defining the experiment's dependent variable.

Clearly, a single data point reveals no tendencies of any kind whatsoever. A single data point simply is where it is, and it makes no more sense to speak of the subject represented in Panel A of Figure 7.3 as someone who "tended" to score 11 than it would make to say that that subject "tended" to be a girl. Yet nothing more than these two facts about this individual subject has been incorporated into the data array that was ultimately subjected to statistical analysis in the hypothetical experiment. Clearly,

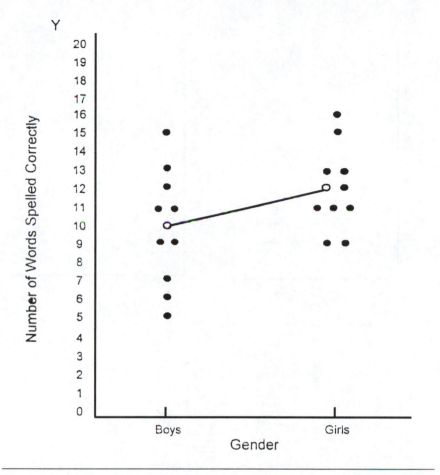

**Figure 7.2**    Plot of Hypothetical Data From Table 6.5 Showing Relationship
Between Gender and Spelling Performance

therefore, no such analysis could reveal anything at all about this individual's
tendencies.[17]

Of course, if this argument applies to some particular one of the 20
subjects in the experiment, then it applies just as well to every particular one
of those subjects, considered individually. For example, the data points
plotted in Panels B, C, and D of Figure 7.3 represent, respectively, a boy
who scored 15, a boy who scored 9, and a girl who scored 9. There is not
the slightest trace of any tendency of any kind whatsoever in empirical evidence for any of these 3 individual subjects or any of the remaining 16 individuals not represented in Figure 7.3. In fact, there is no tendency to speak

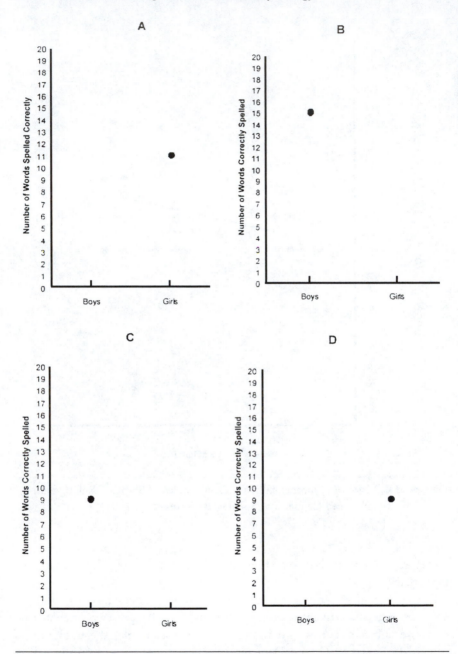

**Figure 7.3**     Plots of Data for 4 Individual Subjects From the 20 Plotted in
                   Figure 7.2

of here at all unless and until the 20 discrete data points of this hypothetical experiment are aggregated into the display of Figure 7.2.

To appreciate this is to gain the central point of the illustration: The establishment of statistical tendencies in data aggregates provides no scientific warrant whatsoever for claims to knowledge of the behavioral/psychological tendencies of *any one* of the individual subjects observed in the course of compiling the aggregates. Clearly, inquiry that by its very nature cannot reveal the tendencies of any one also cannot be said to produce knowledge about "human tendencies" that would be common to all, and this is the logical fact that disqualifies such inquiry as a means of attaining nomothetic knowledge of the psychological tendencies of individuals in the sense of nomothetic intended by Windelband.

## On Probabilistic Thinking as the Basis for Nomothetic Knowledge Claims

One means of circumventing the epistemic problems identified to this point might seem to be afforded by the possibility of couching knowledge claims about individuals in probabilistic language. Conceding, for example, that the accuracy of recursive predictions concerning the criterion variable status of individuals based on empirical laws of the sort illustrated above is unknowable for individuals under the terms of the laws themselves, it might nevertheless be argued that the statistical knowledge conveyed by such laws provides a scientific basis for claims concerning the likelihood or probability that some behavior will occur, or that some designated interval of criterion score values will contain the specific score achieved by any particular individual (Tryon, 1991a; cf. Lamiell, 1991; Tryon, 1991b).

Given trustworthy sample statistics, an investigator might pursue this line of thinking by constructing "confidence intervals" around treatment group means or by calculating "standard errors of estimate" for regression-based predictions. On this basis, it might then be claimed that the probability is, say, .95 that a criterion score interval bounded at the low *(l)* end by $Y_l$ and at the high *(h)* end by $Y_h$ will contain the actual criterion score, $Y_p$, achieved by a given individual research subject in a given instance. The greater the degree of statistical relationship between the criterion variable and the predictor(s), the narrower the interval defined by $Y_l$ and $Y_h$ and hence, presumably, the less the uncertainty about the actual value of $Y_p$ in any given instance.

The fundamental problem with this view can be understood by considering its epistemic ramifications under various probability values in a claim of the sort that "the probability is $P$ that the criterion score interval defined by $Y_l$ and $Y_h$ contains the actual criterion score of person $p$, $Y_p$." The question is this: Under what values of $P$ could a claim of this sort be empirically tested?

Brief reflection suffices to establish that the values $P = 0.00$ and $P = 1.00$ are the only two values that will work here. If $P = 1.00$, then the claim is, in effect, one of certainty that the interval bounded by $Y_l$ and $Y_h$ will be found to have contained $Y_p$. This claim is empirically testable and would be challenged by the observation that the specified interval in fact does not contain $Y_p$. By the same token, if $P = 0.00$, then the claim is, in effect, one of certainty that $Y_p$ will not be contained within the interval bounded by $Y_l$ and $Y_h$. This claim, too, could be subjected to empirical challenge and would be overturned by the observation that the specified interval in fact *does* contain $Y_p$. So far so good.

But what if $P$ is, say, .95 or .80. or .50? Would the empirical discovery that the interval bounded by $Y_l$ and $Y_h$ does not contain $Y_p$ overturn any less than certain claim that that interval would contain that value? If so, how and why? Alternatively: What if $P$ is, say, .30 or .15 or .05? Would the empirical discovery that the interval bounded by $Y_l$ and $Y_h$ does contain $Y_p$ overturn any less-than-certain claim that that interval would not contain that value? Again, if so, how and why?

As noted in Chapter Five, the 19th-century British scholar John Venn cogently explained that the concept of probability depends for its very coherence on the consideration of a *series* of entities or events. To claim, for example, that "the probability is .75 that a designated interval $\{Y_l - Y_h\}$ will contain $Y_p$" is to assert precisely and only that in a series of, say, 100 cases, the interval $\{Y_l - Y_h\}$ will contain $Y_p$ in 75 cases and will not contain $Y_p$ in 25 cases. This claim can be empirically evaluated at the aggregate level and would be falsified through an investigation leading to the discovery that among the 100 cases considered, the hypothesized 75-25 distribution did not obtain.

However such an investigation might turn out, the question as to whether or not the interval $\{Y_l - Y_h\}$ would contain any one particular instance of $Y_p$ is a question in the face of which the original probabilistic claim is necessarily and entirely mute. Probability statements cannot coherently be said to be about individual instances in the first place. This is exactly what insulates social scientists solidly committed to the statistical tenets of neo-Galtonian inquiry from the obligation of folding up their proverbial tents when confronted with some "outlier" or "exception to the rule." Everywhere in social science it is understood that unless $P$ is 1.0 or zero, probabilistic statements issuing from large-scale statistical investigations cannot be overturned by the outcome of any isolated case. But in the present context, this is precisely the problem: The fact that such statements are literally immune from empirical challenge at the level of the individual renders them entirely unfit as claims to scientific knowledge about individuals. This is what finally disqualifies probabilistic claims issuing from neo-Galtonian studies of individual and group differences as claims to nomothetic knowledge about individual behavior.

Recalling the discussion in Chapter Five of Venn's coin-flip example, it should be noted here that an assertion of the form "the probability is 'high' ('low') that person $p$ will (will not) do X under some specified set of circumstances" is an assertion about the strength of a subjective belief held by the individual making the assertion. The danger lies in regarding such an assertion as a valid claim to objective knowledge about person $p$. The statement fails in this latter regard because, for reasons just explained, it is incorrigible: Its validity would be left utterly unchallenged by either of the only two eventualities that could empirically obtain, namely, person $p$'s either doing or not doing X.[18] Ironically, then, we see here that far from guaranteeing a pristine scientific objectivity, probabilistic statements of the sort so casually endorsed by contemporary "nomotheticists" (see, e.g., McCrae & Costa, 1995, p. 234) actually admit into the discipline a deep *subjectivism* of just the sort that on Gigerenzer's (1987) insightful account, reliance on statistical thinking was supposed to seal out.

## On the Alleged Commonality and Heritability of Common Traits

Before concluding this critique of contemporary "nomotheticism," attention is directed briefly toward two aspects of the dominant paradigm identified and discussed in Chapter Six but not specifically mentioned up to now in the present chapter. The first pertains to the effort to identify the most basic "common traits" of "the" human personality, an effort that has culminated (for now) in the isolation of the "Big Five" dimensions of neuroticism, extraversion, openness, agreeableness, and conscientiousness. The second observation to be made here bears on the contemporary "nomothetic" search for the sources of individual differences in the common traits. In this research area, inquiry has long been structured by the categories *nature* and *nurture,* and discussion has revolved around those particular statistical indices known as coefficients of *heritability.*

Regarding the first of these two issues, the point to be stressed in the present context is that nowhere in the factor analytic research and/or convergent and discriminant validation studies described in Chapter Six is the alleged *commonality* of the putatively basic personality "elements" ever empirically tested. On the contrary, the logic of the statistical methods proper to such inquiry requires the assumption that the trait dimensions being sought (through factor analysis) or being submitted to further psychometric evaluation (through studies of convergent and discriminant validity) can be applied meaningfully to all subjects in the research sample.

The correlation coefficients basic to all inquiry in this domain require for their very computation the consideration of standard scores specifying the status of each research subject relative to the others with respect to the variables selected for investigation. To derive these standard scores sensibly, it must be assumed that all variables to be intercorrelated can be applied meaningfully to all individuals being compared. The statistical methods themselves, however, do not provide for any independent check on the validity of this assumption. In fact, in the course of such inquiry, there is no logical possibility whatsoever of discovering that one or more of the variables isolated or selected for study cannot meaningfully be applied to some of the individuals in the research sample. So, the commonality assumption central to contemporary "nomotheticism" has stood throughout the factor analytic and multitrait-multimethod construct validation research discussed in Chapter Six, the results of which are now widely accepted as scientific warrant for regarding the "Big Five" as personality psychology's "periodic table of elements." This is not because some independent body of evidence exists through which that assumption has been empirically tested, but instead simply because the statistical techniques proper to the conduct of neo-Galtonian inquiry have required that assumption procedurally.[19]

As regards the empirical findings issuing from contemporary "nomothetic" investigations into the sources of personality differences in nature and nurture, the single most important point to be made here is that just as is true of the correlations on which they are based, so-called heritability coefficients are aggregate statistics having no scientifically legitimate interpretation of any kind whatsoever at the level of the individual.[20] Most emphatically, such coefficients will not bear interpretation as empirical indicators of the extent to which any individual's personality characteristics have been genetically determined.

In the domain of personality studies, heritability coefficients issuing from well-designed and well-executed research will bear interpretation as empirical indicators of the proportion of total between-person variance in measures of some phenotypic personality characteristic (necessarily assumed to be, but nowhere empirically proven to be, "common to all"; see discussion above) that can be attributed to or "explained" in terms of genotypic differences between the research subjects. Of course, neither phenotypic nor genotypic between-person variance can coherently be said to exist at the level of the individual person; between-person variance is an inherently and irreducibly aggregate level phenomenon, and it follows from this that no discussion of between-person variance, whatever its particulars, could possibly qualify as a discussion of any individual.

Heritability coefficients are no more grounds for inferences concerning the genetic determinants of individuals' personality characteristics than data revealing the birth rate of Caucasian males in the United States in 1950 are grounds for an inference concerning the rate at which this author was birthed in that year (cf. Herrnstein & Murray, 1994). It is important to see that in both these two cases—not just in the latter one—the problem is not merely that the suggested inference is empirically incorrect. The problem is that the suggested inference is literally incoherent. To see this is to grasp that in the quest to understand the source(s) of individuals' personalities (i.e., human individualities), heritability coefficients issuing from population level studies of "phenotypic trait variance" (e.g., Rowe, 1997) are simply and utterly irrelevant.

# Summary

By 1937, when Gordon Allport drew widespread attention among personality investigators to Windelband's (1894/1998) distinction between nomothetic and idiographic knowledge (Allport, 1937a), research psychologists had already embraced a conception of the meaning of "general" that was quite different from that originally intended by the German philosopher. This transformation in meaning was effected through the displacement of the original Wundtian model for psychological research, which was the model known to Windelband, by the neo-Galtonian paradigm and the statistical methods so integral to it. Whereas Windelband had understood general to mean *allen gemein,* or "common to all," Allport's contemporaries, and indeed Allport himself, accepted a meaning of general as referring to the average within a collective.

In a view of statistical knowledge that was prominently championed around the middle of the 19th century by the British historian Henry Thomas Buckle, which subsequently gained ascendance among research psychologists through thinking of the sort exemplified by what I have called the "Thorndike maneuver," the epistemic gap between the two meanings of general seemed bridgeable. According to this view, statistical knowledge capturing aggregate level regularities could validly be taken as grounds for generalizations concerning corresponding individual level phenomena. One very important consequence of this view was that under its terms, the statistical understanding of "general" came to be regarded as consonant with Windelband's conception of nomothetic. From there, it was but a small step to the conclusion that a common trait psychology of personality tethered securely to the statistical methods of neo-Galtonian inquiry would be both appropriate and altogether adequate for purposes of achieving a properly nomothetic understanding of human behavior and personality functioning on the natural science model. Allport's futile critique of "nomo-theticism" was thus reduced to the argument that a psychology of personality tied too exclusively to the common trait approach inevitably would be "too nomothetic" and hence not "sufficiently idiographic."

As the discussion of the present chapter should have made plain, however, the problem with contemporary "nomotheticism" is really quite different from this, and vastly more serious. What mistakenly came to be regarded by virtually all disputants on both sides of the Great Nomothetic vs. Idiographic Debate as the nomothetic approach to personality studies in fact is not, has never been, and could not possibly ever be a nomothetic science of personality on the understanding of nomothetic originally intended by Windelband.

The reason for this is that contrary to a central epistemic tenet of neo-Galtonian inquiry, aggregate level statistical regularities are not valid indicators of corresponding individual level phenomena except under circumstances that, though logically conceivable, are never realized empirically. In practice, therefore, neo-Galtonian inquiry does not constitute an alternative means to the same knowledge objectives as research modeled on the $N = 1$ methods of Wundtian inquiry. The latter kind of research is by its very nature logically suited to the quest for knowledge of what is generally true of persons; hence, it is genuinely suitable for the purposes of a nomothetic psychology of personality in the original Windelbandian sense of the term, precisely because theoretically relevant questions can be framed and then tested individually, on a case-by-case basis. The epistemic force of such inquiry accrues to its formal suitability to the task of empirically evaluating assertions about what is (or might be found to be) *common to all* cases investigated.

Contrary to the long-prevailing view, a comparable epistemic force never accrues to contemporary "nomothetic" studies of individual and group differences. Lawful empirical regularities of the sort that can be discovered through well-designed and well-executed neo-Galtonian research cannot properly serve as grounds for generalizations concerning the predictability of individuals' behavior, because as aggregate phenomena, those regularities do not reveal the predictability of any individual's behavior. Because the pretensions of contemporary "nomotheticists" with regard to the explanation of individual behavior are tied directly to their misunderstanding regarding prediction, the former collapse alongside the latter under the weight of these considerations.

By way of underscoring this argument, several additional points were developed in this chapter. First, it was shown that (and why) the aggregate statistical patterns in data issuing from neo-Galtonian studies of "basic human tendencies" cannot properly be regarded as grounds for generalizations concerning the tendencies of individuals. In fact, such aggregate statistical patterns do not reveal the tendencies of any individual.

Second, it was explained that probabilistic assertions based on neo-Galtonian research findings cannot properly stand as claims to knowledge about individuals—least of all as claims to scientific knowledge—because at the level of the individual, such claims are incorrigible (i.e., in principle immune from empirical challenge). Logically speaking, probabilistic assertions about individuals based on research findings issuing from neo-Galtonian inquiry express nothing more than the strength of investigators' subjective beliefs about their research subjects.

Third, and with specific reference to the "heritability" coefficients and like statistical indices issuing from neo-Galtonian investigations into the nature and nurture of personality differences, it has been noted that such indices are, like the correlation coefficients on which they are based, uninterpretable for individuals. Most pointedly, any attempt to infer on the basis of heritability coefficients the extent to which any individual's personality characteristics have been genetically determined betrays a fundamental misunderstanding of the nature of those coefficients and ultimately leads to assertions that are not merely empirically false, but logically incoherent.

Finally, it has been pointed out that contrary to long-prevailing views, there is not now nor has there ever been any means within the contemporary "nomothetic" framework for empirically testing the thesis that the putatively common traits that lie at the core of the paradigm (for now, at least, the "Big Five") are in fact common. Indeed, the assumption of commonality pervading contemporary "nomotheticism" rests on nothing more than the insistence by researchers that it be made, for without it, the statistical methods proper to neo-Galtonian inquiry cannot sensibly be executed.

Much earlier in this work, notice was taken of Stern's rueful observation, in his 1927 autobiography, that even as he was calling in 1900 for a differential psychology (Stern, 1900a), he realized that human individuality could not be grasped through channels afforded by the assessment and empirical investigation of individual and group differences (Stern, 1927, p. 142). For reasons I have sought to make clear in this chapter, Stern was entirely correct about this, quite possibly even more than he knew. Perhaps, therefore, the time has finally come to more carefully consider the personalistic perspective that, although completely overshadowed to date by the concepts and statistical techniques of neo-Galtonian differential psychology, grounded Stern's thinking about the "problem of individuality" from the very beginning and informed his understanding of that problem throughout his scholarly life.

# Notes

1. Cloninger (1996) went on to state that "in practice, wholly idiographic approaches may be impossible, since any description of a person (for example, 'Mary is outgoing') implies comparison with other people, even if this comparison is only in the memory of the one doing the analysis" (p. 5). In Chapters Nine and Ten, this thesis will be challenged directly on empirical and conceptual grounds, respectively.

2. "Highly regarded gathering! On the celebration of the founding of the University, it is a great privilege for the Rector to have the ear of the institution's guests and members for a subject drawn from the province of the discipline he represents" (Windelband, 1894/1998, p. 8).

3. Nor is the expression "social sciences" an adequate translation of *Geisteswissenschaften*. In German, the social sciences are referred to as *die Sozialwissenschaften*.

4. All of these topics, it should be noted, were featured components of Wundt's *Völkerpsychologie* (e.g., Wundt, 1912). It is, therefore, not inappropriate to see that thinker's "other psychology," as well as its current incarnations in various corners of social and cultural psychology (cf. Moghaddam, Tayor, & Wright, 1993), as embracing essentially idiographic knowledge objectives, at least if idiographic is to be understood as Windelband originally intended it. Note also, however, that it was not Wundt's view that nomothetic knowledge of the sort sought within his general/experimental/individual psychology would be irrelevant to the idiographic objectives of the *Völkerpsychologie*. On the contrary, an understanding of the general laws governing human psychological life would form an important part of the epistemic foundation for investigating the more idiographic—specifically developmental/social/cultural—aspects of human life (cf. Wundt, 1912).

5. Here again, the limits of induction that constrain all scientific inquiry must be kept in mind. It is never possible to know with certainty what *always* is, because mere mortals can never actually test every instance of the phenomenon in question. It must always be understood that to establish scientific "truth" is to determine what may be regarded as true "until further notice." The fact of this matter in no way alters the validity of the point made here concerning the nature of the knowledge needed to empirically support a nomothetic generalization.

6. It is perhaps not coincidental that like Windelband but unlike Allport, both Lewin and Brunswik were native Germans.

7. Technically, the reason for this is that psychologists (and other social scientists) are virtually never working with what they are prepared to regard as *ratio* scales of measurement, having true zero points that can be known and meaningfully articulated. In ANOVA, this is reflected in the fact that the total degrees of freedom is always equal to the total number of observations minus 1. That one degree of freedom could be used to test the null hypothesis that the overall mean of the design is equal to zero, but this is virtually never done because on the nonratio scales of measurement typically employed in psychological investigations, the zero point is arbitrary. In correlation/regression analyses, this same point is reflected in the fact that what are analyzed are not covariances in the technical sense of the term, but rather *standardized* covariances (which is what correlations are). Whereas covariances are defined in terms of "raw" scores, correlations are defined in terms of standard scores, the computation of which entails redefining individual data points in terms of the magnitudes of their respective deviations from the raw score means of the variables. This is why the additive constant term, *a*, is needed in a raw score regression equation for it to "work" properly. When regression equations are written in standard score form, the additive constant terms disappear because, due to the standardization of criterion and predictor variables ahead of time, the numerical value of that constant is always zero, the arithmetic midpoint of the numerical scales in terms of which all of the variables have been (re)defined.

8. For purposes of this discussion, we ignore the fact that in an elementary school spelling exam, a pupil's performance would not ordinarily be scored in such a way as to allow for partial correctness. This simplification will help to streamline the discussion without in any way affecting the logic or conceptual coherence of the points being developed.

9. Perusing the contemporary literature of personality, social, and developmental psychology, the reader will have no difficulty identifying violations of the well-known, and in other contexts oft-proclaimed, principle that "correlation does not imply causation." In fact, the literature is saturated with references to the "effects" on behavior of individual and group difference factors such as age, race, gender, and personality, even though these factors are, obviously, never manipulated experimentally. Given that where there are "effects," there must be corresponding causes, the inferences being invited by these locutions are clear. Be this as it may, the inadequacy of neo-Galtonian inquiry as a framework within which to derive explanations for individual behavior stem from problems much deeper than violations of the aforementioned principle. So, the routine indulgence of such violations by contemporary authors, and by the editors who are supposed to be serving as the gatekeepers of the archival literature of this would-be science, will not be discussed further here.

10. The "starting position" in this instance is 5.525 rather than the actual grand mean, 10.90, simply because the variable $AM$ was defined arbitrarily on a scale admitting of a raw score mean of 50, rather than on one so defined as to guarantee a mean of zero, as was true for each of variables $M$, $G$, and $M \times G$ (see Endnote #7, above). Nevertheless, the analytic procedure here is conceptually identical to that described previously and entails, as always, an explanation for the deviation of

individual criterion scores from some fixed starting point along the scale of measurement defining the criterion variable. The fixed starting point could once again easily be made to equal 10.90 simply by arbitrarily redefining $AM$ so as to make its overall mean zero rather than 50.

11.   Note that except for slight rounding error, this value is identical to the $\hat{Y}$ value shown for Pupil 1 in the first row of Table 6.9.

12.   Measurement error could be among these factors, and were the conclusion reached that such error is the only remaining source of discrepancy between a given individual's outcome and that which would be expected given the law under consideration, the corresponding inference would be that the explanation entailed by that law is in fact complete.

13.   Accordingly, and in just this connection, Pervin (1994) found himself "tempted to ask for the true trait theorist to stand up" (p. 109).

14.   Figure 1 on p. 237 of the article by McCrae and Costa (1995) represents this view very clearly. For a less elaborate but essentially identical representation, see Figure 11 in Cronbach (1957, p. 683).

15.   In contrast, one finds in Stern's (1927/1930) intellectual autobiography his expression of regret at not having availed himself further of Dilthey's tuition when he (Stern) was a student in Berlin. In considering this comment, it is important to bear in mind that Ebbinghaus was, and for some years hence would remain, an intellectually influential and professionally pivotal figure in Stern's professional life (see Chapters One and Two). Just possibly, therefore, the young Stern would have been creating problems for himself had he developed too close an intellectual relationship with Dilthey.

16.   Not included in this count of seven cases is Pupil 16, for whom the residual value reached zero under Equation 6.11 and remained zero under Equation 6.13.

17.   The conceptual problem identified here cannot be circumvented by extending the discussion to the multiple correlation/regression case and incorporating the experimental treatment variable, the gender-by-treatment interaction, and the achievement motivation variable. Under any and all such extensions, the statistical analysis is still such that ultimately, each subject is being represented by a single data point: One of its two coordinates is, as always, that subject's standing on the criterion variable, $Y_p$; the other of the two coordinates is $\hat{Y}_p$, defined as the combination of subject $p$'s standing on multiple predictor variables, whatever they are and however many they may be. In data plots that would incorporate these extended possibilities, the $Y$-axis would remain defined as shown, and the $X$-axis would be demarcated in terms of admissible values of $\hat{Y}_p$. (The simple correlation $rY,\hat{Y}$ is the multiple correlation, $R$, between $Y$ and whatever combination of predictor variables has been chosen to generate values of $\hat{Y}$.)

18.   In his 1961 text, Allport noted,

[T]here is a serious logical error made in discussing actuarial prediction. If six in ten Americans attend the movies every week, you may be tempted to say that I have a 6 in 10 chance of going to the films this week. The statement is really nonsensical. I shall either go or not go, and only a knowledge of my attitudes, interests, and environmental situation will tell you whether or not I will attend. (p. 389)

It would appear from this passage that Allport appreciated the point I am developing here, following Venn (1888). However, and as I noted elsewhere (Lamiell, 1987), Allport either did not grasp the full implications of this point or for some reason chose not to pursue them. Had he done so, he would have pressed his case against the dominant nomothetic paradigm entirely on logical grounds, as is being done here, and not at all on empirical grounds, as he attempted to do.

19.  In the traditional view, some might argue, the empirical check on the commonality assumption is properly regarded as coming later in the research program, within the context of investigations into the temporal consistency (reliability) and transsituational consistency (validity) of measures of the putatively common traits. This view holds that where the "stability coefficients" issuing from such studies are sufficiently high, the prior assumption of commonality is validated, and where these coefficients are low, the validity of that commonality is called into question. As I have explained at some length elsewhere, however (Lamiell, 1981, 1987), the "stability coefficients" issuing from studies of this sort cannot serve as grounds for any generalizations at all about the individuals investigated. Indeed, unless they are perfect, such stability coefficients mean precisely and only that the individuals investigated were *not equally (in)consistent* in their respective relative manifestations of the traits in question, a fact mandating the conclusion that those traits *are not equally applicable* to all individuals investigated. In other words, under a proper interpretation of the stability coefficients by which contemporary "nomotheticists" have set such store, those coefficients always constitute evidence *against* the validity of the commonality assumption. On a related point, see also the recent exchange between Quackenbush (2001a, 2001b) and McCrae (2001).

20.  Of heritability coefficients, it is also vitally important to understand that even if they are perfect, they are not interpretable as evidence that nurture plays no role in the production of whatever phenomenon is under examination. A heritability coefficient could very well be 1.00 and still allow for substantial effects due to nurture, provided that those effects were the same for all individuals.

# Part Three

## Rethinking the Problem

# Chapter Eight
## *An Introduction to Critical Personalism*

*New perspectives become possible either when one offers new answers to questions already being asked, or when one reformulates the fundamental questions themselves, and in so doing restructures the entire problematic. Critical personalism does the latter.*

—Stern (1918b, p. 7)

In light of the somewhat technical nature of the critique of conventional "nomotheticism" mounted in Chapter Seven, the impulse may be great to see the problem now as essentially one of inventing or developing some new or long-neglected research method(s) or procedure(s). Such an impulse would not be entirely groundless, because without doubt, alternative investigative approaches more apposite to the "problem of individuality" than those of neo-Galtonian differential psychology are going to have to be embraced if genuine progress in this domain of inquiry is ever to be made. Accordingly, it will be necessary to consider methodological issues in due course.

But as the philosopher William Barrett once sagely warned, "Beware the illusion of technique!"[1] It is important to appreciate that the problems here are not entirely, or even primarily, technical in nature. To be sure, decades of thinking about human individuality statistically, in terms of variables marking individual and group differences, have produced a discipline fundamentally ill suited to its professed subject matter methodologically. That same thinking, however, has also fostered a disciplinary ethos within which, despite the laudable efforts of some (e.g., Robinson, 1985; Robinson & Mos, 1990; Rychlak, 1976, 1981, 1988; Slife & Williams, 1995, to name just a few), many in the field have become oblivious to the kind of spadework that the subject matter requires conceptually.

One clear example of this was encountered in the quotation of Goldberg (1993) cited in Chapter Six, in which he identified the most fundamental problem within a psychology of personality as being that of establishing a scientifically compelling taxonomy of trait variables. As was mentioned in passing when that quotation was introduced, it might plausibly be contended that the most fundamental problem for a psychology of personality is not taxonomic at all, but rather that of formulating a philosophically sound and theoretically coherent conception of *persons*. Accordingly, it is to a discussion of that particular conception of persons Stern sought to develop within critical personalism that we now turn our attention. In so doing, we encounter some basic theoretical and philosophical issues that within the mainstream of contemporary scientific psychology have been widely overlooked, regarded as long since settled, or simply dismissed out of hand as uninteresting or irrelevant.[2]

## Toward a Critically Personal Individual Psychology

In Chapter Two, notice was taken of the language Stern used to articulate the person-thing distinction. Given the centrality of this distinction to our immediate concerns, his words warrant reintroduction here:

> A person is an entity which, though consisting of many parts, forms a unique and inherently valuable unity and, as such, constitutes, over and above its functioning parts, a unitary, self-activated, goal-oriented being. . . . A thing is the contradictory opposite of a person. It is an entity that likewise consists of many parts, but these are not fashioned into a real, unique, and inherently valuable whole, and so while a thing functions in accordance with its various parts, it does not constitute a unitary, self-activated and goal-oriented being. (Stern, 1906, p. 16)

By pursuing Stern's elaboration of his conception of the person, the larger implications of his personalistic perspective on the problem of individuality can gradually be made clearer.

### The Person in Personalistic Perspective

> *Ich werte, also bin ich . . . Wert.*

This statement appears in Volume III of *Person und Sache*, the *Wertphilosophie* (*Philosophy of Value*; Stern, 1924b, p. 34). The assertion made by Stern there, quite intentionally phrased so as to evoke the famous

"*Cogito, ergo sum!*" of the French philosopher Rene Descartes (1596–1650), translates rather clumsily into English as "I evaluate, therefore I am . . . value." The fuller meaning of this important philosophical assertion may be understood as follows.

To "e-valuate" literally means to send out, project, or radiate value and thus to imbue other entities with value, analogous to the way in which the sun may be said to imbue earthly entities with light and warmth.[3] For an entity to "radiate" value, Stern reasoned, value must in some sense inhere in that entity to begin with. This, Stern believed, is true of persons, but it is not true of things, and this is why a thing can *be evaluated* but can never itself "e-valuate." This notion, from the outset of his attempt to articulate his philosophical worldview *(Weltanschauung),* grounded Stern's conviction that by their very nature, *persons are not things.* Insofar as his contemporaries within scientific psychology were obfuscating this fundamental fact, they were, in Stern's view, not only misrepresenting the essential nature of persons, but actually *devaluing* them in ways that were, ultimately, morally problematic.[4]

To see how Stern sought to meet the challenges presented by these developments within psychology, it is instructive to follow a path taken by Stern himself, in a monograph published in 1917 under the title *Die Psychologie und der Personalismus (Psychology and Personalism;* Stern, 1917). This particular work is especially suited to our present purposes because by Stern's own account, the work was written "to interest researchers coming from empirical psychology in the possibility of a personalistic conception of their problem" (Stern, 1917, p. 5).

Stern opened the 1917 monograph by characterizing as ill advised—and ultimately futile—all attempts to divorce empirical psychology from speculative philosophy. Adopting a decidedly antipositivistic stance, he contended that a conceptually viable personalism would necessarily incorporate metaphysical considerations and so would demand more than could ever be supplied by any empirical psychology alone, least of all by one committed (philosophically!) to the banishment of all metaphysical considerations from discussions of the human condition. Stern thus argued for the reestablishment and maintenance of intellectual ties between psychology and philosophy and specifically nominated critical personalism as a system of thought that could provide and preserve a conception of persons grounded firmly in both disciplines.[5]

## The Unitas Multiplex

The central problematic in personalistic thinking, according to Stern (1917), is a notion for which he chose a Latin expression: *unitas multiplex.* By way of elaboration, Stern asked rhetorically,

# Die Psychologie
# und der Personalismus

Von

## William Stern

Leipzig 1917

Verlag von Johann Ambrosius Barth

---

**Figure 8.1**    Title Page of Stern's 1917 Monograph: *Psychology and Personalism*

How, from the manifold *(multiplex)* of attributes that make up an individual does his/her *unity (unitas)* emerge? Which steps, which directions, which causal and goal relationships exist in these immanent interconnections between the parts and the whole? These questions now circumscribe the basic problematic. (Stern, 1917, p. 6)

Stern then reviewed two historically prominent philosophical positions vis-à-vis these questions. According to one, that which gathers a *multiplex* individual into a *unitas* is his or her *soul (Seele)*, an "I," conceived as "a simple independently existing thing, standing apart from the abundance of characteristics as an accessory to them. . . . This is the conception of personality as we encounter it in folk beliefs about the mind. This is 'naïve personalism'" (Stern, 1917, p. 6).

For Stern, Cartesian dualism generated a philosophical conundrum, the so-called mind-body problem, that somehow had to be overcome, and as a kind of quasi-Cartesian view, "naive personalism" appeared to him as an even less satisfactory alternative. As the second historically prominent stance vis-à-vis the above-stated problem, Stern identified a view that emphasizes the following:

[M]erely the abundance of characteristics, behind and along side of which no special and demonstrable "I" exists at all. The individual is merely a congeries: physically a sum of atoms; psychologically a bundle of perceptions. Clearly, [the individual on this view is] not a real and consequential unity [but is instead] a mechanical by-product of elements, determined by the general laws governing all occurrences. In short, [the individual on this view is] no "person" but a "thing." This is *impersonalism.* (Stern, 1917, pp. 6–7; emphasis added)[6]

Stern's deep-seated convictions concerning the fundamental inadequacy of the impersonalistic view of persons had already been given clear and poignant expression 11 years earlier, with the publication of the first volume of *Person und Sache* (Stern, 1906). There he had written,

The impersonal natural scientist *(Naturphilosoph)* sits at his desk and writes: "What we call a human is physically nothing but an aggregate of atoms or, as the case may be, energy quanta, psychologically an aggregate of consciousness contents; nothing happens with him except that which must occur as a consequence of the blind causal relationship of physical elements; and his so-called psychological life is nothing but the mechanical coupling of those physical elements." But then he steps into the nursery, where his child is lying ill; he braces himself against the thought of losing this beloved being–beloved being? What is it about atom + atom + atom (or energy + energy + energy) and idea + idea + idea that merits love? And: lose? In one case (that of the so-called living individual) the elements are bound more tightly to one another; in the other instance they stand in looser relationship. In the former instance, the influx and outflow of energy is equal, in the latter case it is not. How can this entirely indifferent variability of purely spatial constellation or energy flow mean the difference between joy and despair? And if his other child comes home from school with poor grades, he warns the child: "You should do better!" Better? Is there a better or a worse in the indifferent coupling of indifferent atoms and indifferent ideas? Whence this scale of values all of a sudden? Whence values at all? And: You should? Where mechanical laws and nothing else are at work, how can there be such a thing as "should"? Because "should" signifies nothing other than a determination of one's own doings through the consciousness of a goal. "Should is something that can exist only for a self-activated being. A mere string of elements cannot 'should.'" (Stern, 1906, p. 79)

As his alternative to both naive personalism and impersonalism, Stern (1917) offered a perspective from which one "sees in the confluence of the many into the one a final indispensable basic fact, and sees therefore in the individual a 'person' in the critical sense" (Stern, 1917, p. 7). This "confluence of the many into the one" is just that process whereby (a) diverse sensory-perceptual phenomena are (b) coordinated within meaningful acts, which are in turn (c) organized over extended periods of time through dispositions that are (d) owned by an "I" constituting the psychological makeup of what must finally be regarded as (e) a psychophysically neutral entity, the person. This person must be seen, Stern argued, as a goal-oriented locus of "e-valuations" and hence as an entity that is itself inherently valuable in a way that no mere thing could be. This is the person in the specifically "critical" sense intended by Stern, and it is by virtue of the evaluative powers of this person that he or she must be regarded as an entity whose capabilities exceed the passive responsivity characteristic of things. Those capabilities extend to self-activation and to the genuine purposivity that the power of evaluating, the capacity to imbue value, necessarily entails. Persons must, therefore, be conceived teleologically.

### Phenomena, Acts, Dispositions, and the "I"

Consistent with his intent to persuade readers coming from empirical psychology of the merits of a personalistic perspective on the individual, Stern (1917) chose to elaborate the case for the foregoing in what might be termed a "bottom-up" fashion. That is, rather than starting with broad philosophical notions and principles likely to be foreign to his more experimentally oriented colleagues and then deducing ever more circumscribed and more narrowly psychological notions from them, in "top-down" fashion, Stern (1917) began instead with the consideration of scientific psychology's familiar empirical rudiments, namely, the phenomena of consciousness, and then proceeded "upward" through ever broader and more inclusive notions. All along the way, Stern was at pains to point out how concepts invoked to unify lower-order considerations were themselves in need of unification through still higher-order notions. For Stern, the pinnacle of this theoretical/ philosophical progression would be the *person,* critically conceived.[7]

Stern began his exposition with a definition of *phenomena* that accorded fully with views then prevalent among his experimentally oriented colleagues:

> "Psychological phenomena" or "experiences" are those givens directly accessible to my own perception. In that through introspection I can assert them, "know" about them, they are "conscious." In that they are only "given" to me, they are passive, not active, not directed to goals; they are simply there, expressible in certain qualities, grades, and connections through my own perception; coming, staying, and disappearing in temporal relations likewise recognizable introspectively. (Stern, 1917, p. 11)

Starting with phenomena so understood, as the passively given rudiments of psychological experience, the immediate theoretical problem became that of accounting for their meaningful interrelationships. What is it that coordinates phenomenal experiences, thereby lending them coherence and keeping psychological life from degenerating into sheer chaos? This is the question of *unitas multiplex* as it arises already at the most rudimentary level of human psychological life, and Stern argued that a theoretically satisfactory answer to the question cannot be achieved while remaining wholly within the realm of phenomenal experience. Especially unconvincing in this regard, Stern contended, are answers framed in accordance with mechanistic conceptions of mind invoking,

> [A]bstract interrelationships directly linking, through law-like regularities of connection, one experience to another experience and one phenomenon to another phenomenon. "Associations" and "reproductions" are the two typical primary forms of such phenomenological concepts of relations. In the case of the former, [it is claimed that the] contents of consciousness are bound to one another simply through the fact of their being experienced together temporally. In the latter case, [it is argued], a phenomenon has, simply as a result of its having occurred, the capacity to surface again later in the same or similar form. (Stern, 1917, p. 13)

Without doubt, Stern's critique of these notions was metaphysically "barbed" in just the way that Allport (1937a) would later contend (refer to discussion of Allport's views in Chapter Four). The following passage reveals much not only about the stance Stern took with respect to this specific theoretical issue but also about the philosophical and theoretical basis of his personalistic convictions more broadly:

> Now it is very remarkable that in investigations of the interrelationships of phenomena a shift in perspective occurs. The phenomena, which as givens of self-observation would still have to be entirely passive, are now suddenly spoken of as causal and thus active factors: one idea is said to "pull behind itself" another with which it was previously connected, "suppress" a third, "strengthen" a fourth. One perception "influences" [another], or has the "tendency" to renew itself again as an idea in memory, and so forth. *One sees how much it runs contrary to human nature to conceive of the psychological as pure passivity.* But in order to satisfy the need for causal influences without in the process leaving the chosen level of projection [i.e., the realm of phenomenal experience], the contents of consciousness themselves are made into little active things!
>
> Yet since, on the other hand, one must avoid making ideas and feelings into little spirits functioning personally, their activity is conceived not as personal but instead as something purely objective and mechanical. Just as one link in a chain pulls along the other on the basis of the mechanical law of adhesion, so does one idea call forth another idea in accordance with the general law of association, which is not concerned with the goals and objectives of the person. It is among the older associationistic psychologies, and in the work of Herbart, where this mechanization has found its sharpest expression, but one may well say that the tendency in this direction must inhere in any psychology that orients itself fundamentally to the phenomena of consciousness as its real object. (Stern, 1917, pp. 13–14; emphasis added)[8]

As Stern would eventually express matters, the key to resolving this particular theoretical conundrum is to be found in a form of the principle: *"Keine Gestalt ohne Gestalter!"*—No meaningful perceptual whole *(Gestalt)* absent a meaning-endowing percipient *(Gestalter)!* (Stern, 1938, p. 114). In Stern's view (one amply infused with Kantian rationalism), phenomenological psychology already contained the germ of this very principle within the thesis of phenomena as experiences *given to self-observation.* In the 1917 monograph, Stern argued this case vigorously:

> Phenomenological psychology holds itself to the word "given." But what happens when we focus on the words "self-observation"? The notion of something given in itself is incoherent. *A given must be given to someone.* And this someone knows the given, and only grasps it through self-observation, that is,

through an *act* directed to that given. Thus the basic thesis of phenomenological psychology already includes within it the admission that *every phenomenon has two kinds of preconditions which are not themselves phenomena:* a "someone," that is, an individual subject, and an assertion, that is, an individual act of this subject. (Stern, 1917, pp. 15–16; emphasis added)

Here, Stern was in the midst of articulating a defensible conception of this "someone," this "subject" of scientific psychology's experimental investigations, the person. At this particular point in the exposition under present consideration, however, Stern (1917) invited his readers to temporarily delay the task of considering that entity in its totality. He directed attention instead to the more circumscribed fact of that entity's assertions in the very act of introspection, or "self-observation." It is this concept of *act* that Stern invoked to account for the coherent unification of otherwise wholly disparate and utterly chaotic experiential phenomena. It is through activity, the purposive doing or asserting of something, that "these" rather than "those" phenomenal givens are made salient in a subject's experience at a given point in time and gathered into meaningful, coherent interrelationships. Embedded within acts of attention, or judgment, or discrimination, or recollection, for example, phenomena do not constitute merely a diverse array of passive, isolated, and even chaotic perceptual impressions—but rather components of unified, meaningful experiences.

From a personalistic perspective, all activity is to some degree and in some or other way(s) goal oriented and therefore selective, rendering certain phenomena more salient than others. In Stern's view, there is no way to account for this aspect of human mental life in strictly phenomenal terms. "Phenomena," reiterated Stern, "are themselves not active" (1917, p. 20). On the contrary, as the "givens" of experience, phenomena are by definition passive. On the other hand, while acts are, quite obviously, active, it is also true that "acts are not themselves phenomena of consciousness" (Stern, 1917, p. 20). So, for example, in the act of riding a bicycle, certain perceptual phenomena arise—visual, acoustic, kinesthetic—and are coordinated in and through various goal-oriented acts of attention, judgment, and memory; but at no point is an act of attention or judgment or memory as such a "given" of phenomenal experience.[9] Thus did Stern argue that although an understanding of the psychological functioning of an individual must surely incorporate phenomenal experiences, it cannot be achieved within a theoretical system that considers phenomenal experiences exclusively.

If otherwise disparate and even chaotic phenomenal experiences are coordinated through acts, the question arises as to how disparate acts are organized in turn. The theoretical problem, as Stern understood it, is that acts are temporally "acute," meaning that they are of limited duration. Manifest in individual lives, however, are temporally extended or "chronic" act patterns, and this fact points to the need for a theoretical concept through which to grasp the coherences revealed by such patterns. An act, Stern argued,

[C]annot be regarded as something that rises up out of nothing only to return again into nothing. On the contrary, an act must be thought of as an expression of a more than momentary capability in order to function as such. *No actuality without potent-iality.* (Stern, 1917, p. 24; emphasis added)

As noted briefly in Chapter Two, the concept invoked by Stern to meet this theoretical requirement is that of *the dispositions (die Dispositionen)*, and it was through his conception of dispositions as *potentialities for acts of certain kinds* that Stern explicitly distinguished his personalistic perspective on this matter from that which had been afforded by the earlier faculty psychology:

Contentwise, the disposition does not have a fixed quality [within critical personalism]. This is how the old "faculties" were understood. They were considered as powers through which certain consciousness contents were produced. . . . [F]or us, the unity of each disposition is manifest instead by the likeness of the acts which it enables, *or—since the acts are teleological factors— through the unity of the partial goals which the disposition serves.* On this account, memory is not the capability of producing memoric ideas, but is instead the disposition to make available earlier acquisitions for later life tasks. Intelligence is not the capability to set into course thoughts or thought sequences of a particular kind, but instead the ability to adjust oneself, through acts of thought, to new situations and demands. Character is not the disposition toward certain emotional and willful experiences, but rather the disposition to set certain goals of inner and outer acts of will. (Stern, 1917, pp. 27–28; emphasis added)

It was noted briefly in Chapter Two that Stern distinguished between *labile* and *stable* dispositions. The former category subsumed potentialities still relatively amenable to alteration by outer influences. The latter category subsumed potentialities that over the course of an individual's development become relatively impervious to outer influences. It was specifically for dispositions of this latter sort that Stern reserved the term *traits (Eigenschaften)*. Because the introduction of this term brings critical personalism as close as it ever gets to modern "trait psychology," it bears emphasis that even here, the two frameworks remain, philosophically speaking, worlds apart: From a personalistic theoretical standpoint, traits are psychological potentialities present *within* individuals, not empirical continua invoked by outside observers to differentiate *between* individuals within populations.[10]

From this point forward, with respect to the concept of dispositions, the gulf between critical personalism and contemporary "nomotheticism" only becomes wider. Whereas contemporary thinking is directed, in wholly empiricistic fashion, toward accounts of the manner in and degree to which trait variables defined for populations of persons can be used to "explain" between-person variance in selected domains of human behavior (refer to discussion in Chapter Seven), Stern's thinking was directed toward the theoretical problem of accounting for the unity within the individual of his or her own psychological dispositions—a completely different issue. In addressing this issue, Stern argued as follows:

> A disposition is a causal capacity, but [such] a potentiality does not exist in itself. Rather, *it must inhere in some entity*. We call this required carrier of a basic psychological disposition the "I" or "subject." It is thus simultaneously the last point of relationship of the three lower levels, and this relationship may be described as follows: *The "I" experiences phenomena, executes acts, owns dispositions*. (Stern, 1917, p. 31; emphasis added)

## The Psychophysically Neutral Person, the Telic Nature of Personality Development, and Person-World Convergence

For all his emphasis on the "psychological side" of human existence, Stern was far from oblivious to the fact that individuals are biological creatures as well. Thus, in the 1917 monograph, he offered a scheme for conceptualizing this "side" of human life that directly parallels the treatment discussed above of phenomena, acts, dispositions, and the "I." More specifically, the biological counterparts to these latter four concepts were designated by Stern (1917), respectively, as (a) bodily organs and vessels, (b) biological acts such as respiration, circulation, and digestion, (c) instinctive behavioral dispositions such as fight-or-flight, and finally, (d) the unitary organism as such.

To this point, Stern's analysis seems to culminate in a kind of mind-body duality, with the "I" on one side as "the *unitas multiplex* for everything psychological" and the organism on the other side as "the *unitas multiplex* for everything physical" (Stern, 1917, p. 39). It is precisely here, however, in his crowning conception of the person, that Stern saw critical personalism as transcending the dualistic legacy of Cartesian thought. Stern argued that although individuals are without doubt subject to regard from either a psychological or physical (biological) perspective, a person is the necessary precondition for any mind-body distinction at all and so must be conceived as an entity that exists both prior to and neutrally with respect to any such distinction. Stated otherwise, the person as such is *psychophysically neutral*. Quoting his own 1906 work, Stern (1917) underscored this thesis as follows:

> Not that there is the physical and the psychological, but rather that there are real persons, is the basic fact of the world. That these persons can be present to themselves and to others, and thereby give rise to notions of the psychological and physical, is a fact of the world of second order. (Stern, 1906, pp. 204–205; 1917, p. 42)

Proceeding from this understanding of the person as a psychophysically neutral entity, Stern (1917) sketched the main features of his essentially teleological conception of personality development. In this regard, he postulated two broad categories of ends or goals with respect to which persons orient themselves: the *autotelic* and the *heterotelic*.

As the name suggests, autotelic goals are one's personal objectives, and Stern proposed to understand the most rudimentary of these through a further subdivision into the categories of self-maintenance *(Selbsterhaltung)* and self-unfolding *(Selbstentfaltung)*. In the former case, the person is seen to be striving for the *continuity of being* in relationship to the world (i.e., survival). In the latter case, the goals are more in the nature of the further *realization of potentialities*. Obviously, specific subgoals within each of these categories could be highly individualized or idiosyncratic.

The category of heterotelic goals likewise subsumes various subcategories, but all these pertain to goals that initially lie outside the goal system of the person of regard. As to the question—and it is an important one—of why the consideration of goal systems lying outside the person would be relevant to an understanding of individual persons in the first instance, Stern argued as follows:

> [T]he person who pursues only his/her own narrow individual goals would be an extensionless point in emptiness. Only goals extending beyond the self give the person concrete content and living coherence with the world. Autotelie encounters heterotelie. (Stern, 1917, p. 46)

Among those goal systems initially lying outside a given individual person would be the (in some ways idiosyncratic) autotelic goals of other persons. To the extent that these latter would be incorporated into one's own purposes or objectives (i.e., to the extent that one individual would establish as part of his or her goal system that of facilitating the realization by other individuals of their own goals), the latter would become, for the person of regard, what Stern called *syntelic*.

In some instances, however, the (initially) outer goals are properly regarded not as individual goals at all, but rather as the *transpersonal* goals of larger entities such as "family, folk, humanity, deity" (Stern, 1917, p. 46). To the extent that goals of this sort are incorporated into one's own purposes or objectives, the former are, in Stern's terminology, *hypertelic* for the person of regard.

Finally, Stern (1917) explained, "[T]here are goals which do not pertain directly to other individual persons or transpersonal entities, but instead to the realization of abstract ideals such as truth, morality, justice, holiness, the idea of nationality, etc." (p. 46). To the extent that goals of this sort are made one's own, they are termed *ideotelic*.[11]

Through the consideration of these various goal systems and the individual person's relationship to them, Stern was formulating the basis for an understanding not only of human individuality but also of human diversity *(Mannigfaltigkeit)* and, with that, of *community*. In this connection, Stern (1917) described the reconciliation of self-goals with the goals of other persons and with suprapersonal goals, as follows:

> The basic opposition of autotelie and heterotelie is overcome through an ultimate synthesis. It is a fact not subject to further analysis, perhaps the last and highest secret of the human personality, that it takes up the heterotelic into the autotelic. The (initially) outer goal indeed remains directed to the not-I, but is appropriated within and formed according to one's own self. Only in this way does it become possible that the surrender to suprapersonal and non-personal goals nevertheless does not signify any de-personalization, or any degradation of the personality to a mere thing and mere tool, but that, on the contrary, the personality becomes, through its embodiment of the outer goals in its self activity, a microcosmos. (Stern, 1917, p. 47)

The process of "taking up" the heterotelic into the autotelic and thus appropriating outer goals to the self-system is a process Stern labeled *introception*. Because it refers to an active, purposive process, this concept played a central role in Stern's understanding of the person-world relationship more generally. In his view, that relationship can neither properly be understood as one in which dispositional "faculties" are mechanistically determinative of an individual's actions without regard for external factors nor as one in which the world or "environment," physical or social, somehow presses upon the person in equally mechanistic fashion, buffeting an essentially passive being this way and that, and thus determining how the individual will behave at any given point in time. On the contrary, Stern held, the proper understanding of the person-world relationship requires an appreciation for the manner in which a purposive, goal-oriented, and "e-valuating" entity, a person, *converges* with his or her physical and social milieu. The world, in this view, is not simply a "partial determinant" of an individual's behavior, exerting its effects from without, whether in addition to or in opposition to the determinative effects of inner "faculties," but a genuine codeterminant of behavior in a way described by Stern as follows:

> With his/her inner dispositions, the person is simultaneously goal-striving and *in need of supplementation (ergänzungsbedürftig)*. To this end, room and direction is postulated for the participation of the world in the person's development. Nativism, which attributes to the greatest possible extent all personal happenings to the preconditions given in the person, and empiricism, which allows world influences the greatest possible degree of power over the person, are superceded through convergence. On this view, it is due to the incompleteness and breadth of latitude of every personal disposition that in its realization factors residing in the external world necessarily play a role, while yet at the same time, the power of this influence is circumscribed and colored through the goals of the person. (Stern, 1917, p. 51; emphasis added)[12]

Stern's conception of persons as entities that although inherently purposive and evaluative are nevertheless in need of supplementation by others provides an important point of philosophical and theoretical contact with at least some understandings of social constructionism (cf. Gergen, 1991, 1992, 1999; Harré, 2000; Lamiell, 1992; Lamiell & Deutsch, 2000; Renner & Laux, 2000), and this is a point to which we will return in Chapter Ten. Our immediate purposes are better served, however, by considering a specific example of personalistic inquiry carried out by Stern himself in collaboration with his wife, Clara (1878–1945).

# An Early Example of Personalistic Inquiry: Recollection, Testimony, and Lying in Early Childhood

As mentioned in Chapter One, the Stern couple kept diaries in which they recorded extensive observations of their three children from 1900 until 1918, and William Stern made explicit note of the importance of the diary material for the refinement of his personalistic outlook (Stern, 1927). This being the case, we should not be surprised to find in *Recollection, Testimony, and*

*Lying in Early Childhood* (C. Stern & W. Stern, 1909/1999, one of the two published monographs based on the diary material and the only one thus far available in English translation) various features of the work that can serve to concretely illustrate some important aspects of personalistic thinking. Of course, no single work of the sort exemplified by *Recollection, Testimony, and Lying in Early Childhood* could be expected to illustrate all facets of critical personalism, and no secondary treatment of the present sort could do justice to such a wealth of material, in any case. Still, the following discussion should serve to concretize some significant features of the personalistic perspective.

## Some Methodological Considerations in the Conduct of Personalistic Research

Certainly, as an exercise in personalistic inquiry, *Recollection, Testimony, and Lying in Early Childhood* is noteworthy in part for methodological reasons. Of primary importance in this regard is the attention the Sterns paid to the individual case. Part I of the book, which includes chapters on "Recognition as the Basis of Recollection," "The Chronological Development of Recall and Testimonial Ability," and "False Testimony: Mistaken Recollections, Pseudo-Lies, and Lies," is based exclusively on observations of daughter Hilde that had been recorded in the diaries from 1900 until August of 1907.

The Sterns' focus here on a single case was of course entirely appropriate given that the subject matter of interest pertained to psychological processes being played out, in one way or another, at the level of the individual person. And yet it is telling that even as early as 1909, Clara and William Stern found it necessary to explicitly defend their use of the *psychographic* method of research, that is, the investigative scheme that William Stern would soon incorporate into his broad vision of differential psychology (Stern, 1911) as an approach entailing the study of one individual in terms of many attributes (refer to Chapter Two of this volume, esp. Figure 2.3). In the very first paragraph of Part I of *Recollection, Testimony, and Lying in Early Childhood*, the Sterns directly addressed themselves to this methodological issue as follows:

> In opposition to the method of portraying the individual in child psychology, critics have often maintained that the results of such investigations are not scientifically useful, because the findings obtained with a single child cannot be generalized. This view, however, overlooks an important use of child psychography, because the very issues warranting psychological investigation cannot

be regarded as if they were somehow obvious from the start. On the contrary, the issues themselves emerge in their fullness only if one continuously follows the course of development of a particular individual. Moreover, the conditions giving rise to a specific phenomenon—in our case *testimony,* or the giving of some sort of report about something that has in some way been experienced— are probed quite differently when one studies individuals than when one studies large groups, in which any given individual is tested and observed only on an *ad hoc* basis. (Stern & Stern, 1999, p. 3)

The Sterns were far from blind to the important question of generalization. On the contrary, Part II of the 1909 monograph is titled "Comparative Psychology of Testimony in Early Childhood." Here, guided in part by considerations that had been taken up in Part I, the bandwidth of the inquiry was broadened to include not only observations that the Sterns had made of their other two children, Günther and Eva, but also material—some of it published in the professional literature—based on observations that other investigators had made, independently, of their own children. Worthy of comment in this regard is the fact that as they expanded their inquiry to include more than one case, the Sterns were not abandoning the "single subject" or "$N = 1$" approach, but were *repeating* it. It is in this way that one logically gains warrant for such generalizations across individual cases as might in fact prove *empirically* justified. In contrast, for the Sterns to have shifted over from the sequential or parallel study of individual cases—the proper empirical basis for what Stern (1911) designated "comparison research"—into an aggregate, statistical framework, with its attendant focus on group means, variances, intercorrelations, and tests of statistical significance, would have been for them to embark on a completely different investigative enterprise—one that, for reasons which at this point should be manifest, would have been fundamentally incompatible with the personalistic outlook. In *Recollection, Testimony, and Lying in Early Childhood,* therefore, one finds no trace whatsoever of the aggregate statistical thinking proper to neo-Galtonian inquiry.

A second aspect of this work that is particularly noteworthy from a methodological standpoint is its reliance on nonlaboratory procedures. Given the subject matter of *Recollection, Testimony, and Lying in Early Childhood,* and given also the close personal and professional ties that existed between William Stern and Hermann Ebbinghaus (the latter of whom died in the very year that the work under present consideration was published), one is struck by the absence in the Sterns' work of references to Ebbinghaus's laboratory studies of memory. In the Sterns' view, however, much of worth—and indeed, of truly scientific worth—could be learned by carefully and systematically observing persons engaging in meaningful actions in their natural milieus. To this issue, as well, the Sterns addressed themselves directly in *Recollection, Testimony, and Lying in Early Childhood*:

> In this work, it was not necessary to adhere to a pre-established observational scheme. . . . The reason for this is that life in the nursery, with all of its pleasures and pains, all of its routine and special occasions, was occurring around the parents, and more specifically around the mother, all the time, and thus offered countless opportunities to follow and to pinpoint the psychological development of the young person in a wide variety of respects. . . . Only rarely did we resort to experiments, and then only in ways that were engaging to the child. To this end, pictures proved very helpful to us in many connections, as means of testing perception, testimony, intelligence, and speech. Tiring experiments—for example, on color recognition, learning to count, and so forth—were avoided, not just because such procedures are only burdensome to the children, but also because we did not wish to artificially hasten or otherwise alter the natural course of development. (Stern & Stern, 1999, pp. xxxv-xxxvi)

As this passage indicates, the Sterns did not eschew experimentation altogether. What they did instead was arrange circumstances in such a way that the children could be observed systematically while engaging in activities that could easily and unobtrusively be incorporated into their usual daily routines.[13] So, for example, inasmuch as looking at picture books and discussing their contents was very much a part of family life in the Stern household, it was fairly easy for the parents to set up observational sessions during which one of the children (at a time) would examine a novel picture for some specified period of time and then be asked to report on its contents.

In one such experiment, the Sterns used the "Breakfast Picture" (Dürr-Borst, 1906; see Stern & Stern, 1999, p. 76). Working independently, each of the children was asked to examine the picture silently for 1 minute and then repeat back every feature of the picture he or she could freely recall. The child was then prompted according to a predesigned list of questions, some of which were phrased as "leading questions" designed to induce false answers. After a 1-week interval, the child was again asked to freely recall the contents of the picture. This session was immediately followed by a self-correction period in which the child was once again shown the picture and permitted to compare his or her recollections with the actual contents of the picture.

In a second experiment, also involving a picture, the Sterns wished to investigate "the children's ability to recall material that, unlike the 'Breakfast Picture,' had been more or less continuously present to them" (Stern & Stern, 1999, p. 90). For this purpose, they selected the image that appeared on a tapestry that for some 2 1/2 half to 3 years had been prominently displayed in the children's room (see Stern & Stern, 1999, p. 92). "Without any advance warning," the Sterns wrote, "we would take one of the children to a different room and asked him/her to tell us what she/he knew about the picture" (Stern & Stern, 1999, p. 91).[14] The basic procedure designed for these studies was the same as that described above for the "Breakfast Picture" experiments.

In the course of these experiments, the Sterns kept verbatim (or nearly verbatim) records of each child's statements during the free-recall sessions and of their respective answers to the prompting questions. These records were then used to tabulate certain results for comparative purposes. Readers interested in the specific findings are referred to the original source (see Stern & Stern, 1999, Chapter 8). With respect to our present methodological concerns, however, the following points are of greater moment.

To be noted first of all is the fact that in the case of Eva, the Sterns found it necessary to somewhat modify the procedure described above to accommodate the difference between her age and the ages of her siblings. Thus, in connection with the "Breakfast Picture" experiment, conducted when Hilde was 7 years, 8 months, and Günther was 5 years, 5 months, but little Eva was but 2 years and 11 months of age, the Sterns wrote,

> With Eva, it was not possible to carry out the experiment exactly as we had done with her two older siblings, because it is impossible to get a child of this age to look at a picture and say nothing. So in Eva's case, we presented the picture and asked if she would like to tell us everything she saw in the picture. The exposure time was 2 minutes rather than 1 minute, as had been the case for the other two children. We then took the picture away and proceeded to her report and then to the questioning. (Stern & Stern, 1999, p. 87)

We see here that in light of an important aspect of Eva's individuality, in this case, her age, the Sterns found it necessary to alter the investigative procedure they had used with Eva's older siblings so as to take this fact about Eva into account. Certainly, Clara and William Stern were not blind to the possibility that an alteration of this sort could to some extent compromise the comparability of the results obtained with Eva to those obtained with Hilde and Günther. Nevertheless, from a personalistic standpoint, the requirements of psychographic inquiry trump those of comparative studies.

Another principle of personalistic inquiry vividly illustrated in the Sterns' discussion of the findings of these experiments is their refusal to treat the tabulated data as if they somehow spoke for themselves or as if those data should for some reason uncritically be given more weight than seemingly more "subjective" observations provided by the investigators. We learned in Chapters Two and Three of the stress William Stern repeatedly placed on the importance, in personalistic inquiry, of systematically incorporating "the observations of sensitive persons who have spent some extended time with the person whose psychological profile is being constructed" (Stern, 1921, p. 3). Such observations were prominently displayed by the Sterns at the conclusion of Chapter 8 of *Recollection, Testimony, and Lying in Early Childhood,* where they commented on the overall similarity between Hilde and Günther projected by the tabulated (i.e., quantitative) findings:

> The substantial convergence in the performances of the two older children might seem surprising at first, but it would be a mistake to generalize these results either across age or gender. Certainly, there is no moratorium between the ages of 5 and 7 in the development of the ability to testify, nor should the comparability of Günter's[15] performance with that of his older sister be taken as evidence that, in general, boys have some sort of an advantage over girls. We believe we are simply dealing with an individual difference between Günter and Hilde. Günter's strong visual sense, especially his perception of colors, had such a powerful effect that it overcompensated for his deficiency–in comparison to his sister–with respect to suggestibility. Evidence of this comes from the study involving the often-seen picture of the geese, where he not only equaled but surpassed his sister (30 versus 25 correct statements; 4 versus 6 false statements). In this case, where it was not a matter of a one-time concentration of attention but rather of a habitual and recurrent exposure, conditions were especially favorable for his natural inclination toward the visual and his great interest in images. (Stern & Stern, 1999, pp. 98–99)

Reading these lines, one can scarcely fail to appreciate the way in which the Sterns sought to weave into the interpretation of their quantitative research findings the fruits of their extensive, personal familiarity with their research "subjects." Without question, William Stern maintained for the duration of his scholarly life the deep conviction that no psychology of personality worthy of the name could flourish without interpretive efforts of this sort.

We see here also that although the Sterns were determined to accommodate the facts (as they saw them) of certain differences between Hilde and Günther in their interpretation of the experimental results, at no point did the Sterns make, or propose to make, those differences themselves the objects of study. The experiments were designed to shed light on *the psychology of recollection,* not to track individual differences in some "recollective faculty."

## Some Theoretical and Philosophical Issues
## Highlighted by a Personalistic Conception of Lying

Beyond its serviceability as a window onto certain methodological aspects of personalistic inquiry, *Recollection, Testimony, and Lying in Early Childhood* is also a very useful work within the context of which to highlight certain important theoretical and philosophical aspects of personalistic thought more generally. Though much could be said in this regard with specific reference to recollection and testimony, the Sterns' 1909 work is richest in these respects in its consideration of lying. The reason for this is soon grasped after considering the manner in which the Sterns defined lying:

> Lies are consciously false assertions made with the intention of deceiving others. Both features are required: If a speaker is unaware that what she or he is saying is false, then there is no lie. Moreover, if the speaker is aware that what she is saying is false, but has no intention of deceiving, then again there is no lie. (Stern & Stern, 1999, p. 31)

It is perhaps safe to assume that few, if any, would find quarrel with the notion that absent awareness that an assertion is false, a speaker cannot be regarded as having lied through that assertion. The third sentence in this passage, however, may seem a bit more problematic, in that it may not be immediately obvious what is meant by speaking of an assertion that is consciously false yet made without intention to deceive. Here, however, the Sterns' analysis of lying by children became quite nuanced as they went to some lengths to distinguish between "genuine" lies, on one hand, and what they termed "pseudo lies" *(Scheinlügen),* on the other. In playful fantasy, for example, a child will often invent mates and imagine happenings and then relate his or her fantasies to parents or others in full awareness that what is being said does not refer to actual people or events. Instances of this sort qualify as pseudo lies in that what is being said is known to be false and yet is not being said with the intention to deceive. The relevant intention might very well be, for example, to *entertain.*[16]

What is most relevant about all of this to our present concerns is the crucial role played by intentionality. "Genuine lies," as the Sterns would reiterate, are "consciously false assertions in which a *purposive* and *deliberate* attempt is made to deceive others" (Stern & Stern, 1999, p. 112; emphasis added). Clearly, a teleological conception of the person is, in this account, a philosophical prerequisite for any coherent discussion at all of lying. A being unable to act in a truly intentional, purposive, and deliberate way—that is, *freely*—is likewise incapable of lying to begin with. In a sense, therefore, the very engagement of this topic as a subject for psychological investigation brings with it a teleological conception of the person. Such a conception is fundamental to personalistic thinking (though, as we have seen, it is foreign to the mechanistic and hence ultimately impersonal theoretical perspectives against which Stern was struggling).

Still greater insight into the nature of personalistic thinking about psychological problems is provided by Chapter 12 of *Recollection, Testimony, and Lying in Early Childhood,* titled "The Origins of Lying and Its Prevention." In treating of this topic, the Sterns brought the personalistic conception of person-world convergence into bold relief and in so doing also made clear the relevance of personalistic thinking to questions of character, and hence to issues of moral consequence.[17]

The Sterns opened their discussion of the developmental course of lying as follows:

> Different perspectives on the moral aspects of early childhood are nowhere in greater conflict than with respect to the pedagogical problem presented by lying. On the one hand, the belief prevails that the small child is by nature not merely amoral but indeed antimoral, and that therefore lying is among the earliest manifestations of an egoism that has yet to be brought under control. On the other hand, there is the conviction that the naïveté of the child entails an innocence and lack of guilt, and that therefore the caretakers alone must bear the responsibility for the child's lies: *"Tout est bien sortant des mains de l'auteur des choses; tout dégénere entre les mains de l'homme"* (Rousseau).[18] (Stern & Stern, 1999, p. 129; untranslated French in original)

Consistent with their view of convergence as a concept through which to overcome the nativism-empiricism duality, the Sterns proceeded to discuss those basic psychological features of persons, on one hand, and those socioenvironmental factors, on the other, that in certain patterns of convergence could lead to the development of lying as a chronic character trait, or to the avoidance of same.[19]

Concerning the psychological features of persons, the Sterns rejected the notion that lying per se could be regarded as a natural human tendency. Instead, they argued, there are certain basic human psychological tendencies that could play an important role in the development of lying as a chronic character trait under certain environmental circumstances. Among the basic human tendencies identified by the Sterns were (a) the natural inclination to defend oneself from unpleasant experiences (an autotelic goal having to do with *Selbsterhaltung* or "self-maintenance"), (b) the very capacity for fantasy (an autotelic goal having more to do with *Selbstentfaltung* or "self-development"), and (c) the tendency to imitate (also an autotelic goal oriented toward self-development). Among the environmental circumstances most consequential in this regard, the Sterns pointed to the untoward effects of harsh corporal punishment and excessive inquisitiveness on the part of parents and other adults. In addition, special emphasis was placed on the ill-advised practice among adults of telling young children "white lies." The Sterns elaborated this latter concern as follows:

> Even the [supposedly] harmless "white lies" that children must listen to, or into which they are sometimes recruited (e.g., being told to say that "Mother is not at home" when mother does not wish to be visited) perhaps draw the child's attention for the first time to the fact that there is such a thing as an intentional deviation from the truth. In any case, these experiences deprive children of their unquestioning trust in what adults say.
>
> It is surprising to see how highly educated persons engage in activities that they regard as harmless to their children. To save 10 cents on the streetcar, a mother will risk damaging what is most precious in the child. She requires the child to lie about his age, and in the process she herself sows the seeds of untruthfulness. Then, later, when the same child lies to his mother at home, he will receive a lecture about lying and will be punished. "Children's lies are the work of the child-raiser" (Rousseau). (Stern & Stern, 1999, p. 131)

We see here that far from shying away from socioethical questions or from viewing considerations of human values as somehow lying outside the boundaries of an objective scientific psychology, the Sterns regarded commentary of this sort as part and parcel of their proper contribution, as psychological scientists, to the larger society of which they were a part.[20] The following passage serves to further underscore this important point. Concluding their discussion of the developmental origins of lying and of ways of preventing it, the Sterns referred once again to the views of the French philosopher and pedagogue, Jean Jacques Rousseau (1712–1778):

> Rousseau . . . goes too far when he teaches, in his *Émile*, that one should not demand the truth from a child and in the process induce the child to conceal the truth, or that one should not demand a promise so that it will not be broken, or that in the case of some or other incident one should never ask "Did you do that?" and so forth. He states, "The more the child's well-being is made independent, be it of the will of others or of their judgment, the less will be the child's interest in lying." This artificial isolation, discussed in talk of "natural" child-rearing, is essentially a kind of pampering that will exact its cost as soon as the unnatural conditions maintaining isolation no longer hold. One can well understand Rousseau's views as a reaction to prevailing, overly strict child-rearing

practices. But in struggling against excessive discipline, he also undermines, to a considerable extent, self-discipline; and it is precisely those child-rearing practices that foster self discipline that offer the best possibility of recruiting the child him- or herself to the collective struggle against lying. Even in the most sheltered environment, real life does not insulate the child from the lies of others, or from his or her own attempts to lie. A child whose parents teach him about the importance of maintaining self-control in general, a child who has learned to curb his own anger, or to forego a pleasure out of consideration for others, or to tolerate an unfairness—yes, one who can take satisfaction in having achieved self-control—will also overcome his own inclinations to lie. (Stern & Stern, 1999, p. 137)

The concern expressed in this last passage for questions having ultimately to do with personal character is obvious enough. Beyond this, however, the reader might sense an undertone of anti-individualism in the stance taken by the Sterns vis-à-vis Rousseau. In the light of William Stern's relentless concern over the entire course of his professional life for what he called the "problem of individuality," the presence of this undertone might seem surprising. It is indeed there, however, and in fact is not out of place, at least as far as Stern himself was concerned.

In the foreword to *The Human Personality,* the second volume of *Person and Thing,* published in 1918, Stern wrote that it would be his task to show how critical personalism is a system of thought,

[A]s distant from a one-sided individualism which recognizes only the rights and happiness of the single individual, as from a socialism, in which individual uniqueness and freedom are choked by the pressure of supra-personal demands. (Stern, 1918a, p. x)

For all our concern in the present chapter with the personalistic conception within scientific psychology of the individual person, an entire aspect of personalistic thinking has been left largely unexplored. To be sure, hints in this direction have been provided by mention of (a) domains of human values lying beyond those of the individual person, (b) the notion that in the course of personality development, the individual is supplemented by the external world, including the social world, and (c) the concept of introception, conceived by Stern as a process whereby certain of those aforementioned values lying outside the individual are appropriated by him or her in the course of personality development. These are matters of considerable moment, to be explored further in Chapter Ten. For the present, it is sufficient to simply take note of the fact that at least from Stern's perspective, "personal-ism" cannot be equated with "individual-ism."

## Summary

Given the utter and irremediable inadequacy of neo-Galtonian thinking as a basis from which to approach what William Stern (1900a) called "the problem of individuality" within scientific psychology, the need exists for a fundamentally different approach to the problem based on a philosophically sound and theoretically coherent conception of *persons*. Accordingly, the present chapter has been devoted to a discussion of the view Stern sought to develop within that system of thought he called *critical personalism*.

Fundamental to critical personalism is the distinction between *persons* and *things*. The former are entities that can, do, and indeed must "e-valuate" actively, whereas the latter are entities that can only *be evaluated*, passively. Evaluation itself is a purposive act presupposing certain goals or objectives. Hence, evaluating entities, or *persons,* must be regarded as fundamentally teleological in nature and so cannot properly be conceived in purely mechanistic, or *impersonalistic,* fashion. Through the goals of *acts,* persons render coherent what would otherwise be chaotic phenomena; through the objectives of *dispositions,* persons coordinate what would otherwise be disjointed acts; and it is through the purposivity of the *self,* or "I," that persons synthesize their more or less enduring dispositions into certain characteristic ways of being.

Speaking at a very general level, the purposivity of human beings can be understood in terms of two broad categories: self-maintenance (or survival; *Selbsterhaltung*) and self-development (or "unfolding"; *Selbstentfaltung*). Within each of these broad categories, an individual's goals or objectives can be classified further as *autotelic* and *heterotelic*. The former reflect one's personal goals, whereas the latter reflect goals originating outside of oneself, in other individuals, and/or in the values propagated by the human institutions of which one is inevitably a part. Through a process Stern called *introception,* individuals can and do embrace as their own certain purposes originating outside themselves. Pursuit of such *syntelic* goals is seen within critical personalism as *person-world convergence* and thus emerges as a means of fostering community without compromising individuality.

In the latter half of this chapter, discussion centered around a work published in 1909 by Clara and William Stern, *Recollection, Testimony, and Lying in Early Childhood* (Stern & Stern, 1909/1999). This work provides a very useful context within which to illustrate certain points relevant to personalistic thinking, both from a substantive standpoint and from the standpoint of research methods. Particularly noteworthy in the latter regard are (a) the Sterns' manifest appreciation for the importance of investigating individual cases, (b) the absence of standardized laboratory manipulations, statistical analyses, and null hypothesis testing procedures proper to modern neo-Galtonian inquiry, and (c) the preparedness on the part of the investigators to supplement the presentation of objectively documented experimental results with interpretations based on extended familiarity with the subjects of the investigations.

With regard to substantive considerations within critical personalism, *Recollection, Testimony, and Lying in Early Childhood* (Stern & Stern, 1909/1999) is also illuminating by virtue of (a) its focus on the crucial role of intentionality in any coherent treatment of the act of lying and (b) its suitability as a medium with which to draw out the relevance of personalistic thinking to issues of socioethical consequence. Through the discussion of this latter point, a brief glimpse was gained of critical personalism's rejection of a one-sided "individual-ism," its clear and unwavering commitment to the concept of "individual-ity" notwithstanding.

# Notes

1.   Apologies to Barrett, who used this expression for the title of his fine book (Barrett, 1978).

2.   In this latter connection, the following anecdote speaks shrilly for itself. One contemporary investigator, asked by the publisher of this work to provide an anonymous review of the prospectus, replied as follows:

> I am a traditional Individual Difference psychologist. The philosophical and historical approach taken by [this author] was of no interest to me and, I suspect, is of little interest to most people in the field. . . . I tried to read the manuscript and I found it of no interest and of little relevance to the kinds of issues I address in my work. (Anonymous, October, 1999)

3.   Throughout his writings, Stern made extensive use of the word *Ausstrahlung* and its cognates to convey a sense of *radiance* analogous to the sun's aura.

4.   To be recalled in this regard is the discussion in Chapter Three of Stern's deep misgivings about psychotechnicians embracing that perspective on *Menschenbehandlung* urged by Hugo Münsterberg (1913). In Münsterberg's view, research subjects would properly be regarded as *means to others' ends*, that is, as objects or resources to be treated or deployed in the interest of achieving economic or institutional goals specified by others. For one contemporary representation of Münsterberg's views, see Hogan, Hogan, and Roberts (1996).

5. Within a year of the publication of *Psychology and Personalism* (Stern, 1917), there would appear a parallel piece of comparable length under the title *Foundations of Personalistic Philosophy* (Stern, 1918b). This publication is the printed version of a lecture that Stern delivered on October 17, 1917, before the Kant Society of Berlin. Together, these two works give further testimony to the extent to which Stern's scholarly interests and intellectual concerns were rooted not only in psychology but in the broader discipline of philosophy as well.

6. Stern's characterization here of the impersonalistic view of persons as a "bundle of perceptions" was surely an allusion to the views of the British philosopher David Hume (1711-1776) and, by implication, to that entire philosophy of mind known as *empiricism* (Robinson, 1995). It was noted in Chapter Seven that contemporary thinking about personality is quintessentially empiricist on just this model, and this is why such thinking is properly regarded as mechanistic and impersonal in precisely the sense described by Stern in this passage.

7. It is interesting to note that in the aforementioned *Foundations of Personalistic Philosophy* (Stern, 1918b), a work intended for an audience of philosophers (see Endnote #6), Stern organized his exposition of critical personalism in "top-down" fashion and so in a manner directly opposite to that adopted in *Psychology and Personalism* (Stern, 1917) for an audience of psychologists.

8. This last sentence can perhaps be read not only as an articulation by Stern of his own position but also as a way of deflecting any subsequent criticism of his views along the same lines invoked many years earlier by his own mentor, Ebbinghaus (1896b), in the latter's critique of Dilthey (1894). We saw in Chapter Seven that Dilthey had voiced doubts about the ability of scientific psychology to achieve meaningful accounts of human actions by starting from the analysis of psychological elements. We saw further that Ebbinghaus quickly dismissed Dilthey's arguments as having been directed against a "straw man" psychology that by 1894 had long since been displaced by positivistic thinking along lines drawn by Ernst Mach. In that context, Ebbinghaus specifically mentioned Herbart's ideas as representative of the older, outdated psychology. Perhaps, therefore, Stern was wary of being dismissed on the same grounds and for this reason may have felt compelled to emphasize that his concerns would apply to *any* psychology, which, if it did not attempt to sidestep the problem of explanation altogether, could offer only associationistic accounts for the phenomena of consciousness.

9. Certainly, it is possible to make acts of attention, judgment, memory, and so forth the objects of one's own consciousness, but doing this while in the act of riding a bicycle is a very dangerous proposition.

10. It will be recalled that Allport (1937a) tried to accommodate both of these two radically different conceptions of *trait* within his theory of personality (refer to Chapter Four). For reasons that I have sought to make clear in Chapter Seven, Allport's admission of the latter notion, that is, of traits as empirical continua marking between-person differences, was a profound mistake on his part, given what he himself was trying to accomplish theoretically vis-à-vis mainstream scientific psychology.

11.   The spelling of this term should be noted carefully. The root meaning from which the expression *ideotelic* springs is that of *ideal,* and not that of *idio-* in the previously discussed sense of *idiosyncratic* or (following Windelband) *idiographic.*

12.   There is a certain superficial resemblance between this conception of convergence and the orientation within modern personality psychology known as *interactionism* (see, e.g., Ekehammar, 1974; Endler & Magnusson, 1976). One major difference between these two views, however, lies in the fact that the modern interactionist conception of the "confluence" of person factors with environmental factors is mechanistic, whereas the personalistic conception of this process as represented by Stern is not. In addition, there is the fact that from an epistemic standpoint, modern interactionism is firmly embedded within the neo-Galtonian conception of psychological inquiry. Indeed, following Cronbach (1957), modern interactionism may be seen as the very epitome of this view. For both of these reasons, therefore, the superficial resemblance between interactionism and Stern's understanding of person-world convergence is just that—superficial—and nothing more.

13.   Some readers might find interesting in this respect some rather more recent observations by J. J. Gibson (1985). Commenting critically on a century of experimental research on perception, Gibson stated,

> We have assumed that the controlling of the physical variables of stimuli at the sense organs of a perceiver would relate the physical to the psychical, as if what he needed to perceive was physics. The experiments we need to design in future should control the display of stimulus information, not the physical variables of stimuli. *Or, for that matter, perfectly good experiments can be done outdoors under the sky without having to construct an artificial display.* (1985, p. 230; emphasis added).

14.   In reporting on this experiment, the Sterns noted that it was not conducted with the children at the same time. Instead, whereas Hilde was studied when she was 7 years and 8 months of age, and so at about the same time that the "Breakfast Picture" experiment was carried out, the other two children were not studied until several months later: Günther at the age of 6 years and 0 months and Eva at the age of 3 years, 6 1/2 months.

15.   For reasons I have not to date discovered, the spelling of the name of the Sterns' son actually changed over the course of the text of *Recollection, Testimony, and Lying in Early Childhood,* from *Günther* (with an *h*) to *Günter* (without an *h*). I incorporated that change into my English translation of the work and do the same in quoted passages here.

16.   Other categories of pseudo lies discussed by the Sterns are (a) untruths uttered defensively, simply as a way of warding off some unpleasant emotional state, and (b) certain instances of scapegoating. The reader interested in a detailed treatment of these topics is referred to Stern and Stern (1999), especially Chapters 3 and 10.

17.   The reader may contrast in this regard Allport's (1937a) critical commentary on the studies of honesty conducted by Hartshorne and colleagues in the late

1920s. Allport expressed regret that those investigators had allowed themselves to be guided in the design of their research not by a definition of honesty framed from the scientific perspective of child psychology, but instead by one framed "in the usual ethical terms," that is, "from the point of view of society and its conduct values." Allport went on to say that "the study of personality is difficult enough without complicating it at the beginning with ethical evaluation" (Allport, 1937a, p. 252). It was noted in Chapter Four that this stance by Allport was altogether foreign to Stern's personalistic perspective on such matters, and the discussion that ensues here should serve to underscore this point.

18.   "Everything is good when it leaves the hands of the creator, but degenerates in the hands of man."

19.   The Sterns also addressed themselves to the possibility that a personality disposition diametrically opposite to chronic lying could develop. They called this disposition "truth fanaticism," and noted that an exaggerated concern for telling the truth could finally be as personally and interpersonally problematic as pathological lying.

20.   Consistent with this understanding, the Sterns devoted the final chapter of *Recollection, Testimony, and Lying in Early Childhood* to a discussion of the implications of their research findings for the proper treatment and interrogation of young children in legal proceedings.

# Chapter Nine

## Some Models of Personalistic Inquiry in Contemporary Psychology

O n first consideration, the present effort toward reviving Stern's personalistic outlook on human individuality will perhaps strike many readers as both anachronistic and impractical. After all, critical personalism as a system of thought has been in place since early in the 20th century, and if for no other reason than the clear affinity between Stern's thinking and the romantic idealism so prominent in 19th-century German philosophy, many will find his perspective hopelessly out of step with modern, and even "postmodern," sensibilities. Beyond this, and quite apart from critical personalism per se, the argument for reinstituting some variant of the original Wundtian approach to empirical investigation—meaning that theoretical questions about individual psychological functioning would once again be investigated at the level of the individual—seems diametrically opposed to the objective, arguably as prominent now as ever, of producing knowledge about human behavior that is "practically useful." As noted in Chapter Five, the salience of just this objective figured prominently in the demise of the Wundtian research model to begin with. By these lights, the stance implied by the present challenge to the dominant neo-Galtonian framework may well appear pragmatically untenable, even to those who would finally concede the soundness of the challenge itself.

What must be kept firmly in mind, however, is the fact that that challenge is *warranted*. It brings into focus very real and utterly fundamental epistemic problems that cannot be made to disappear simply by ignoring them—nor can those problems possibly be neutralized from within the prevailing framework. Whatever else it is and however useful it might be for various actuarial/demographic purposes, the knowledge of aggregates yielded by statistical analyses of variables marking individual and group differences simply is not knowledge about individuals. Perseverance in the interpretive errors and conceptual confusions discussed in Chapter Seven merely perpetuates the illusion that matters are otherwise.

So, the following question begs: how finally to break free of the neo-Galtonian research framework in pursuit of a more personalistic scientific psychology? In the present chapter, I point in the direction of some possible answers to this question without presuming to resolve satisfactorily, or even to address, all relevant issues. What is offered here is more in the nature of a sketch, broadly indicative of two general fronts along which personalistic inquiry might well advance. The discussion is guided by three fundamental principles warranting emphasis from the very start.

The first of these is that if some or another form of insight into what is transpiring with individual persons is the sort of knowledge to be sought—and it is difficult to imagine how matters could be otherwise in any *psychology* worthy of the name—then the relevant empirical investigations must be carried out on individual persons. In this matter, there is no alternative, and this is true regardless of how "impractical" or "inefficient" such investigations might be, or might at first glance seem to be.

The second guiding principle here is that no logical incompatibility whatsoever exists between the study of individual persons, on one hand, and the scientific quest for laws or "law-like" regularities pertaining to persons in general, on the other. This is not to say that all studies of individuals are formally suited to this objective. It does serve, however, to reiterate for emphasis what was obvious to Wundt and other early practitioners of the general/experimental/*individual* psychology: A test of the hypothesis that some individual level psychological phenomenon pertaining to, say, sensation or perception or judgment or memory is governed by some specified law or captured by some law-like empirical regularity (e.g., in the case of memory, Ebbinghaus's well-known "forgetting curve") logically requires that relevant empirical evidence be sought at the level of the individual case, for there is no other way to empirically evaluate the proposition that the law or law-like regularity does indeed hold true for *persons in general*.[1]

The third guiding principle to be emphasized here has primarily to do with avoiding a potential red herring. Specifically, the objective of achieving a more personalistic approach to psychological inquiry does not require a categorical rejection of quantitative methods in favor of "qualitative" techniques. On the contrary, and as I shall endeavor to make abundantly clear, personalistic inquiry makes ample room for both approaches.

To be sure, and as we saw in Chapters Two and Three, Stern argued emphatically over the entire course of his career for incorporating direct observations of research subjects into *psychographic* studies, made by "sensitive persons who have spent some extended time with the individual whose psychological profile is being constructed" (Stern, 1921, p. 3). It was obvious to Stern that in a great many instances, it would be impossible to express such qualitative observations quantitatively, but in his view this would never be grounds for dismissing qualitative observations altogether. Indeed, he was actually more of the view that when qualitative findings ran counter to quantitative results, such as might be obtained with mental tests, for example, the qualitative findings would often be the ones warranting greater credence. In just this spirit, Stern argued that mental tests "by no means . . . render [qualitative methods] . . . superfluous" and that in many instances tests "must give way to what is revealed by the other methods" (Stern, 1911, p. 106; refer to discussion of this point in Chapter Three).

At the same time, however, Stern manifested in many of his works a deep respect and abiding appreciation for the important functions, conceptual as well as methodological, that would properly be served by measurement concepts and quantitative techniques in the advancement of a personalistic psychological science.[2]

Consistent with these three guiding principles, the remainder of this chapter is devoted to a discussion of some contemporary research focused on individuals and illustrating both quantitative and qualitative approaches to personalistic inquiry. First to be considered is research of a decidedly quantitative nature designed to shed light on the psychology of subjective personality judgments (cf. Lamiell & Durbeck, 1987; Lamiell, Foss, Larsen, & Hempel, 1983; Weigert, 2000). Discussion of this line of investigation will serve to clarify some conceptual issues of broader significance in the measurement of personality dispositions and will also highlight the manner in which quantitative data analysis techniques can be used in hypothesis testing from a personalistic perspective (Lamiell, 1995). Following discussion of this research, attention will be directed to recent work by Sabat (2001) investigating qualitatively, largely by means of extensive interview material, the experiences of persons suffering from Alzheimer's disease. This work serves not only to illuminate the crucial role of qualitative analysis in personalistic research methods but also to illustrate certain key concepts within critical personalism as a theoretical/philosophical system of thought.

## Some Illustrative Quantitative Research: Modeling the Psychology of Subjective Personality Judgments on Alternative Rationales for the Measurement of Personality Dispositions

It will be remembered from the discussion in Chapter Four that Gordon Allport's convictions concerning the possibility of fruitful "idiographic" inquiry were fueled in part by his belief that clinical and other subjective impressions about individuals' personality characteristics might well be grounded in intuitive judgments that do not necessarily, or even routinely, entail the comparison of individuals with one another along dimensions presumed "common to all" (Allport, 1937a). We also saw, however, that this notion of Allport's was summarily (and often harshly) dismissed by critics such as Lundberg (1941), Sarbin (1944), and Holt (1962) on the grounds that scientifically meaningful statements about an individual's personality characteristics *require* the comparison of that individual with others. We have already noted Epstein's (1983) reiteration of this conviction, and it has found still more recent expression in the writing of Cloninger (1996), who wrote,

> [I]n practice, wholly idiographic approaches [to person characterization] may be impossible, since any description of a person (for example, "Mary is outgoing") implies comparison with other people, even if this comparison is only in the memory of the one doing the analysis. (p. 5)

For all the stress placed by mainstream "nomotheticists" on the importance of prosecuting the psychology of personality scientifically, it is remarkable that the question raised by Allport (1937a) concerning the psychology of subjective personality judgments was never deemed worthy of empirical investigation. His hypothesis was then refuted and has since been ignored, not on the basis of evidence, but instead on the basis of dogma. In the research to be discussed below, however, Allport's hypothesis was taken seriously, and the findings of that research point rather emphatically toward the conclusion that his intuitions in this domain may very well have been correct. To set the stage properly for a consideration of that research, it is necessary to provide some additional background pertaining to issues in the measurement of personality dispositions more generally. We may begin by sketching Stern's own early efforts to articulate the personalistic perspective on psychological measurement.

## Preliminary Considerations

That all effort in the direction of quantification might seem at first glance to be antithetical to the personalistic perspective in psychological inquiry is a possibility of which Stern himself was fully aware. "No science," he once wrote, "seems more impersonal than mathematics" (Stern, 1906, p. 398). Elaborating this notion more than a decade later, he began the sixth chapter of *The Human Personality,* titled "Principles of Personality Measurement," as follows:

Of all ways of thinking, the mathematical way is the most impersonal. The application of amount and number to personal being and doing seems to signify the reduction [of the person] to an entity merely comparable [to other entities], to a mere instance of a stiff lawfulness, in short, to a thing. It is a fact that in virtually every instance where mathematical methods—measurement, experiment, statistics—have been applied to personal life and experience as well as to the cultural and social manifestations of personal communities, such a depersonalization has been the consequence. What is truly personal—the wholeness and individual specialness of being, the inner origin and goal-striving nature of doing—has been submerged, and persons have been made over into mere pieces of the measurable and countable larger world. (Stern, 1918a, p. 183)

And yet, Stern urged,

[We] should not adopt blindly a position against the possibility and fruitfulness of mathematization. We must only understand and approach it properly.... *[I]t is the convergence of the person with the world that must come to expression in specific measurable relationships and measurement principles.* (Stern, 1918a, pp. 183-184; emphasis added)

Stern's general approach to this problem was grounded in the concepts of Fechnerian psychophysics, and for reasons that will become apparent below, it is instructive to consider briefly how Stern tried to adapt those concepts to the requirements of his personalistic orientation.

For Stern, the most elementary measurement problem was to quantitatively represent the personal significance to a particular individual of some specified stimulus event. To address this problem, Stern (1918a) introduced the concepts of the *personal range (der persönliche Umfang)* and the *personal midpoint (die persönliche Mitte)* of a continuum of stimulation. The personal range would encompass alternative possible levels of stimulation extending between opposite extremes, referred to by Stern as the "personal range thresholds" *(die persönlichen Umfangsschwellen)*. The lower threshold would specify that extreme of the continuum of stimulation below which the person in question could not detect further decreases in stimulus intensity. Conversely, the upper threshold would specify that extreme of the continuum of stimulation above which that person could not detect further increases in stimulus intensity. As its name suggests, the personal midpoint of the continuum would be that point along the dimension of stimulation exactly halfway between the two personal range thresholds. With these concepts in place,[3] Stern continued as follows:

> Let L, M, N, O . . . represent the physical values of various stimuli, and $L_1$, $M_1$, $N_1$, $O_1$ . . . their respective polar opposites. Further, let $\Omega$ represent the personal midpoint of the stimulus continuum, likewise expressed in physical terms. Finally, let Z and $Z_1$ represent, respectively, the polar extremes [personal thresholds] of the stimulus continuum. Accordingly, quantity $(M - \Omega)$ defines the physical effect of stimulus M on the individual for whom $\Omega$ has been defined, and quantity $(Z - Z_1)$ defines the full range of effective physical stimulation for that same individual. The potential psychological significance of stimulus M for the individual in question is thus given by the expression $(M - \Omega)/(Z - Z_1)$. (Stern, 1918a, p. 210, footnote)

The quotient $(M - \Omega)/(Z - Z_1)$, Stern emphasized, thus indexes the psychological significance, to a specific person, of a given stimulus as "the ratio of its *actual* effect to the range of its *potential* effects" on that particular person (Stern, 1918a, p. 210; emphasis added). Such ratios, then, would formally represent *person-world convergence* in its most basic form.

Extending this line of reasoning in accordance with his conception of personality dispositions as *potentialities*, Stern (1918a) then added to the foregoing the concept of *personal preference (der persönliche Vorzugswert)*. Stern used this concept to refer to that position between the extremes of an individual's personal thresholds toward which that individual would strive purposely, in accordance with his or her goals, on one hand, and the demands/affordances of the environment, social and physical, on the other. Through this notion of personal preference, then, Stern introduced a teleological element to psychological measurement conceived in terms of person-world convergence.

In light of the foregoing, it appears very much as if Stern was aiming toward a theoretical understanding of the problem of dispositional measurement according to which what *is* said to be the case about an individual would properly be understood in terms of a context defined not by what is found to be the case about other individuals—again, Stern explicitly dismissed such between-person comparisons as irrelevant to the problem of representing person-world convergence—but rather in terms of what *has not but might otherwise have been* said to be the case about that individual, given his or her aspirations (objectives, preferences) and prevailing circumstances within the external world. However, and as noted in Chapter Three, Stern (1918a) made his concerns clear about the technical difficulties that such an approach to psychological measurement would present, and the historical fact is that he never made appreciable headway in this direction. Normative measurement operations (i.e., those tied to between-person comparisons) became, and have remained, the preferred method for measuring personality characteristics.

Nearly three decades after Stern's 1918 work, however, a perspective on matters very similar in certain formal respects to his own found expression in the discussion by Raymond B. Cattell (1944) of an approach to psychological measurement he called "interactive." We turn now to a consideration of what would be entailed by that approach to the measurement of personality dispositions and how it would differ from traditional normative procedures.

## Measuring Personality Dispositions

### I. From Behavioral Observations to "Raw Score" Assessments

Personality dispositions are not observed directly (Goldfried & Kent, 1972). What is observed are various overt behaviors—for practical reasons often taking the form of verbal statements about behavior—that are regarded as empirical indicators of the underlying dispositions. Brought to bear on records of these empirical indicators (as might exist, for example, in the form of a person's answers to the items of a professionally constructed paper-and-pencil "test" or inventory), personality measurement is essentially a formal exercise in *person characterization*. That is, it is a procedure for deriving meaningful quantitative expressions, here termed *measures,* of the respective levels at which a given personality is endowed with various dispositions of interest.

To achieve these desired measures, it is first necessary to derive from their putative empirical indicators what are here termed *raw score assessments.* As explained more thoroughly elsewhere (Lamiell, 1987), this step in the quantification process, from observations to assessments, has traditionally been executed in a way that can be formally represented in terms of the following general model (see also Hase & Goldberg, 1967):

$$A_{pd} = \sum (B_{pi}) (W_{id}) \qquad [9.1]$$

where

$A_{pd}$ represents the raw score assessment of person $p$ with respect to some underlying disposition $d$,

$B_{pi}$ represents the "$i$-th" member of a set of $m$ observations conveying information about the *behavior* of person $p$,

$W_{id}$ represents the conceptual *weight* or significance attached by the assessor to the "$i$-th" observation as an empirical indicator of disposition $d$, and

$\sum$ represents the summative operation through which the assessor combines the $m$ weighted observations concerning the behavior of person $p$ into the overall raw score assessment of that person with respect to disposition $d$.

To illustrate, we may once again use as a model the *NEO Personality Inventory* (Costa & McCrae, 1992) discussed in Chapter Six. As noted previously, this inventory consists of a total of 240 items, with 48 items designed to convey information about an individual relevant to each of the five traits of neuroticism, extraversion, openness, agreeableness, and conscientiousness. Each of the 240 items on the *NEO Personality Inventory* is written as a declarative sentence and is designed to relate to some aspect of an individual's typical behavior or characteristic psychological state. Illustrative items that in form and content are similar to (but not identical with) actual *NEO* items were given in Table 6.11, and it will be recalled from our earlier discussion of this instrument that an individual answers each item by selecting one of five possible responses: *strongly disagree, disagree, neither disagree nor agree, agree,* and *strongly agree.*

Numerical coding of a respondent's answers on the *NEO Personality Inventory* ensues using the consecutive integers 0 through 4 (refer to Table 6.12). In the calculation of an individual's scores on the inventory, these numerical codes, in effect, constitute the $B_{pi}$ component of Equation 9.1. The simple sum of these numerical values across the 48 items designated for assessing one of the "Big Five" traits defines an individual's total raw score assessment with respect to that trait. Note that this means, in effect, that the $(W_{id})$ component of Equation 9.1 (i.e., the numerical "weight" by which each numerically coded observation, $B_{pi}$, is cross-multiplied in the assessment of disposition $d$ is 1.0 for each of the 48 observations designated to assess that particular disposition and zero (0.00) for each of the other 192 items.[4]

With all this in mind, let us now suppose that as raw score assessments of neuroticism, extraversion, openness, agreeableness, and conscientiousness, some given respondent's *NEO Personality Inventory* protocol has yielded, respectively, the values 90, 128, 110, 100, and 92. What then?

## II. From "Raw Score" Assessments to
## Traditional Normative Measures

In the face of this question—What then?—the need for a clear distinction between raw score *assessments* and interpretable *measures* becomes apparent. The psychometrician's overriding goal here, it must be remembered, is to quantitatively express the level at which each of a number of dispositions is present within the personality of the target individual, and though numerical values of the sort just given represent a necessary step along the way to this objective, they clearly do not realize that objective completely. What remains to be more fully specified is the context within which each of these numerical values is to be interpreted. Measurement may thus be thought of as a formal procedure for *contextualizing* raw score assessments (Lamiell, 1987).

Throughout the 20th century, thinking about this problem within the mainstream has been thoroughly dominated by the conviction that "all meaning for a given score of a person derives from comparing his score with those of other persons" (Kleinmuntz, 1967, p. 47). Consistent with this view, and incorporated directly into the statistical methods proper to conventional neo-Galtonian inquiry, raw score assessments have been routinely contextualized in accordance with normative measurement operations defined by Equation 9.2:

$$Z_{pd} = (A_{pd} - \bar{A}_{.d}) / sd_{.d} \qquad [9.2]$$

where

$Z_{pd}$ represents the normatively computed *standard score* of person $p$ with respect to some underlying trait $d$, disposition.

$A_{pd}$ is defined by Equation 9.1,

$\bar{A}_{.d}$ represents the arithmetic mean computed for an *aggregate* of individuals by summing across those individuals their respective raw score assessments and then dividing that sum by the number of individuals in the aggregate, and

$sd_{.t}$ represents the standard deviation within the group of the set of assessments just named, computed as the square root of the average, across persons, of the squared deviations from $\bar{A}_{.d}$ of the individual $A_{pd}$ values.[5]

To illustrate Equation 9.2, let us consider again the five raw score assessments obtained for the complete 240-item *NEO Inventory* by the hypothetical individual mentioned above. For the domains of neuroticism, extraversion, openness, agreeableness, and conscientiousness, respectively,

**Table 9.1**    Combined Male-Female Population Means and Standard
Deviations for Form S of the (Revised) NEO *Personality Inventory*

| Domain | Mean | Standard Deviation |
|--------|------|--------------------|
| Neuroticism | 79.1 | 21.2 |
| Extraversion | 109.4 | 18.4 |
| Openness | 110.6 | 17.3 |
| Agreeableness | 124.3 | 15.8 |
| Conscientiousness | 123.1 | 17.6 |

SOURCE: Adapted from Costa & McCrae (1992).

these values were identified as 90, 128, 110, 100, and 92. Inserting these $A_{pd}$ values, in turn, into Equation 9.2 along with the appropriate mean and standard deviation in each case, taken from Table 9.1, the reader can verify that the resulting normative measures are +.51, +1.01, −.03, −1.54, and −1.77. Hence, compared to the others with reference to whom this individual is being characterized, it is found that he or she has measured *above* the population mean on neuroticism (by roughly .5 standard deviation; $Z = +.51$) and on extraversion (by 1 full standard deviation; $Z = +1.01$); almost exactly *at* the population mean on openness ($Z = −.03$); and *below* the population means on agreeableness (by about 1.5 standard deviations; $Z = −1.54$) and conscientiousness (by 1.75 standard deviations; $Z = −1.77$).

To represent measures of this kind graphically, it is customary to reexpress z scores as "*T* scores."[6] This is commonly done in accordance with Equation 9.3 (Garrett, 1966):

$$T_{pd} = 10(Z_{pd}) + 50 \qquad [9.3]$$

Note that by Equation 9.3, the "bottom" of the normative scale of measurement, where $T = 0$, is effectively fixed at $Z = −5.00$, while the "top" of that scale of measurement, where $T = 100$, is fixed at $Z = +5.00$.[7] An individual whose raw score assessment is exactly equal to the population mean and hence equivalent to a z score of 0 (zero) would thus measure halfway between these two extreme $T$ values, where $T = 50$. By now reexpressing the aforementioned z scores, +.51, +1.01, −.03, −1.54, and −1.77 as $T$ scores in accordance with Equation 9.3, the normative measures assume, respectively, the values 55, 60, 50, 35, and 32 (rounded to nearest whole number). These are the measures used to construct the trait profile displayed in Figure 9.1.

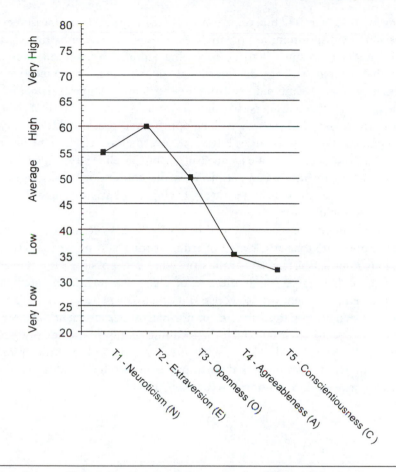

**Figure 9.1**    Illustrative "Big Five" Personality Profile Based on Normative
Measurements

*III. From "Raw Score" Assessments to Interactive Measures*

In the aforementioned work by Cattell (1944), the measurement rationale
he called "interactive" was defined as measurement,

> [W]ithin a restricted framework defined by the test. It recognizes the oneness
> of the organism-environment and pays tribute to the oft-forgotten fact that a
> trait is never resident only in the organism but is *a relation between the organ-*
> *ism and the environment.* (Cattell, 1944, p. 293; emphasis added)

On its face, at least, this alternative rationale for dispositional measurement
would seem to offer good prospects for realizing, or at least more faithfully

approximating, Stern's notion of person-world convergence in the measurement of personality dispositions as potentialities. This is not to suggest that Cattell (1944) understood himself to be following Stern's lead. Indeed, it is not clear that Cattell had any familiarity at all with Stern's perspective on measurement issues, and judging from the thoroughly empiricistic nature of Cattell's own approach to personality research (see e.g., Cattell, 1957), it seems safe to say that he would have appreciated precious little of what Stern had to say on this matter, anyway. Nevertheless, it is here being suggested that the basic rationale for measurement Cattell (1944) called "interactive" is fundamentally compatible with the conception of dispositional measurement toward which Stern was striving as a basis for quantification in psychographic inquiry.

To see how interactive logic could be applied in this context, it is important to appreciate that any formal instrument for assessing personality dispositions imposes certain constraints on what can possibly be discovered about an individual through the use of that instrument. In interactive measurement, one views those constraints themselves (rather than sample statistics/population parameters, as in normative measurement) as circumscribing the context within which the meaning of any particular raw score assessment is articulated. This is what it means to speak of measurement "within a restricted framework defined by the test itself," an idea that finds formal expression in Equation 9.4 (Lamiell, 1981):

$$I_{pd} = (A_{pd} - A'_{pd\,min}) \, / \, |\, A'_{pd\,max} - A'_{pd\,min}\,| \qquad\qquad [9.4]$$

where

$I_{pd}$ represents an interactive measure of person $p$ with respect to disposition $d$,

$A_{pd}$ is defined by Equation 9.1, and

$A'_{pd\,max}$ and $A'_{pd\,min}$ represent, respectively, the highest and lowest values that any actual $A_{pd}$ could possibly assume given the assessment procedure itself (i.e., given the constraints imposed by the operative parameters of Equation 9.1).

In Equation 9.4, the denominator defines, in effect, the total length of the continuum over which admissible raw score assessments of a person are defined with respect to dimension $d$. For example, given the structure and scoring conventions of the *NEO Personality Inventory* as discussed above, the reader will perhaps have discerned that for each of the five traits putatively measured by that inventory, $A'_{pd\,min}$ equals 0 (zero), while $A'_{pd\,max}$ equals 192. The former value would be achieved if an individual were to answer all 48 items for assessing a given trait in a manner which scored

0 (zero), while the latter value would be achieved were the individual's answers on those same 48 items scored 4.[8] For each trait putatively measured by the *NEO Personality Inventory*, then, the total length of the continuum is $|192 - 0| = 192$.

The numerator of Equation 9.4 specifies the distance of person $p$'s raw score assessment, $A_{pd}$, from the functional "bottom" or zero point of the scale, $A'_{pd\ min}$. Thus, any given $I_{pd}$ value expresses an individual's position along a scale of measurement for disposition $d$ as a ratio of the distance from functional zero to the total length of the scale. This locates the person of regard along the scale of measurement for disposition $d$, not in comparison with the locations of other persons along that same scale of measurement—considerations that from the personalistic perspective are seen as secondary at best, and often irrelevant—but instead in consideration of other locations on that scale of measurement that *might possibly* have been assumed by person $p$ had his or her responses on the items of the inventory been other than they were. The obtained measure, $I_{pd}$, literally emerges from an interaction between the individual being measured and the device through which the measure is achieved.[9]

To illustrate Equation 9.4 concretely, let us now recall that the five hypothetical raw score assessments of an individual on the *NEO Personality Inventory* were specified above as 90, 128, 110, 100, and 92. Bearing in mind that in the case of this instrument, the value of the denominator in Equation 9.4 is 192 for each of the five measured dispositions, the values of $I_{pd}$ corresponding to these five raw score assessments are (after multiplication by 100 and subsequent rounding to nearest whole number) 47, 67, 57, 52, and 48, respectively.

Figure 9.2 presents the "Big Five" profile defined by these five interactive measures, graphed in terms of the same $y$-axis as the profile in Figure 9.1 so as to facilitate comparison of the two (and not because interactive measurement has anything to do with the derivation of $T$ scores). Note that by interactive measurement, the hypothetical person portrayed by this profile appears rather lower on the dimension of neuroticism than is suggested by the corresponding normative measure, somewhat higher on extraversion and openness, and appreciably higher on agreeableness and conscientiousness. In any event, viewed personalistically, the interactive profile shown in Figure 9.2 is thought of properly not as some sort of neutral, objective record of some individual's more or less fixed standing with respect to a set of "faculties" presumed relevant to the characterization of "people in general," but as one temporally circumscribed empirical realization of a kind of person-world convergence: Certain potentialities deemed relevant to the specific person under consideration have found (limited) expression through an artifact of the world external to that person, that is, through a projection by that person of his or her dispositions into a framework constrained by the parameters of an assessment device created by some other person(s) for the purpose of reflecting precisely those projections.

Quite obvious in Figure 9.2 is the fact that one and the same individual can appear rather differently depending on which measurement rationale, normative or interactive, is used to contextualize the "raw" assessments made of that individual. The fact of this matter led the present author and various colleagues, some years ago, into programmatic research bearing on the question that had been raised many years earlier by Gordon Allport (1937a) concerning the nature of "idiographic" personality judgments.

## Revisiting the Question of "Idiographic" Intuitions: Studies on the Psychology of Subjective Personality Judgments

Although they differed in various procedural details, the early studies in this line of work (Lamiell & Durbeck, 1987; Lamiell, Foss, Larsen, & Hempel, 1983; Lamiell, Foss, Trierweiler, & Leffel, 1983) were all designed in accordance with the following basic notion: If, as has traditionally been assumed, the psychology of subjective personality judgments is well captured by the logic of normative measurement operations, then applying the arithmetic of those operations (i.e., Equation 9.2) to the information in target protocols presented to research subjects should generate trait measures of the targets that correspond well with ratings that subjects actually make of those targets. If, on the other hand, the subjective judgment process is better described in a fashion more consonant with Allport's (1937a) speculations, then quite possibly subjects' ratings of targets would correspond more closely to trait measures of the targets generated nonactuarially[10] by the arithmetic of interactive measurement (i.e., Equation 9.4). Hence, in these studies, Equations 9.2 and 9.4 do not serve as a means of generating numerical "tags" to be pinned onto the research subjects, the usual goal in trait measurement. Rather, they provide alternative—and competing—formal representations of the cognitive process through which those individual subjects characterize the manifest personality characteristics of the targets.

In one such study (Lamiell & Durbeck, 1987), 67 research subjects (university students) were asked to rate 40 target peers on each of three attributes. The ratings were to be made on numerical scales ranging from 0 (zero) at one end to 20 at the other and were to be based on information about each target's characteristic engagement in each of 16 different

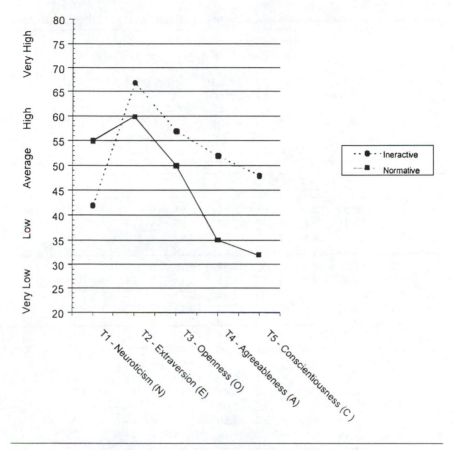

**Figure 9.2**    Illustrative "Big Five" Personality Profile Based on Interactive Measurements, Juxtaposed With Previously Derived Normative Profile

activities proper to college student life. Results for one subject are shown in Table 9.2.

Panel I in the table displays the ratings predicted of the subject in question for each of the 40 targets on the theoretical assumption that those ratings were mediated by considerations formally corresponding to the arithmetic of traditional normative measurement operations. Panel II displays the ratings predicted of the same subject for each of the same 40 targets on the theoretical assumption that the ratings were mediated by considerations better modeled by the arithmetic of interactive measurement operations. Panel III displays the ratings actually made of each of the 40 targets by the subject in question. Panel IV quantifies, target by target, the validity of each of the two measurement models for predicting the subject's

**Table 9.2**    Results for One Subject Study of Subjective Personality Judgments

*Predicted Rating, Actual Rating,*
*and Proportional Profile Dissimilarities*

| Target | PANEL I Predictions From Normative Model (N) Attribute | | | PANEL II Predictions From Interactive Model(N) Attribute | | | PANEL III Actual Ratings (A) Attribute | | | PANEL IV Profile Dissimilarities | |
|---|---|---|---|---|---|---|---|---|---|---|---|
|   | 1 | 2 | 3 | 1 | 2 | 3 | 1 | 2 | 3 | N vs. A | I vs. A |
| 1. | 17.32 | 0.00 | 10.39 | 12.01 | 7.14 | 12.54 | 10 | 8 | 13 | .55 | .11 |
| 2. | 8.65 | 19.81 | .22 | 9.19 | 12.67 | 7.95 | 5 | 15 | 4 | .27 | .23 |
| 3. | 13.57 | 16.39 | 8.41 | 10.79 | 12.67 | 7.95 | 4 | 9 | 8 | .53 | .36 |
| 4. | 9.09 | 5.40 | 19.34 | 9.33 | 8.65 | 16.58 | 8 | 8 | 12 | .38 | .23 |
| 5. | 0.00 | 4.23 | 13.99 | 6.37 | 8.32 | 14.16 | 8 | 12 | 11 | .57 | .25 |
| 6. | 20.00 | 4.07 | 9.56 | 12.88 | 8.28 | 12.16 | 9 | 14 | 8 | .69 | .38 |
| 7. | 14.27 | 6.76 | 6.43 | 11.01 | 9.03 | 10.75 | 14 | 8 | 8 | .09 | .19 |
| 8. | 7.90 | 20.00 | 5.54 | 8.95 | 12.72 | 10.35 | 7 | 13 | 7 | .32 | .17 |
| 9. | 10.95 | 12.72 | 11.36 | 9.94 | 10.69 | 12.98 | 7 | 8 | 7 | .34 | .33 |
| 10. | 3.67 | 7.16 | 12.38 | 7.57 | 9.14 | 13.66 | 6 | 5 | 8 | .24 | .30 |
| 11. | 14.09 | 9.88 | 12.30 | 10.96 | 9.90 | 13.40 | 7 | 8 | 8 | .40 | .32 |
| 12. | 7.57 | 2.34 | 8.46 | 8.34 | 7.80 | 11.67 | 8 | 8 | 7 | .27 | .22 |
| 13. | 8.08 | 4.94 | 12.49 | 9.00 | 8.52 | 13.49 | 8 | 13 | 8 | .43 | .33 |
| 14. | 8.63 | 6.11 | 7.23 | 9.18 | 8.84 | 11.11 | 7 | 10 | 8 | .21 | .20 |
| 15. | 10.60 | 10.25 | 6.78 | 9.82 | 10.00 | 10.91 | 7 | 10 | 12 | .31 | .15 |
| 16. | 3.91 | 8.67 | 1.28 | 7.64 | 9.56 | 8.42 | 6 | 13 | 4 | .22 | .23 |
| 17. | 2.83 | 14.48 | 4.43 | 7.30 | 11.18 | 9.85 | 6 | 14 | 8 | .21 | .16 |
| 18. | 2.79 | 8.46 | 19.58 | 7.28 | 9.50 | 16.69 | 8 | 8 | 14 | .35 | .14 |
| 19. | 9.51 | 18.64 | 11.14 | 9.47 | 12.34 | 12.88 | 9 | 14 | 9 | .24 | .20 |
| 20. | 16.71 | 12.50 | 5.94 | 11.81 | 10.632 | 10.53 | 7 | 9 | 11 | .57 | .25 |
| 21. | 12.84 | 5.37 | 14.54 | 10.55 | 8.64 | 14.42 | 12 | 7 | 9 | .28 | .28 |
| 22. | 11.26 | 8.91 | 11.21 | 10.04 | 9.63 | 12.91 | 12 | 8 | 11 | .06 | .16 |
| 23. | 7.24 | 7.96 | 7.78 | 8.73 | 9.36 | 11.36 | 8 | 12 | 12 | .28 | .14 |
| 24. | 15.21 | 2.13 | 14.13 | 11.32 | 7.73 | 14.23 | 10 | 7 | 12 | .37 | .13 |
| 25. | 15.81 | 6.08 | 10.65 | 11.52 | 8.84 | 12.66 | 10 | 12 | 14 | .43 | .18 |
| 26. | 8.01 | 11.57 | 5.73 | 8.98 | 10.37 | 10.44 | 8 | 12 | 10 | .22 | .10 |
| 27. | 9.02 | 7.53 | 5.99 | 9.31 | 9.24 | 10.55 | 8 | 12 | 7 | .22 | .22 |
| 28. | 13.34 | 11.02 | 4.90 | 10.72 | 10.22 | 10.06 | 7 | 13 | 4 | .28 | .31 |
| 29. | 10.19 | 12.07 | 0.00 | 9.69 | 10.51 | 7.84 | 6 | 13 | 6 | .31 | .20 |
| 30. | 15.70 | 7.68 | 7.38 | 11.48 | 9.28 | 11.18 | 13 | 13 | 7 | .26 | .26 |
| 31. | 19.67 | 8.21 | 7.35 | 12.78 | 9.43 | 11.17 | 11 | 7 | 5 | .40 | .30 |
| 32. | 13.46 | 2.13 | 12.77 | 10.75 | 7.73 | 13.62 | 8 | 7 | 8 | .41 | .29 |
| 33. | 13.80 | 11.05 | 8.10 | 10.87 | 10.22 | 11.50 | 8 | 13 | 12 | .34 | .19 |
| 34. | 9.42 | 5.57 | 8.58 | 9.44 | 8.70 | 11.72 | 7 | 8 | 12 | .23 | .12 |
| 35. | 9.90 | 10.25 | 11.64 | 9.60 | 10.00 | 13.10 | 12 | 8 | 11 | .12 | .15 |
| 36. | 10.16 | 12.84 | 10.29 | 9.68 | 10.73 | 12.49 | 8 | 8 | 11 | .26 | .17 |

**Table 9.2** Continued

Predicted Rating, Actual Rating,<br>and Proportional Profile Dissimilarities

| Target | PANEL I Predictions From Normative Model (N) Attribute | | | PANEL II Predictions From Interactive Model(N) Attribute | | | PANEL III Actual Ratings (A) Attribute | | | PANEL IV Profile Dissimilarities | |
|---|---|---|---|---|---|---|---|---|---|---|---|
| | 1 | 2 | 3 | 1 | 2 | 3 | 1 | 2 | 3 | N vs. A | I vs. A |
| 37. | 5.53 | 7.44 | 14.94 | 8.17 | 9.22 | 14.60 | 7 | 14 | 11 | .35 | .28 |
| 38. | 17.19 | 9.38 | 12.08 | 11.97 | 9.75 | 13.30 | 9 | 11 | 15 | .41 | .17 |
| 39. | 6.43 | 0.74 | 20.00 | 8.47 | 7.35 | 16.88 | 7 | 12 | 18 | .45 | .20 |
| 40. | 6.10 | 4.56 | 9.90 | 8.36 | 8.42 | 12.32 | 7 | 12 | 9 | .36 | .24 |

SOURCE: Adapted from Lamiell & Durbeck (1987).

| | | |
|---|---|---|
| Means of the profile dissimilarity values: | .33 | .22 |
| Standard deviations of the profile dissimilarity values: | .13 | .07 |
| $t$ value for differences between correlated means ($N$ vs. 1) | 5.71 | ($p < .01$) |

actual ratings in terms of a variation on the Cronbach-Gleser profile dissimilarity index (Cronbach & Gleser, 1953) suggested by Budescu (1980). By this method, a set of predictions that corresponded perfectly with the subject's actual ratings of a given target would yield a profile dissimilarity index of zero (0.00). A set of predictions maximally discrepant from actual ratings would yield an index of 1.00. Hence, in any given row of the table, the lower of the two dissimilarity values in Panel IV is associated with the measurement model that worked better as a basis for predicting the subject's actual ratings of that particular target.

Comparing, target by target, the dissimilarity values shown in Panel IV of Table 9.2, it can be seen that the interactive measurement model more accurately predicted the subject's ratings of the targets in 31 out of 40 cases, whereas the normative model out-predicted the interactive model in 9 of the 40 cases. To evaluate this distribution statistically for *this individual subject*, one might sensibly employ a simple chi-square test, entering 31 in one cell of the chi-square table to represent the 31 "hits" for the interactive model, and 9 in the other cell to represent the 9 "hits" for the normative model. This distribution of "hits" and "misses" can in turn be tested for statistical significance against chance expectations of 20 "hits" for each model.

The value of chi-square in this case is $X^2 = 12.1$, a value that at one degree of freedom would occur by chance alone much less often than 1 time in 100.

This finding points decisively toward the conclusion that at least in the case of this one subject, the logic of interactive measurement much better represents the psychology underlying the subjective judgments than does the logic of normative measurement. A $t$ test for the difference between the average dissimilarity values associated with the two models—in which the respective averages were computed for this individual subject across the 40 targets—was also carried out on these data, pointing to the same conclusion (refer to bottom of Table 9.2).

Now, what of the fact that for all the foregoing, only one subject has been investigated? To explore the generality of the findings obtained in this one case, the procedures just described were repeated for each of the 66 other subjects individually. The reader may thus imagine 66 additional tables, each formally identical to Table 9.2. Of the total of 67 subjects thus investigated (including the one represented by Table 9.2), there were 57 for whom interactive measurement proved to be the better model of the psychology of subjective personality judgments, 10 for whom the data revealed no clear superiority of one model over the other, and none—not one—for whom the competing hypothesis that normative measurement operations would better model the subjective judgment process was confirmed.

On the evidence, therefore, it appears that Allport's (1937a) speculations about the "idiographic" nature of clinical intuitions and other informal personality characterizations warrant, at the very least, serious reconsideration. Contrary to Lundberg (1941), Sarbin (1944), Holt (1962), Epstein (1983), Cloninger (1996), and many others, the relevant empirical evidence now available points toward the conclusion that the psychology of subjective personality judgments is not normative in the usual psychometric sense of that term, but instead conforms more closely to the logic of interactive measurement. The suggestion here is that (a) the judgment process in question involves a mental process of negation, through which the rater generates subjective analogues of the $A'_{pd\,min}$ and $A'_{pd\,max}$ parameters of Equation 9.4, and that (b) ideas roughly correspondent to these values, rather than anything analogous to the $\overline{A}_{.d}$ and $sd_{.d}$ parameters of normative measurement operations as specified by Equation 9.2, serve the rater as the psychological reference points against which the characteristics of individual targets are judged. What is seen to be the case about "this" target is judged not in terms of what *is* or *has been* found to be the case about *other* targets, but rather what *is not* but *might otherwise* have been the case about *this same* target. From the point of view of the subject making the judgments, the "reference ideas" supplying the needed context are not passively recorded *memories of prior experiences* (Cloninger, 1996), but actively constructed *negations of a present experience*.

In an important extension of this line of research, Weigert (2000) has recently completed a series of studies oriented around this basic question: Which method for deriving trait measures from *NEO Personality Inventory* protocols, normative or interactive, yields "Big Five" profiles more closely corresponding to those obtained when subjects are provided with "thumbnail" descriptions of each of the five traits putatively measured by that instrument and asked to simply rate themselves and/or others on numerical scales corresponding to each of the five dimensions?

In one of these studies, 36 husband-wife couples whose respective marriages had lasted a minimum of 10 years served as subjects. In one set of analyses carried out on Form S of the revised *NEO Inventory* (Costa & McCrae, 1992), in which each subject's responses refer to himself/herself, Weigert (2000) found in 62 of 72 cases that an interactive scoring of the inventory (following the method described above) yielded a "Big Five" profile that better predicted the subject's simple self-ratings than did the profile defined for the same subject via conventional normative-measurement operations ($X^2 = 37.55$; $p < .001$).[11]

When the simple ratings of a given subject made by his or her spouse defined the profile to be predicted, interactive scoring of the subject's responses on Form S of the *NEO* outperformed normative scoring of those same responses in 64 of the 72 cases ($X^2 = 43.55$; $p < .001$).

When an individual subject's simple self-ratings were predicted from his or her respective partner's responses on Form R of the inventory (in which items are worded in the third person so that the person answering the inventory is describing another), interactive scoring of the protocol out-predicted normative scoring in 63 of 71 cases ($X^2 = 46.72$; $p < .001$). And when these same alternative sets of measures were used to predict the simple ratings that the partner made of his or her spouse, the interactive model outperformed the normative model in 68 of the 71 cases ($X^2 = 56.88$; $p < .001$).[12] These findings, and many more reported by Weigert (2000), suggest that the psychology of laypersons' subjective characterizations of their own and one another's personality characteristics is reflected with much greater fidelity by the logic of interactive measurement procedures than by the logic of normative measurement procedures, even when the former procedures are applied to instruments originally designed with the latter procedures in mind.

## Some General Observations on Hypothesis Testing in Personalistic Inquiry

In drawing the present discussion to a close, it may be well to call attention to certain methodological aspects of the work just discussed.

The first of these highlights a crucial feature of what might be termed "neo-Wundtian" inquiry: Throughout the research discussed above, the hypotheses of interest concerned psychological processes presumably transpiring at the level of the individual; therefore, tests of those hypotheses were properly carried out at that same level, just as was true of Wundtian general/experimental/individual psychology more than 100 years ago.[13]

A second point to be stressed here is that although the investigation of individuals manifestly did not preclude the use of conventional statistical analysis techniques (e.g., chi-square analyses, *t* tests), it did alter the role of those techniques in an epistemically important way.

In the research by Lamiell and Durbeck (1987), for example, formal models representing alternative theoretical conceptions of the subjective judgment process were used to generate alternative predictions as to where a given subject would mark a series of rating scales in characterizing himself/herself or another individual. The adequacy of these alternative predictions was then investigated by empirically indexing their degree of correspondence with the ratings the subject actually made in characterizing specific individual targets. In the case of the individual whose data are displayed in Table 9.2, the substantive hypothesis was investigated once by comparing the dissimilarity values shown in the last two columns of the first row of the table. There, it was found that the dissimilarity index for the interactive model, .11, was lower (indicating less dissimilarity) than that for the normative model (.55). The substantive hypothesis that the interactive model would prove superior was thus empirically corroborated *in that instance,* and it is important to see that this conclusion does not appeal to any null hypothesis test or inferential statistic of any sort (cf. Bakan, 1966; Meehl, 1978). At this point in the analysis, there was no null hypothesis to reject or fail to reject, and this was true as well for each of the other 39 targets with respect to which the comparison of dissimilarity values was carried out.

There came then a point in the procedure when statistical analyses were executed, but it is important to appreciate that at this juncture, the analyses were carried out on that subject's data *individually.* The analyses did not entail the "sampling" of subjects from "populations" toward the end of determining what held true on average within one subgroup of subjects as compared with another. As an example of "neo-Wundtian" inquiry, the Lamiell and Durbeck (1987) research is not properly understood as a single study with an *N* of 67, but rather a series of 67 studies, each with an *N* of 1.

Through the methods described, Lamiell and Durbeck (1987) found that in 57 of their 67 studies of individual cases, the results favored the conclusion that the interactive measurement model had better represented the subjective judgment process under investigation than had the normative model, whereas in no case did findings point to the opposite conclusion that the normative model had worked significantly better in this regard. Though it was scarcely necessary to go through the motions given such a one-sided pattern of findings, this result could in turn have been subjected to a conventional chi-square analysis, with an outcome as decisive as the outcomes of the comparable chi-square analyses that were in fact carried out and reported by Weigert (2000) using a similar research design. The point to be stressed in this context is that in neo-Wundtian inquiry, such aggregate level analyses, if and when they are undertaken at all, do not function as tests of the substantive theoretical propositions under examination. Rather, they function as a means of establishing whether *serial tests of theoretical propositions already accomplished by other and entirely independent means at the level of the individual* either corroborate or challenge the propositions with a degree of regularity sufficient to suggest some (appropriately tentative) generalization concerning the phenomenon under investigation.

Without question, it is a long way from these neo-Wundtian studies of subjective personality judgments to the elaboration of a full complement of investigative procedures adequate to the methodological challenges presented by personalistic inquiry more broadly conceived. By the same token, however, the logic of interactive measurement operations is formally compatible with certain heretofore neglected aspects of Stern's conception of psychological measurement from a personalistic standpoint (refer to discussion earlier in this chapter); and if that logic is serviceable as a formal representation of the psychology of "subjective" personality judgments, as the research discussed above seems to indicate, then it is at least plausible that the same logic could be made serviceable to personality investigators as the basis for "objective" personality measurement. The pursuit of this possibility by coming generations of personality investigators may well serve to revive those person-centered investigative disciplines, psychography and comparison studies that, though prominent components of Stern's (1911) initial vision of differential psychology, were effectively subverted as mainstream investigators gravitated ever more exclusively and fatefully toward the attribute-centered disciplines, variation studies, and correlational research.

Meanwhile, as noted at the outset of this chapter, the fact that quantitative methods can be embraced as one means of advancing personalistic investigation does not mean that the need for qualitative methods is overlooked. The following discussion is intended to highlight this point.

## Some Illustrative Qualitative Research: Personalistic Studies of the Experience of Alzheimer's Disease

It is not entirely without reason that Alzheimer's Disease (AD) is viewed by many as an essentially organic disorder. Postmortem examinations comparing the brains of subjects who presumably had been healthy with those of individuals who had been diagnosed as "demented" have pointed to the heightened presence within the latter group of *beta-amyloid tissue,* an abnormal protein, as well as so-called *neurofibrillary tangles,* which are strands of axonal material that displace normal neurons in the cerebral cortex. It is possible that the pathological process entailed by these biological abnormalities may damage neurons in the brain in such a way that the reception and transmission of neural impulses are compromised (Sabat, 2001).

This organic degeneration could well have untoward effects on the cognitive abilities and behavior of afflicted persons, and it is in this connection that research psychologists and psychiatrists have played such an important role in the formulation of contemporary understandings of individuals suffering from AD and other forms of dementia.[14] Through studies comparing memory and other cognitive functions (including language and perceptual-motor skills) of apparently healthy subjects with those of subjects appraised as demented, programmatic empirical research is aimed at documenting the untoward psychological and behavioral effects of various neuropathological conditions with ever increasing precision. In virtually all this research, extensive reliance is placed on standardized mental tests as instruments for revealing aspects of psychological functioning that have been compromised or lost altogether, presumably as a consequence of organic degeneration.

The Mini-Mental State (MMS) test (Folstein, Folstein, & McHugh, 1975), for example, is a short, standardized instrument designed to tap various rudimentary aspects of cognitive functioning, including orientation in place and time, ability to accurately register objects and events in one's immediate environment, simple recall, speech production, and speech comprehension. Possible scores on the MMS range from 0 (zero), a score that would indicate extremely deficient level of cognitive functioning, to 30, indicating full competence across the range of tested functions. In an article describing this instrument and discussing its basic psychometric properties, Folstein et al. (1975) reported a mean MMS score of 27.6 (standard deviation 1.7) in a sample of 63 "normal" subjects averaging 73.9 years of age, compared with a mean MMS score of 9.6 (standard deviation 5.8) in a sample of 29 "demented" persons averaging 80.8 years of age.

In his personalistic studies of individuals who had been diagnosed as "probable" AD sufferers in the "moderate" to "severe" stages of the disease

(MMS scores in the 5-7 range), Sabat (2001) was concerned with going beyond the results of this and other standardized tests, engaging in discourse with afflicted individuals notwithstanding their speech difficulties and in this way discovering, among other things, what was *enduring* in their respective psychological lives despite the losses that, undeniably, were manifest as well. Sabat's objective in this work was to identify aspects of the psychological lives of individual sufferers that not only were left unrevealed by the standardized tests, but in some instances could scarcely have been deemed possible given the test results alone.

Sabat's interest in pursuing such personalistic studies stemmed from his growing concern that the professional literature was projecting not only to the scientific and medical practitioner communities but to the lay public as well, an image of dementia sufferers (including but not limited to those suffering specifically from AD) that was far too limited. Indeed, the image being projected was often demeaning of sufferers in ways that were neither scientifically warranted nor practically beneficial to the sufferers themselves or to their caregivers. In this connection, Sabat (2001) specifically pointed to descriptions in the scientific literature of AD victims as "suffering from deficiencies in problem-solving, word-finding, conveying information, and concept formation" and as "unable to perceive, attend, and recall" (Sabat, 2001, p. 162).

After explaining the actual empirical basis for such characterizations, that is, statistical evaluations of average differences between aggregates of "normal" and "demented" research subjects on various standardized measures such as the MMS, Sabat (2001) then articulated one of his central concerns by noting that on this basis, AD sufferers are stereotyped as follows:

> [I]n defectological terms—they are viewed primarily in terms of their deficits and those deficits are assumed to have been caused principally by the disease process. And, to the extent that conceptions of this mythic *average* AD sufferer inform the actions, attitudes, and interpretations of clinicians and caregivers, *particular* AD sufferers' actual intact abilities will necessarily be rendered more or less invisible, because afflicted people will be reacted to principally in terms of their deficits. Social interactions which have defects as their focus necessarily limit the range and quality of those interactions and often result in malignant social psychology. (Sabat, 2001, p. 166; emphasis added)

What, then, Sabat wondered, might be learned when one decides to view AD sufferers as *persons* rather than merely as instances of the psychometric categories defined by tests designed to differentiate sufferers from "normals" using cognitive, emotional, and behavioral deficits of the former? Sabat's

(2001) book offers the most thorough answer to this question that is to be found in the contemporary professional literature, and no secondary discussion of the work could possibly do justice to its richness. At the same time, however, much of the material contained in the book serves to highlight themes of central importance within critical personalism, so our purposes here are well served by looking closely at some relevant segments of Sabat's (2001) work.

## The AD Sufferer as an Evaluating and Intentional Person

*Doc, you gotta find a way to give us purpose again.*

This sentiment, notes Sabat (2001, p. 161), was expressed by a "moderately" afflicted AD sufferer to whom Sabat was about to administer a battery of neuropsychological tests in a hospital outpatient clinic. Sabat found the sufferer's statement to be of special interest because on the surface at least, it seemed to run contrary to conventional wisdom. More specifically, the statement pointed to an enduring concern on the part of the sufferer to find purpose in his life, whereas prevailing views, based largely on psychometric (statistical) considerations of the sort described above, suggested, in Sabat's words,

> [T]hat people with AD in the moderate to severe stages of the disease do not have the cognitive abilities required to behave in ways that would reflect deliberate action which is guided by the meaning of the situations which they confront. (Sabat, 2001, p. 162)

In other words, the sufferer's statement suggested to Sabat that there might well be merit in viewing that individual—as well as other AD sufferers, including those whose routine cognitive functioning is even more severely compromised—not merely as medical patients displaying inferior mental ability when statistically compared with "normals" according to their respective average performances on standardized mental tests; rather, they might be seen as *semiotic subjects,* that is, as persons who despite their deficiencies nevertheless continue to act in ways properly understood as *meaning driven* (Sabat & Harré, 1994). In Sabat's (2001) view,

> Semiotic subjects are individuals who can act intentionally given their interpretations of the circumstances in which they find themselves; they are people who can evaluate their own behavior and the behavior of others in accordance with socially agreed-upon standards of propriety and reason. (p. 171)

It is not difficult to see in this definition of the "semiotic subject" an essential compatibility with the tenets of critical personalism, given the resolutely teleological thrust of Stern's thinking and his commitment to a view of persons as evaluative, intentional beings (refer to previous chapter)—nor was Sabat (2001) himself blind to these possibilities.[15] Although it is neither feasible nor necessary to discuss here all of Sabat's many relevant observations (to this end, the reader can and should consult Sabat's work directly), it is instructive for present purposes to further probe some of the details of the case of a certain "Dr. B," for this case vividly illustrates some of the possibilities offered by qualitative personalistic inquiry of this sort.

Dr. B, who held a Ph.D. degree in biology, was 68 years old when Sabat met him. Dr. B had been diagnosed at age 64 as a "probable" Alzheimer's sufferer and had since then earned a score of 5 on the MMS, placing him in the "severely afflicted" range. Sabat indicates that at the time he met the man,

> [Dr. B] was unable to drive, had great difficulty dressing himself, had significant problems in the areas of word-finding (naming), spelling, reading, and auditory comprehension, as seen on standard tests such as the Boston Diagnostic Aphasia Examination, could not recall the day of the week, the month, the year, and couldn't copy a simple drawing, nor could he perform simple calculations. Often, he had difficulty recalling the names of particular staff members at the day care center as well as the center's location. There was great variability in his signature and he had great difficulty with writing in general. Toward the middle months of our association, when he was at home and dusk approached, his wife reported that he insisted upon carrying a flashlight with him. (Sabat, 2001, p. 26)

Viewed in terms of these symptoms, Dr. B certainly does appear markedly defective both cognitively and behaviorally. Nonetheless, his interviews with Sabat showed that he remained fully attuned to the importance of having *goals* in his life, and thus of acting coherently for the sake of purposes he personally valued. As will be seen, Dr. B also demonstrated a continuing ability to evaluate interpersonal circumstances in a way that showed exquisite sensitivity to concerns of others and to the meanings embedded in certain social contexts.

Dr. B was himself keenly aware of the dramatic declines in his own cognitive functioning. As a person who in earlier years had enjoyed both a high level of intellectual accomplishment and the professional recognition that goes with same, these changes were very difficult for him to accept. The opportunity to participate in a scientific project with a psychology professor from a highly regarded university thus proved very appealing to Dr. B, at least partly because it offered, to his way of thinking, prospects for reviving to some degree the scientific/intellectual life he had once known and in which he had once prospered.[16]

Interview material further revealed that Dr. B saw his participation in the project as a way of enhancing his status among professional friends and acquaintances, including some who did not attend the adult day care center where the project was being conducted. Alas, one obstacle that surfaced for Dr. B in this regard was that, due to his word-finding problems, it was becoming increasingly difficult for him to make known to his peers, in conversations with them, the fact that he was collaborating in such a significant scientific undertaking. To this extent, his efforts toward achieving a measure of status were being thwarted. What did the severely afflicted Dr. B do then? In search of an answer this question, let us consult Sabat's data.

Dr. B:    I think I was very much wanting the project should go like faster and that I've lost something um which I may or may not really need. Again, the project is one that I feel very much uh, but from the professionals, they don't feel that is much status. Is there any name we could call for a project or would you rather not?

Steven R. Sabat (SRS):    You mean somebody to talk with about this?

Dr. B:    No, no, no, no—what is the name of this project? So what we can take a very decent project that, uh, something like a coordinous thing.

SRS:    Like a title?

Dr. B:    A title or a project or you—what's your name and what is it?

SRS:    I think we should work on a title.

Dr. B:    Let's think about it because it would bring a little more something.

SRS:    Focus?

Dr. B:    Focus. Now having said that, do you, we want that? Because I've had this, people talk to me and then I'm blum, blum, blum, what do I do? Well, blum, blum, blum. So it may I think, my God this is *real* stature to do! This is maybe picky, picky, picky, stuff.

SRS:    I don't think so.

Dr. B:    That's stature and what, who can be attached to somebody uh, in agreeable thing. Now if you don't like it . . .

*SRS:*    Do you have any ideas for a title for this?

*Dr. B:*    That's . . . I've been thinking about it for a long, long time. I thought about this before. I thought I had and now it's *tsuris* [Yiddish for grief: He's saying that he thought about it, but that now it's not retrievable. SRS]

*SRS:*    But it's in there somewhere.

*Dr. B:*    Somewhere—where we can do status. If somebody calls me and says "What are you doing?" and then I write this thing, what is it? Now it could be a very long, long thing in the project from your university or something else. Do you think I'm silly?

*SRS:*    No. No, not at all.

*Dr. B:*    Some sort of status.

*SRS:*    If you're going to write something it's a good idea to have a title.

*Dr. B:*    Am I picky on this thing?

*SRS:*    No, you're an active participant.

*Dr. B:*    Oh sure, and I was thinking to myself, "Hey now wait a minute, I'm involved in this thing and it doesn't matter what it's called."

*SRS:*    I was thinking about a title. It's got to be something that will grab the attention.

*Dr. B:*    Okay, because I can be set or attached to some, some project, you know, a senior project or something like that so that I would have this sort of status. (Sabat, 2001, pp. 138-139)

At this point in his exposition of Dr. B's case material, Sabat (2001) notes that at about the time of this interview, he had been thinking about a title for his project, anyway (i.e., quite independently of this conversation with Dr. B), and partly for this reason failed to see as soon as he might have that what Dr. B was seeking was a not a title for the project but rather one *for himself*, as a collaborator in that project. That is, what Dr. B needed, under the circumstances created by the difficulties he was having with speech, was an alternative way of communicating his participation in the project to friends and acquaintances when they asked him what he was doing. As things were, he could only respond to their questioning with "blum, blum, blum." This was simply not adequate to his purposes and, his severe affliction notwithstanding, *he knew this*. Dr. B needed a title if he was to achieve the "*real* stature" he was seeking. Finally grasping this, Sabat (2001) adopts, as psychological scientist, the role of (to borrow Stern's phrasing) a "sensitive observer who has spent some extended time" with Dr. B, and articulates his predicament as follows:

1. Working on the project provides [Dr. B] with stature, with status, which is important to him.
2. Yet, given his linguistic and other problems due to AD, he cannot describe clearly to others exactly what he's doing, and thus cannot be looked upon favorably by others as one who has a certain admirable status despite AD. . . .
3. He then hints at what he needs—something in writing from my university which would, essentially, "do the talking for him," by explaining to others exactly what he has done and is doing to have achieved the "status" that he desires and believes he deserves. (Sabat, 2001, p. 139)

These observations serve to vivify (a) Dr. B's enduring sense of his own value as a person, (b) his intention to maintain that sense of self-worth even in the face of declining cognitive capacities, (c) his continuing capacity to evaluate his social world for opportunities to pursue that meaningful objective, and (d) his lasting ability not only to act intentionally toward the end of realizing that objective but also to discern some alternative means to the desired end when the more customary means were failing.

Once Dr. B's true intentions in the foregoing interchange became apparent to Sabat, he arranged for his dean to provide, on official letterhead of the College of Arts and Sciences, a commendation to Dr. B taking formal notice of his important contribution to the scientific project. In the meantime, however, Dr. B had become extremely unhappy about developments and, feeling disrespected, quit the project. Happily, the commendation from the Dean did eventually reach Dr. B, and he then rejoined the project. Sabat's commentary on these developments with Dr. B is highly personalistic in its theoretical and philosophical spirit and reminds one tellingly of the importance Stern long ago placed on probing beyond the relatively superficial information provided by standardized tests and delving into a more thorough, qualitative examination of the individual case:

Here we have a man who had a number of serious problems in the cognitive realm and who, in addition, was experiencing great frustration about those problems and his own lack of ability to do anything about them. And yet . . . [Dr. B] was clearly capable of acting in a way to preserve his feelings of self-worth. He was exercising control in the situation. His sensibilities had been assaulted, and he was not about to accept that treatment for another day. . . . [Now] in formal assessments of cognitive ability, physicians and neuropsychologists ask people to do all sorts of tasks, from naming objects, to spelling, to reading, to following commands, to interpreting proverbs, and more. Yet, far more fundamental and, perhaps, complex, than any of the test based elements of cognitive function, is the cognitive function that is involved in the assertion of one's sense of dignity, of self worth. . . . Feeling slighted or feeling as though one has been treated in an undignified way requires a highly complex combination of functions involving memory, attention, emotion, and abstract thought—such as the idea of fairness. And even though Dr. B could not dress himself, he was still able to assert, and work to maintain, his sense of proper pride, and to understand and ask for reciprocity. (Sabat, 2001, pp. 142-143)

## Introception and the Establishment of Syntelic Goals in the Case of Dr. B

In his personalistic interpretation of the case material pertaining to Dr. B, Sabat (2001) has accurately characterized the objectives of Dr. B described above as *autotelic* in nature: They were Dr. B's individual goals, having primarily to do with the maintenance of social status and self-esteem. However, it would be misleading to leave the impression that Dr. B's intentions were exclusively autotelic. On the contrary, and once again despite his severely compromised cognitive capacities, Dr. B was highly attuned to what are regarded from the perspective of critical personalism as *heterotelic* goals. Furthermore, he was able to realize the possibility of appropriating certain of these latter goals into his own goal system and through this process, called *introception* by Stern, frame what are referred to as *syntelic* goals (refer to previous chapter).

Illustrative of this, Sabat notes, was Dr. B's attempt to enhance the project by directing Sabat to another person who, in Dr. B's opinion, would be able to make an important contribution to the work. Sabat's problem was to figure out who this third person was, given the difficulty Dr. B was having in his attempts to make that clear. When in the course of a conversation with Sabat, Dr. B picked up a pamphlet published by the Alzheimer's Disease Association, it at last became clear to Sabat that Dr. B had a person in mind who was working for that association. Dr. B had visited the offices of the association sometime previously, and he was remembering a woman he had met there as a person who both could and would provide valuable information. Once this was clear to Sabat, his conversation with Dr. B continued as follows:

*Dr. B:*    But we can match . . . we can meld this, this, this, this. We can, we can get material like this (snaps his fingers) just like this.

*SRS:*    Oh, so she can help us get information.

*Dr. B:*    Yes! Here it is (waving pamphlet from the Alzheimer's Association).

*SRS:*    She can help us get information about dementia and that kind of stuff.

*Dr. B:*    There it is . . . If we could get things together we would have a very sophisticated thing. . . . It's, it's worth it that you and I go look, look at it.

*SRS:*    Was she a nice person?

*Dr. B:*    Awfully nice. We could work with her with, like that (snaps fingers).

*SRS:*    So if there's some information that we might be able to use or need, she could help get it.

*Dr. B:*    Right. And it's only five cents a piece.

*SRS:*    Oh, so she can make copies?

*Dr. B:*    Sure! And she has a copy machine . . . we could meld together, to meld Alzheimer's. I think, I think we, we can have sort of a tri-ite (*triad;* SRS) thing.

*SRS:*    We can try it out and see.

*Dr. B:*    I'm not, I'm not pushing you for push, push, push, you know that.

*SRS:*    Oh ya, I know. We're working together to find out some information about this.

*Dr. B:*    That's right. (Sabat, 2001, pp. 257-258)

Striking in these data is the wealth of evidence that despite his cognitive deficits as revealed by standardized tests, Dr. B was quite able to remember certain things that were relevant to his present purposes. That is, he might not have been able to remember what day or month it was, but he was able to remember having met a woman who could significantly contribute to an important project on which he was working in collaboration with a university professor. Dr. B could remember where that woman worked, and that she was a nice person, and that she would be easy to work with, and that she had access to a photocopying machine, and that making copies on that machine would cost 5¢ a page. In the life situation in which Dr. B found himself, these things *mattered* to him in ways that the day of the week and other items of information probed in standardized tests simply did not.

Beyond all this, what is also salient in these data is Dr. B's desire to engage in a genuinely *collaborative* enterprise. Commenting on this, Sabat notes,

> [Dr. B] was acting as a member of a research team, trying to provide all he could, to do his part, for the good of the research itself. Dr. B had come upon a situation which he was able to see as having great potential for the advancement of the Project. *He had made what was initially my goal, his goal as well.* (Sabat, 2001, pp. 258-259; emphasis added)

This last statement captures the very essence of *syntelie* as Stern conceived of it within the framework of critical personalism, and as noted in Chapter Eight, through this concept and the allied notion of introception, critical personalism leads away from a purely individualistic conception of individuality toward one in which *community* plays a critical role as well. Warranting notice here is the further fact that in his eagerness to pursue his genuinely syntelic objective, Dr. B was careful to act in a way that was polite and fully considerate of the perspective of the other person—his collaborator. Thus do we find Dr. B assuring Sabat that it was not his (Dr. B's) intention to "push, push, push." Sabat comments insightfully on this as follows:

> [W]hen Dr. B evinced urgent interest in making a connection with [the person] at the Alzheimer's Disease Association, he seemed extremely interested in communicating that he wasn't "dictating" to me. In so doing, he had to be: (1) monitoring his own behavior on a moment-by-moment basis; (2) evaluating its meaning and potential meaning insofar as how his behavior *might* appear to me (dictatorial), while (3) calling into play his knowledge of the standards of proper behavior established by the social community of which we both were a part, and then (4) acting in a way so as to assure me that his behavior was not to be interpreted as being outside those standards, and willing and able to communicate that any appearance that he might be acting in an impolite way was hardly his intention. (Sabat, 2001, pp. 270-271)

## Comment

Dr. B was not the only AD sufferer with whom Sabat (2001) explored the experience of the disease. Material obtained through extensive interviews with five other individuals is also presented in his book, and every case is rich in observations that lend themselves readily to interpretation within the framework of critical personalism. Sabat (2001) made no claim, and none is made here, that his research serves to *test* in any decisive way any specific theoretical assertion of critical personalism (or any other conceptual framework). What his research unquestionably does, however, is provide the reader with a perspective on the psychological functioning of Alzheimer's sufferers *as persons*, a perspective that cannot be approximated, even remotely, through the methods of conventional neo-Galtonian studies of average differences between "normal" subjects and their "demented" counterparts on standardized tests of cognitive functioning. In doing this, Sabat's research findings also serve to check many unwarranted inferences that have been made about Alzheimer's sufferers "in general" on the basis of statistical comparisons of aggregates. In short, Sabat's (2001) work vividly illustrates what can be accomplished through careful qualitative observations made by a "sensitive observer who has spent some time with the subjects" of his or her investigation. The work thus stands as one excellent model for personalistic inquiry in contemporary psychological research.

## Summary

The discussion in the present chapter was organized around two lines of empirical investigation that may be taken as models for the kinds of inquiry now needed as alternatives to the long-dominant neo-Galtonian approach to the "problem of individuality." Considered together, these two models reflect three basic principles that, in the view being defended here, should guide such choices generally.

The first of these principles is that if insight into what is transpiring at the level of the individual is the sort of knowledge sought and/or theoretically required—and it is not at all clear how a discipline officially indifferent to such knowledge could qualify as a *psychology*—then empirical investigation must be carried out at the level of the individual subject. In this matter, *there is no epistemically viable alternative*.

The second guiding principle here is that no logical incompatibility exists between the study of individual persons and the scientific quest for laws or "law-like" regularities pertaining to persons in general On the contrary, when *general* is understood to mean "common to all" *(allen gemein)*, as was true in the original Wundtian model of experimentation, then in the "neo-Wundtian" model called for here, the study of individuals not only does not undermine the search for the general but is logically mandated by that search. All that must be surrendered here is the false notion that the accumulation of knowledge about what is true *on average* somehow serves this same objective.

The third guiding principle here is that the objective of achieving a more personalistic scientific psychology does not require a categorical rejection of quantitative methods in favor of so-called qualitative techniques. On the contrary, personalistic investigation might incorporate either or both, depending on considerations such as the current state of knowledge in a given domain of inquiry and the specific knowledge objectives of the research. These latter might at certain times and in certain respects be idiographic, but at other times and in other respects be nomothetic. In either case, it is always *persons,* and never *person variables,* that are the foci of investigation.

To illustrate quantitative personalistic inquiry, a substantial portion of this chapter was devoted to a discussion of studies carried out by the present author and various colleagues on the psychology of subjective personality judgments (Lamiell & Durbeck, 1987; Lamiell, Foss, Larsen, & Hempel, 1983; Lamiell, Foss, Trierweiler, & Leffel, 1983). In these studies, the traditional *normative* model for personality trait measurement has been compared with an alternative model, termed *interactive* (Cattell, 1944), in terms of their respective validities as formal models of the manner in which laypersons formulate subjective judgments of their own and others' personality characteristics. The findings of these studies emphatically point toward the conclusion that the subjective judgment process in question does not entail the comparison of judged targets with one another along the attribute dimensions in question (the logic of normative measurement), but rather involves the appraisal of each target individually against the judge's understanding of how *that same target is not but might otherwise be* (the logic of interactive measurement).

These findings suggest that Allport's (1937a) speculations concerning the psychology of personality judgments made by counselors and clinicians—speculations never empirically evaluated, which were flatly and dogmatically rejected by Allport's critics—may well have been valid after all. The same findings point suggestively in the direction of a model for personality measurement fundamentally compatible with the personalistic approach to the problem that, decades ago, William Stern (1906, 1918a) sketched but was never able to bring to fruition. More recent evidence obtained by Weigert (2000) in studies involving the application of interactive measurement logic to the scoring of *NEO Personality Inventory* protocols (Costa & McCrae 1992) also points in this direction.

Apart from these theoretically important substantive issues, the quantitative research considered in this chapter also illustrates the proper role of conventional statistical analysis procedures in neo-Wundtian personalistic inquiry, a role quite different from that played by the same procedures in conventional neo-Galtonian investigations.

In the second half of this chapter, the focus shifts to a consideration of Sabat's (2001) qualitative research into the experience of Alzheimer's disease (AD). This work vividly and poignantly illustrates the fruitfulness of probing beyond what is revealed by standardized tests—in this case, of cognitive (dis)functioning commonly used to assess patients diagnosed as demented—and engaging Alzheimer's patients as *persons* who despite clear declines in certain rudimentary cognitive abilities continue to function as *evaluative entities* in precisely the sense of the term embraced by Stern within critical personalism.

Drawing largely on excerpts from Sabat's (2001) interviews with "Dr. B," the intent here has been to provide the reader with a sense for Sabat's (2001) clear and convincing demonstration that even in the stage of "severe" affliction, AD sufferers are able to act in accordance with meaningful evaluations of their present life circumstances, taking into account their personal pasts, their hopes for the future, and socially accepted standards of conduct. To see this, as Stern himself argued decades ago, requires "a sensitive observer who has spent some time" with the individuals being studied and in this way succeeds in penetrating beyond the superficial and inherently stereotypical information provided by standardized tests to the more consequential aspects of each subject's personal life and being.

Though inquiry of the sort undertaken by Sabat (2001) may not be well suited to the requirements of formal hypothesis testing, it can provide valid and perhaps indispensable insights into the functioning of persons that cannot possibly be achieved through the conventional methods of psychological assessment. Such work also serves very well to check unwarranted inferences often made about "people in general" on the basis of statistical comparisons of aggregates. In short, work of this sort serves vitally important functions from the perspective of a personalistic scientific psychology.

## Notes

1. In the interest of completeness, let it also be emphasized once again that this principle is in no way challenged by the obvious fact, reflecting the limits of induction constraining all scientific inquiry, that it is not humanly possible to investigate *all* persons.

2. For example, in Chapter 17 of Volume 1 of *Person and Thing,* the *Rationale and Basic Tenets,* Stern (1906) discussed "Intensity relationships and measurement," and in further pursuit of the ideas introduced there, he devoted Chapter 6 of Volume 2 of *Person and Thing, The Human Personality* (Stern, 1918a) to a discussion of "Principles of personality measurement."

3. Following the lead of psychophysics, Stern (1918a) also discussed personal difference thresholds *(persönliche Unterschiedsschwellen)*, but that discussion need not concern us here.

4. At first glance, it might appear that framing the discussion of assessment in terms of Equation 9.1 needlessly complicates the treatment of a very simple procedure, because under the scoring convention here described, the process of "weighting" each of the observations either 1 or 0 (zero) is clearly arithmetically superfluous. Nevertheless, there is a good reason for formally representing the logic of assessment in the manner indicated, because there is nothing in that logic that *requires* either that all observations scored for a given disposition have equal weight or that the weight of every observation be 0 (zero) for all dispositions save one. Without question, matters are arithmetically simplified under such conditions, and it is true that these are the conditions imposed by current conventions for scoring *NEO Personality Inventory* protocols. Still, other and possibly much more nuanced weighting schemes could be introduced without altering in any way the logic of the assessment procedure (Lamiell, 1987). In consideration of this possibility, it is important to recognize that the specific procedure discussed for illustrative purposes here is a special case of a more general approach in some applications of which the "weighting" process symbolized in Equation 9.1 would not be arithmetically superfluous (cf. Hase & Goldberg, 1967; Lamiell, 1987).

5. For purposes of estimating a population standard deviation from a sample value, the denominator in this computation is normally $(N - 1)$ rather than $N$.

6. The inventor of the "$T$ scale," William A. McCall, chose the designation $T$ in honor of two predecessors who were historically prominent advocates of this approach to the measurement of personality dispositions and whose surnames began with the letter $T$. One of these two individuals was Lewis Terman (1877-1956); the other was E. L. Thorndike (1874-1949), whose ideas on this topic were discussed at some length in Chapter Three (McCall, 1939, pp. 498-499).

7. Technically speaking, this "fixing" of a "top" and a "bottom" to the scale of $z$ score measurements is treasonous to the logic of such measurement because theoretically, the scale by which such normative measures are defined extends to infinity in either direction from the midpoint (mean). Practically speaking, however, the transgression is necessary, for without it, the seemingly simple task of constructing a trait profile cannot be executed. For a more detailed discussion of this point, see Lamiell (1987, Chapter Five).

8. In either case, this would mean responding *strongly disagree* on half of the 48 items and *strongly agree* on the other half, the difference here being attributable to the "direction" in which the items are worded (refer to discussion of item wording and scoring direction in Chapter Six).

9. Parroting criticisms of interactive measurement made by Paunonen and Jackson (1986a, 1986b) without attending to the rejoinder to those criticisms offered by Lamiell and Trierweiler (1986), Asendorpf (1991) has noted that under the logic of interactive measurement, no account is taken of the population base rates of various raw score assessments. In effect, Paunonen and Jackson (1986a,

1986b) and Asendorpf (1991) have criticized a rationale for dispositional measurement that was proposed as a needed alternative to rationales guided by statistical considerations on the grounds that the proposed alternative "fails" to incorporate statistical considerations!

10.  The difference between actuarial and nonactuarial approaches to this question is one that has been obfuscated by some critics of this line of research (e.g., Conger, 1983; Dar & Serlin, 1990; Ozer, 1990; Woody, 1983), and this is one of the reasons that the criticisms are rather less trenchant than their authors took them to be (cf. Lamiell, 1990b; Lamiell, Trierweiler, & Foss, 1983).

11.  Here and throughout this discussion of Weigert's (2000) work, the quantitative index of predictive validity employed was the same Cronbach-Gleser index of profile dissimilarity discussed above in connection with the research by Lamiell and Durbeck (1987).

12.  One of the 72 subjects who participated in Weigert's research was unable to provide NEO Form R data.

13.  That the substantive questions examined in this research concerned psychological processes considerably more complex than Wundt himself deemed amenable to experimental inquiry—something also true of the experimental research on memory carried out by Ebbinghaus (1885/1964)—does not alter the distinctly Wundtian nature of the research design.

14.  Although nearly 100 years have passed since AD was first described for the medical profession by the physician after whom the affliction was named, Alois Alzheimer (1864-1915), a definitive diagnosis is still exceedingly difficult to achieve and to this day is made only when the results of a biopsy or autopsy are viewed in conjunction with additional clinical evidence (Sabat, 2001). In many instances, therefore, studies of individuals clearly suffering from some form of dementia must be carried out prior to any determination that those individuals are, or are not, suffering from AD in particular.

15.  On the contrary, Sabat (2001) devoted an entire chapter of his book to a discussion of "goals, intentions, and the Alzheimer's sufferer's predicament in light of critical personalism" (pp. 224-273), and this is not the only section of the work in which observations illustrative of personalistic thinking are made. See also in this regard Sabat (2000).

16.  One of the enduring myths about Alzheimer's sufferers is that as rudimentary cognitive skills fail, the sense of self or identity, dependent as it is on memory, must necessarily fade accordingly. Sabat's (2001) research provides a wealth of evidence that this is not the case. One of many poignant illustrations of this was provided by "Mr. K," an AD sufferer. Sabat relates an instance in which the director of the adult day care center, "Mr. G," was introducing Mr. K to a third party. Mr. G said, "This is Mr. K. Mr. K was a lawyer." Immediately, the severely afflicted Mr. K interrupted, saying, "I am a lawyer."

# Chapter Ten

## Our Differences Aside

### *Persons, Things, Individuality, and Community*

By his own account, William Stern centered his entire intellectual life around "the problem of individuality." The challenge, as he saw it, was to incorporate into the "New Science" of psychology a philosophically sound and theoretically viable conception of the human being (Stern, 1927), and the distinction between persons and things was fundamental to his thinking in this regard. In critical personalism, this distinction turns ultimately on the concept of *value:* A thing is an entity that can *be evaluated,* passively, whereas a person is an entity that actively "e-valuates"—or "radiates value," as Stern often put it—in accordance with his or her purposes. In combination, the notions of value and purpose lead, finally, to a conception of the individual personality, or one's individuality, as *character.*

We have seen that as a vehicle for systematically advancing the aspects of critical personalism that could be regarded as amenable to empirical exploration at all, Stern proposed, as a complement to the general-experimental psychology of his day, a new subdiscipline he called "differential" psychology (Stern, 1900a). Much of the present work has been devoted to a discussion of how the project Stern thus initiated was derailed. Of surpassing importance in this historical development was the widespread endorsement among Stern's contemporaries of the notion that studies yielding knowledge

about the covariation of attribute measures in populations—studies of the
sort Stern termed "correlational"—open a "window" onto what is transpiring at the level of the individual. In the shadow cast by this notion, the
components of Stern's original differential psychology that installed *individuals* rather than attributes as the foci of investigation appeared superfluous at best, and unscientific at worst. Accordingly, but against Stern's
repeated and increasingly strenuous objections, those aspects of his thinking were simply ignored, and the differential psychology that came to dominate "personality studies" was no longer the differential psychology Stern
had founded. Meanwhile, critical personalism as a framework for conceptualizing the problem of individuality in its broader philosophical as well
as specifically psychological dimensions faded quietly from the disciplinary
scene.

Demonstrably, however, it is not true that studies of the covariation of
attribute measures in populations yield knowledge about what is transpiring at the level of the individual. For this reason, as a means of advancing
our understanding of human individuality, the project that displaced Stern's
is itself fatally flawed. In fact, what has been proffered for most of the
20th century as a "psychology of persons" is scarcely anything of the sort:
Its subject matter is not persons but *person variables*, and the knowledge it
delivers is not psychological, but essentially *demographic* (Lamiell, 2000).
By these lights, it is fair to say that fully 10 decades after Stern proclaimed
individuality "the problem of the 20th century" (Stern, 1900a), the challenge he saw still looms, waiting to be met properly.

It was noted in Chapter One that at the time of Stern's death, Allport
(1938) wrote admiringly of Stern's optimism that other thinkers would
eventually be persuaded of the merits of his views, and Allport confidently
forecast for critical personalism a day that would be "long and bright"
(Allport, 1938, p. 773). Thus far, both Stern's optimism and Allport's confidence have gone unrequited. Stern himself continues to be known, if at all,
mainly as "the IQ guy" (Lamiell, 1996), and critical personalism remains as
obscure as ever. In light of arguments developed in the present work, however, some will perhaps agree that for its true breadth and depth, Stern's
thinking on the "problem of individuality" merits a great deal more attention than it has thus far received. With this in mind, my purpose in this concluding chapter is to reemphasize and elaborate certain basic conceptual
points relevant to critical personalism and to draw out still others, not only
to make critical personalism's implications clearer as a foundation for
personality theory but also to suggest its relevance as a framework for
contemporary social thought.

# On Critical Personalism as a Foundation for Personality Theory

## Reviving the Project Within the Contemporary Context

A point of emphasis in Chapter Two was that when Stern called in 1900 for a differential psychology, his primary concern was not that his experimentally oriented contemporaries were systematically ignoring what could be captured statistically through the investigation of variables marking individual and group differences. What concerned Stern most was the mechanistic and hence impersonal theoretical conception of human psychological life that was being projected by the experimental psychology of the day. Cast in the language of critical personalism, Stern was concerned about *die Versächlichung von Personen,* the turning of persons *(Personen)* into things *(Sachen),* and this concern fueled his resolve to direct the attention of his contemporaries to the "problem of individuality" in the first instance (Stern, 1900a).

Clearly, Stern believed at the turn of the 20th century that empirical documentation of such enduring between-person differences as might be found with respect to basic psychological functions, such as attention, perception, judgment, and memory, would help to display the need within scientific psychology for a viable conception of human individuality. However, Stern never believed that such studies could effectively meet that need. Unfortunately, the vast majority of his contemporaries (and successors) did not see things his way. So, whereas Stern's ultimate goal was to achieve a personalistic individual psychology within the context of which empirical facts about individual and group differences would be *theoretically accommodated,* what flourished instead was a neo-Galtonian "hybrid" discipline (Danziger, 1987) that displaced the study of individuals altogether and installed the empirical study of individual and group differences as "the" agenda. In a discipline in which method was soon dictating theory, it was perhaps inevitable that even when the ultimate objective would be an empirically derived "portrait" of an individual (e.g., in the construction of a multiattribute personality profile or in clinical diagnosis), virtually universal agreement would congeal around the notion that "it is meaningless to interpret the behavior of an individual without a frame of reference of others' behavior" (Epstein, 1983, p. 381).

As we saw in Chapter Nine, however, this widespread and long-standing conviction is fundamentally incompatible with critical personalism. Consequently, the blinders that that conviction has imposed on contemporary understanding of the process of person characterization, formal or informal, must be removed if there is to be any hope at all of reestablishing the personalistic perspective in modern times.

## Person Characterization Without Between-Person Comparisons

The issue here is perhaps best seen by casting it in very concrete terms. To this end, suppose that on the basis of valid information about the recurrent act patterns of a man named Smith, we wish to characterize him in terms of his single most salient personality characteristic. Stated more precisely, the goal here is to position Smith *(S)* with respect to some underlying attribute dimension, *D*. Should he be situated somewhere around the middle of the dimension, as in Line *a?*

$$\backslash\underline{\hspace{4cm}S\hspace{4cm}}/ \quad (a)$$
$$D$$

Or would it in fact be more accurate to locate Smith appreciably to the left end of center, as in Line *b?*

$$\backslash\underline{\hspace{0.5cm}S\hspace{5cm}}/ \quad (b)$$
$$D$$

Or again, might it be determined that Smith is most appropriately positioned somewhat to the right of center, as in line *c?*

$$\backslash\underline{\hspace{5cm}S\hspace{0.5cm}}/ \quad (c)$$
$$D$$

Now, by the conventional truism that meaningful person characterization logically requires between-person comparisons, we should have to concede at this point that an intelligible statement about Smith with respect to attribute dimension *D* cannot be formulated outside the context of statements about other individuals with respect to that same attribute dimension. In effect, this maxim asserts that until Smith is compared with others, he has no location at all with respect to dimension *D*. So, our situation at the moment is as depicted in Line *d*.

$$\backslash\underline{\hspace{6cm}}/ \quad (d)$$
$$D$$

The problem is now apparent: If with respect to attribute dimension, *D*, Smith is *nowhere at all* prior to being compared with others, then no comparison of Smith with others in terms of that attribute dimension could ever be made. For an individual to be "higher," "lower," or "equal to" some other(s) with respect to some dimension of characterization, that individual, and each of the others, *must be somewhere along that dimension to start with* (Lamiell, 1990b). Accordingly, if between-person comparisons are possible at all, and obviously they are, then there must also be some rationale for characterizing individuals that does not appeal to such comparisons and that, indeed, is recognized as an epistemic precondition for them.

In Chapter Nine, an approach to dispositional measurement termed *interactive* was discussed as providing such a rationale. Philosophically speaking, interactive measurement is grounded in a *rationalist* conception of person characterization. Under its terms, what *is* said to be the case about some given individual at some particular point in time has meaning by virtue of its implications concerning what *might otherwise have been* said to be the case about that same individual at that point in time.

At first blush, it might seem cogent to object that knowledge about how "this" individual "is not but might otherwise be" must itself be grounded in acquaintance with how other individuals actually are. This is an *empiricist* conception of person characterization. It was on such a conception that Thorndike (1911) based his seminal assertions about "what kinds of individuals there *can* be" (refer to discussion of this point in Chapter Three), and in the domain of formal trait measurement, this same conception has long driven the notion that "all meaning for a given ["raw"] score of a person derives from comparing [that] score with those of other persons" (Kleinmuntz, 1967, p. 47). Let us examine the empiricist thesis more closely.

Certainly, it would be possible, through the arithmetic of the normative measurement operations discussed in Chapter Six, to determine that with respect to some intended measure of, say, introversion versus extraversion, the "raw" score realized by Smith is, say, 1 standard deviation above the group mean. This would make Smith's standard score, *Z*, equal to +1.0. At the same time, it could be determined that the "raw" score realized by some other individual, Jones *(J)*, is, say, 1 standard deviation below the group mean, making his standard score, *Z*, equal to −1.0. However, such knowledge alone would not yet suffice for a meaningful characterization either of Smith or of Jones, for the question would still beg as to whether the derived standard scores marked Smith as relatively extraverted *(E)* and Jones as relatively introverted *(I)*, or *vice versa*. Our situation would be as depicted in Line *(e)*.

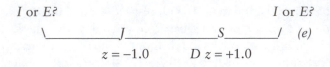

$$I \text{ or } E? \qquad\qquad\qquad\qquad I \text{ or } E?$$
$$\backslash_____/_____S_____/ \quad (e)$$
$$z = -1.0 \qquad D \; z = +1.0$$

To finally interpret the standard scores realized by Smith and Jones as normative measures (i.e., impose *substantive meaning* on those scores), it is necessary to know which end of the scale is which. Clearly, this knowledge is not achieved by examining "more data" or statistics compiled of them, or anything empirical at all. It is achieved through a rational consideration of how the device is scored, that is, by conceptually grasping the alternative possibilities built into the assessment instrument itself. Only in this way could it ever be determined that, for example, Smith's standard score of $Z$ = +1.0 positions him not only 1 standard deviation above the group mean but also, should it be the case, *toward that end of the scale conceptualized as extreme introversion;* and Jones's standard score of $Z = -1.0$ positions him not only 1 standard deviation below the group mean but also, should it likewise be the case, *toward that end of the scale conceptualized as extreme extraversion.*

We see, then, that even when one seeks attribute measures of the traditional normative variety, ideas corresponding, in effect, to the $A'_{min}$ and $A'_{max}$ terms of interactive measurement (refer to Equation 9.4) are present "in the wings" and must be invoked, even if only implicitly, for the meaning of the resulting measures to emerge. This is why Cattell (1944) was correct in observing that "true normative measurements are bound to be founded on interactive measurement" (p. 299)—not vice versa—and this is also why the claim by Kleinmuntz (1967) quoted above concerning the source of *"all* meaning of a given score of a person" could not possibly be valid.

By these considerations, we are led back to the validity of the thesis that it is, as indeed it must be, possible to meaningfully characterize persons *prior* to comparing them with one another, and this suffices to establish that persons can be characterized meaningfully whether or not they are ever compared with one another at all. This is the epistemic position toward which Stern (1918a) was striving in his attempt, discussed briefly in Chapter Nine, to articulate a theoretical conception of psychological measurement at once liberated from considerations of between-person differences and formally compatible with the personalistic thesis that in human psychological life, *actuality presupposes potentiality.* A person's individuality, in this view, is *what distinguishes that person from the persons he or she is not but might otherwise be.* To be sure, it may often be possible to identify empirically persons who *are* as the person in question *is not,* but such considerations are never of fundamental epistemic importance, and as we shall see, they are quite often of no importance at all. Our individualities are and remain recognizable quite irrespective of whatever differences might also exist.

## Individuality Versus Uniqueness

In Chapter Four, attention was focused on the controversy sparked by Gordon Allport's quasi-personalistic arguments in favor of supplementing studies of the sort mistakenly termed *nomothetic* with inquiry of a more *idiographic* nature. Through that discussion, it was explained both that and why Allport's historic efforts in this direction failed. In light of the immediately preceding discussion, however, there is another important point to be made regarding Allport's views that was passed over in the earlier discussion.

In a monograph by Allport published in 1955 under the title *Becoming: Basic Considerations for a Psychology of Personality* (Allport, 1955), there is a subsection headed "The Dilemma of Uniqueness," in which we read the following:

> If there is to be a science of personality at all it should do better than it has in the past with the feature of personality that is most outstanding—its manifest *uniqueness* of organization. (Allport, 1955, p. 21; emphasis added)

A few paragraphs later, we read,

> Nor is it helpful to take refuge in the example of the other sciences. . . . [On the contrary . . . ] we should refuse to carry over the indifference of other sciences to the problem of *individuality*. (Allport, 1955, p. 22; emphasis added)

What merits our attention here is the ease with which Allport moved from the term *uniqueness* to the term *individuality*. There is nothing in these passages (or to the best of my knowledge, elsewhere in the corpus of Allport's writings) to suggest that he saw any need to distinguish these two concepts from one another. A major implication of the foregoing discussion of the rationalist approach to person characterization, however, is that a clear distinction between these concepts both can and should be made.

To say that an individual is unique (within the inevitably limited population under consideration) is to say that none of the others with whom that individual is being compared is identical to him or her. But we have just seen that to carry out the between-person comparisons that would be necessary to establish this, meaningful characterizations of all individuals to be compared would already have to be in place, and this is why a distinction between individuality and uniqueness is necessary. The former concept is properly reserved for statements asserting *what is* rather than *is not* the case about individuals, whereas the latter concept refers to the question of whether what has been said to be the case about some one individual happens to be identical with what has been said to be the case about some other individual.

Note that under either of the two possible answers to this question, the individualities being compared in any given instance would remain as they were: Smith would not somehow become more the individual he had been found to be simply by virtue of our failing to find any other individual just like him, nor would he become any less the individual he had been found to be simply if we happened to identify another just like him in all respects under consideration. Smith is who he is, whether he is "unique" or not. Moreover, questions of genuine theoretical and practical consequence about the course of his personality development (i.e., questions concerning the emergence, maintenance, and change in the various features of his individuality; cf. Levy, 1970), would remain to be addressed, regardless of the outcome of inquiry diverted to the question of his uniqueness.

In the present view, then, what Allport (1955) called "the dilemma of uniqueness" is a red herring (Lamiell, 1997). This is not to deny that individuals are unique. Plainly, however, empirical inquiry designed to *establish* (within unavoidable limits) individual uniqueness inevitably leads back into between-person comparisons, and as should now be abundantly clear, this is precisely where a discipline genuinely concerned with the "problem of individuality" should not wish to be.

## Positioning, Position Taking, and Personal Identity

Above, the process of person characterization was referred to as *positioning:* To speak of the salient attributes of one's individuality is, after all, to make assertions that "locate" that individual with respect to certain dimensions (and at times, categories) of meaning. In a very similar vein, modern social constructionists (see, e.g., Harré, 1984; Harré & Gillett, 1994; Shotter, 1993) draw attention to the language of interpersonal discourse as an instrument by means of which individuals are situated vis-à-vis one another, or positioned, within the context of their relationships.

In Chapter Nine, it was noted that Sabat (2001) used the concept of positioning to discuss the untoward consequences of characterizing an Alzheimer's disease sufferer in *defectological* terms, that is, in terms of what is missing or lacking in the person's capacities. When this happens, attention is necessarily deflected away from abilities the sufferer retains, and as Sabat (2001) has masterfully shown, these latter are often considerable. Practically speaking, therefore, the end result of defectological positioning is often a relationship between the sufferer and his or her caretaker(s) that is of rather poorer quality than it might otherwise be.

Be this as it may, however, a personalistic understanding of positioning emphasizes that it is not exclusively a passive process whereby persons are *given* positions but also, and more fundamentally, an active process whereby they *take* positions. Stern (1917) specifically discussed "position taking" *(die Stellungnahme)* as an intentional act through which, in the face of a multiplicity of alternative possibilities, one strives to realize certain preferred states of affairs and thus to preclude or negate others (cf. Bamberg, 2000). Indeed, it is sometimes the case that what the person strives to preclude or negate is the way in which he or she has been positioned by another. Here, too, we found in Sabat's (2001) work a simple but poignant illustration of this: When a day care center staff member referred to the Alzheimer's sufferer Mr. K as someone who *was* (had been) a lawyer, Mr. K immediately protested "I *am* a lawyer!" (see Endnote #16 in Chapter Nine). In the event, Mr. K rejected the position of former lawyer to which he had been relegated by the staff member and insisted on positioning himself in accordance with his *continuing* identity as a lawyer.

Viewed personalistically, this example underscores the importance of regarding persons as autonomous, "e-valuative" agents in their own social construction. The point bears emphasis here because not all contemporary versions of social constructionism endorse this view. From the "postmodernist" perspective adopted by Kenneth Gergen, for example, social relationships are taken to be ontologically fundamental, and the individuals "constructed" under the terms of those relationships are thus strictly derivative entities. Persons as autonomous, evaluative agents are explicitly "deontologized" (Gergen, 1992, p. 17), and in their places are substituted beings viewed as "saturated selves," that is, congeries of the social roles into which the circumstances of their lives have thrust them (see, e.g., Gergen, 1991, 1994). Renner and Laux (2000) have discussed at length the fact that from such a theoretical perspective, the unity of self postulated by Stern does not exist. In effect, therefore, this postmodernist view reduces persons to things, and this is the very antithesis of personalistic thinking.

It does not follow, however, that critical personalism is incompatible with all versions of social constructionism (Harré, 2000, 2002). In Chapter Eight, we noted Stern's commitment to the view that even as persons are purposive, goal-oriented beings, they are at the same time beings *"in need of supplementation"* (Stern, 1917, p. 51). More specifically, Stern held that "it is due to the incompleteness and breadth of latitude of every personal disposition that, in its realization, factors residing in the external world necessarily play a role" (Stern, 1917, p. 51). Obviously, the "external world" includes (though is not limited to) the social world, and this is why in critical personalism, special emphasis is placed on the process of *introception* as the personal act through which the values reflected by the prevailing customs and mores in one's cultural milieu can be taken up, or not, by the individual and be made into, or rejected as, part of his or her personal value system (Hermans, 2000). The discussion by Clara and William Stern of the development of lying in childhood (Stern & Stern, 1909/1999) provides one clear example of this perspective (refer to Chapter Eight; see also Tissaw's, 2000, discussion of psychological symbiosis in critical personalism and social constructionism).

We see, then, that the personalistic conception of social construction (a) rejects the postmodernist notion that persons can properly be regarded as mere congeries of attributes resulting from constructions imposed from without and (b) retains a view of persons as purposive, goal-oriented bearers and co-constructors of their own individual identities (Lamiell, 1992).

Writing nearly 40 years after Stern's death and apparently without any direct knowledge of critical personalism, Rychlak (1976) expressed a view entirely consistent with the spirit of Stern's thinking on this matter:

> It is the ability to both have an idea or be doing something and yet at the same time grasp transcendentally that one is thinking and doing these things, to comment on them, *and to know that one could be doing and thinking otherwise,* that leads a personality theorist to postulate the identity factor. (Rychlak, 1976, p. 220; emphasis added)

## Teleology Reconsidered

In light of this understanding of personal identity, the need for an explicitly teleological conception of the person becomes manifest. To know even as one is doing/thinking something that one might very well be doing/thinking otherwise is to grasp that personal being not only allows for but also demands the exercise of will in the pursuit of goals set in accordance with one's values. This is as true of the rudimentary act of attending to the immediately present stimulus world as it is of what might be regarded as more "elevated" acts, such as choosing a spouse, settling on a career path, or practicing a religion. This is the philosophical orientation Stern quite properly saw as threatened by the mechanistic conception of human thought and behavior that was gaining wide currency among the experimentalists of his day—and as noted repeatedly throughout this work, this concern prompted his efforts toward a critical personalism.

It is worthy of mention in this context that the theoretical perspective of "the" preeminent turn-of-the-century experimentalist, Wilhelm Wundt, also could not easily be reconciled with ascendant mechanistic views (cf. Blumenthal, 1975). On the contrary, the *voluntarism* that centered Wundt's understanding of human consciousness was actually more compatible with Stern's teleological views than with those of many of their more mechanistically inclined contemporaries (e.g., Ebbinghaus), and this is true even if Stern himself was not entirely satisfied with certain aspects of Wundt's theorizing. In particular, Stern criticized the conception of *will* embedded in Wundt's voluntarism as "too broad" and hence too imprecise (1938, p. 398), and in the monograph discussed in Chapter Eight of the present work, Stern (1917) made clear what he meant by this:

> [In] Wundt's psychology, . . . the border between act and conscious experience was not clearly drawn: when he sets up the will as characteristic of all psychological life, he means in one instance the goal-striving act of will, in another instance the experience of willing present in consciousness. (Stern, 1917, p. 20)

Such theoretical nuances were soon rendered moot. The same positivist-empiricist outlook on psychological science that eventually would prove so nurturant of neo-Galtonian inquiry—and in the process marginalize Stern's views—led to the repudiation of Wundt's voluntarism as well (Danziger, 1979; see also Blumenthal, 1975) and to the creation of an intellectual environment decidedly inhospitable to any conception of will or genuine purposivity in the production of behavior (cf. Rychlak, 1981).

Nevertheless, and consistent with his determination to oppose this trend despite its rapidly increasing popularity, Stern concluded Volume 2 of *Person and Thing,* titled *The Human Personality* (Stern, 1918a), with the following observation:

> Long-standing concerns about the excesses and inadequacies of a false teleology have led many to doubt that a teleological perspective could ever be justified at all. But those areas of research and daily life that are related in any way to the human personality have been greatly hampered by this, because the idea of purpose *(Zweck)* is the very key to a true understanding of personal being. Having now acquainted ourselves with a correct understanding of teleology, with its justification and its limits, we have reached a time when the aforementioned concerns—which have actually developed into a kind of "teleophobia"—can be allayed. The way has now been opened for making a critically teleological conception of human nature fruitful both for work in the human sciences and for the grounding of cultural life. (Stern, 1918a, p. 270)

The optimism expressed in this passage notwithstanding, Stern had every reason to believe that his teleological outlook would yet meet with stiff resistance. He knew, after all, that most of his experimentalist contemporaries regarded a mechanistic conception of human psychological life as positively mandated by the ground rules of the science they were so determined to ape, namely, Newtonian physics (Leahey, 2001). In this view, persons had to be regarded as mere instances—however complex—of *matter in motion* (Robinson, 1995), in principle fully understandable according to causal laws that incorporated no reference at all to personal goals or genuine purposivity in thought or action. This view has remained dominant up to the present day.

It should be noted here that against this dominant view, the *rigorous humanism* staunchly defended by the contemporary scholar Joseph F. Rychlak is philosophically entirely compatible with critical personalism (see, e.g., Rychlak, 1979, 1981, 1988, 1991, 1997). Rychlak's logical learning theory is explicitly teleological, and within that theory, his concepts of *affective assessment* and *predication* are fully in accord with Stern's understanding of position taking. Underscoring the point here, however, is the unfortunate fact that Rychlak's contributions, like those of Stern, have thus far received very little attention within the mainstream of personality psychology.

One reason for this is surely that work carried out within the neo-Galtonian paradigm that replaced Wundtian-style experimentation has only seemed to further validate the mechanistic view. The reason for this is not difficult to see: If the aggregate level order to be discerned in statistical knowledge afforded by neo-Galtonian inquiry is taken to confirm a corresponding individual level order, then the thought and action patterns of individuals appear to have been rendered empirically predictable, and hence explainable, without any help from teleological theoretical concepts such as goals, purposes, and reasons. Nor is the presence of residual ("error") variance seen to challenge this stance, because such variance can always be understood from within the accepted paradigm as a failure to take all relevant causal mechanisms into account.

From the discussion in Chapter Five, it is evident that this outlook fully corresponds with the position on the question of will explicitly defended by Henry Thomas Buckle (1898/1857) as he parlayed Adolphe Quetelet's "social physics" into a view of social science that would become the epistemic foundation for neo-Galtonian psychology. We saw in Chapter Seven, however, that this entire approach to the problem of individuality is predicated on a mistake: Close analysis reveals that the aggregate level order reflected by statistical findings generated through neo-Galtonian studies of individual and group differences is not a "window" onto individual level phenomena at all—and so entitles no knowledge claims whatsoever concerning the degree to which any individual's thoughts or behaviors have been rendered predictable and hence explained. Certainly, therefore, there is nothing in the sizable corpus of knowledge presently defining modern "personality psychology" (cf. Hogan, Johnson, & Briggs, 1997) that decisively contraindicates a reconsideration of the teleological conception of persons developed by Stern within the framework of critical personalism.

# On Critical Personalism as a Framework for Social Thought

## *Menschenkenntnis* and *Menschenbehandlung* Revisited

Without question, Stern's scholarly efforts vis-à-vis the problem of individuality gave expression to what he himself described as his *furor metaphysicus* (Stern, 1927), his ambition to formulate a conception of the individual human person that would reflect and convey his philosophical worldview. Just as clear, however, is the fact that Stern regarded the intellectual product of his efforts in this direction, critical personalism, as a platform from which to launch endeavors of practical consequence in the world outside the academy. He deplored an ivory tower experimental psychology that had "condemned itself to sterility *(Unfruchtbarkeit)* in relation to socio-cultural issues *(kulturelle Aufgaben)*" (Stern, 1911, p. 6), and he called for a differential psychology that would advance the *understanding of people*, or *Menschenkenntnis*, in ways that could and should inform the *treatment of people*, or *Menschenbehandlung*, including their deployment as "human resources." In this way, a philosophically grounded scientific psychology could pursue its basic knowledge objectives and still be relevant within the context of various social institutions such as schools and universities, the legal system, governmental agencies, the military, health care, business, and industry.

We saw in Chapter Three that although many of Stern's contemporaries shared his enthusiasm for constructing a discipline that would be practically consequential, their efforts in this direction also came to be dominated by a very limited version of the differential psychology he originally envisioned. In particular, and due in no small part to the efforts of Stern's contemporary Hugo Münsterberg, the view ascended that the interests of officials in various social institutions, on one hand, and those of applied differential psychologists, on the other, articulated best in *correlational* studies. In such studies, psychologists could investigate in a systematic, quantitative way the manner and extent to which variables marking individual and group differences were statistically related to criterion measures of interest in those various institutional settings. Knowledge of this sort could be used to guide institutional policies and decision making so as to optimize, in the long run, desired outcomes concerning, for example, admissions, placements in different programs of study, alternative career paths, job assignments, clinical diagnoses and medical treatment regimens, advertising campaigns, and so on.

Formally speaking, this conception of applied differential psychology is perfectly coordinate with the vision of a basic science of personality committed to examining and discovering the sources of individual and group differences. Both agendas conform to, and are furthered by, the same set of measurement methods and statistical data analysis techniques, namely, those proper to neo-Galtonian inquiry; this is what accounts for the symmetry of Figure 6.1 schematizing the so-called nomothetic paradigm for scientific personality studies. In the accepted view, then, the applied, practical agenda of *Menschenbehandlung,* on one side, and the more basic, theoretical agenda of *Menschenkenntnis,* on the other, are but two aspects of one central project: the assessment and systematic study of individual and group differences.

The critique of contemporary "nomotheticism" mounted in Chapter Seven was intended to clarify the fundamental inadequacy of neo-Galtonian inquiry as a means of realizing Stern's philosophical and theoretical objectives in the domain of *Menschenkenntnis.* However, and just because of the symmetry just mentioned, that critique also has important implications for widely accepted views and practices in the domain of *Menschenbehandlung.*

Consider the use of standardized personality tests as "preemployment screening" devices (Hogan, Hogan, & Roberts, 1996), that is, as a basis for deciding whether individual job applicants should or should not be considered further for employment in some particular line of work. For example, through carefully designed and competently executed neo-Galtonian inquiry, one might make observations such as the following:

> [T]ruck driver performance is predicted by high scores for prudence and adjustment and low scores for sociability, because high sociability is associated with impulsivity, and impulsive truck drivers get in trouble on the job. (Hogan, Hogan, & Roberts, 1996, p. 472)

Suppose that in knowledge of the statistical relationships alluded to here, under retention as a (doubtless well-compensated) consultant to a major trucking company, a psychotechnician recommends to the chief personnel officer of the company that applicant Charles not be hired as a driver. Pursuant to receiving his rejection notice, Charles requests a meeting to discuss the reason(s) for his not having been hired. The trucking company arranges for Charles to speak directly with the psychotechnician, and on the assumption that the latter is fully conversant with the epistemic limitations of his own statistical techniques (an assumption that, alas, cannot always safely be made; cf. Hake, 2001; Valsiner, 1986), we may imagine the conversation unfolding as follows:

*Charles:*   I'm here to ask why my application to be hired as a truck driver has been rejected.

*Psychotechnician:*   On the battery of personality tests that you took as part of the application process, you scored high on sociability.

*Charles:*   Yes, and?

*Psychotechnician:*   In this instance, I'm afraid, your high sociability is a liability, because psychological research has shown that high sociability is statistically predictive of impulsivity, and impulsivity in truck drivers leads to trouble.

*Charles:*   I see. So, given my highly sociable nature, just how much trouble would I cause were I to be hired?

*Psychotechnician:*   Well, it is not really possible to say in any individual case, but what we do know based on the scientific research is that, on average, highly sociable people have more trouble in this profession than do their less sociable counterparts.

*Charles:*   But in my particular case, you really can't say what the outcome would be?

*Psychotechnician:*   Correct.

*Charles:*   So in other words, I as an individual have been denied employment as a truck driver on the basis of a statistically guided prediction that has been made about me as an individual but whose accuracy in my individual case is completely unknown.

*Psychotechnician:*   Correct.

We can imagine that Charles's next comment would be something like "I think I'll call my lawyer." Just in case he did, and suit was brought, how might the trucking company defend its practice of basing preemployment screening decisions on statistical considerations of the usual and widely accepted sort? We know from the discussion in Chapter Seven that there is no real recourse in the argument "We might not know for certain what Charles will do, but research has revealed to us his *tendencies* and those of other individuals like him." Neo-Galtonian studies of individual and group differences do not, in fact, reveal *any individual's* psychological or behavioral "tendencies," and this is no less true in the domain of *Menschenbehandlung* than in the domain of *Menschenkenntnis*. Nor can the psychotechnician reach safe haven through the argument that "We can't say for sure that Charles will get into trouble, but we know that the *probability* that he will get into trouble is high." As claims to knowledge about Charles, or any other individual, probabilistic statements based on neo-Galtonian studies of individual and group differences are incorrigible and hence scientifically vacuous. Such claims can stand as statements about the strength of the decision maker's personal conviction about what will happen in Charles's case, but thus understood, the basis for Charles's rejection is, transparently, a subjective opinion held by the decision maker and not knowledge of some objective, scientific truth about Charles.

In the last analysis, justification for handling Charles's application (that is, for treating Charles) in the manner described must ultimately be sought in practical considerations. It might be argued, for example, that the in-depth studies of Charles and other persons that would be necessary to reveal their respective individual psychological and/or behavioral tendencies are precluded by time and resource constraints and, perhaps, by considerations having to do with the personal privacy of the subjects themselves. Without contesting that in many contexts, this "argument-from-practicality" might reasonably carry the day, it is nevertheless important to make explicit what the argument means from a personalistic standpoint.

First of all, it should be clear that the argument in no way rescues the thesis that aggregate statistical knowledge about individual differences constitutes scientific knowledge about individuals. On the contrary, the argument explicitly concedes that gaining the latter sort of knowledge is not feasible, and if aggregate statistical knowledge already *were* that sort of knowledge, then no such concession would be necessary.

Second, it is important to see that the argument-from-practicality requires that persons be regarded as mere instances of categories, fully interchangeable for other instances of the same categories. From this perspective, each person is properly treated in accordance with the dictates of a statistical scheme (e.g., a regression model) that, if followed, will optimize certain pay-off functions and hence serve the best long-term interests of the exercisers of the scheme. It is understood that through the exercise of the statistical scheme, decisions will be made and actions taken that will disserve some of the affected persons (e.g., some will be barred from jobs in which they would have done well, and others will be directed to jobs for which they will prove to be ill suited), but it is accepted that concern for such inequities must be subordinated to the concern for the greater overall interests of the institution (school, corporation, state, etc.) in the service of which the scheme is being exercised. Individual persons are treated as *commodities,* to be handled, deployed, and even manipulated in consideration of those other, superordinate interests (Hanson, 1993).

The tension here seems to be relieved, if not made altogether indiscernible, by "forgetting" the above-noted concession to practicality and readopting the epistemic position—logically untenable but nevertheless obstinately maintained by the vast majority of mainstream investigators—that aggregate statistical knowledge is knowledge about the individuals within the aggregate. From that position, statistically defined rules of decision making followed in the best long-term interests of the institution appear also to be in the best interests of the individuals affected, and objectively justifiable as such, even if the individuals in question would subjectively disagree. Charles might not believe that he would be headed for trouble as a truck driver, but scientific research seems to have established that he would be, and so rejecting his application apparently serves not only the best interests of the trucking company but also the very worthy objective of saving Charles from himself.

Of course, it is acknowledged (as it must be) by the psychotechnical "experts" that mistakes will occur. But from the neo-Galtonian perspective, this is never seen as an inevitable outcome of the fact that statistical laws are not knowably applicable to this or that individual case to begin with. Seen (improperly) as *general* laws in the sense of *allen gemein,* they are considered applicable to *all* individual cases, to be imposed on each and every one in the same way, and when "exceptions" or "outliers" occur, it is because more laws of the same basic kind have yet to be discovered and implemented accordingly. The statistically guided decision scheme is epistemically privileged, and so although it can be *mistaken* in this or that individual case, its application per se cannot be regarded as fundamentally *inappropriate* in any individual case. In *Menschenbehandlung* in the neo-Galtonian model, all mistakes are "honest" ones—regrettable, perhaps, as a kind of collateral damage, but finally eradicable only by further and more thorough applications of the same model. In the meantime, it is not only practically necessary but scientifically justifiable to subordinate the interests of adversely affected individuals to the larger, long-term interests of the institution(s).

When exercises in *Menschenbehandlung* framed exclusively within the neo-Galtonian framework are viewed in this light, it is easy to see the basis for Stern's concerns about the excesses of psychotechnics. We took notice in Chapter Three of his repeated warnings about how psychotechnicians' *intercessions* in the lives of others, however well intentioned, can degenerate into *interference* in those lives, justified on grounds won via methods that do not respect human individuality and require instead that persons be regarded as things. Just as other aspects of Stern's *Weltanschauung* were grounded in Kantian philosophy, so were his moral sensibilities aligned closely with Kantian thought. Specifically, critical personalism embraces the moral imperative that persons be regarded as inherently valuable ends in and of themselves, never merely as means to the ends of others. Clearly, ascendant practices in psychotechnology were violating this imperative, and from Stern's perspective, that was a very troublesome matter.

A rather different model of practically useful intervention, one decidedly more compatible with the tenets of critical personalism, is provided by the work of Sabat (2001) discussed in the previous chapter, and in this connection, it is instructive to consider the comments of a medical practitioner named Michael Gordon. In a review of Sabat's book in the *Canadian Medical Association Journal*, Gordon (2002) wrote,

> It's not often that I encounter a book that changes the way I look at a clinical problem, especially one so familiar to me as Alzheimer's disease. With 25 years' experience as a geriatrician, I had become comfortable with the concepts and issues surrounding the care of people with dementia. . . . [Yet] even in the midst of reading this book for review, I started to communicate differently with patients with Alzheimer's disease and their families. I began to take note of evidence of strengths in my patients and evidence of impatience and the misreading of cues by caring family members. . . . This is a "must read" for any practitioner whose clientele includes patients with Alzheimer's disease. Sabat's book is unlike others that recount personal and family experiences, or professional works that help practitioners understand the mechanisms of the disease. It combines humanity, humility and a clear conceptual framework that can be put to practical use. . . . His fundamental message is that each person afflicted with Alzheimer's disease is an individual whose special essence we must endeavor to find and to nurture for as long as possible. (Gordon, 2002, pp. 1-2)

Clearly, practical and effective *Menschenbehandlung* need be neither actuarial nor otherwise impersonal.

## Personalism Without Individualism

For all of the foregoing, it would nonetheless be mistaken to view critical personalism as a framework within which the interests of the individual would always take precedence over those of social institutions. On the contrary, and as noted at the conclusion of Chapter Eight, Stern himself viewed critical personalism as a system of thought no more compatible with a one-sided "individual-ism" concerned exclusively with the rights and happiness of the single person, than with a socialism in which human "individual-ity" would be ignored if not suppressed altogether.

It will be recalled from that earlier discussion that in elaborating his teleological conception of the person, Stern argued as follows:

> [T]he person who pursues only his/her own narrow individual goals would be an extensionless point in emptiness. Only goals extending beyond the self give the person concrete content and living coherence with the world. Autotelie encounters heterotelie. (Stern, 1917, p. 46)

He recognized an irreducibly sociocultural aspect of personal being in this actuality:

> [E]ach person is a member of higher unities, which for their part have the character of living wholes with their own goals . . . family, folk, humanity, deity. The partaking in these higher unities signifies for the individual a serviceability with respect to their goals. [This is] hypertelie. (Stern, 1917, p. 46)

Stern introduced the concept of introception relating to participation in the pursuit of goals other than—and in some cases higher than—one's individual objectives, and he was at pains to point out that this is not a passive process. Certainly, it is not simply a matter of becoming "saturated" with the mores and customs that just happen to prevail in one's particular social milieu. Were that the case, then the socialization process would be, literally, depersonalizing. The individual, molded entirely by suprapersonal social forces, would be, to paraphrase Stern, "degraded into a mere thing and tool." In contrast to this, Stern believed that through the *active*—and hence, by definition, *critical*—appropriation of certain human values represented by interests extending beyond the self, the person becomes, as Stern put it, a *microcosmos*. Thus did he argue,

> [T]he self-directed personal sphere and personal action [must be related] to the personal spheres and personal actions of other equal and higher personal unities. People must, therefore, incorporate the ends of others into their self ends. (Stern, 1923, p. 63)

One clear example of the understanding within critical personalism of individuals' obligations to others may be seen in the work carried out by

Clara and William Stern on the topic of lying in early childhood (refer to Chapter Eight). Explicitly distancing themselves from the highly individualistic views on child rearing advanced by Jean Jacques Rousseau, the Sterns emphasized that children must be brought to see the importance of *disciplining themselves*—meaning, in this case, regulating their own immediate self-interests in favor of lying—out of respect for the greater common good within their families and communities.

Critical personalism's nonindividualistic tenor is sounded further in the following passage, especially illuminating in the present context because its content pertains to correlational studies that were being directed by Stern in Hamburg relevant to the problem of identifying gifted and talented youth (refer to Chapter One):

> The insight that the advancement of highly capable children would be a socio-ethial task of the first order has spread further and further in recent years. . . . We stand before an "ethics of ability," such that, on the one hand, the people at large recognize their duties with regard to those talents growing within our midst and, on the other hand, that individuals blessed with a special ability not be permitted to see in it a private privilege which they enjoy, but a special duty to themselves and to the entire society. (Stern, 1928, quoted in Feger, 1991, p. 98)

Moral voice, however, was a casualty as 20th-century differential psychologists divorced their own correlational research efforts from the philosophical tenets of critical personalism and instead embraced the mechanistic conception of behavior that finds such clear expression in contemporary "trait psychology." In the emergent (and still hegemonic) view, human individuality is conceived strictly in terms of variables with respect to which individuals can be differentiated from one another empirically. To "have a personality" simply means *to be different* from specified others in specified ways. The constellation of personality attributes that a given individual happens to "have" is seen as something determined for that individual by some combination of genetic endowment (nature) and upbringing (nurture), and the consequences of "having" precisely those attributes are understood as lawfully determined causal effects on thought and behavior, unmediated by the will of the individual in question.

So, modern differential psychologists can, as did Stern, bring their technical expertise to bear on the problem of discriminating the "gifted and talented" from their less blessed peers, and as social science "experts," they can also advise public policymakers on initiatives that would advance the interests of the different groups (see, e.g., Herrnstein & Murray, 1994). There is not, however, any basis on which modern differential psychologists could say that gifted and talented individuals (or any other individuals, for that matter) have any obligation at all to the larger society. In the accepted view, persons are things, and things have no moral obligations.

From the personalistic standpoint, however, individuality is not fundamentally a matter of having been passively constituted, by nature and nurture, in a way that makes one different from others, and perhaps even unique. It is a matter of actively taking on a character that makes one different from the person one would otherwise be. Individuality is not a congeries of sociobiological forces that (somehow) cause one's behavior to follow certain empirically discernable patterns—but rather, in the last analysis, comprises a set of *values* by which the person regulates his or her conduct vis-à-vis others. Because in this view, being different from others is not the essence of one's individuality to begin with, neither is one's individuality in any way compromised by being like others to the extent of sharing certain values *in common*. In critical personalism, individuality accords with rather than contests community.

## Individuality, Diversity, and Community

In contemporary social discourse in the United States, there is perhaps no theme more prominent than that of *diversity*. In schools and universities, in businesses and corporate boardrooms, in social and recreational organizations, and in activities of virtually every kind, the way participant groups are constituted across categories of variables, such as race, gender, ethnicity, socioeconomic class, and religious confession, is a highly salient issue. Quite obviously, considerations about diversity are bound up tightly with modern sensibilities concerning what is equitable in the distribution of society's resources, but beyond this, such considerations are also prominent in contemporary notions about what is right and good—that is, valuable— in human affairs. In this connection, the requisite personal virtue is *tolerance,* and much modern discourse presumes, if it does not explicitly claim, that diversity at the organizational/institutional level will strengthen communities by engendering virtuous tolerance in individuals.

As comforting as it might be to believe that this presumption warranted, it is not at all clear that it functions in reality. In their well-known work *Habits of the Heart,* Bellah, Madsen, Sullivan, Swidler, and Tipton (1985) treat the "culture of separation" that prevails in modern American life as being problematic for an ethos of community. Indeed, inasmuch as discussions of diversity necessarily highlight differences rather than commonalities, the rhetoric of diversity is quite possibly fostering that very culture of separation rather than nurturing community. Anecdotal evidence can serve to illustrate what is problematic in this regard.

Consider, for example, the observations of Ms. Ilke Bauer, who studied as a Fulbright exchange student at the School of the Art Institute of Chicago (1998-1999). In a short essay titled "Thoughts About Race and Multi-culturalism in the U.S.A.," published in *The Funnel: The Newsmagazine of the German-American Fulbright Commission,* Ms. Bauer (2000) wrote,

> As soon as I arrive, it starts: the first form to fill out, and in the space for giving information about oneself it says: Race. To help me, the alternative possible answers were provided, one of which I was supposed to check. I look for "White," but it is not there. Well, what am I, anyway? Probably Caucasian, because none of the others fits, and it seems improbable that I should classify myself as "other" and then invent on my own the proper term to designate my race. Hesitantly, I make my choice. . . . That would not be the only time during my 18 month stay in the U.S.A. that the issue of race would come up. To the contrary, questions about what one is and to what group one belongs seem to have enormous importance here. I am very irritated by the relentless inclination among Americans to differentiate people according to their race or ethnicity. Race: the very word makes me wary, because I immediately associate it with Nazi Germany or with the Klu Klux Klan. (pp. 30-31)

Mr. Lars Winkler (2000), another Fulbright exchange student studying in the United States, also contributed an essay to *The Funnel,* titled "Culture Shock, or What I Wasn't Prepared For," and on the topic of diversity observed the following:

> I find it very interesting that, really, almost everyone finds it most comfortable simply to stay within their own little groups. The Chinese students stick with the Chinese, those from India stick with others from India, etc., etc. One's own culture and identity is, apparently, much more important than "the American culture." . . . It seems as if everyone here has a clear negative image of some-one. . . . The multicultural society functions, but apparently only on the surface. (p. 10)

In light of such observations, the question is at least worth posing: Might an uncritical celebration of diversity—of individual and group differences—actually be furthering the culture of separation, and to this extent under-mining rather than enhancing communities?

On the 15th of March, 1900, William Stern delivered a lecture before the membership of an organization known as "The Society of Brothers." The lecture was titled "On the Ethical Meaning of Tolerance," and in it, he developed a number of points that have an uncanny relevance to the con-cerns expressed in the quotations above and to contemporary discourse on diversity and tolerance more generally.

Early in the lecture, Stern (1900b) posed the question "What is tolerance *(Toleranz)*?" and then commented as follows:

The word has a variety of connotations that can be grouped into two main categories. . . . [One is] *forbearance (Duldung),* [the other is] *tolerance (Duldsamkeit).* Forbearance is a behavior which one practices; tolerance is a sentiment that one has. Tolerance is an aspect of character relating to our judgments. It makes it possible for us to make sense of and to find value in and relative justification for an opinion or perspective that deviates from our own. Forbearance is a practical stance adopted by an individual or a collective, e.g., the state, with respect to the representatives of a view that does not correspond to the individual's or collective's own. For example, the minimal tolerance shown to Jews in earlier times was forbearance, in that non-Jews permitted the Jews to live in the cities. This forbearance was not based on tolerance, but emerged instead for other reasons, from the insight that in certain areas of life, such as trade and business, Jews were indispensable. Later, every movement that carried the Jew toward emancipation and civil rights emerged from a sentiment of tolerance which, as a characteristic of the larger people, was a product of the period of Enlightenment. (Stern, 1900b, p. 5)

Of course, writing in 1900, Stern could not possibly have fathomed the approaching horror, and in retrospect, his suggestion in this passage that thanks to the Enlightenment, the situation of the Jews had safely progressed beyond mere forbearance to genuine tolerance appears tragically naive. But the fact that Stern so drastically misread the circumstances of the Jews in early 20th-century Germany only serves to underscore the importance of the distinction he was drawing between a merely superficial form of tolerance, forbearance, which is a kind of public posturing in the interest of social or economic expediency, and a truly virtuous tolerance that is a deep and principled conviction extending well beyond considerations of a practical nature.

Conceiving of true tolerance as a virtue, Stern explicitly followed Aristotle in situating that virtue between the opposite and equally vicious extremes of *intolerance* and *indolence (Indolenz).* The latter, Stern argued,

[I]s, literally, painlessness, that is, the inability to be moved. [It is] the deficiency in the ability to get worked up or even enraged. . . . Is it still a virtue if one is neither cold nor warm but always lukewarm, inclined to accept anything, and to view everything with a kind of indifference? Truly, I believe that the damage that can be done by hateful intolerance is not greater than that which can result from indolence. . . . If one proclaims absolute tolerance a virtue, then one would have to abandon every evaluation, every judgment, every criticism. Should we forbid ourselves to be able to say: This is good, and that is bad? or: This is precious and that is outrageous injustice? or: This must be promoted, that must be stopped? . . . No, if we want to say that, we would surrender the best aspect of our human nature and of human ability: the ability to evaluate. (Stern, 1900b, pp. 12-13)

From the personalistic standpoint, then, tolerance is something quite other than the mere absence of intolerance. The latter amounts to an ever tentative forbearance that can be exploitative or even degenerate into indolence. In any case, no true and lasting community can be based on mere forbearance.

Virtuous tolerance is predicated finally on a genuine respect for human individuality, that is, on individuals' principled regard for other individuals as *persons,* whose thoughts and actions convey what they have and have not embraced in the realm of human values. Unlike mere forbearance, which encourages the uncritical acceptance of "difference" for its own sake, virtuous tolerance is demanding. It requires the active engagement of each person in the critical appraisal of one's own values and those of other persons—seen individually and not in the stereotypic fashion licensed by the rampant *statisticism* of modern social science—to establish the proper place of those values in civic life.

Contrasting his views to the abstract idealism of Hegel, Stern explicitly referred to critical personalism as a "concrete idealism" (Stern, 1924b, p. 65), and in the foregoing, the romantic facet of the framework is evident as well. This alone might seem reason enough to dismiss personalistic thinking as hopelessly out of step with modern/postmodern sensibilities. And yet in the world that was changed so radically by the attacks on the World Trade Center and the Pentagon, on September 11, 2001, perhaps some will agree that it is time to penetrate beyond the undeniable differences that separate persons and peoples from one another—to the realization that the fundament of our respective individualities does not lie in what differentiates us *from one another,* but rather in what differentiates each of us *from what we would otherwise be were our values other than what they are.* With this idea firmly in grasp, it is but a short step to the realization that the quest for community need not and indeed ought not compromise individuality, and that a crucial aspect of our respective individualities as human persons is to be found in the values we share in common, our differences aside.

# References

Achilles, P. S. (Ed.). (1932). *Psychology at work.* New York: McGraw-Hill.

Alexander, I. (1993). Science and the single case. In K. H. Craik, R. Hogan, & R. N. Wolfe (Eds.), *Fifty years of personality psychology* (pp. 119-129). New York: Plenum.

Allport, G. W. (1937a). *Personality: A psychological interpretation.* New York: Holt, Rinehart & Winston.

Allport, G. W. (1937b). The personalistic psychology of William Stern. *Character and Personality, 5,* 231-246.

Allport, G. W. (1938). William Stern: 1871-1938. *The American Journal of Psychology, 51,* 770-773.

Allport, G. W. (1946). Personalistic psychology as science: A reply. *Psychological Review, 53,* 132-135.

Allport, G. W. (1955). *Becoming: Basic considerations for a psychology of personality.* New Haven, CT: Yale University Press.

Allport, G. W. (1961). *Pattern and growth in personality.* New York: Holt, Rinehart & Winston.

Allport, G. W. (1962). The general and the unique in psychological science. *Journal of Personality, 30,* 405-422.

Allport, G. W. (1966). Traits revisited. *American Psychologist, 21,* 1-10.

Allport, G. W. (1968). *The person in psychology: Selected essays by Gordon W. Allport.* Boston: Beacon.

Allport, G. W., & Odbert, H. S. (1936). Trait names: A psycholexical study. *Psychological Monographs, 47*(Whole No. 211).

Anders, G. (1950). "Bild meines Vaters" ("Portrait of my father"); a foreword to William Stern's *Allgemeine Psychologie auf personalistischen Grundlage* (zweite unveränderte ed., pp. xxiii-xxxii). Den Haag, Netherlands: Nijhoff.

Anders, G. (1971). Die geköpfte Lilie: Erinnerung an den Vater [The beheaded lily: A recollection of my father]. *Süddeutsche Zeitung,* pp. 115.

Angleitner, A. (1991). Personality psychology: Trends and developments. *European Journal of Personality, 5,* 185-197.

Asendorpf, J. (1991). *Die differentielle Sichtweise in der Psychologie* [The differential perspective in psychology]. Göttingen: Hogrefe.

Ash, M. (1995). *Gestalt psychology in German culture, 1890-1967*. Cambridge: Cambridge University Press.

Bakan, D. (1966). The test of significance in psychological research. *Psychological Bulletin, 66*, 423-437.

Bamberg, M. (2000). Critical personalism, language, and development. *Theory and psychology, 10*, 749-767.

Barrett, W. (1978). *The illusion of technique*. New York: Anchor Books.

Bauer, I. (2000). Thoughts about race and multiculturalism in the U.S.A. *The Funnel: The Newsmagazine of the German-American Fulbright Commission, 36*, 2, 30-32.

Beck, L. W. (1941). William Stern's philosophy of value. *The Personalist, 22*, 353-363.

Beck, S. J. (1953). The science of personality: Nomothetic or idiographic? *Psychological Review, 60*, 353-359.

Behrens, H., & Deutsch, W. (1991). Die Tagebücher von Clara und William Stern [The diaries of Clara and William Stern]. In W. Deutsch (Ed.), *Über die verborgene Aktualität von William Stern* (pp. 19-37). Frankfurt am Main: Peter Lang Verlag.

Bellah, R. N., Madsen, R., Sullivan, W. M., Swidler, A., & Tipton, S. M. (1985). *Habits of the heart: Individualism and commitment in American life*. New York: Harper & Row.

Bem, D. J., & Allen, A. (1974). On predicting some of the people some of the time: The search for cross-situational consistencies in behavior. *Psychological Review, 81*, 506-520.

Binet, A., & Henri, V. (1896). La psychologie individuelle [Individual psychology]. *Annee psychologie, 2*, 411-465.

Blumenthal, H. (1975). A reappraisal of Wilhelm Wundt. *American Psychologist, 30*, 1081-1088.

Brand-Auraban, A. (1972). William Stern's philosophy of personalism and value. *Korort (Hebrew) Quarterly for the History of Medicine and Science, 5*, 808-813.

Brunswik, E. (1943). Organismic achievement and environmental probability. *The Psychological Review, 50*, 255-272.

Buckle, H. T. (1898). *A history of civilization in England* (2nd London ed.). New York: D. Appleton. (Original work published 1857)

Budescu, D. (1980). Some new measures of profile dissimilarity. *Applied Psychological Measurement, 4*, 261-272.

Bühring, G. (1996a). *William Stern oder Streben nach Einheit* [William Stern, or the quest for unity]. Frankfurt am Main: Peter Lang Verlag.

Bühring, G. (1996b). *Titelbibliographie zu und über William Stern* [Bibliography of works by and about William Stern]. Unpublished manuscript, Berlin.

Bühring, G. (1997). Dem Psychologen und Philosophen William Stern (1871-1938) zum 125. Geburtstag [To the psychologist and philosopher William Stern (1871-1938) on the 125 anniversary of his birth]. *Report Psychologie, 22*, 366-373.

Burt, C. L. (1937). Correlation between persons. *British Journal of Psychology, 28*, 59-96.

Buss, D. M., & Craik, K. H. (1983). The act frequency approach to personality. *Psychological Review, 90,* 105-126.

Campbell, D. T., & Fiske, D. W. (1959). Convergent and discriminant validation by the multitrait-multimethod matrix. *Psychological Bulletin, 56,* 81-105.

Carlson, R. (1971). Where is the person in personality research? *Journal of Personality and Social Psychology, 75,* 203-214.

Cattell, J. M. (1890). Mental tests and measurements. *Mind, 15,* 373-380.

Cattell, R. B. (1944). Psychological measurement: Normative, ipsative, interactive. *Psychological Review, 51,* 292-303.

Cattell, R. B. (1950). *Personality.* New York: McGraw-Hill.

Cattell, R. B. (1952). The three basic factor-analytic research designs—their inter-relations and derivatives. *Psychological Bulletin, 49,* 499-520.

Cattell, R. B. (1957). *Personality and motivation: Structure and measurement.* New York: World Book Company.

Cloninger, S. C. (1996). *Personality: Description, dynamics and development.* New York: Freeman.

Cohn, J. (1932). *Wertwissenschaft* [Science of values]. Stuttgart: Frommans.

Cohen, J. (1968). Multiple regression as a general data analytic system. *Psychological Bulletin, 70,* 292-303.

Conger, A. (1983). Toward a further understanding of the intuitive personologist: Some critical evidence on the diabolical quality of subjective psychometrics. *Journal of Personality, 51,* 292-303.

Costa, P. T., & McCrae, R. R. (1992). *Revised NEO Personality Inventory (NEO-PI-R) and NEO Five-Factor Inventory (NEO-FFI) professional manual.* Odessa, FL: Psychological Assessment Resources.

Cronbach, L. J. (1957). The two disciplines of scientific psychology. *American Psychologist, 12,* 671-684.

Cronbach, L. J., & Gleser, G. (1953). Assessing similarity between profiles. *Psychological Bulletin, 50,* 456-473.

Cronbach, L. J., & Meehl, P. E. (1955). Construct validity in psychological tests. *Psychological Bulletin, 52,* 281-302.

Danziger, K. (1979). The positivistic repudiation of Wundt. *Journal of the History of the Behavioral Sciences, 15,* 205-230.

Danziger, K. (1987). Statistical method and the historical development of research practice in American psychology. In L. Krueger, G. Gigerenzer, & M. S. Morgan (Eds.), *The probabilistic revolution, Vol. 2: Ideas in the sciences* (pp. 35-47). Cambridge: MIT Press.

Danziger, K. (1990). *Constructing the subject: Historical origins of psychological research.* New York: Cambridge University Press.

Dar, R., & Serlin, R. C. (1990). For whom the bell curve toils: Universality in individual differences research. In D. N. Robinson & L. P. Mos (Eds.), *Annals of theoretical psychology* (Vol. 6, pp. 193-199). New York: Plenum.

Darlington, R. (1968). Multiple regression in psychological research and practice. *Psychological Bulletin, 69,* 161-182.

Daston, L. (1988). *Classical probability in the Enlightenment*. Princeton, NJ: Princeton University Press.

Deutsch, W. (1997). Im Mittelpunkt die Person: Der Psychologe und Philosoph William Stern (1871-1938) [In the center the person: The psychologist and philosopher William Stern (1871-1938)]. In M. Hassler & J. Wertheimer (Eds.), *Der Exodus aus Nazideutschland und die Folgen: Jüdische Wissenschaftler im Exil* (pp. 73-90). Tübingen: Attempto.

Digman, J. M. (1989). Five robust trait dimensions: Development, stability, and utility. *Journal of Personality, 57*, 195-214.

Digman, J. M. (1990). *Personality structure: Emergence of the five-factor model* (Vol. 41). Palo Alto, CA: Annual Reviews.

Dilthey, W. (1894). Ideen über eine beschreibende und zergliedernde Psychologie [Toward a descriptive and analytical psychology]. *Sitzungsberichte der Akademie der Wissenschaften zu Berlin*, zweiter Halbband, 1309-1407.

Drobisch, M. W. (1867). *Die moralische Statistik und die menschliche Willensfreiheit: Eine Untersuchung* [A study of moral statistics and human free will]. Leipzig.

Dürr-Borst, M. (1906). Die Erziehung der Aussage und Anschauung des Schulkindes [Training school-aged children with respect to testimony and perspective]. *Die experimentelle Pädagogik, 3*, 1-30.

Ebbinghaus, H. (1885/1964). *Memory: A contribution to experimental psychology* (H. A. Ruger & C. E. Bussenius, Trans.). New York: Dover.

Ebbinghaus, H. (1896a). Über eine neue Methode zur prüfung geistige Fähigkeiten und ihre Anwendung bei Schulkindern [A new method for testing mental abilities and its application with school children]. *Zeitschrift für Psychologie der Sinnesorgane, 13*, 401-457.

Ebbinghaus, H. (1896b). Über erklärende und beschreibende Psychologie [On explanatory and descriptive psychology]. *Zeitschrift für Psychologie und Physiologie der Sinnesorgane, 9*, 161-205.

Ebbinghaus, H. (Ed.). (1897). *Grundzüge der Psychologie* [Foundations of psychology] (Vols. 1 & 2). Leipzig: Feit.

Ebbinghaus, H. (1908). *Psychology: An elementary textbook* (M. Meyer, Trans.). Boston: D.C. Heath.

Ekehammar, B. (1974). Interactionism in personality psychology from a historical perspective. *Psychological Bulletin, 81*, 1026-1048.

Endler, N. S., & Magnussoon, D. (1976). Toward an interactional psychology of personality. *Psychological Bulletin, 83*, 956-974.

Epstein, S. (1977). Traits are alive and well. In N. S. Endler & D. Magnusson (Eds.), *Personality at the crossroads: Current issues in interactional psychology* (pp. 83-98). Hillsdale, NJ: Erlbaum.

Epstein, S. (1979). The stability of behavior: I. On predicting most of the people most of the time. *Journal of Personality and Social Psychology, 37*, 1097-1126.

Epstein, S. (1980). The stability of behavior: II. Implications for psychological research. *American Psychologist, 35*, 790-806.

Epstein, S. (1983). Aggregation and beyond: Some basic issues in the prediction of behavior. *Journal of Personality, 51*, 360-392.

Eysenck, H. J. (1952). *The scientific study of personality.* London: Routledge & Kegan Paul.

Eysenck, H. J. (1954). The science of personality: Nomothetic! *Psychological Review, 61,* 339-342.

Eysenck, H. J. (1990). Differential psychology before and after William Stern. *Psychologische Beiträge, 32,* 249-262.

Fancher, R. E. (1985). *The intelligence men: Makers of the IQ controversy.* New York: W. W. Norton.

Feger, B. (1991). William Sterns Bedeutung für die Hochbegabungsforschung—die Bedeutung der Hochbegabungsforschung für William Stern [William Stern's significance for research on the highly talented—and the significance of research on the highly talented for William Stern]. In W. Deutsch (Ed.), *Die verborgene Aktualität von William Stern* (pp. 93-108). Frankfurt am Main: Peter Lang Verlag.

Folstein, M., Folstein, S., & McHugh, P. R. (1975). Mini-mental state: A practical method for grading the cognitive state of patients for the clinician. *Journal of Psychiatric Research, 12,* 189-198.

Freud, S. (1900). *Die Traumdeutung* [The interpretation of dreams]. Leipzig und Wien: Deuticke.

Galton, F. (1865). Hereditary talent and character. In R. Jacoby & N. Glauberman (Eds.), *The bell curve debate: History, documents, opinions* (pp. 393-409). New York: Times Books/Random House.

Garrett, H. E. (1966). *Statistics in psychology and education.* New York: David McKay Company.

Gergen, K. J. (1991). *The saturated self: Dilemmas of identity in contemporary life.* New York: Basic Books.

Gergen, K. J. (1992). Social construction and moral action. In D. N. Robinson (Ed.), *Social discourse and moral judgment* (pp. 9-27). New York: Academic Press.

Gergen, K. J. (1994). *Realities and relationships.* Cambridge, MA: Harvard University Press.

Gergen, K. J. (1999). *An invitation to social construction.* London: Sage.

Gibson, J. J. (1985). Conclusions from a century of research on sense perception. In S. Koch & D. E. Leary (Eds.), *A century of psychology as science* (pp. 224-230). New York: McGraw-Hill.

Gigerenzer, G. (1987). Probabilistic thinking and the fight against subjectivity. In G. Gigerenzer, L. Krueger, & M. S. Morgan (Eds.), *The probabilistic revolution, Vol. 2: Ideas in the sciences* (Vol. 2, pp. 11-33). Cambridge: MIT Press.

Goldberg, L. R. (1993). The structure of phenotypic personality traits. *American Psychologist, 48,* 26-34.

Goldfried, M. R., & Kent, R. N. (1972). Traditional versus behavioral personality assessment: A comparison of methodological and theoretical assumptions. *Psychological Bulletin, 77,* 409-420.

Gordon, M. (2002). Veiled meanings. *Canadian Medical Association Journal, 166,* 482.

Graf-Nold, A. (1991). Stern versus Freud: Die Kontroverse um die Kinder-Psychoanalyse—Vorgeschichte und Folgen [Stern versus Freud: The controversy over childhood psychoanalysis—Background and consequences]. In W. Deutsch (Ed.), *Die verborgene Aktualität von William Stern* (pp. 49-91). Frankfurt am Main: Peter Lang Verlag.

Graumann, C. F. (1980). Wundt vor Leipzig—Entwürfe einer Psychologie [Wundt before Leipzig—Outlines of a psychology]. In W. Meischner & A. Metge (Eds.), *Wilhelm Wundt: Progressives Erbe, Wissenschaftsentwicklung und Gegenwart* (pp. 63-77). Leipzig: Verlag Karl-Marx-Universität.

Graziano, W. G., & Eisenberg, N. H. (1997). Agreeableness: A dimension of personality. In R. Hogan, J. Johnson, & S. Briggs (Eds.), *Handbook of personality psychology* (pp. 795-824). New York: Academic Press.

Grünwald, H. (1980). *Die sozialen Ursprünge psychologischer Diagnostik* [The social origins of psychological diagnosis]. Darmstadt: Steinkopf.

Guilford, J. P. (1954). *Psychometric methods.* New York: McGraw-Hill.

Guilford, J. P. (1959). *Personality.* New York: McGraw-Hill.

Hacking, I. (1990). *The taming of chance.* Cambridge: Cambridge University Press.

Hake, A. (2001). *Was sagen gruppenstatistische Kennwerte über den Einzelfall aus? Ein Text-und Übungsbuch* [What do aggregate statistics reveal about the single case? A text and workbook]. Landau: Verlag Empirische Pädagogik.

Hanfmann, E. (1952). William Stern on "projective techniques." *Journal of Personality, 21,* 1-21.

Hanson, F. A. (1993). *Testing testing: Social consequences of the examined life.* Berkeley: University of California Press.

Hardesty, F. P. (1976). Louis William Stern: A new view of the Hamburg years. *Annals of the New York Academy of Sciences, 270,* 31-44.

Hardesty, F. P. (1977). William Stern and American psychology: A preliminary analysis of contributions and contexts. *Annals of the New York Academy of Sciences, 291,* 33-46.

Harré, R. (1984). *Personal being.* Cambridge, MA: Harvard University Press.

Harré, R. (2000). Personalism in the context of a social constructionist psychology. *Theory and Psychology, 10,* 731-748.

Harré, R. (2002). Public sources of the personal mind: Social constructionism in context. *Theory and Psychology, 12,* 611-623.

Harré, R., & Gillett, G. (1994). *The discursive mind.* London: Sage.

Harrington, A. (1996). Reenchanted science: Holism in German culture from Wilhelm II to Hitler. Princeton, NJ: Princeton University Press.

Hartshorne, H., & May, M. A. (1928). *Studies in the nature of character, Vol 1: Studies in deceit.* New York: Macmillan.

Hartshorne, H., & May, M. A. (1929). *Studies in the nature of character, Vol. 2: Studies in service and self-control.* New York: Macmillan.

Hartshorne, H., May, M. A., & Shuttleworth, F. K. (1930). *Studies in the nature of character, Vol. 3: Studies in the organization of character.* New York: Macmillan.

Hase, H. D., & Goldberg, L. R. (1967). Comparative validity of different strategies of constructing personality inventory scales. *Psychological Bulletin, 67,* 231-248.

Hermans, H. (2000). Valuation, innovation and critical personalism. *Theory and Psychology, 10,* 801-814.

Herrnstein, R. J., & Murray, C. (1994). *The bell curve: Intelligence and class structure in American life*. New York: Free Press.

Hogan, J., & Hogan, R. (1989). How to measure employee reliability. *Journal of Applied Psychology, 74*, 273-279.

Hogan, R., Hogan, J., & Roberts, B. W. (1996). Personality measurement and employment decisions: Questions and answers. *American Psychologist, 51*, 469-477.

Hogan, R., Johnson, J., & Briggs, S. (Eds.). (1997). *Handbook of personality psychology*. New York: Academic Press.

Hogan, R., & Ones, D. S. (1997). Conscientiousness and integrity at work. R. Hogan, J. Johnson, & S. Briggs (Eds.), *Handbook of personality psychology*. New York: Academic Press.

Holt, R. W. (1962). Individuality and generalization in the psychology of personality. *Journal of Personality, 30*, 377-404.

Hothersall, D. (1995). *History of psychology* (3rd ed.). New York: McGraw-Hill.

Huber, R. J., Edwards, C., & Heining-Boynton, D. (Eds.). (2000). *Cornerstones of psychology: Readings in the history of psychology*. New York: Harcourt Brace.

Hug-Hellmuth, H. von. (1913). Aus dem Seelenleben des Kindes: Eine psychoanalytische Studie [From the psychological life of the child: A psychoanalytic study]. In S. Freud (Ed.), *15, Heft der schriften zur angewandten Seelenkunde*. Wien.

Jacoby, R., & Glauberman, N. (Eds.). (1995). *The bell curve debate: History, documents, opinions*. New York: Times Books.

John, O., & Robins, R. W. (1993). Gordon Allport: Father and critic of the five-factor model. In K. H. Craik, R. Hogan, & R. N. Wolfe (Eds.), *Fifty years of personality psychology* (pp. 215-236). New York: Plenum.

Johnson, J. A. (1997). Units of analysis for the description and explanation of personality. In R. Hogan, J. Johnson, & S. Briggs (Eds.), *Handbook of personality psychology* (pp. 73-93). New York: Academic Press.

Kerlinger, F. N., & Pedhazur, E. J. (1974). *Multiple regression in behavioral research*. New York: Holt, Rinehart & Winston.

Kimble, G. A. (1993). Evolution of the nature-nurture issue in the history of psychology. In R. C. Plomin, & G. E. McClearn (Eds.), *Nature, nurture, & psychology* (pp. 3-25). Washington, DC: American Psychological Association Books.

Kleinmuntz, B. (1967). *Personality measurement: An introduction*. Homewood, IL: Dorsey.

Kreppner, K. (1992). William L. Stern: A neglected founder of developmental psychology. *Developmental Psychology, 28*, 539-547.

Krueger, F., & Spearman, C. (1906). Die Korrelation zwischen verschiedenen geistigen Leistungsfähigkeiten [The correlation between various mental abilities]. *Zeitschrift für Psychologie und Physiologie der Sinnesorgane, 44*, 50-114.

Lamiell, J. T. (1981). Toward an idiothetic psychology of personality. *American Psychologist, 36*, 276-289.

Lamiell, J. T. (1987). *The psychology of personality: An epistemological inquiry*. New York: Columbia University Press.

Lamiell, J. T. (1990a). Explanation in the psychology of personality. In D. N. Robinson & L. P. Mos (Eds.), *Annals of theoretical psychology* (Vol. 6, pp. 153-192). New York: Plenum.

Lamiell, J. T. (1990b). Let's be careful out there: Reply to commentaries. In D. N. Robinson & L. P. Mos (Eds.), *Annals of theoretical psychology* (Vol. 6, pp. 219-231). New York: Plenum.

Lamiell, J. T. (1991). Problems with the notion of uncertainty reduction as valid explanation. *Theoretical and Philosophical Psychology, 11,* 99-105.

Lamiell, J. T. (1992). Persons, selves, and agency. In D. N. Robinson (Ed.), *Social discourse and moral judgment* (pp. 29-41). San Diego: Academic Press.

Lamiell, J. T. (1995). Rethinking the role of quantitative methods in psychology. In J. Smith, R. Harré, & L. van Langenhove (Eds.), *Rethinking methods in psychology* (pp. 143-161). London: Sage.

Lamiell, J. T. (1996). William Stern: More than "the IQ guy." In G. A. Kimble, C. A. Boneau, & M. Wertheimer (Eds.), *Portraits of pioneers in psychology* (Vol. II, pp. 73-85). Washington, DC: American Psychological Association Books; Mahwah, NJ: Lawrence Erlbaum.

Lamiell, J. T. (1997). Individuals and the differences between them. In R. Hogan, J. Johnson, & S. Briggs (Eds.), *Handbook of personality psychology* (pp. 117-141). New York: Academic Press.

Lamiell, J. T. (1998). "Nomothetic" and "idiographic": Contrasting Windelband's understanding with contemporary usage. *Theory and Psychology, 10,* 715-730.

Lamiell, J. T. (2000). A periodic table of personality elements? The "Big Five" and trait "psychology" in critical perspective. *The Journal of Theoretical and Philosophical Psychology, 20,* 1-24.

Lamiell, J. T., & Deutsch, W. (2000). In the light of a star. An introduction to William Stern's critical personalism. *Theory and Psychology, 10,* 715-730.

Lamiell, J. T., & Durbeck, P. (1987). Whence cognitive prototypes in impression formation? Some empirical evidence for dialectical reasoning as a generative process. *Journal of Mind and Behavior, 8,* 223-244.

Lamiell, J. T., Foss, M. A., Larsen, R. J., & Hempel, A. (1983). Studies in intuitive personology from and idiothetic point of view: Implications for personality theory. *Journal of Personality, 51,* 438-467.

Lamiell, J. T., Foss, M. A., Trierweiler, S. J., & Leffel, G. M. (1983). Toward a further understanding of the intuitive personologist: Some preliminary evidence for the dialectical quality of subjective personality impressions. *Journal of Personality, 53,* 213-235.

Lamiell, J. T., & Trierweiler, S. J. (1986). Interactive measurement, idiothetic inquiry, and the challenge to conventional "nomotheticism." *Journal of Personality, 54,* 460-469.

Lamiell, J. T., Trierweiler, S. J., & Foss, M. A. (1983). Theoretical vs. actual analyses of personality ratings, and other rudimentary distinctions. *Journal of Personality, 51,* 259-274.

Leahey, T. H. (2001). *A history of modern psychology* (3rd ed.). Upper Saddle River, NJ: Prentice-Hall.

Levy, L. (1970). *Conceptions of personality.* New York: Random House.

Lewin, K. (1935). *Dynamic theory of personality.* New York: McGraw-Hill.

Loehlin, J. C. (1992). *Genes and environment in personality development.* Newbury Park, CA: Sage.

Lück, H. E., & Löwisch, D.-J. (Eds.). (1994). *Der Briefwechsel zwischen William Stern und Jonas Cohn: Dokumente einer Freundschaft zwischen zwei Wissenschaftlern* [Letters between William Stern and Jonas Cohn: Documents of a friendship between two scientists]. Frankfurt am Main: Peter Lang Verlag.

Lundberg, G. A. (1941). Case-studies vs. statistical methods—An issue based on misunderstanding. *Sociometry, 4,* 379-383.

MacLeod, R. B. (1938). William Stern (1871-1938). *Psychological Review, 45,* 347-353.

May, M. A. (1932). The foundations of personality. In A. S. Achilles (Ed.), *Psychology at work* (pp. 81-101). New York: McGraw-Hill.

McCall, W. A. (1939). *Measurement.* New York: Macmillan.

McClelland, D. C. (1951). *Personality.* New York: Sloane.

McCrae, R. R. (2000). Trait psychology and the revival of personality and cultural studies. *American Behavioral Scientist, 44,* 10-31.

McCrae, R. R. (2001). Facts and interpretations of personality trait stability: A reply to Quackenbush. *Theory and Psychology, 11,* 837-844.

McCrae, R. R., & Costa, P. T. Jr. (1986). Clinical assessment can benefit from recent advances in personality psychology. *American Psychologist, 41,* 1001-1003.

McCrae, R. R., & Costa, P. T. Jr. (1987). Validation of the five-factor model of personality across instruments and observers. *Journal of Personality and Social Psychology, 52,* 81-90.

McCrae, R. R., & Costa, P. T. Jr. (1995). Trait explanations in personality psychology. *European Journal of Personality, 9,* 231-252.

McCrae, R. R., & Costa, P. T. Jr. (1997). Conceptions and correlates of openness to experience. In R. Hogan, J. Johnson, & S. Briggs (Eds.), *Handbook of personality psychology* (pp. 826-847). New York: Academic Press.

Meehl, P. E. (1978). Theoretical risks and tabular asterisks: Sir Karl, Sir Ronald, and the slow progress of soft psychology. *Journal of Consulting and Clinical Psychology, 46,* 806-834.

Michaelis-Stern, E. (1991). Erinnerungen an meine Eltern [Recollections of my parents]. In W. Deutsch (Ed.), *Die verborgene Aktualität von William Stern* (pp. 131-141). Frankfurt am Main: Peter Lang Verlag.

Mischel, W. (1968). *Personality and assessment.* New York: Wiley.

Moghaddam, F., Taylor, D. M., & Wright, S. (1993). *Social psychology in cross-cultural perspective.* New York: Freeman.

Münsterberg, H. (1900). *Grundzüge der Psychologie* [Foundations of psychology]. Leipzig: Barth.

Münsterberg, H. (1913). *Psychology and industrial efficiency.* Boston and New York: Houghton-Mifflin.

Murchison, C. (Ed.). (1930). *A history of psychology in autobiography.* New York: Russell & Russell.

Nunnally, J. C. (1967). *Psychometric theory.* New York: McGraw-Hill.

Ozer, D. J. (1990). Individual differences and the explanation of behavior. In D. N. Robinson, & L. P. Mos (Eds.), *Annals of theoretical psychology* (Vol. 6, pp. 201-209). New York: Plenum.

Paunonen, S. V., & Jackson, D. N. (1986a). Idiothetic inquiry and toil of Sisyphus. *Journal of Personality, 54,* 470-477.

Paunonen, S. V., & Jackson, D. N. (1986b). Nomothetic and idiothetic measurement in personality. *Journal of Personality, 54,* 447-459.

Pawlik, K. (1992). *Don't worry! Traits exist.* Paper presented at the Sixth European Conference of Personality, Groningen, the Netherlands.

Pawlik, K. (1994). Einleitung (Introduction). In K. Pawlik (Ed.), *Die Differentielle Psychologie in ihren methodischen Grundlagen* (pp. 13-21). Göttingen: Hans Huber.

Pearson, K. R. (1901-1902). Editorial. *Biometrika, 1, 3.*

Pearson, K. R. (1903). On breeding good stock. In R. Jacoby, & N. Glauberman (Eds.), *The bell curve debate: History, documents, opinions* (pp. 410-416). New York: Times Books/Random House.

Pekrun, R. (1996). Geschichte von Differentieller Psychologie und Persönlichkeitspsychologie [History of differential psychology and personality research]. In K. Pawlik & M. Amelang (Eds.), *Enzyklopädie der Psychologie, Serie 8: Differentielle Psychologie und Persönlichkeitsforschung, Band I: Grundlagen und Methoden der differentiellen Psychologie* (pp. 83-123). Göttingen: Hogrefe.

Pervin, L. (1994). A critical analysis of current trait theory. *Psychological Inquiry, 5,* 103-113.

Plomin, R. C. (1993). Nature and nurture: Perspective and prospective. In R. C. Plomin & G. E. McClearn (Eds.), *Nature, nurture, & psychology* (pp. 459-485). Washington, DC: American Psychological Association Books.

Plomin, R. C. (1994). *Genetics and experience: The interplay between nature and nurture.* Thousand Oaks, CA: Sage.

Porter, T. M. (1986). *The rise of statistical thinking: 1820-1900.* Princeton, NJ: Princeton University Press.

Porter, T. M. (1995). *Trust in numbers.* Princeton, NJ: Princeton University Press.

Probst, P. (1989). Ernst Meumann als Begründer der empirischen Psychologie in Hamburg [Ernst Meumann as founder of empirical psychology in Hamburg]. *Psychologie und Geschichte, 1,* 6-16.

Probst, P. (1997). The beginnings of educational psychology in Germany. In W. G. Bringmann, H. E. Lück, R. Miller, & C. E. Early (Eds.), *A pictorial history of psychology* (pp. 315-321). Chicago: Quintessence.

Quackenbush, S. W. (2001a). Trait stability as a noncontingent truth: A pre-empirical critique of McCrae and Costa's stability thesis. *Theory and Psychology, 11,* 818-836.

Quackenbush, S. W. (2001b). Reliability as a value in personality research: A rejoinder to McCrae. *Theory and Psychology, 11,* 845-851.

Renner, K.-H., & Laux, L. (2000). Unitas multiplex, purposiveness, individuality: Contrasting Stern's conception of the person with Gergen's saturated self. *Theory and Psychology, 10,* 831-846.

Ringer, F. (1969). The decline of the German Mandarins: The German academic community, 1890-1933. Cambridge, MA: Harvard University Press.

Robinson, D. N. (1985). *Philosophy of psychology*. New York: Columbia University Press.

Robinson, D. N. (1989). *Aristotle's psychology*. New York: Columbia University Press.

Robinson, D. N. (1995). *An intellectual history of psychology* (3rd ed.). Madison: University of Wisconsin Press.

Robinson, D. N., & Mos, L. P. (Eds.). (1990). *Annals of theoretical psychology*. New York: Plenum.

Rosenzweig, S. (1958). The place of the individual and of idiodynamics in psychology: A dialogue. *Journal of Individual Psychology, 59*, 339-345.

Rowe, D. C. (1997). Genetics, temperament, and personality. In R. Hogan, J. Johnson, & S. Briggs (Eds.), *Handbook of personality psychology* (pp. 369-386). New York: Academic Press.

Rucci, A. J., & Tweney, R. D. (1980). Analysis of variance and the "second discipline" of scientific psychology: A historical account. *Psychological Bulletin, 87*, 166-184.

Rümelin, G. (1875). Über den Begriff eines sozialen Gesetzes [On the concept of a social law]. In G. Rümelin (Ed.), *Reden und Aufsätze* (pp. 1-31). Freiburg.

Runyan, W. M. (1982). *Life histories and psychobiography*. New York: Oxford University Press.

Rychlak, J. F. (1976). Personality theory: Its nature, past, present, and—future? *Personality and Social Psychology Bulletin, 2*, 209-224.

Rychlak, J. F. (1979). *Discovering free will and personal responsibility*. New York: Oxford University Press.

Rychlak, J. F. (1981). *A philosophy of science for personality theory* (2nd ed.). Malaber, FL: Krieger.

Rychlak, J. F. (1988). *The psychology of rigorous humanism* (2nd ed.). New York: New York University Press.

Rychlak, J. F. (1991). *Artificial intelligence and human reason: A teleological critique*. New York: Columbia University Press.

Rychlak, J. F. (1997). *In defense of human consciousness*. Washington, DC: American Psychological Association.

Sabat, S. R. (2000). Time past, time present, time future: The Alzheimer's disease sufferer as Stern's unitas multiplex. *Theory and psychology, 10*, 787-800.

Sabat, S. R. (2001). *The experience of Alzheimer's disease: Life through a tangled veil*. Oxford, UK: Blackwell.

Sabat, S. R., & Harré, R. (1994). The Alzheimer's disease sufferer as a semiotic subject. *Philosophy, Psychiatry, Psychology, 1*, 145-160.

Samelson, F. (1977). World War I intelligence testing and the development of psychology. *Journal of the History of the Behavioral Sciences, 13*, 274-282.

Samelson, F. (1979). Putting psychology on the map: Ideology and intelligence testing. In A. R. Buss (Ed.), *Psychology in social context* (pp. 103-168). New York: Irvington.

Sanborn, H. (1939). An examination of William Stern's philosophy. *Character and Personality, 7*, 318-330.

Sanford, N. (1963). Personality: Its place in psychology. In S. Koch (Ed.), *Psychology: A study of a science* (Vol. 5, pp. 488-592). New York: McGraw-Hill.

Sarbin, T. R. (1944). The logic of prediction in psychology. *Psychological Review, 51*, 210-228.

Saudino, K. J., & Eaton, W. O. (1991). Infant temperament and genetics: An objective twin study of motor activity level. *Child Development, 62*, 1167-1174.

Schmidt, R. (Ed.). (1927). *Philosophie der Gegenwart in Selbstdarstellung* [Contemporary philosophy in self-portraits]. Leipzig: Barth.

Schmidt, W. (1991a). Sehnsucht nach Weltanschauung: William Stern um die Jahrhundertwende [The longing for a worldview: William Stern at the turn of the century]. *Psychologie und Geschichte, 3*, 1-8.

Schmidt, W. (1991b). William Stern—Günther Anders: Zwei Generationen, zwei Welten [William Stern—Günther Anders: Two generations, two worlds]. In W. Deutsch (Ed.), *Die verborgene Aktualität von William Stern* (pp. 117-129). Frankfurt am Main: Peter Lang Verlag.

Schmidt, W. (1994). William Stern (1871-1938) und Lewis Terman (1877-1956): Deutsche und amerikanische Intelligenz-und Begabungsforschung im Lichte ihrer andersartigen politischen und ideologischen Voraussssetzungen [William Stern (1871-1938) and Lewis Terman (1877-1956): German and American research on intelligence and aptitude in the light of different political and ideological circumstances]. *Psychologie und Geschichte, 6*, 3-26.

Shotter, J. (1993). *Conversational realities: Constructing life through language*. London: Sage.

Skaggs, E. B. (1945). Personalistic psychology as science. *Psychological Review, 52*, 234-238.

Slife, B., & Williams, R. N. (1995). *What's behind the research? Discovering hidden assumptions in the behavioral sciences*. Thousand Oaks, CA: Sage.

Sokal, M. M. (1990). James McKeen Cattell and mental anthropometry: Nineteenth century science and reform and the origins of psychological testing. In M. M. Sokal (Ed.), *Psychological testing and American society* (pp. 21-45). New Brunswick, NJ: Rutgers University Press.

Spearman, C. (1904). "General intelligence" objectively determined and measured. *American Journal of Psychology, 15*, 201-292.

Spoerl, H. D. (1938). William Stern. *The Personalist, 19*, 309-311.

Staeuble, I. (1983). *William Stern's research program of differential psychology: Why did psychotechnics outstrip psychognostics?* Paper presented at the Cheiron Society, Toronto, Canada.

Stephenson. (1952). Some observations in Q-methodology. *Psychological Bulletin, 49*, 483-498.

Stern, C., & Stern, W. (1907). *Die Kindersprache* [Children's speech]. Leipzig: Barth.

Stern, C., & Stern, W. (1909). *Erinnerung, Aussage, und Lüge in der ersten Kindheit* [Recollection, testimony, and lying in early childhood]. Leipzig: Barth.

Stern, C., & Stern, W. (1999). *Recollection, testimony, and lying in early childhood* (J. T. Lamiell, Trans.). Washington, DC: American Psychological Association.

Stern, W. (1894). Die Wahrnehmung von Bewegungen vermittelst des Auges [The visual perception of movements]. *Zeitschrift für Psychologie und Physiologie der Sinnesorgane, 7,* 321-385.

Stern, W. (1899). Ein Beitrag zur differentiellen Psychologie des Urtheilens [A contribution to the differential psychology of judgment]. *Zeitschrift für Psychologie und Physiologie der Sinnesorgane, 22,* 13-22.

Stern, W. (1900a). *Über Psychologie der individuellen Differenzen (Ideen zu einer "differentiellen Psychologie")* [On the psychology of individual differences (Toward a "differential psychology")]. Leipzig: Barth.

Stern, W. (1900b). *Über die ethische Bedeutung von Toleranz* [On the ethical significance of tolerance]. Unpublished manuscript, Breslau.

Stern, W. (1901). S. Freud. Die Traumdeutung (Rezension). [S. Freud. The interpretation of dreams (A review)]. *Zeitschrift für Psychologie und Physiologie der Sinnesorgane, 26,* 130-133.

Stern, W. (1906). *Person und Sache: System der philosophischen Weltanschauung. Erster Band: Ableitung und Grundlehre* [Person and thing: A systematic philosophical worldview. Volume 1: Rationale and basic tenets]. Leipzig: Barth.

Stern, W. (1908). Tatsachen und Ursachen der seelischen Entwicklung [Facts about and causes of psychological development]. *Zeitschrift für angewandte Psychologie und psychologische Sammelforschung, 1,* 1-43.

Stern, W. (1910). Abstracts of lectures on the psychology of testimony and on the study of individuality (E. C. Sanford, Trans.). *The American Journal of Psychology, 21,* 270-282.

Stern, W. (1911). *Die Differentielle Psychologie in ihren methodischen Grundlagen* [Methodological foundations of differential psychology]. Leipzig: Barth.

Stern, W. (1912). *Die psychologischen Methoden der Intelligenzprüfung* [The psychological methods of intelligence testing]. Leipzig: Barth.

Stern, W. (1914a). *Psychologie der frühen Kindheit bis zum sechsten Lebensjahr* [Psychology of early childhood up to the sixth year of life]. Leipzig: Quelle & Meyer.

Stern, W. (1914b). Die Anwendung der Psychoanalyse auf Kindheit und Jugend. Ein Protest. Mit einem Anhang von Clara und William Stern: Kritik einer Freudschen Psychoanalyse [The application of psychoanalysis to children and adolescents. A protest. With an appendix by Clara and William Stern: Critique of a Freudian psychoanalysis]. *Zeitschrift für angewandte Psychologie und psychologische Sammelforschung, 8,* 71-101.

Stern, W. (1914c). Psychologie [Psychology]. In D. Sarason (Ed.), *Das Jahr 1913: Ein Gesamtbild der Kulturentwicklung* (pp. 414-421). Leipzig: Teubner.

Stern, W. (1915). *Vorgedanken zur Weltanschauung* [Preliminary ideas toward a worldview]. Leipzig: Barth.

Stern, W. (1916). Der Intelligenzquotient als Maß der kindlichen Intelligenz, insbesondere der Unternormalen [The intelligence quotient as a measure of intelligence in children, with special reference to the sub-normal child]. *Zeitschrift für angewandte Psychologie, 11,* 1-18.

Stern, W. (1917). *Die Psychologie und der Personalismus* [Psychology and personalism]. Leipzig: Barth.

Stern, W. (1918a). *Person und Sache: System der philosophischen Weltanschauung. Zweiter Band: Die menschliche Persönlichkeit* [Person and thing: A systematic philosophical worldview. Volume Two: The human personality]. Leipzig: Barth.

Stern, W. (1918b). Grundgedanken der personalistischen Philosophie [Conceptual foundations of personalistic philosophy]. In A. Liebert (Ed.), *Philosophische Vorträge*. Berlin: Reuther & Reichard.

Stern, W. (1921). Richtlinien für die Methodik der psychologischen Praxis [Guidelines for a method of psychological pratice]. *Beihefte zur Zeitschrift für angewandte Psychologie, 29,* 1-16.

Stern, W. (1923). *Person und Sache. System der philosophischen Weltanschauung. Zweiter Band: Die menschliche Persönlichkeit (dritte unveränderte Auflage)* [Person and thing: A systematic philosophical worldview. Volume 2: The human personality (3rd unrev. ed.)]. Leipzig: Barth.

Stern, W. (1924a). *Psychology of early childhood up to the sixth year of age* (A. Barwell, Trans.). London: Allen & Unwin.

Stern, W. (1924b). *Person und Sache: System der kritischen Personalismus. Dritter Band: Wertphilosophie* [Person and thing: The system of critical personalism. Volume 3: Philosophy of value]. Leipzig: Barth.

Stern, W. (1925a). *Anfänge der Reifezeit: Ein Knabentagebuch in psychologischer Bearbeitung* [Beginnings of maturity: A psychological analysis of a boy's diary]. Leipzig: Quelle & Meyer.

Stern, W. (1925b). Aus dreijährige Arbeit des Hamburger Psychologischen Laboratoriums [3-year report on work at the Hamburg Psychological Laboratory). *Zeitschrift für pädagogische Psychologie, 26,* 289-307.

Stern, W. (1927). Selbstdarstellung [Self-portrayal]. In R. Schmidt (Ed.), *Philosophie der Gegenwart in Selbstdarstellung* (Vol. 6, pp. 128-184). Leipzig: Barth.

Stern, W. (1929). Persönlichkeitsforschung und Testmethode [Personality research and the methods of testing]. *Jahrbuch der Charaketerologie, 6,* 63-72.

Stern, W. (1930a). William Stern autobiography (S. Langer, Trans.). In C. Murchison (Ed.), *A history of psychology in autobiography* (Vol. 1, pp. 335-388). Worcester, MA: Clark University Press.

Stern, W. (1930b). *Studien zur Personwissenschaft. Erster Teil: Personalistik als Wissenschaft* [Studies in the science of persons: Personalism as science]. Leipzig: Barth.

Stern, W. (1933). Der personale Faktor in Psychotechnik und praktischer Psychologie [The personal factor in psychotechnics and practical psychology]. *Zeitschrift für angewandte Psychologie, 44,* 52-63.

Stern, W. (1935). *Allgemeine Psychologie auf personalistischer Grundlage* [General psychology from the personalistic standpoint]. Den Haag, Netherlands: Nijhoff.

Stern, W. (1938). *General psychology from the personalistic standpoint* (H. Spoerl, Trans.). New York: Macmillan.

Stigler, S. M. (1986). *The history of statistics: The measurement of uncertainty before 1900.* Cambridge, MA: Belknap Press, Harvard University Press.

Thorndike, E. L. (1909). A note on the accuracy of discrimination of weights and lengths. *Psychological Review, 16,* 340-346.

Thorndike, E. L. (1911). *Individuality.* New York: Houghton-Mifflin.

Tissaw, M. (2000). Psychological symbiosis: Personalistic and constructionist considerations. *Theory and psychology, 10,* 847-876.

Toulouse, E. (1896). *Enquete medico-psychologie sur les rapports de la superiorite intellectuelle avec la nevropathie. I. Introduction generale. Emile Zola* [A psycho-medical survey of the relationship between intellectual superiority and nervous disorder. I. General introduction. Emile Zola]. Paris: Flammarion.

Toulouse, E. (1910). *Enquete medico-psychologie sur la superiorite intellectuelle. Henri Poincaré* [A psycho-medical survey of intellectual superiority. Henri Poincaré]. Paris: Flammarion.

Tryon, W. W. (1991a). Uncertainty reduction as valid explanation. *Theoretical and Philosophical Psychology, 11,* 91-98.

Tryon, W. W. (1991b). Further support for uncertainty reduction as valid explanation. *Theoretical and Philosophical Psychology, 11,* 106-110.

Tyler, L. E. (1959). Toward a workable psychology of individuality. *American Psychologist, 14,* 75-81.

Tyler, L. E. (1978). *Individuality: Human possibilities and personal choice in the psychological development of men and women.* San Francisco: Jossey-Bass.

Tyler, L. E. (1984). *Some neglected insights in personology.* Unpublished manuscript, Eugene, OR.

Valsiner, J. (1986). Between groups and individuals: Psychologists' and laypersons' interpretations of correlational findings. In J. Valsiner (Ed.), *The individual subject and scientific psychology* (pp. 113-151). New York: Plenum.

Venn, J. (1888). *The logic of chance.* London/New York: Macmillan.

Wagner, A. (1864). *Die Gesetzmäßigkeit in den scheinbar willkürlichen menschlichen Handlungen vom Standpunkt der Statistik* [Lawfulness in deceptively arbitrary actions from the standpoint of statistics]. Hamburg.

Watson, D., & Clark, L. A. (1997). Extraversion and its positive emotional core. In R. Hogan, J. Johnson, & S. Briggs (Eds.), *Handbook of personality psychology* (pp. 767-793). New York: Academic Press.

Weigert, S. C. (2000). *The predictive accuracy of normative and interactive frameworks for personality measurement.* Unpublished doctoral dissertation, Georgetown University, Washington, D.C.

Werner, H. (1939). William Stern's personalistics and psychology of personality. *Character and Personality, 7,* 109-125.

Wiggins, J. S. (1973). *Personality and prediction: Principles of personality assessment.* Reading, MA: Addison-Wesley.

Wiggins, J. S. (1979). A psychological taxonomy of trait descriptive terms: The interpersonal domain. *Journal of Personality and Social Psychology, 37,* 395-412.

Wiggins, J. S., & Trapnell, P. D. (1997). Personality structure: The return of the Big Five. In R. Hogan, J. Johnson, & S. Briggs (Eds.), *Handbook of personality psychology* (pp. 737-765). New York: Academic Press.

Windelband, W. (1998). *History and natural science* (J. T. Lamiell, Trans.). Strassburg: Heitz. (Original work published 1894)

Winkler. L. (2000). Culture shock, or what I wasn't prepared for. *The Funnel: The Newsmagazine of the German-American Fulbright Commission, 36,* 10.

Wissler. (1901). The correlation of mental and physical tests (Series of Monograph Supplements). *The Psychological Review 3*(6).

Woody, E. Z. (1983). The intuitive personologist revisited: A critique of dialectical person perception. *Journal of Personality, 51,* 236-258.

Wundt, W. (1912). *Elemente der Völkerpsychologie* [Elements of a cultural psychology]. Leipzig: Alfred Kröner Verlag.

Wundt, W. (1913). *Die Psychologie im Kampf ums Dasein* [Psychology's struggle for existence]. Leipzig: Kröner.

# Author Index

Allen, A., 118, 196
Allport, G. W., 23, 39, 84, 86, 87, 88,
    91, 92, 95, 96, 97, 102, 103, 104,
    160, 176, 183, 205, 222, 246, 256,
    275, 280, 285, 286
Anders, G., 18, 20, 21
Angleitner, A., 159, 161

Bakan, D., 191, 262
Bauer, I., 300
Beck, S. J., 42, 97, 98, 100
Behrens, H., 14
Bellah, R. N., 299
Bem, D. J., 118, 196
Binet, A., 61
Blumenthal, H., 289
Briggs, S., 171, 291
Brunswik, E., 183
Budescu, D., 259
Bühring, G., 3, 4, 5, 8, 9, 11, 13, 14, 15,
    16, 17, 21, 22, 39, 64, 83
Burt, C. L., 100
Buss, D. M., 171

Campbell, D. T., 166
Carlson, R., 83
Cattell, J. M., 58, 59
Cattell, R. B., 99, 100, 249, 253, 275, 284
Clark, L. A., 171
Cloninger, S. C., 180, 181, 246, 260
Costa, P. T., Jr., 119, 159, 160, 165, 166,
    167, 171, 172, 189, 190, 198, 203,
    250, 261, 275
Craik, K. H., 171
Cronbach, L. J., 114, 121, 122, 135, 141,
    149, 166, 259

Danziger, K., 44, 64, 69, 77,
    114, 115, 120, 121, 123, 124,
    172, 183, 281
Dar, R., 196
Deutsch, W., 9, 14, 228
Digman, J. M., 159, 160
Dilthey, W., 190
Drobisch, M. W., 133
Durbeck, P., 245, 256, 259, 262, 275
Dürr-Borst, M., 231

Eaton, W. O., 169
Ebbinghaus, H., 32, 39, 40, 115, 190
Eisenberg, N. H., 171
Epstein, S., 83, 196, 246, 260, 281
Eysenck, H. J., 58, 97, 98, 99,
    100, 181

Fancher, R. E., 58, 59, 60, 61
Feger, B., 64, 298
Fiske, D. W., 166
Folstein, M., 264
Folstein, S., 264
Foss, M. A., 245, 256, 275
Freud, S., 12

Garrett, H. E., 252
Gergen, K. J., 228, 287
Gigerenzer, G., 72, 203
Gillet, G., 286
Gleser, G., 259
Goldberg, L. R., 159, 160, 216, 249
Goldfried, M. R., 249
Gordon, M., 296
Graf-Nold, A., 12, 15
Graumann, C. F., 32

Graziano, W. G., 171
Grünwald, H., 44, 64
Guilford, J. P., 99

Hacking, I., 125, 126
Hake, A., 293
Hanson, F. A., 295
Hardesty, F. P., 17
Harré, R., 228, 266, 286, 287
Harrington, A., 41
Hartshorne, H., 90
Hase, H. D., 249
Hempel, A., 245, 256, 275
Henri, V., 61
Hermans, H., 288
Herrnstein, R. J., 205, 298
Hogan, J., 119, 292
Hogan, R., 119, 171, 291, 292
Holt, R. W., 39, 100, 101, 102, 181,
    184, 246, 260
Hug-Hellmuth, H. von, 13, 14

John, O., 159
Johnson, J. A., 119, 171, 291

Kent, R. N., 249
Kimble, G. A., 168
Kleinmuntz, B., 251, 283, 284

Lamiell, J. T., 61, 83, 140, 177,
    191, 197, 201, 228, 245, 249,
    251, 256, 259, 262, 275, 280, 283,
    286, 288
Larsen, R. J., 245, 256, 275
Laux, L., 228, 287
Leahey, T. H., 290
Leffel, G. M., 256, 275
Levy, L., 286
Lewin, K., 183
Loehlin, J. C., 169, 170
Löwisch, D. -J., 5, 9, 11, 14, 17, 19,
    20, 21, 22, 40, 41
Lück, H. E., 5, 9, 11, 14, 17, 19, 20, 21,
    22, 40, 41
Lundberg, G. A., 93, 94, 246, 260

Madsen, R., 299
May, M. A., 90

McClelland, D. C., 93, 99
McCrae, R. R., 119, 159, 160, 165, 166,
    167, 171, 172, 189, 190, 198, 203,
    250, 261, 275
McHugh, P. R., 264
Meehl, P. E., 166, 262
Michaelis-Stern, E., 5, 18, 20, 22
Mischel, W., 83, 106, 159
Mos, L. P., 215
Münsterberg, H., 69, 70, 79, 122
Murray, C., 205, 298

Nunnally, J. C., 104, 161, 181

Odbert, H. S., 160
Ones, D. S., 171
Ozer, D. J., 171

Pawlik, K., 39, 83
Pearson, K. R., 118
Pekrun, R., 44, 64
Pervin, L., 190
Plomin, R. C., 169
Porter, T. M., 125, 126, 127, 128,
    129, 133, 189
Probst, P., 11

Renner, K. -H., 228, 287
Roberts, B. W., 119, 292
Robinson, D. N., 32, 215, 290
Robins, R. W., 159
Rosenzwieg, S., 83
Rowe, D. C., 169, 170, 205
Rucci, A. J., 121
Runyan, W. M., 83
Rychlak, J. F., 215, 288, 290

Sabat, S. R., 245, 264, 265, 266, 267,
    269, 270, 271, 272, 273, 274, 276,
    286, 287, 296
Samelson, F., 61, 115
Sanford, N., 104, 105, 181
Sarbin, T. R., 94, 246, 260
Saudino, K. J., 169
Schmidt, W., 4, 19, 20, 61, 73
Serlin, R. C., 196
Shotter, J., 286
Shuttleworth, F. K., 90

Skaggs, E. B., 95, 181
Slife, B., 215
Sokal, M. M., 58, 60
Staeuble, I., 74
Stephenson, 97, 100
Stern, C., 6, 229, 231, 232, 233, 234,
    235, 236, 237, 238, 239, 288
Stern, W., 3, 4, 6, 8, 10, 13, 14, 17, 21,
    29, 31, 34, 35, 36, 37, 38, 44, 46,
    48, 49, 50, 51, 55, 57, 58, 59, 60,
    61, 62, 63, 64, 67, 71, 72, 73, 74,
    75, 77, 98, 100, 207, 215, 216,
    217, 219, 220, 221, 222, 223, 224,
    225, 226, 227, 228, 229, 230, 231,
    232, 233, 234, 235, 236, 237,
    238, 239, 245, 247, 248, 249, 263,
    275, 279, 280, 284, 287, 288, 289,
    291, 297, 298, 301, 302
Sullivan, W. M., 299
Swidler, A., 299

Thorndike, E. L., 65, 66, 67, 68, 74, 75,
    78, 87, 123, 135, 283
Tipton, S. M., 299
Tissaw, M., 288
Trapnell, P. D., 159, 160, 171
Trierweiler, S. J., 256, 275
Tryon, W. W., 201
Tweney, R. D., 121
Tyler, L. E., 1, 10, 18, 83

Valsiner, J., 293
Venn, J., 133, 134, 135

Watson, D., 171
Weigert, S. C., 3, 245, 261, 263, 275
Wiggins, J. S., 94, 159, 160, 171, 198
Williams, R. N., 215
Windelband, W., 39, 179, 180
Winkler, L., 300
Wissler, C., 60

# Subject Index

Achenwall, Gottfried, 125
Acts, 49–50, 130–131, 133, 223–224
Adler, Alfred, 15
Aggregate level reality, 122, 123–124,
    130–132, 137, 183–184, 191,
    195, 201
Allport, G. W., 39, 82–92, 105–106, 160
Alzheimer's Disease (AD) study,
    264–274, 276, 296
Analysis-of-variance (ANOVA)
    techniques, 121–122, 143, 172
Applied psychology, 8–10, 56–57
    occupational decisions and, 16–17,
        64, 292–295
    organizational psychology, 72–73,
        119, 122–123
    psychoanalysis, children/adolescents
        and, 13–15
    standardized testing, 36
Attributes, 46–49, 47 (figure), 55
    psychographic investigation and, 62–64
    testing/ranking of, 58, 61–62
    unitas multiplex concept, 217–220
    See also Traits
Autotelic goals, 271

Between-person variance, 191, 205, 225,
    248–249, 281
Binet, Alfred, 36–37, 61
Breslau Proclamation, 14–15
Brunswik, Egon, 183–184
Buckle, Henry Thomas, 130–132, 135,
    149, 184, 189, 205, 290

Cattell, James McKeen, 58, 59–60
Causal inferences, 120–123, 132, 136

Character studies, 90–91, 91 (figure),
    282–285
Child psychology:
    infantile sexuality, 14, 15
    mental testing, 61
    psychoanalytic practice and, 12–15
    See also Critical personalism
Chronological age (CA), 61
Clark University Conference, 9–10
Cohn, Jonas, 4, 52
Commission for Youth Studies, 12, 14
Common trait perspective, 82–83, 87–88,
    94–95, 105–106, 177, 183,
    203–205
Community, 48, 227–228, 273,
    299–300, 302
Complex types, 37–38, 68
Contemporary nomothetics, 176–177
    aggregate reality and, 183–184,
        195–196, 206–207, 244
    basic human tendencies, 197–201,
        199–200 (figures), 207
    between-person variance, 191, 205
    explanatory function of, 185–191
    general laws and, 182–184, 205
    heritability, common traits and,
        203–205, 207
    historical foundation of, 177–184,
        178 (figure)
    human psychological functioning,
        191–205
    idiographic knowledge and, 180–181
    predictive laws, 191–197, 193 (table),
        206–207
    probabilistic thinking and,
        201–203

significance, test of, 191
Thorndike maneuver and, 184,
    195–196, 205–206
See also Nomothetic personality
    research; Personalistic inquiry
Convergent/discriminant validity,
    166–168, 167 (table)
Correlational research, 46–48, 47
    (figure), 56, 58, 280
    aggregate level reality, individual level
        reality and, 123–124
    intelligence testing, 60–61
    Pearson r, 116–119
    Q-technique and, 97–98
    trait/character studies, 90–91, 91
        (figure), 106
    See also Nomothetic personality
        research; Standardized testing
Critical personalism, 2, 15, 85, 86,
    215–216, 238
    acts, 223–224
    anti-individualism and, 237, 299–302
    community diversity and, 227–228
    development of, 17–18, 43
    diary work and, 5–8, 7 (figure)
    dispositions, 224–225
    early childhood study, 228–237
    introception and, 227–228
    lying, personalistic conception of,
        234–237
    personality theory, foundation for,
        281–291
    person in, 216–225, 218 (figure)
    phenomenal experience and, 221–223
    psychophysically neutral person,
        225–228
    research methodology issues, 229–233
    self-observation and, 222–223
    social thought, framework for,
        291–302
    standardized testing and, 71–78
    teleological personality development,
        226–227
    tendencies and, 235–236
    unitas multiplex concept and,
        217–220
    See also Common trait perspective;
        Personalistic inquiry;

Personalistic perspective;
    Personality theory; Psychology of
    personality
Cronbach-Gleser profile dissimilarity
    index, 259
Cultural influence, 86, 130–132

Darwin, Charles, 118
Descartes, Rene, 217
Diary writings, 5–8, 7 (figure)
Differential psychology, 1–2, 52, 280
    development of, 78–79
    general experimental psychology and,
        31–34
    individuality, problem of, 29–31,
        30 (figure), 33, 42–43
    measurement/statistical techniques
        and, 56
    mechanistic/reductionist perspective
        and, 38–43
    personalistic perspective within, 43–51
    research disciplines in, 46–48,
        47 (figure)
    scope/mission of, 34–38
    type complexes vs. complex types and,
        37–38, 68
    See also Critical personalism;
        Personality theory; Standardized
        testing
Dilthey, Wilhelm, 190
Direct observation, 72–73, 222–223, 245,
    249–250
Discriminant validity, 166–168, 167
    (table)
Dispositions, 49–51, 224–225
    behavioral observations of, 249–250
    interactive measures of, 253–256,
        257 (figure), 283–284
    measurement of, 249–256
    raw score assessments of, 251–253,
        252 (table), 253 (figure)
Diversity, 227–228, 299–302
Dream interpretation, 12–13
Drobisch, M. W., 133

Ebbinghaus, Hermann, 4, 32, 33, 39, 244
Empathic understanding, 100–102,
    106, 256–261

Empirical inquiry, 123–124, 132, 135, 180
Epistemic problem, 123–124, 132,
   135, 136
Explanatory psychology, 189–191

Factor analysis, 58, 97–100, 160
Fechner, Gustav, 4, 32
Ferenczi, Sandor, 9
Fisher, R. A., 121
Five factor model, 163–168, 198,
   203–204
Forgetting curve, 32, 34, 244
Free will, 49, 130–131, 132–133, 289
Freud, Sigmund, 9

Galton, Francis, 59, 115–116, 118–119
Galtonian research model, 115–116,
   118–119
   causal inferences, metaphysical
      problem of, 120–123, 132
   empirical inquiry, epistemic problem
      of, 123–124, 132, 135
   treatment groups in, 120–121, 136
   See also Nomothetic personality
      research; Statistical methods
General experimental psychology, 31–34
   general laws in, 33, 182–184
   individual differences and, 35–36, 43
   See also Differential psychology
Generalizations. See Lawful regularities
Goddard, H. H., 61
Group difference variable, 149–154,
   150–151 (tables), 153 (table)

Hall, G. S., 9
Helmholtz, Hermann, 32
Heritability, 169–170, 203–205, 207
Heterotelic goals, 271
Humanities, 179–180
Humanization movement, 11
Human psychological functioning:
   basic tendencies, 197–201,
      199–200 (figures), 207
   common traits, heritability of,
      203–205
   predictive laws, 191–197, 193 (table),
      206–207
   probabilistic thinking and, 201–203

Idiographic inquiry, 89–92, 92–105, 106,
   176–177, 180–181, 256–261
Individual differences variable, 154–158,
   155 (table), 157 (table)
Individual level reality, 122, 123–124,
   130–132, 137
Individuality, 10, 29–31, 33, 35–36, 280
   diversity, community and, 299–302
   general laws and, 33, 182–184
   inherent value and, 42–43, 296
   mechanistic/reductionist view of,
      38–43
   psychographic investigation of, 62–64
   psychological functioning, 129–132,
      191–205
   quantitative vs. qualitative nature of,
      65–68, 67 (figure), 245
   type complexes vs. complex types and,
      37–38
   versus uniqueness, 285
   See also Critical personalism; Human
      psychological functioning;
      Personalistic perspective;
      Standardized testing
Industrial psychology, 70–71, 119,
   122–123
Infantile sexuality, 14, 15
Inherent human value, 42–43, 296
Institute for Youth Studies, 16
Intelligence quotient (IQ), 1, 2, 58
   correlational testing and, 60–61, 118
   development of, 61
   See also Standardized testing
Introception, 271–273, 296–299
Intuition, 100–102, 106, 256–261

Jung, Carl, 9

Krueger, Felix, 58

Lawful regularities:
   contemporary nomothetics and,
      182–184, 205
   human psychological functioning,
      predictive laws and, 191–197,
      193 (table), 206–207
   individuality and, 33,
      182–184, 244

statistically-guided decisions and, 295–296

trait manifestation, 170–171

Lazarus, Moritz, 4

Lewin, Kurt, 183

Lexical hypothesis, 160–162, 162 (table)

Lipmann, Otto, 8, 21

Lying, 234–237

Mandarin tradition, 41

Mechanistic conceptualization, 38–43

Memory studies, 32, 34, 244

Mental age (MA), 61

Mental processes, 15
  general psychology and, 31–34, 51–52
  mechanistic/impersonalistic conception of, 39–40, 43
  See also Standardized testing

Metaphysical problem, 120–123, 132, 136

Mini-Mental State (MMS) test, 264–265

Moral responsibility, 179–180, 296, 298, 301–302

Morphogenic psychology, 102–103

Muchow, Martha, 21

Multitrait-multimethod matrix, 166

Münsterberg, Hugo, 40–41, 56, 69–73, 79, 291

Natural sciences, 179–180, 219–220

Nature vs. nurture debate, 168–170, 298–299

Nazi regime, 20–23

Neo-Galtonian inquiry. See
  Contemporary nomothetics;
  Nomothetic personality research;
  Statistical methods

NEO Personality Inventory, 163–168, 250, 251, 254, 255

Neo-Wundtian inquiry, 262–263

Newtonian perspective, 41, 290

Nomothetic knowledge, 89, 92–105, 106

Nomothetic personality research, 135, 140–142, 141 (figure), 158
  computational formulae in, 142, 143 (table)
  differences, sources/behavioral manifestations of, 168–171

five factor model, validity of, 163–168, 163 (table), 165 (table), 167 (table)

group difference variable and, 149–154, 150–151 (tables), 153 (table)

heritability, coefficient of, 169–170, 204–205

individual differences variable, 154–158, 155 (table), 157 (table)

lawful regularities, behavioral manifestations of traits, 170–171

lexical hypothesis, factor analysis and, 160–162, 162 (table)

nature vs. nurture debate, 168–170

personality trait taxonomy, 159–168

treatment groups, statistical comparison of, 142–149, 144–145 (tables), 148 (table)

See also Contemporary nomothetics

Observation, 72–73, 222–223, 245, 249–250

Occupational decisions, 16–17, 64, 292–295

Odbert, Henry S., 160

Organizational psychology, 72–73, 119, 122–123

Paulsen, Friedrich, 4

Pearson product-moment correlation coefficient, 116–119, 122, 144

Personalism versus individualism, 296

Personalistic inquiry, 243–244
  Alzheimer's disease subjects, 264–274, 276
  behavioral observations, 249–250
  disposition, measurement of, 249–256
  foundational principles in, 244–245, 274–275
  hypothesis testing in, 261–263
  idiographic intuitions, subjective personality judgments and, 256–261, 258–259 (table)
  idiographic vs. nomothetic research and, 246
  interactive measures, 253–256, 257 (figure), 275

introception, syntelic goals and,
    271–273
person-world convergence, measures
    of, 248–249, 255–256
qualitative research, 264–271
quantitative measurement in, 247–249
raw score assessments, 251–252,
    252 (table), 253 (figure)
*See also* Critical personalism;
    Personality theory
Personalistic perspective, 18–20, 23,
    43–46, 45 (figure)
acts, 49–50
communities of people and, 48
differential psychology research,
    46–48, 47 (figure)
dispositions and, 49–51
individual/attribute, concepts of,
    46–49
phenomena, 48–49
psychotechnics and, 72–78
*See also* Common trait perspective;
    Critical personalism; Differential
    psychology; Personality theory
Personality psychology. *See*
    Contemporary nomothetics;
    Nomothetic personality research;
    Psychology of personality
Personality theory, 281–282
aggregate statistical knowledge,
    294–295
applied differential psychology,
    291–296
between-person differences and,
    281, 283
diversity, community/individuality
    and, 299–302
general laws and, 295–296
individuality vs. uniqueness, 285–286
inherent value and, 296
interactive measurement and, 283–284
introception, teleological
    conceptualization and, 296–299
nature vs. nurture debate and,
    298–299
person characterizations in, 282–285
person-world convergence and,
    287–288

positioning/position taking, identity
    development and, 286–288
social constructionist thought and,
    287–288
teleological outlook and, 288–291
tolerance, virtue of, 301–302
trait psychology, 298–299
*See also* Critical personalism;
    Psychology of personality
Person-world convergence, 168–170,
    248–249, 255–256, 287–288
Petty, William, 125
Phenomena, 48–49, 221–223
Political arithmetic, 124–128
Positioning/position-taking, 286–288
Potentiality, 248
Practical psychology, 77–78
Predictive laws, 191–197, 193 (table),
    206–207
Probability, 133–135, 201–203, 294
Profiling, 64
Psychoanalysis, 12–15
Psychognostics, 46, 55, 64–68,
    88–89, 119
Psychography, 62–64
Psychological functioning. *See* Human
    psychological functioning
Psychological testing. *See* Standardized
    testing
Psychology of personality, 56,
    84–85, 280
actuarially-based prediction, 93–94
character studies and, 90–91,
    91 (figure)
common traits/individual traits and,
    87–89, 92
definition of, 85–87
factor analysis and, 97–100
morphogenic psychology and,
    102–103
nomothetic-idiographic debate,
    92–105
nomothetic knowledge, idiographic
    inquiry and, 89–92
romantic science, empathic
    understanding and,
    100–102, 106
scientific status of, 95–100

*See also* Critical personalism; Human
    psychological functioning
Psychophysically neutral person, 225–228
Psychotechnics, 46, 55–56, 69
    applied psychology and, 69–70, 88
    Galtonian research model and, 119
    industrial/organizational psychology
        and, 70–71
    personalistic perspective and, 72–78

Q-technique, 97–100
Qualitative inquiry, 65–68, 67 (figure),
    245, 264–271
Quantitative measurement. *See*
    Personalistic inquiry
Quetelet, Adolphe, 126–128, 129,
    131, 290

Regression analysis. *See* Nomothetic
    personality research
Rousseau, Jean Jacques, 235,
    236–237, 298
R-technique, 100

School reform movement, 10–12
Scientific psychology, 114, 132
    five factor model, 163–168
    Galtonian model, 115–116
    Wundtian model, 114–115
    *See also* Nomothetic personality
        research
Self-observation, 222–223
Sexuality, 14, 15
Simon, Theodore, 61
Sinclair, John, 125
Social constructionist thought, 287–288
Social physics, 127–129, 131–132,
    290–291
Society for School Reform, 11–12
Spearman, Charles, 58
Standardized testing, 36–37
    attributes, quantitative indexing
        of, 61–62
    correlational test results and,
        60–61
    critical personalist perspective and,
        71–78
    differential psychology and, 55–56

individualities, psychographic
    investigation of, 62–64
individuality, quantitative measure of,
    65–68, 67 (figure)
intelligence testing movement, 61
limitations of, 58–62
observational methods and, 72–73
personality dimensions and,
    73–75, 76–77
practical psychology and, 77–78
psychodiagnostics and, 64–68
psychotechnics and, 69–71, 74–76
technical improvements in, 59–60
test experiment method, 57–58
*See also* Common trait perspective;
    Correlational research
Statistical methods, 57–58, 93–94,
    113–114
aggregate level reality, individual level
    reality and, 122, 123–124,
    130–132, 137
analysis-of-variance techniques,
    121–122
average man, physical measures,
    126–127
bell-shaped curve, 126
causal inferences, metaphysical
    problem of, 120–123, 132, 136
empirical inquiry, epistemic problem
    of, 123–124, 132, 135
error variance and, 126, 133
free will and, 49, 130–131, 132–133
historical development of, 124–135
individual psychological functioning,
    129–132
Pearson product-moment correlation
    coefficient, 116–119, 122
probability concept, 133–135
social physics, 127–129, 131–132
treatment groups and,
    120–121, 136
Wundtian vs. Galtonian research
    models and, 114–116, 118–119,
    121–122
*See also* Contemporary nomothetics;
    Nomothetic personality
    research
Stern, Clara, 228–237, 298

Stern, William:
    applied psychology initiatives, 8–10,
        16–17
    Breslau years, 4–16
    childhood of, 2–3
    diary work, early child psychology,
        5–8, 7 (figure)
    Hamburg years, 16–20
    influences on, 3
    Nazi regime and, 20–23, 78, 79
    personalistic worldview of, 18–20, 23
    psychoanalytic methods, debate on,
        12–15
    psychological-philosophical union,
        17–18, 22
    school reform movement and, 10–12
    university studies of, 4
    See also Differential psychology
Syntelic goals, 271–273

Teleological personality development,
    226–227, 248, 288–291
Tendencies, 197–201, 199–200 (figures),
    207, 235–236, 294
Terman, Lewis, 61
Testing. See Standardized testing
Thorndike, Edward L., 56, 65–68, 78–79,
    123–124
Thorndike maneuver, 135, 184, 195–196,
    205–206
Tolerance, 300–302
Traits, 87, 298
    common traits, 87–88, 105–106
    correlational studies of, 90–91,
        91 (figure)
    individual traits, 88–89, 106
    manifestation of, lawful regularities in,
        170–171
    potentialities and, 224–225
    See also Contemporary nomothetics;
        Nomothetic personality research
Treatment groups, 120–121, 136
    group difference variable and,
        149–154, 150–151 (tables),
        153 (table)
    individual differences variable,
        154–158, 155 (table),
        157 (table)
    statistical comparison of, 142–149,
        144–145 (tables), 148 (table)
T tests, 143, 172
Type complexes, 37–38, 68, 87

Unconscious mental processes, 15
Understanding. See Psychognostics
Uniqueness, 285–286
Unitas multiplex concept, 217–220, 225

Venn, John, 133–135, 184

Wagner, Adolph, 133
Windelband, Wilhelm, 39, 48, 64, 87, 89,
    106, 130, 177–184, 205
Wissler, Clark, 58, 60
Worldview, 2, 17–18, 40
Wundtian research model, 114–116, 183,
    243, 262–263
Wundt, Wilhelm, 4, 31, 32, 57, 289

# About the Author

**James T. Lamiell** is Professor of Psychology at Georgetown University in Washington, D.C. Born and raised with his eight sisters in Canton, Ohio, he earned a Bachelor of Liberal Studies degree at Bowling Green State University in 1972, concentrating in psychology and philosophy. He pursued his graduate studies in psychology at Kansas State University, earning his M.S. degree in 1974 and his Ph.D. in 1976. After 6 years at the University of Illinois at Urbana-Champaign, he joined the Georgetown faculty in 1982. A two-time Fulbright Senior Scholar to Germany, Lamiell has held guest professorships at the University of Heidelberg (1990) and at the University of Leipzig (1998).

Lamiell is the author of *The Psychology Of Personality: An Epistemological Inquiry* (Columbia University Press, 1987) and translator of Clara and William Stern's 1909 monograph, *Erinnerung, Aussage und Lüge in der ersten Kindheit*, published in English as *Recollection, Testimony, and Lying in Early Childhood* (American Psychological Association Books, 1999). His numerous scholarly publications have primarily to do with theoretical and philosophical issues in the psychology of personality, and he has lectured on these topics at many universities both in the United States and in Europe.

Lamiell has served as Associate Editor of the *Journal of Personality* and the *Journal of Theoretical and Philosophical Psychology*. He was elected Fellow of APA Division 1 (General Psychology) in 1987, and Division 24 (Theoretical and Philosophical Psychology) in 1988. He was the honored recipient of the Psi Chi Award for Excellence in Undergraduate Teaching at the University of Illinois in 1979, and of the Edward B. Bunn Award for Faculty Excellence at Georgetown University in 2001.

In his spare time, Lamiell enjoys picking bluegrass banjo and long-distance bicycle touring. He lives in Oakton, Virginia, with Leslie, his wife of 30 years. Together they have raised a son, Kevin (26), and a daughter, Erika (24).